Isurium Brigantum

an archaeological survey of Roman Aldborough

The authors and publisher wish to thank the following individuals and organisations for their help with this publication:

Historic England
Society of Antiquaries of London
Thriplow Charitable Trust
Faculty of Classics and the McDonald Institute for Archaeological Research, University of Cambridge
Chris and Jan Martins

Historic England

UNIVERSITY OF CAMBRIDGE

Isurium Brigantum

an archaeological survey of Roman Aldborough

Rose Ferraby and Martin Millett

with contributions by Jason Lucas, James Lyall, Jess Ogden, Dominic Powlesland, Lieven Verdonck and Lacey Wallace

Research Report of the Society of Antiquaries of London No. 81

SOCIETY OF
ANTIQUARIES
OF LONDON

For RWS Norfolk – RF

First published 2020 by
The Society of Antiquaries of London
Burlington House
Piccadilly
London W1J 0BE

www.sal.org.uk

ISBN: 978 0 8543 1301 3

British Cataloguing in Publication Data
A CIP catalogue record for this book is available from the British Library.

Library of Congress Cataloguing in Publication Data
A CIP catalogue record for this book is available from the Library of Congress, Washington DC

Cover illustration: © Rose Ferraby
Design and layout: Sue Cawood
Printing and binding: Ashford Colour Press, Gosport

Contents

List of figures

Chapter 4

Appendix 1

Preface

This project at Aldborough came about through a combination of circumstances. One of the authors (MM) had been conducting fieldwork in Yorkshire concerned with understanding the impact of Roman imperialism on local societies, and was seeking to extend this to the urban sphere. He had been also running major urban survey projects in Italy developing the use of surface survey techniques. The other (RF) had worked as a geophysicist in Italy and as a co-director of a project at Thwing. Returning to her home town after working on urban surveys in Italy, the opportunity that Aldborough offered became clear.

Work started on a small scale in 2009 with a geophysical survey, first, with student trainees from Cambridge, then, on a larger scale, in collaboration with James Lyall and Dominic Powlesland. The spectacular success of this work led to the growth of the project as presented in this volume, which provides a systematic new synthesis of knowledge of the Roman town and a wide-ranging discussion of the implications of this research. The work has stimulated a renewed interest in the site, with the Friends of Roman Aldborough now well established to promote it.

This volume is an entirely collaborative work. The academic input of others involved in the fieldwork and processing of the survey results is acknowledged in the text as appropriate, but the text and illustrations are the product of joint work between the two authors.

Acknowledgements

A project like has only worked through collaboration between the survey team and local people. The authors have been extremely lucky at Aldborough to have been allowed unfettered access to survey on farmland and in private gardens. They are particularly grateful to Neil Bailes, Robert Bailes, Edward Craggs, Sir Andrew Lawson-Tancred and Tom Sanderson, as well as the many villagers who enthusiastically welcomed them into their gardens. Reverend Phillip Smith, Nick Kirkwood and David Vose kindly gave permission for the authors to work in the churchyard.

Key members of the survey team were Susan Holmes, Jason Lucas, James Lyall, Hanneke Reijnierse-Salisbury, and Elin Simmonson. Jess Ogden (LP Archaeology) and Lieven Verdonck (University of Ghent) undertook the GPR surveys, whilst Donna McCallay and Gigi Signorelli (LS Archaeology) played a key role in the excavations of 2017–18. Dave Haldenby, Roy Doughty and Chris Hannard undertook metal-detecting for the authors on their excavations. Specialist contributions to the project (some of which will be published elsewhere) came from Richard Brickstock, Charly French, Jerry Evans, Phil Mills, James Rackham and Vida Rajkovača. Helen Goodchild and Anthony Massington (Department of Archaeology, University of York) kindly helped with the loan of equipment. Lacey Wallace also undertook significant work on the project in the early stages of preparing this publication. Dominic Powlesland has been a key friend, collaborator and supporter throughout.

The work would not have been possible without the friendly help and support of English Heritage, Historic England and North Yorkshire County Council. The authors are particularly grateful to Mel Dalton, Mark Douglas, Keith Emerick, Gail Falkingham, Leonora Goldsmith, Susan Harrison, Peter Rowe, Hannah Saxton, and Pete Wilson. Colin Dobinson, who undertook pioneering work on the site in the 1980s and 1990s, has been most generous in sharing his information and knowledge with the authors.

The enthusiastic help and support of the Friends of Roman Aldborough (especially Jane Barber, David Roberts and Sir Andrew Lawson-Tancred) has been very much appreciated throughout.

In writing this volume the authors have benefited greatly from comments and advice from Ian Haynes and especially John Creighton.

Finally, the authors are most grateful to the following bodies for funds that have made this research possible: the Society of Antiquaries of London, the Thriplow Charitable Trust, the University of Cambridge (Faculty of Classics and the McDonald Institute for Archaeological Research). Historic England have kindly provided a publication grant for this volume.

Very substantial financial support for this project, including a publication grant, was kindly donated by Chris and Jan Martins. Chris Martins very sadly died in July 2018, so did not see the fruits of his generosity. The authors dedicate this volume to his memory.

Summary

Aldborough (in North Yorkshire) was the site of the Roman town of *Isurium Brigantum*, the administrative centre of the *civitas* of the Brigantes and one of the most northerly cities of the Roman Empire. The site has long been known, and was extensively explored by antiquarians in the seventeenth–nineteenth centuries. However, since the middle of the nineteenth century, it has received comparatively little archaeological attention. This book seeks to rectify this by providing a new synthesis of its archaeology and a discussion of its historical significance in the context of the history of Roman Britain.

This book draws together all the evidence from previous antiquarian and archaeological work on the site alongside a presentation of the authors' new work. This evidence is summarised in a gazetteer that accurately locates all past interventions, and which provides a summary and references to that work. Drawing on this material, there is a discussion of this earlier research which pays particular attention to the context of discoveries in the period between the 1680s and 1720s. It then discusses the unusually extensive exploration of the site under the patronage of Andrew Lawson between the 1830s and 1852. This period saw the construction of an antiquarian garden, part of which uniquely survives today, and culminated in the publication of Henry Ecroyd Smith's *Reliquae Isurianae* (1852) and the opening of a museum on the site. Subsequently, there was little further work on the site, although there were significant campaigns of excavations in the 1920s and 1930s as well as an important field-survey in the environs of the town in the 1980s and 1990s. Alongside this, small amounts of development-led archaeology have taken place since the 1950s, with such work becoming systematic in the 1990s.

The core of this volume presents the results of a geophysical survey of the town and its environs that was initiated in 2009, and has covered about 100ha. The results of this work (primarily using fluxgate gradiometers but complemented by ground-penetrating radar) are presented in an area-by-area description and discussion. By relating these survey results to information from past excavations and antiquarian research, the book provides a detailed new understanding of the topography of the town. This includes evidence of the town plan, a wide variety of buildings and the defences and structures lining the approaching roads. Importantly, it also provides a clear indication of the differing character of various areas outside the town walls, clarifies the courses of the Roman roads and provides new evidence for a Roman bridge over the River Ure.

Based on this evidence, a new synthesis of the site is presented. The authors argue that the town originated as a settlement of traders in the wake of the Roman conquest of the region around AD 70. It developed to become an important administrative centre, arguably before the end of the first century AD. Sometime around AD 120 there was a major phase of re-planning, which included the laying out of a street grid with terracing of the hill slope, the construction of a *forum* and the building of a new bridge over the River Ure. At about the same time a large amphitheatre was built just to the south east of the town. The town was provided with a town wall in the latter part of the second century, and over the next 150 years or so, the settlement thrived, with the development of suburban cemeteries and settlement and the occupation of some substantial town-houses. There is strong evidence to suggest that the town's economy was closely connected to military supply and taxation, with the provision of huge warehouses just inside the North Gate. The town's defences were enhanced in several phases during the fourth century, with the construction of external towers, new defensive ditches, and the addition of annexes outside the North and East Gates. The final phase of these defences seems to date to the late fourth or early fifth century. There are various strands of evidence to suggest that Aldborough remained as a key centre of power into the early medieval period.

Rose Ferraby
Martin Millett

Résumé

Aldborough, dans le nord du Yorkshire, était le site de la ville romaine de *Isurium Brigantum*, centre administratif de la *civitas* des Brigantes et l'une des cités de l'empire romain les plus au nord. Le site est connu de longue date et fut extensivement exploré par des amateurs d'antiquités aux 17ième-19ième siècles. Toutefois, depuis le milieu du 19ième siècle, il n'a reçu que relativement peu d'attention de la part des archéologues. Ce livre cherche à rectifier cela en offrant une nouvelle synthèse de son archéologie et une discussion de son importance historique dans le contexte de l'histoire de la Grande-Bretagne romaine.

Ce livre rassemble tous les témoignages des travaux des amateurs d'antiquités et des archéologues effectués précédemment sur le site à côté d'une présentation de nos nouveaux travaux. Ces témoignages sont résumés dans unrépertoire géographique qui situe avec précision toutes les interventions passées et fournit un résumé et des références à ces travaux. S'appuyant sur ces matériaux, il y a une discussion de ces recherches antérieures qui accorde une attention particulière au contexte des découvertes de la période entre les années 1680 et 1720. Elle discute ensuite l'exploration exceptionnellement étendue du site sous le patronage d'Andrew Lawson entre 1830 et 1852. Celle-ci comprenait la construction d'un jardin d'antiquités, dont une partie a singulièrement survécu jusqu'à nos jours, et a culminé dans la publication du *Reliquae Isurianae (1852)* de Henry Ecroyd Smith et l'ouverture d'un musée sur le site. Par la suite, il n'y eut que peu d'autres travaux entrepris sur le site bien qu'il y eut d'importantes campagnes de fouilles dans les années 1920 et 1930 ainsi qe d'importants relevés de terrain aux alentours de la ville dans les années 1980-90. En parallèle à cela de petites quantités d'archéologie liée à des travaux d'aménagement ont eu lieu depuis les années 1950, ces travaux devenant systématiques à partir des années 1990.

Le coeur du volume présente les résultats d'une prospection géophysique de la ville et de ses environs qui commença en 2009 et couvrit environ 100 ha. Les résultats de cette entreprise (utilisant essentiellement des sondes gradiométriques à porte de flux mais accompagnées de radar à pénétration de sol) sont présentés dans une description et une discussion zone par zone. En associant les résultats de ces prospections aux renseignements provenant des fouilles passées et aux recherches des amateurs d'antiquités, ce livre offre une nouvelle compréhension détaillée de la topographie de la ville. Ce qui comprend des témoignages d'un plan urbain, d'une grande variété de bâtiments, de défenses, et de structures qui bordent les voies d'accès. Tout aussi important, il donne une claire indication du caractère varié des différentes zones à l'extérieur des remparts de la ville, clarifie le tracé des voies romaines et apporte la preuve de l'existence d'un pont romain sur la rivière Ure.

Sur la base de ces témoignages, les auteurs présentent une nouvelle synthèse du site. Les auteurs présentent que la ville était à l'origine une implantation de marchands dans la foulée de la conquête romaine de la région vers environ 70 ap.J.-C . Elle s'est agrandie pour devenir un important centre administratif, probablement avant la fin du premier siècle ap.J.-C. A un certain moment vers 120 ap.J.-C. eut lieu une importante phase de planification qui comprenait le tracé d'un quadrillage des rues avec la construction de terrasses sur le flanc de la colline, la construction d'un *forum* et celle d'un nouveau pont sur la rivière Ure. A peu près au même moment, un grand amphithéâtre fut érigé juste au sud-est de la ville. La ville fut dotée d'un rempart dans la seconde moitié du 2ième siècle et au cours des plus ou moins 150 années qui suivirent, l'implantation prospéra avec le développement d'implantations et de cimetières en périphérie et l'occupation de maisons de ville substantielles. Il existe de solides témoignages qui donnent à penser que l'économie avait de forts liens avec le ravitaillement militaire et la taxation avec la mise a disposition d'immenses entrepôts juste à l'intérieur de la porte nord. Les défenses furent renforcées en plusieurs phases au cours du 4ième siècle avec la construction de nouvelles tours extérieures, de nouveaux fossés défensifs et l'addition d'annexes à l'extérieur des portes nord et est. La phase finale de ces défenses semble dater de la fin du 4ième ou du début du 5ième siècle. Il existe diverses sources de témoignages qu indiquent que Aldoborough est resté un siège clé du pouvoir jusqu'au début de la période médiévale.

Annie Pritchard

Zusammenfassung

Aldborough (in North Yorkshire) war als römische Stadt *Isurium Brigantum* das Verwaltungszentrum der Civitas der Brigantes und eine der nördlichsten Städte des Römischen Reiches. Die Stätte ist seit langem bekannt und wurde zwischen dem 17. und 19. Jahrhundert von Altertumsforschern intensiv erkundet. Seit Mitte des 19. Jahrhunderts hat sie jedoch vergleichsweise wenig archäologische Beachtung gefunden. Dieser Band versucht, dies mit einer neuen Synthese zur Archäologie der Stadt und einer Diskussion ihrer historischen Bedeutung vor dem Hintergrund der Geschichte des römischen Britannien zu korrigieren.

Mit diesem Buch werden alle Ergebnisse bisheriger altertumswissenschaftlicher und archäologischer Arbeiten an diesem Ort zusammengefasst und zugleich die neuen Arbeiten der Autoren vorgestellt. Die Ergebnisse sind in einem Fundverzeichnis zusammengefasst, das alle vorangegangenen Untersuchungen genau lokalisiert und eine Übersicht sowie Quellennachweise zu den jeweiligen Maßnahmen bietet. Auf Grundlage dieses Materials werden diese früheren Forschungen unter besonderer Berücksichtigung der Entdeckungen aus dem Zeitraum zwischen den 1680er und 1720er Jahren diskutiert. Hieran schließt sich eine Betrachtung der außergewöhnlich umfangreichen Erkundung der Fundstätte unter der Schirmherrschaft von Andrew Lawson zwischen den 1830er Jahren und 1852 an. In dieser Zeit wurde ein archäologischer Garten angelegt, von dem ein Teil einzigartiger Weise bis heute erhalten ist. Diese Periode gipfelte mit der Veröffentlichung von Henry Ecroyd Smiths *Reliquae Isurianae* (1852) und der Eröffnung eines Museums vor Ort. In der Folgezeit fanden nur wenige weitere Arbeiten am Fundort statt, es wurden jedoch in den 1920er und 1930er Jahren bedeutende Ausgrabungskampagnen sowie in den 1980er und 1990er Jahren wichtige Geländeaufnahmen im Umfeld der Stadt durchgeführt. Daneben gab es seit den 1950er Jahren eine geringe Anzahl baubegleitender archäologischer Maßnahmen, die seit den 1990er Jahren systematisiert wurden.

Das Hauptaugenmerk des Bandes liegt auf der Vorlage der Ergebnisse einer 2009 begonnen geophysikalischen Untersuchung der Stadt und ihrer Umgebung, die etwa 100 Hektar umfasst. Die Ergebnisse dieser Arbeit (hauptsächlich mit Fluxgate-Gradiometern, aber ergänzt durch Bodenradar) werden bereichsspezifisch beschrieben und erörtert. Durch die Verknüpfung dieser Untersuchungsergebnisse mit Informationen älterer Ausgrabungen und altertumswissenschaftlicher Forschungen liefert der Band ein detailliertes neues Verständnis zur Topografie der Stadt. Dazu gehören Hinweise zum Grundriss der Stadt, einer Vielzahl von Gebäuden sowie der Verteidigungsanlagen und Bauwerke entlang der Zufahrtsstraßen. Wichtig sind auch die deutlichen Anhaltspunkte auf den unterschiedlichen Charakter der verschiedenen Bereiche außerhalb der Stadtmauern, die Klärung des Verlaufs der Römerstraßen sowie neue Belege für eine römische Brücke über den Fluss Ure.

Auf Grundlage dieser Erkenntnisse wird eine neue Entwicklungsgeschichte des Fundorts vorgestellt. Nach Meinung der Autoren gehen die Anfänge der Stadt auf eine Siedlung von Händlern im Zuge der römischen Eroberung der Region um 70 n. Chr. zurück. Sie entwickelte sich zu einem wichtigen Verwaltungszentrum, wohl noch vor Ende des 1. Jahrhunderts n. Chr. Um 120 n. Chr. fand eine umfangreiche Neuplanung statt, die u. a. die Anlage eines Straßenrasters mit Terrassierung der Hügelhänge, sowie den Bau eines Forums und einer neuen Brücke über die Ure umfasste. Etwa zur gleichen Zeit wurde ein großes Amphitheater im Südosten der Stadt errichtet. In der zweiten Hälfte des 2. Jahrhunderts wurde die Stadt mit einer Mauer versehen, und in den folgenden 150 Jahren florierte die Siedlung, was sich z. B. an der Entwicklung von Vorstadtfriedhöfen und -siedlungen und der Anlage einiger bedeutender Stadthäuser zeigt. Es gibt deutliche Hinweise auf eine enge Verbindung der Wirtschaftsgrundlage der Stadt mit der militärischen Versorgung und dem Steuerwesen, was an der Anlage riesiger Lagerhallen innerhalb der Stadtmauern in unmittelbarer Nähe des Nordtores abzulesen ist. Die Verteidigungsanlagen der Stadt wurden im 4. Jahrhundert in mehreren Phasen ausgebaut, einschließlich des Baus von Außentürmen, neuen Wehrgräben und Anbauten außerhalb des Nord- und Osttores. Die Endphase dieser Verteidigungsanlagen scheint bis in das späte 4. oder frühe 5. Jahrhundert zu reichen. Aufgrund verschiedener Anzeichen ist davon auszugehen, dass Aldborough auch im frühen Mittelalter ein wichtiges Machtzentrum blieb.

Jörn Schuster

Notes on referencing and archives

In order to be economical with space and to make this volume easier to navigate for the reader, all the key information about past archaeological work on the site has been presented within the Gazetteer (Appendix 1) at the end of the volume. This also includes the fundamental bibliographical references. In the text all references to these sites is made by Gazetteer number in bold (for example, **G1**).

Additional archive material relating to this project is available in the University of Cambridge Digital Archive: Apollo https://www.repository.cam.ac.uk/handle/1810/275723. This includes a digital version of the survey plan, which can be examined at different scales. The DOI for this archive material is https://doi.org/10.17863/CAM.39574. The same archive also contains the details for finds from past fieldwalking and reports on the authors' recent excavations:

2016 excavation https://doi.org/10.17863/CAM.39571
2017 excavation https://doi.org/10.17863/CAM.39572
2018 excavation https://doi.org/10.17863/CAM.39573
fieldwalking data https://doi.org/10.17863/CAM.21743

1 Introduction

1.1 Background to this study

Aldborough, in North Yorkshire, is today a genteel village that lies in an agricultural landscape close to the market town of Boroughbridge, where the old Great North Road crosses the River Ure. It is one of many such villages in the Vale of York, but is distinguished as having been the site of the Roman town of *Isurium Brigantum*, which was the *civitas* capital of the *Brigantes*. As such, it was once the most northerly Roman administrative centre on the eastern side of Britain (figs 1.1 and 1.2). However, unlike many of the other major towns of Roman Britain, Aldborough has not benefited from much archaeological research. It has been overshadowed by the perception that its role was secondary in relation to the legionary fortress and later *colonia* at York (*Eburacum*). This lies only *c* 25km to Aldborough's south east, and had a key function both as a military and an administrative centre, becoming the provincial capital of *Britannia Inferior* under the Severan dynasty in the early third century.[1] It is also significant that the indigenous peoples of the north of Britain have generally been viewed in a negative manner by many studying the Roman Empire – often seen as being underdeveloped and lacking the sophistication of their contemporaries in the south. This view has been reinforced by a dominant narrative that sees the long-term military occupation of Hadrian's Wall and its hinterland in terms of a failure to control rebellious indigenous peoples who were ungovernable.[2] Paradoxically, such interpretations have come to the fore again in recent post-colonial scholarship, which places emphasis on the resistance of populations to Roman imperialism.[3] Both traditional scholarship and such post-colonial approaches have neglected to question both the extent to which Roman texts might have exaggerated indigenous rebellion for political reasons, and equally the potentially destabilising impact of long-term military occupation on a previously settled local people. In this context, a better understanding of the Roman town of *Isurium Brigantum* has the potential to contribute broadly to wider debates about the history of Roman Britain and about the impact of Roman imperialism.

The present project at Aldborough seeks to enhance knowledge of the Roman town. This involved two strands of initial work: the first, to conduct geophysical and topographic surveys of the available areas of the Roman town; the second, to analyse the results of field-walking surveys conducted in the extra-mural areas of the town under the aegis of the Roman Antiquities Section of the Yorkshire Archaeological Society in the 1980s and early 1990s. The results of the analysis of the field-walking finds are published elsewhere with information used in the discussion here and summarised in fig 4.6.[4] The present volume presents the results of the authors' geophysical and topographic survey work undertaken between 2009–17 as the basis for a new interpretation of the Roman town. To allow the fullest possible understanding of the site, the authors have also drawn together, mapped and summarised here the results of all previous antiquarian and archaeological work. Further research on the site is continuing, and this will be published elsewhere.

1.2 Geographical setting

Aldborough is located on the west side of the River Ure in the Vale of York, *c* 25km to the north west of York (fig 1.1). The southern part of the Roman town lies on a north-east facing slope, with the ground falling away from a ridge towards the river terrace, which is occupied by the northern part of the town (fig 1.2). This overlooks flood meadows that flank the river and has commanding views over the landscape to the north, east and west. The meadows are still prone to major flooding which, even in recent years, has inundated the area almost up to the Roman Town Wall. The ridge on which the southern part of the town lies is formed from Sherwood Sandstone dating from the late Permian–mid Triassic era. This solid geology is covered by glacial and alluvial deposits, predominantly sands in the area occupied by the Roman town (fig 1.3). These form rich, well-drained soils, although on the floodplain beside the river they are overlain by silty clays. Details of the local topography are shown on the LiDAR image (fig 1.4) produced from the Environment Agency data. This image reveals that the natural topography has been much altered, most visibly by the extensive ridge and furrow cultivation that survives across much of the site. It also shows that a slight ridge runs north from the Roman town towards the Ure, a feature that was followed by the route of the Roman road from the North Gate to the river.

1.3 Historical background

To understand the significance of Aldborough, it is useful to summarise the broader historical setting, noting that the authors will return to a more detailed review in Chapter 4. The Iron Age archaeology of the area remains poorly understood, although it seems clear that there was no major centre in the vicinity of the later Roman town. Settlement during this period in this part of the Vale of York appears marginal to the more intensively exploited landscapes of the Yorkshire Wolds to the east and on the

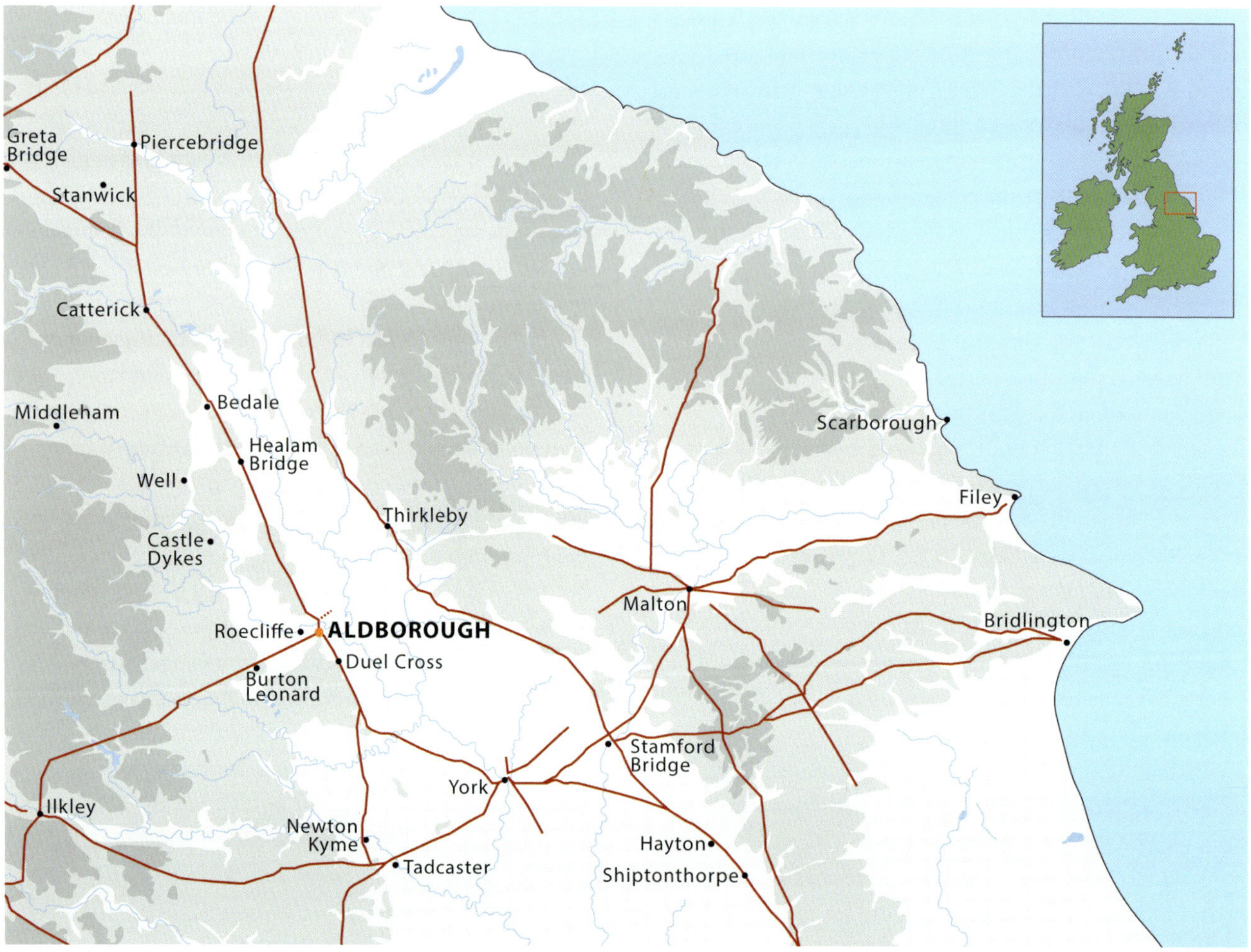

Fig 1.1 Map showing the location of Aldborough, North Yorkshire, in relation to topography and Roman roads with the principal sites mentioned in the text. *Drawing:* Rose Ferraby (using data from Digital Atlas of the Roman Empire, CC BY–SA 3.0)

Magnesian Limestone ridge – in particular, in the area a little distance to the south west. This may represent a real pattern although allowance should be made for the likelihood of some bias in the evidence with sites in the Vale of York being less archaeologically visible than those on the limestone and chalk.[5] Although the region lay outside the zone of direct contact with Rome in the period immediately after the Claudian invasion of AD 43, there is good evidence for interactions that had a major impact on the indigenous population.

These contacts, which figure in Roman sources, need to be understood in the broader context of the nature of Roman intervention in Britain. The Roman annexation of the south east in AD 43 had followed a long period of interaction between this region and the near continent.[6] Certainly, by the time of Augustus, around the end of the first century BC, there were regular political and economic links with the emergent Roman provinces of Gaul. This allowed some indigenous leaders to enhance their own social positions, with some perhaps becoming *de facto* clients of the Romans.[7] A similar pattern emerges within the British Isles after Rome's conquest of south-eastern Britain.

Amongst those who developed links with the Roman province was Cartimandua, described by Tacitus as Queen of the Brigantes.[8] Her pro-Roman stance caused internal conflict, and we are told that this resulted in Roman military support being sent to her, first in AD 57[9] and again in AD 69[10]. Although there has been some debate about whether Tacitus' account duplicates a single series of events in AD 69,[11] it seems on balance that there were two periods of conflict. Archaeological work has confirmed that Cartimandua's territory was focused on the substantial earthwork complex at Stanwick, in the Tees Valley.[12] Probably as early as the end of the first century BC, the settlement here was receiving goods from the Roman world, most likely within the context of diplomatic exchanges.[13] By the period between *c* AD 40 and 70 it was receiving significant quantities of high-quality goods.[14] The texts also show that Roman troops were sent to the region, but the overthrow of Cartimandua by an anti-Roman faction eventually took place around AD 69.[15]

Fig 1.2 Aerial photograph showing the village of Aldborough, North Yorkshire, in its local landscape, viewed from the north east. *Photograph:* Dominic Powlesland

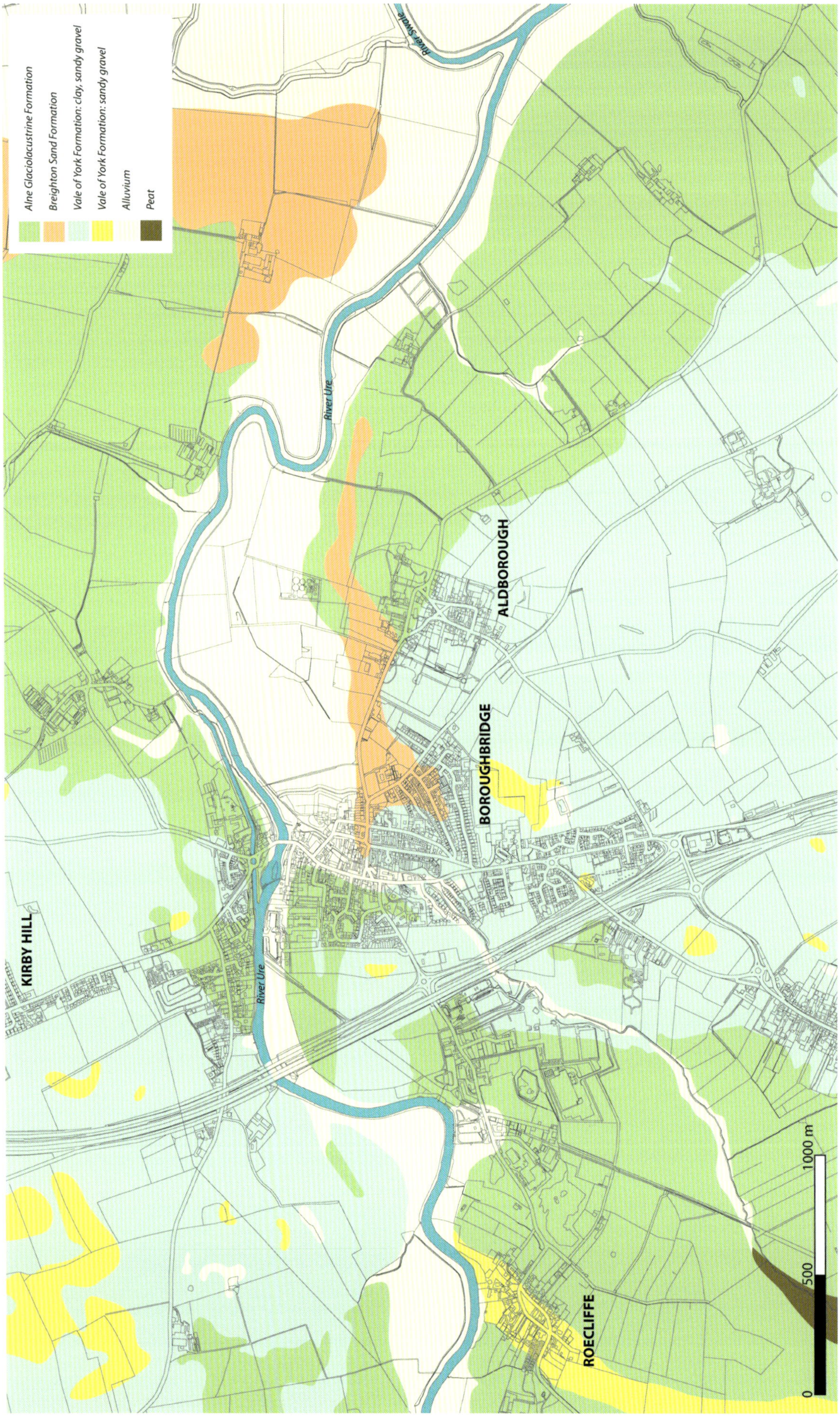

Fig 1.3 Map showing the drift geology of the area around Aldborough, North Yorkshire. *Drawing*: Rose Ferraby using DiGMapGB-50 Rock Unit 1:10,000. © Crown copyright and database rights 2018 Ordnance Survey (100025252)

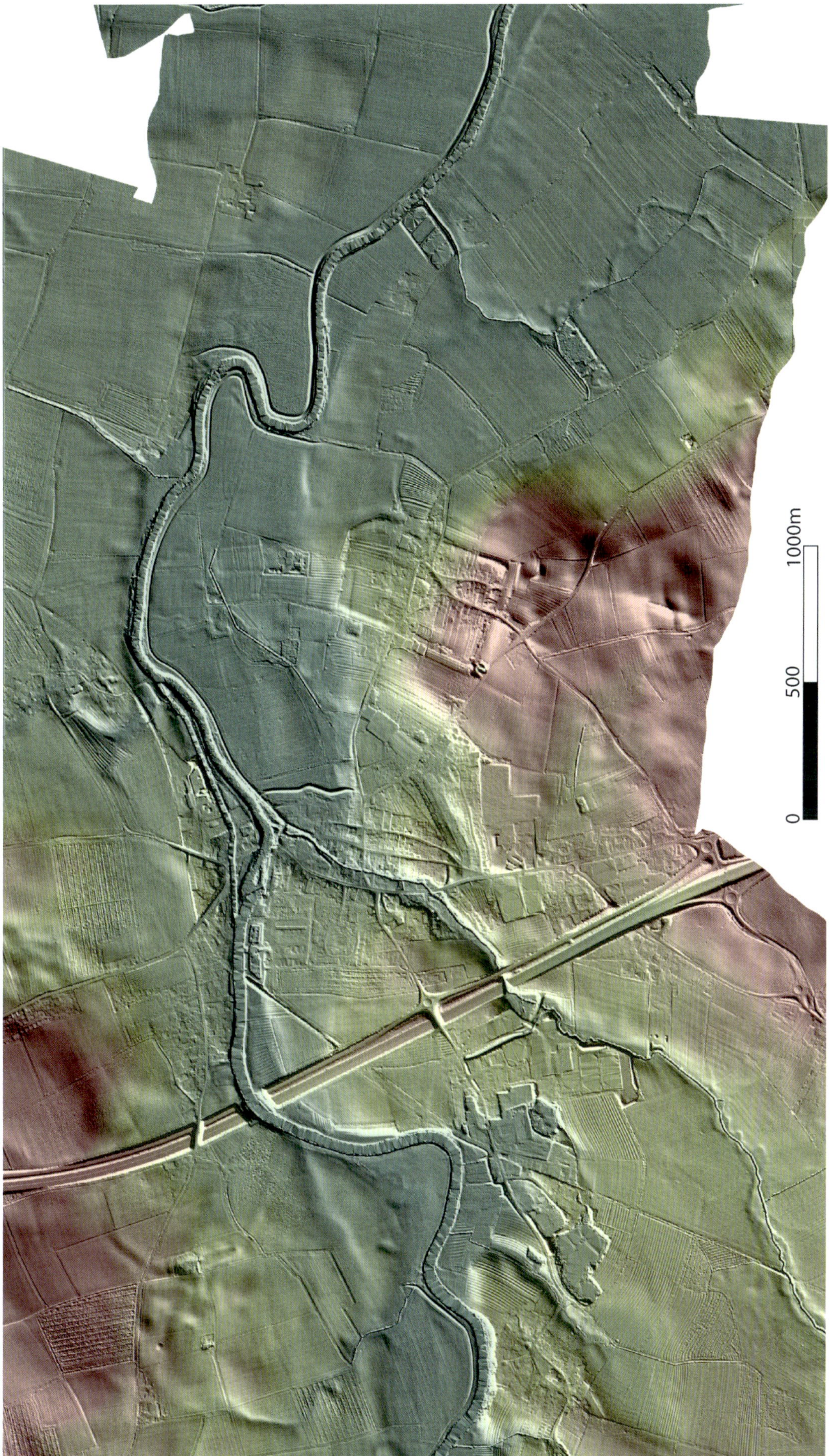

Fig 1.4 LiDAR image of the area around Aldborough, based on Environment Agency data. (Contains public sector information licensed under the Open Government Licence v3.0.). *Image:* Lacey Wallace

The people led by Cartimandua were called the Brigantes, although the character of their society is uncertain. By analogy with other areas, it seems likely that proximity to Roman power and the processes of military conflict as well as diplomatic, political and economic exchange led to social and political centralisation within indigenous societies. This may have brought people together into a larger agglomeration rather than the loosely related kinship or allied groupings that had existed previously. The extent of the territory controlled by Cartimandua is unknown, but the later evidence implies that the term 'Brigantia' was used to refer to a considerable area, extending from the Vale of York northwards to County Durham and westwards up into the Pennines.[16] Whether this was ever a coherent territory, and whether the later *civitas* coincides with the area controlled by Cartimandua, remains uncertain.

Roman military annexation of the region took place under the governor Q Petilius Cerialis from about AD 71.[17] Prior to this date, the limit of Roman military control seems to have been marked by the forts at Doncaster and Templeborough, established in the early 50s, and the Humber estuary to the east. Details of the Flavian military campaigns remain obscure, but a legionary base was established on a new site at York, and auxiliary forts across the region, including a string that ran northwards through the Vale of York up to the Tees. One of these controlled the crossing of the River Ure at Roecliffe, just to the west of Aldborough.[18] Parts of a network of military control continued in existence through the rest of the Roman period as York remained a key centre of Roman power. Elsewhere, individual forts went out of use, with that at Roecliffe abandoned *c* AD 85.[19]

The process of the Roman conquest of the north did not go smoothly, and despite a concerted push to control the whole of the island in the 80s, there followed a period of retrenchment that culminated in the construction of Hadrian's Wall in the 120s.[20] In the area behind the frontier, there was a constant military presence and substantial lines of communication and military supply were also maintained. The principal route on which Aldborough was located (known as Dere Street)[21] followed the line of the later A1 road up to the River Tees, where it continued to the frontier at Corbridge, whilst another road branched off to cross the Pennines via Bowes and Brough under Stainmore[22] connecting on to Carlisle. In conformity with her general practice, Rome also moved to engage local aristocracies in the process of provincial government. The general pattern involved the establishment of a network of self-governing territories (*civitates*), each with its own urban capital. In the south east, these were generally formed out of pre-existing Iron Age territories, with the capital being established at an existing settlement.[23] In the north and west, in the absence of an existing centre, former military settlements were sometimes developed as towns.[24]

In this region, it is known from later sources that the *civitas* of the Brigantes was formed with its administrative centre at *Isurium*, which can be identified with Aldborough (below, p. 7). This raises a series of questions: about the nature of the process of establishing the town; about the extent of its territory; and why the centre was established at Aldborough and not at the pre-existing centre of Stanwick, 50km to the north. It is these questions that have prompted interest in the early development of Aldborough.

1.4 Previous inferences on urban origins

Knowledge of the origins and early development of *Isurium Brigantum* is thus key to understanding of northern Britain during the Roman period. In the nineteenth century it was clearly understood that urban development was a direct product of Roman colonisation, and this is reflected unproblematically in Ecroyd Smith's volume, which provides an account of the early nineteenth-century exploration of Aldborough,[25] and the 1948 guidebook to the site.[26] Interestingly, R G Collingwood, writing in 1927, suggested for the first time that the town was founded *de novo* in the 70s as a civil centre.[27] By the 1950s, archaeological thought about the origin of Roman towns was becoming more nuanced, and the evidence from Aldborough was seen as suggesting that the site originated as a *vicus* beside an auxiliary fort established to control the crossing of the River Ure during the governorship of Q Petilius Ceralis in AD 71–4.[28] The evidence adduced to support this included finds of Vespasianic coins, stamped tiles of *Legio* IX,[29] and the dated structures excavated in the northern part of the town, although structural evidence for a fort was missing.[30] This interpretation chimed with broader understanding of Roman Britain at the time, as reflected in the Leicester conference on *civitas* capitals in 1963,[31] and remained as the basic framework down to the 1990s.[32] Evidence was interpreted within this paradigm, so here J S Wacher interpreted a building just inside the East Gate as a possible first-century military bathhouse, associated with a hypothesised early fort.[33]

In his 1988 assessment of the site, Colin Dobinson refined these ideas further, identifying more of the layout of the town grid and also, building on a suggestion by

Wacher, tentatively concluding that the situation of the *forum* might imply that it lay on the site of the *principia* of an earlier fort.[34] This emerging consensus was undermined by the discovery of a fort at Roecliffe, 2km west of Aldborough, during the widening of the A1 road in 1993. This fort controlled the river crossing and is dated by excavation to the period from *c* AD 70–85.[35] This discovery clearly meant that the hypothesis that there was a fort beneath Aldborough at this date needed reconsideration. In his discussion of this issue, Bishop suggested that there were consecutive forts at the two sites, with that at Aldborough replacing Roecliffe in the late 80s and lasting until after AD 122, on the basis of the presence of three stamped tiles of *Legio* VI and one of the *Cohors* IIII *Breucorum* – both units first posted to Britain under Hadrian.[36] Whilst this hypothesis might explain the evidence, it is based on a model of relations between the Roman army and indigenous peoples that may need revision. This debate will be explored below (p. 94).

1.5 Textual evidence

Relevant to any discussion about the origins of Aldborough is the limited textual evidence for its Roman place name. This is relatively consistent, with three principal sources critically discussed by Rivet and Smith.[37] *Isurium* is listed by Ptolemy as a *polis* of the Brigantes.[38] This reference dates to the middle of the second century AD, but probably draws upon a Flavian source for this area.[39] The Antonine Itinerary (likely compiled in the early third century AD) mentions the town on three routes, in each case on the road between Catterick and York. In *Iter I* and *Iter II*, it is referred to simply as *Isurium*, whilst in *Iter V* it appears as *IsuBrigantum*, reasonably interpreted as a corruption of *Isurium Brigantum*, providing the sole evidence for the role of the town as the *civitas* capital of the Brigantes. Finally, it has been suggested that the name *Coguveusuron* that is listed amongst the rivers in the Ravenna Cosmography (dated to shortly after AD 700, but incorporating at least three earlier sources) is the result of a river name (perhaps *Coccuveda*) being conflated with *Usuron* – a corrupted version of the town's name, *Isurium*.[40]

Recently, the discovery of writing tablets at Vindolanda has provided new evidence for the use of the place name *Isurium*, which appears in two of the texts dated to between *c* AD 92–122. *Tab Vind* II,185, has one certain mention of *Isurium* (line 23) and another suggested (line 6), both concerning the purchase of wine. The text appears to be a set of accounts from a journey along Dere Street, with the next stopping place being Catterick. *Tab Vind* III, 595 (line 3), apparently also a series of accounts, similarly mentions *Isurium*. These references indicate that both the settlement and a road existed by that period and were in regular use for those moving to and from the Roman frontier. Whether there was a fort at Aldborough at this date, or some other form of settlement is not clear, but this evidence is returned to in the debate below (Chapter 4).

1.6 History of the town

There is very little historical evidence to aid in the understanding of the town, so we rely on the archaeological evidence and analogy with other sites. The dates of its foundation as a *civitas* centre remain uncertain. John Wacher fitted it into his schematic reconstruction of urban development in Roman Britain under the heading of 'Hadrianic stimulation'.[41] However, he adduced very little evidence to support this dating, which is largely derived from his general reading of the historical context, and an implausible suggestion that Hadrian himself took a direct interest in urban foundation in Britain when he toured the Empire. A key question for research is thus whether it can be established when the town was founded, and how this was achieved.

It seems clear that the Roman town acted as a nodal centre for the region (see fig 1.1). From the south, one road came via Newton Kyme,[42] the other joining it from York,[43] both then leading via Aldborough to the northern frontier. It was also positioned on the River Ure, which was navigable up to just below Boroughbridge in the eighteenth century, with a wharf at Aldborough.[44] This suggests that Aldborough was at the point where goods could be transferred between road to river during the Roman period. There is also evidence for a road leading south west towards Ilkley,[45] whilst the authors' survey (below, p. 78) confirms that there was a road linking it to Malton in the east. Furthermore, its location also gave access to the routes leading west into the Yorkshire Dales, whether or not these were formalised as Roman roads.

Previous archaeological work has shown that once established the town shows evidence for some prosperity, in the form of a fine collection of mosaics, architectural fragments and other finds. The urban centre was also surrounded by walls (probably constructed in the second century AD), which were strengthened with the addition of external towers in the fourth century, indicating its continued importance. However, we have little more to inform us of the character or history of the town in late antiquity. Equally, unlike some of the *civitas* capitals in southern Britain, there is comparatively little evidence for the growth of villas – associated with the governing elites – in the immediate vicinity of *Isurium*, perhaps because of the difficulty in detecting them in the environment of the Vale of York. The nearest well-known villas are located a distance up the Ure Valley at Castle Dykes (North Stainley) and Well.[46] A recently discovered villa at Aiskew (Bedale) lies close to a tributary to the River Swale, not far from the road between Aldborough and Catterick.[47] Others are probably waiting to be found elsewhere in the hinterland of the town. It is perhaps likely that the *mausoleum* found *c* 4km south of the town at Hundayfield Farm[48] as well as the nearby barrow discovered in the eighteenth century at Duel Cross[49] are associated with another villa. Aerial photographic evidence also confirms that there were other farming settlements in the surrounding landscape.[50]

Evidence for the ending of the Roman town and its subsequent fate is also lacking. Coinage continued to be supplied to the site down to the cessation of supplies in the early fifth century.[51] However, the lack of high-quality modern excavation means that we have no good evidence for the nature of occupation at this time or into the early medieval period. It is notable that at Domesday the settlement, then called Burc, remained important and was only eclipsed by the foundation of Boroughbridge at a new river crossing in the twelfth century.[52]

1.7 Previous archaeological work

The pattern of past archaeological exploration of the Roman town is unusual in that after flourishing in the eighteenth, nineteenth and early twentieth centuries fieldwork slowed, and has been very limited in the past fifty years or so. In Chapter 2 of this volume is a detailed review of previous work, and in Appendix 1 a Gazetteer of known archaeological interventions (**G1–106**, pp. 127–58) is given, so here it is only appropriate to offer a brief overview.

Eighteenth-century antiquarians were aware of the identification of Aldborough as *Isurium Brigantum* on the basis of the Antonine Itinerary, and there was a steady interest in the site.[53] After a series of discoveries, including a number of mosaics, in the early eighteenth century the first major archaeological discovery was of the northern range of the *forum* in 1770 (**G6**). Several mosaics were kept open for display within purpose-built structures, establishing a tradition of antiquarian visits.[54]

The second quarter of the nineteenth century marks a high point in work at the site. Andrew Lawson, a prominent member of a local family, purchased much of the town and developed Aldborough Manor and its gardens, the property remaining with this family today (see fig 1.5). He was a keen antiquarian and the Roman history of the site became a major interest for him. His work included both the presentation of past finds and new discoveries, including a series of other mosaics and architectural fragments.[55] Several Roman buildings were cleared and planned, with the gardens of the Manor laid out to include some of the exposed buildings within its design (below, pp. 18–19). In 1852, a volume describing the finds and entitled *Reliquae Isurianae* was compiled and published by Henry Ecroyd Smith.[56] It drew together earlier information and provided an impressive series of illustrations produced by M N Hessey of York.[57] The 'Museum Isurianum' established by Andrew Lawson presented the material found. It was initially displayed in his house, but a purpose-built museum was opened on the site in 1863.[58]

After the death of Andrew Lawson in 1853 there was little archaeological work at Aldborough until after the First World War. New excavations (**G33–G38**) were started as a local initiative in 1924, yet were never fully published.[59] Later, an influential group within the Roman Antiquities Section of the Yorkshire Archaeological Society came together to organise a programme of new work. These campaigns (1934–5 and 1937–8) were led by Mrs A M H Chitty jointly with Mr J N L Myres for the first two seasons, and Dr K A Steer for the latter two.[60] This work formed part of a broader programme on Roman sites in Yorkshire at the time. It primarily involved cutting a series of trenches to explore and date the town defences, to establish their course in the north-western part, and to examine their south-western corner (**G34**, **G39–G43**). Other trial trenches were also excavated, but they are not the subject of any very full report.[61]

In the years following the Second World War work at Aldborough was very limited indeed. In contrast to the carefully defined research agenda of the 1930s, excavation was limited to interventions either occasioned by the construction of new buildings, or to investigate the southern defences that had been put into the Guardianship of the then Ministry of Public Buildings and Works (MPBW) by the Dowager Lady Lawson-Tancred in 1952. These small excavations were conducted between 1959 and 1974, first by the Royal Commission on Historical Monuments for England (RCHME) and then by the Ministry of Public Buildings and Works, largely under the supervision of Dorothy Charlesworth. One project completed in 1964, saw a major excavation just outside the South Gate (**G51**), together with

Fig 1.5 Photograph of an excavated Roman building (**G10**) and architectural fragments displayed in the garden of Aldborough Manor, *c* 1910. The Roman Town Wall (**G9**) lies just beyond the path, covered in ivy. Viewed from the west. *Photograph:* T J Hanstock. Reproduced by courtesy of Sir Andrew Lawson-Tancred

observations on a sewer trench that cut across the land to the east and north of the town (**G52**), which was fully published by Mrs M U Jones.[62] The remainder of the work remained unpublished until it was dealt with as part of a back-log project by English Heritage many years later.[63] Charlesworth herself explained her understanding of the town in her guidebook,[64] and also summarised her work on the town defences in a paper published in 1971.[65] The team responsible for publishing Charlesworth's work did a sound job, but the poor quality of the surviving archive limited what they were able to report. Work on the Guardianship site also included further investigation of a mosaic found in the nineteenth century – commonly referred to as the Helicon pavement – which was also published in 2002.[66] In the 1990s, under the initiative of English Heritage, research was also undertaken on certain categories of finds from the site. The most notable product of this work was a catalogue of small finds published by Mike Bishop in 1996. This publication allowed Bishop to offer some brief comments on the history of the town.[67]

Through the 1980s and early 1990s new field-survey work was initiated by members of the Roman Antiquities Section of the Yorkshire Archaeological Society. This work, initially undertaken by adult education students under the direction of Jennifer Price, and later developed by Colin Dobinson, involved systematic field-walking: first, immediately to the north of the town; later, in other areas of arable cultivation within its environs. The work by Dobinson's team was unusually systematic, with each individual findspot carefully recorded. At the time, the material and data on finds locations was so voluminous that processing was not completed. Nevertheless, as the finds and archive were carefully retained, this evidence has been available for use in the current project.[68]

Finally, with the advent of developer-funded archaeological work, a series of small projects has recorded interventions and limited excavations undertaken since 1990. The 'grey literature' resulting from this work is curated by the North Yorkshire County Council within their Historic Environment Record. The extent of these interventions has generally been limited since the walled area of the Roman town is a Scheduled Ancient Monument. Nevertheless, they provide a range of information, which has been drawn upon where appropriate in the work within this volume.

1.8 Organisation of this volume

The authors' research is presented in the three following chapters. In Chapter 2, the results of past antiquarian and archaeological work are discussed and evaluated. This is supported by a detailed Gazetteer (Appendix 1), which provides information on all past work along with appropriate illustrations and references to the key sources. Chapter 3 then provides an account and discussion of the results of the survey, presenting and interpreting the results, and cross-referencing and integrating them with the evidence from previous work. This chapter is organised topographically, with detailed plans of the survey data and the authors' interpretations of these. Finally, in Chapter 4, the evidence is drawn together to provide a new chronological account of the whole site as well as a full reassessment of its development within the broader context of Roman Britain.

2

Previous antiquarian and archaeological work

Aldborough has been known as a key Roman site, identified with *Isurium* in the Antonine Itinerary, since the sixteenth century and, unusually for a major Roman site in Britain, much of our most significant knowledge of it was recovered before the development of modern archaeology. For this reason, it is important to present a clear account of early work about the Roman town. This chapter thus begins with a review of work down to the publication of Henry Ecroyd Smith's *Reliquae Isurianae* in 1852. This discussion focuses on the information obtained during that period, whilst also offering incidental insights into the methods of working during that period as this helps to evaluate the evidence. For the period since 1852, this chapter provides a more straightforward overview of the different phases of exploration and their results. The chapter is complemented by a gazetteer (below, pp. 127–58) that provides details of every known intervention on the site with a full bibliography and, where appropriate, an explanation of how the authors have established its exact location. For ease and economy of referencing, all sites and finds are referred to using the volume's gazetteer number (**G1**, etc) and can be located on the maps of the separate survey areas within Chapter 3.

2.1 Knowledge up to the mid eighteenth century

The earliest antiquarian discussion of Aldborough appears to come from John Leland whose account relates to the period 1535–43.[1] The village was already identified with *Isurium Brigantum* and Leland reports the discovery of Roman coins (of silver and 'brass'), as well as 'sepultures, *aquae ductus* and *tessellata pavimenta*'; he also identifies Studforth Hill (then called 'Stothart') with the site of a medieval castle. Aside from the castle, precise locational information is not provided, but there is no reason to doubt the veracity of his information. Leland's account is noted by most subsequent writers and is quoted in full by Francis Drake.[2] In the later seventeenth century, an inscription found in a wall in Boroughbridge was linked with the Roman settlement at Aldborough.[3]

The first set of really significant information comes from the late seventeenth and early eighteenth century, when the Reverend Edward Morris (sometimes spelt 'Maurice') was evidently active as an antiquarian. He was the incumbent of the parish, and also a canon of Ripon, from 1676/7 until his death in 1719, as recorded on his monument that was in the chancel of St Andrew's church. This is no longer extant but was quoted by Gough.[4] Although Morris does not appear to have written anything at length about the site himself, he clearly knew much about it and became an informant and a guide to various other antiquaries. He was a significant letter-writer, and various of his communications provide information for later writers. He is explicitly noted as the informant of Edmund Gibson, who quotes a letter from him in his edition and translation of Camden's *Britannia*,[5] later quoted in full by Francis Drake.[6] The letter reads:

> The ancient town (as appear'd by a late survey) contain'd within the walls, sixty acres, being almost a

direct square, upon a declining hill towards Ure on the north-side; Road-gate, leading to the old *Cataractonium*, went through it to Milby; and the way through the meadows may yet be discover'd, bearing the name of Brig-gates, near half a mile east of the present bridge. Under the South-wall, there seems to have been an old camp, or about two acres, the only place on the outside, where coins are found. The old walls are about four yards thick, founded upon large pebbles laid on a bed of blue clay, four or five yards deep. The soil is black, which makes the tradition probable that it was burnt by the Danes when York was almost destroy'd by them; and also, upon opening the ground, bones are seen half-burnt, with other black ashes. Here have been found also fragments of aquaeducts cut in great stones, and cover'd with Roman tile; and in the late Civil wars, as they were digging a Cellar, they met with a sort of vault, leading as it is said, to the river; if it was of Roman work (for it has not yet met with any one curious enough to search it) it might probably be a repository for the dead. The coins (generally of brass, but some few of silver) are rarely elder than Claudius, yet some are of Augustus Caesar, and so down to the Antonines with Carausius and Allectus, and two of the thirty tyrants, *viz* Posthumus and Tetricus; but those of Constantine are most common. They meet also with little Roman heads of brass and have formerly found coin'd pieces of gold with chains of the same metal; but none of late. Here have likewise been found, within the circuit of the old walls, about twenty little polish'd signet-stones, of diverse kinds and cuts, particularly one had a horse upon it, and a stamp of laurel shooting five branches; another, a Roman fitting, with a sacrificing dish in one hand, and resting his other on a spear; a third, a Roman (if not Pallas) with a spear in one hand, wearing a helmet, and a shield on the back, or on the other arm, and under that something like as quiver hanging to the knee; a fourth (of purple colour) has a Roman head like Severus or Antonine; a fifth hath the head of Jupiter Ammon; a sixth an eagle, with a civic crown in its bill; a seventh, a winged victory crowning a trophy. Several pavements have been found about a foot under ground, and compose'd with stones of about an inch square; but within are little stones of a quarter that bigness, wrought into knots of flowers, after the mosaic fashion. No altars are met with; but pieces of urns and old glass are common; and they also have found vessels of red earth, wrought with knots, flowers, heads, birds and beasts, and lately a lamp of earth, and a Cothon or Poculum Laconicum, which the soldiers did use, in their marches, for cleaning of water, by passing it into several concavities made therein. In the vestry wall of the church, is plac'd a figure of Pan or Silvanus, in one rough stone niched.

The absence of reference to this letter in Gibson's first edition of Camden[7] suggests that the letter dates to after 1695. A very slightly different version of it, which omits the section prior to the description of the vault found in the Civil War, cites a different selection of coins, and lists only the first four intaglios, is quoted in a manuscript written in 1714 and now held in the British Library.[8] The coins listed there are: '…most of Constantine and Carausius, tho there are too of Maximian, Diocletian, Valerian, Severus, Pertinax, Arcadius and other emperors, as also of Faustina and Julia.'[9]

The British Library manuscript, entitled *An Explanation of the survey of the Mannour of Aldborough*, written by someone with the initials 'WD',[10] provides an introduction to the estate to accompany the two maps of Aldborough surveyed in 1708 by Robert Smithson (figs 2.1 and 2.2). This survey seems to have been commissioned following the Duke of Newcastle's acquisition of Aldborough in 1701 and in connection with it, as the principal content is a list of the land-holdings. The maps provide an invaluable resource for understanding Aldborough at this date, and additionally are annotated with letters, apparently added by 'WD'.

In relation to the wider estate map (see fig 2.1), the text explains:

> There is tradition of a famous highway that was between **A** at the Town's End and **B** in the river, where it's said there was a bridge, and I am induced to believe it; because there are many heavy stones & others to be found in the river at this place and not any where else as the fishermen did assure me. The River Ure is navigable from York to **C**, from whence abundance of lead is water born and a repository is built at **D** for the Merchants Goods brought back: Tis navigable likewise for the very most to **E** where very much lead is also taken on board; and the like conveniency built....'[11]

The location of the bridge on this estate map matches the evidence from the survey (below, p. 77), although the route of the Roman road leading to it is not that suggested in the manuscript.

In the section relating to the village map (see fig 2.2), the text reads: 'At **A** and **B** in this draught I saw the pavement that is mentioned in Mr Morris' letter; and at **C**

Fig 2.1 Map of the Manor of Aldborough drawn by R Stephenson in 1708. © The British Library Board (Stowe MS 883)

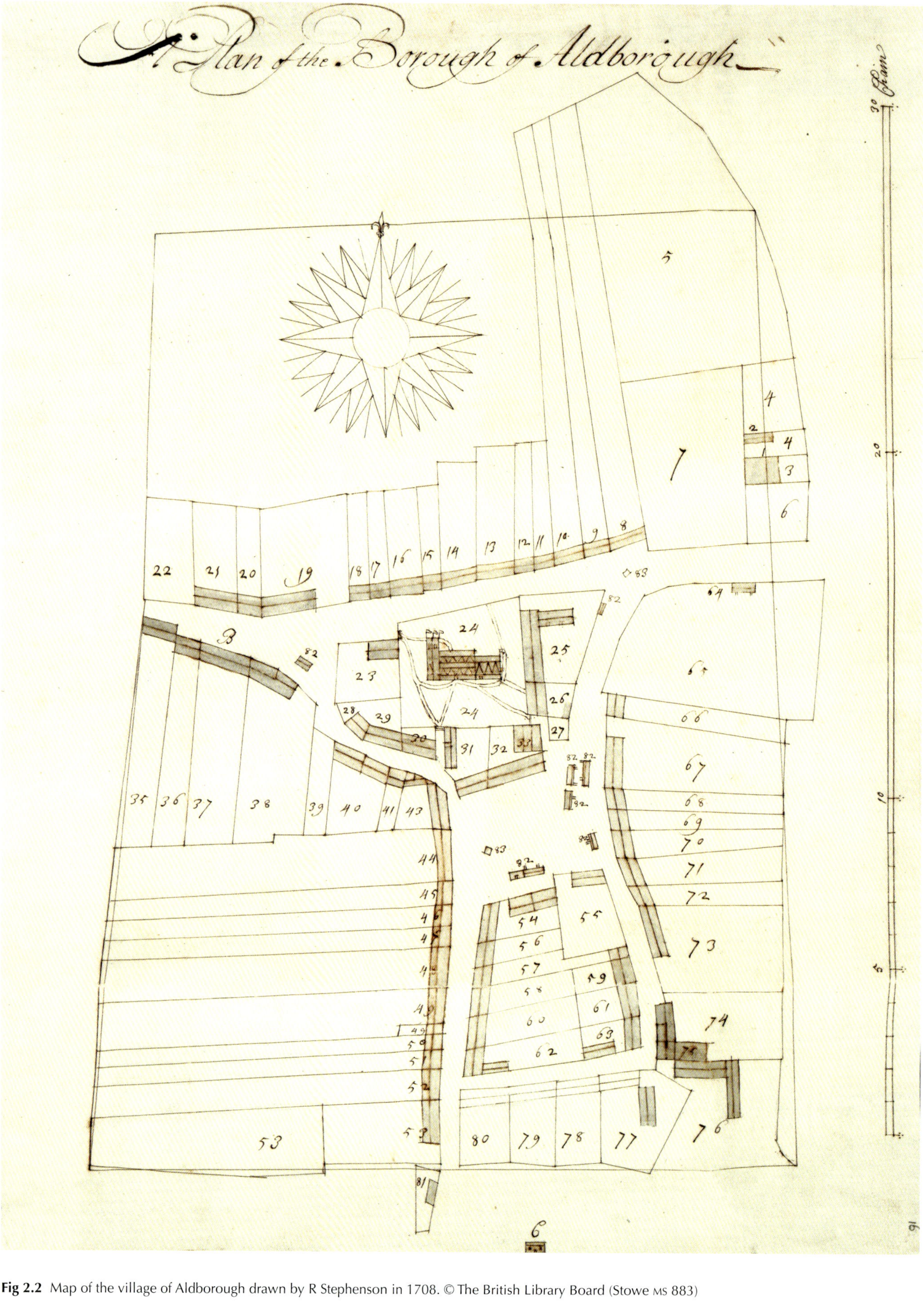

Fig 2.2 Map of the village of Aldborough drawn by R Stephenson in 1708. © The British Library Board (Stowe MS 883)

> found an urn, and at ***a*** a gold coin of Trajan, IMP. TRAIANO AVG. GER. DAC. P. M. TR. P. COS. VI. P.P. rev. a figure standing holding in its right hand a patera, in its left an ear of corn, S. P. Q. R. OPTIMO PRINCIPI. This seems to be the great building in the street before the church-yard described by Dr Stukeley, of which many stones had been taken up and many remained.[32]

Gough then goes on to repeat Stukeley's words (as quoted above) before continuing to describe some stones that he himself had seen. His plan is reproduced here (fig 2.4), although it should be noted that the printed plan does not label ***a*** or ***e*** mentioned in his text. The remaining paragraphs of his account largely follow the letter from Morris cited by Gibson and Drake that have been quoted above, with the addition of material from Stukeley. The only additional detail is his note about an onyx from the site exhibited at the Society of Antiquaries in 1749.

It has long been recognised from Gough's description that the remains outside the church (**G6**) are best interpreted as one range of the *forum,*[33] but how Gough obtained his information is unclear. Some light is cast on this by the unpublished manuscript of William Hargrove, a York publisher who set out to produce a revised edition of Drake's *Eboracum*, eventually published as the *History and description of the ancient City of York* in 1818, but which largely excluded material from beyond the city.[34] He does note the discovery of burials at Aldborough,[35] whilst amongst his manuscript notes are other entries relating to Aldborough[36] that appear to result from his research on updating Drake. Most of this information derives from the earlier sources discussed above, perhaps via his father, Ely Hargrove, author of the *History of Knaresborough,*[37] although there are indications that he had access to a wider range of original material. This includes a letter, dated 9 April 1757, from Stukeley to Roger Gale regarding the Devil's Arrows and which does not seem to derive from any of these sources.[38] More significantly regarding Aldborough, the manuscript includes two plans that are otherwise unknown.

The first is a drawing of the Roman milestone[39] found at Duel Cross, to the south of Aldborough, in March 1776,[40] as well as a plan showing its findspot. Hargrove's manuscript has some overlap with the information about this find provided in Gough's edition of Camden (see above), but he includes more information, such as the map, implying access to a primary source. Significantly, a contribution to the *Gentleman's Magazine* reports additional finds at Duel Cross in 1787, including a coin of Vespasian, and states that the tumulus was 18ft high with a circumference of 370ft (giving a radius of 59ft).[41] This entry (initialled 'EH') is known to have been authored by Ely Hargrove,[42] whilst a correction to the reading of the inscription in the same magazine initialled 'DH' was written by Richard Gough.[43] This suggests that William Hargrove's information about Duel Cross, as well as that used by Richard Gough, derived from Hargrove's father, Ely, who died in 1818.[44]

The second drawing is a plan of the excavated remains of the Aldborough *forum* (**G6**) discovered in front of the church in 1770[45] as were also reported by Gough (see above). There is no significant accompanying text (although the text of the legend on the gold coin noted by Gough is repeated), but the plan (fig 2.5) and annotations include letters showing the findspots for the urn and gold coin as reported by Gough, though not located on his plan (see above). The illustration also includes vignettes of the buildings opposite, and details of the layouts of the walls that appear less schematised than in Gough's illustration (see fig 2.4). As the vignettes can be identified with some of the surviving houses, its

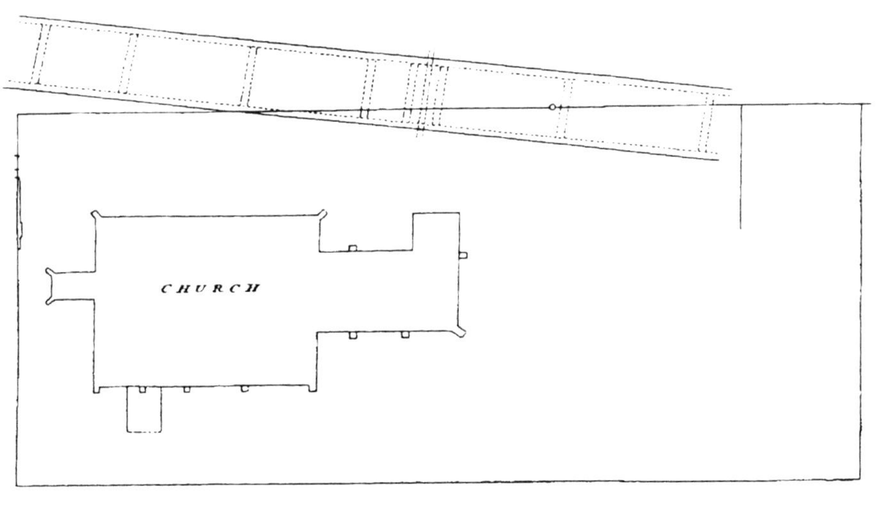

Fig 2.4 Plan of the *forum* remains excavated in 1770 (**G6**) from Gough 1789

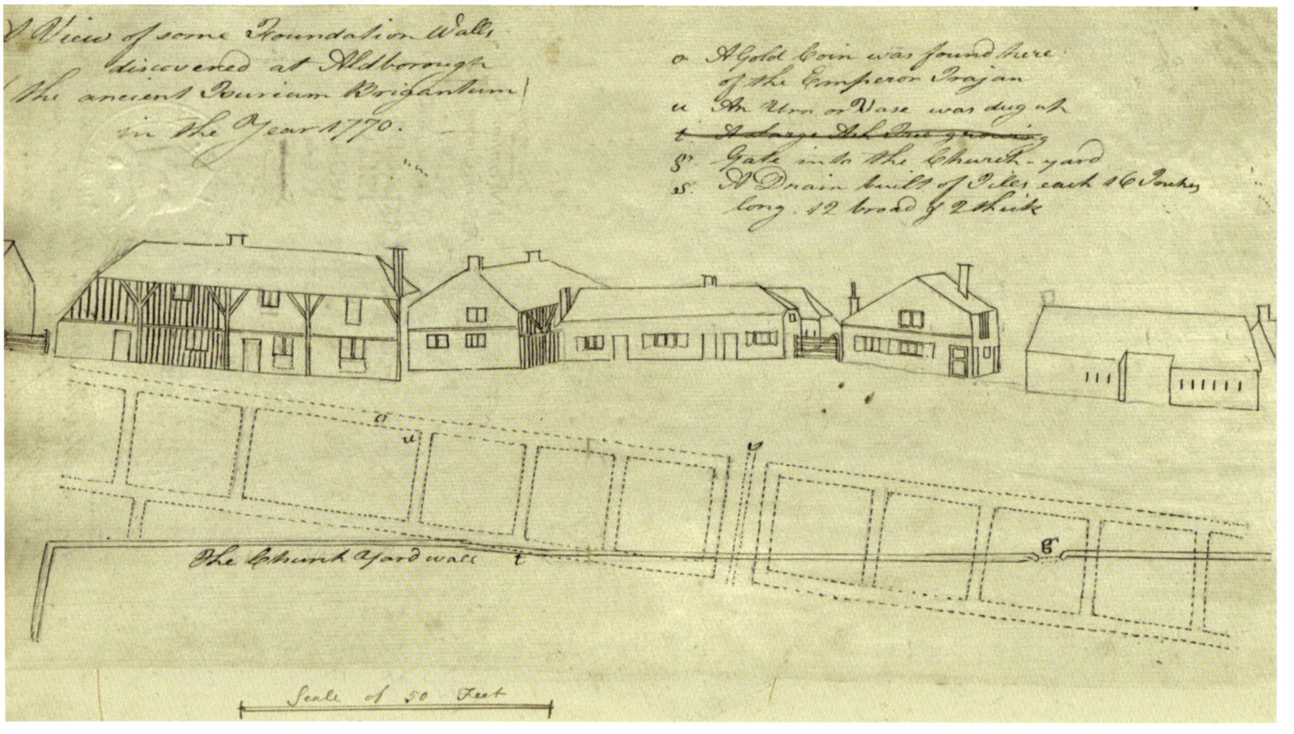

Fig 2.5 Unpublished plan of the *forum* remains excavated in 1770 (**G6**) from the Hargrove MS. The plan is thought to have been made by Ely Hargrove. *Image:* reproduced from an original held by City of York Council/Explore Libraries and Archives Mutual, York: Manuscript GB 192 HAR

evidential value is clear. This plan must have been copied from a primary source but, as it differs from Gough's figure in also omitting the location of the church, this suggests that the two illustrations, although related, are independent. It thus provides very significant new evidence about the *forum*. Who made this record remains unknown, but given the evidence of the Duel Cross plan, it too may well have come from Ely Hargrove.

In 1811, another correspondent to the *Gentleman's Magazine* (calling himself Viator Militaris) reports the discovery of a tombstone at Aldborough,[46] whilst lamenting the neglect of the site's antiquities and mentioning various other finds including burials.[47] These burials (the discovery of which is dated to 1808) may be those alluded to by William Hargrove[48] and also included in a short discussion of the site some forty years later where the burials are located just south of the town.[49] Their attribution to the widening of the road at Chapel Hill (**G7**) is confirmed by Turner,[50] whose text perhaps suggests that the inscription came from the same site.

2.3 The first half of the nineteenth century

The golden age of antiquarian exploration of Aldborough came about during this period, culminating in the publication of Henry Ecroyd Smith's *Reliquae Isurianae* in 1852. The bulk of this work was the result of the patronage of Andrew Lawson. He had previously lived at Boroughbridge Hall, and had come to reside at the Manor from *c* 1823–5; in 1834 he bought most of the estate from the Duke of Newcastle.[51] The sale of the estate followed the Great Reform Act of 1832, which led to the parliamentary boroughs of Aldborough and Boroughbridge losing their right to return four members of parliament, despite having only a handful of electors.[52]

Andrew Lawson was a keen antiquarian who not only encouraged the exploration of the site, but also incorporated the remains in the gardens of Aldborough Manor, which he had built in 1825[53] and remodelled around 1840.[54] Lawson created a walk through the garden which passed excavations open to display (fig 2.6) with items including inscriptions (and the shaft of a Saxon cross brought from Cundall) placed for the visitor to admire. The walk up to, and through the pinetum planted along the south wall of the town and including a Roman quarry, culminated in a prospect tower situated on the wall by the South Gate, providing a view back over the town (fig 2.7).[55] The creation of a museum and the production of Ecroyd Smith's volume[56] formed an integral part of Andrew Lawson's enterprise. This book is one of the earliest accounts of any town in Roman Britain and remains a key work of reference: where it can be

Fig 2.6 Nineteenth-century photograph of the Roman Town Wall (*in front*) and 'barracks' (*to the left*) (**G11**) laid out in the garden of Aldborough Manor. Viewed from the north. *Photograph:* unknown photographer; reproduced by courtesy of Sir Andrew Lawson-Tancred

Fig 2.7 View of Aldborough from the 'prospect tower'. Frontispiece from Ecroyd Smith 1852. Note that the new plan of the Roman town is featured in the foreground along with a copy of the volume itself. Original illustration by M N Hessey

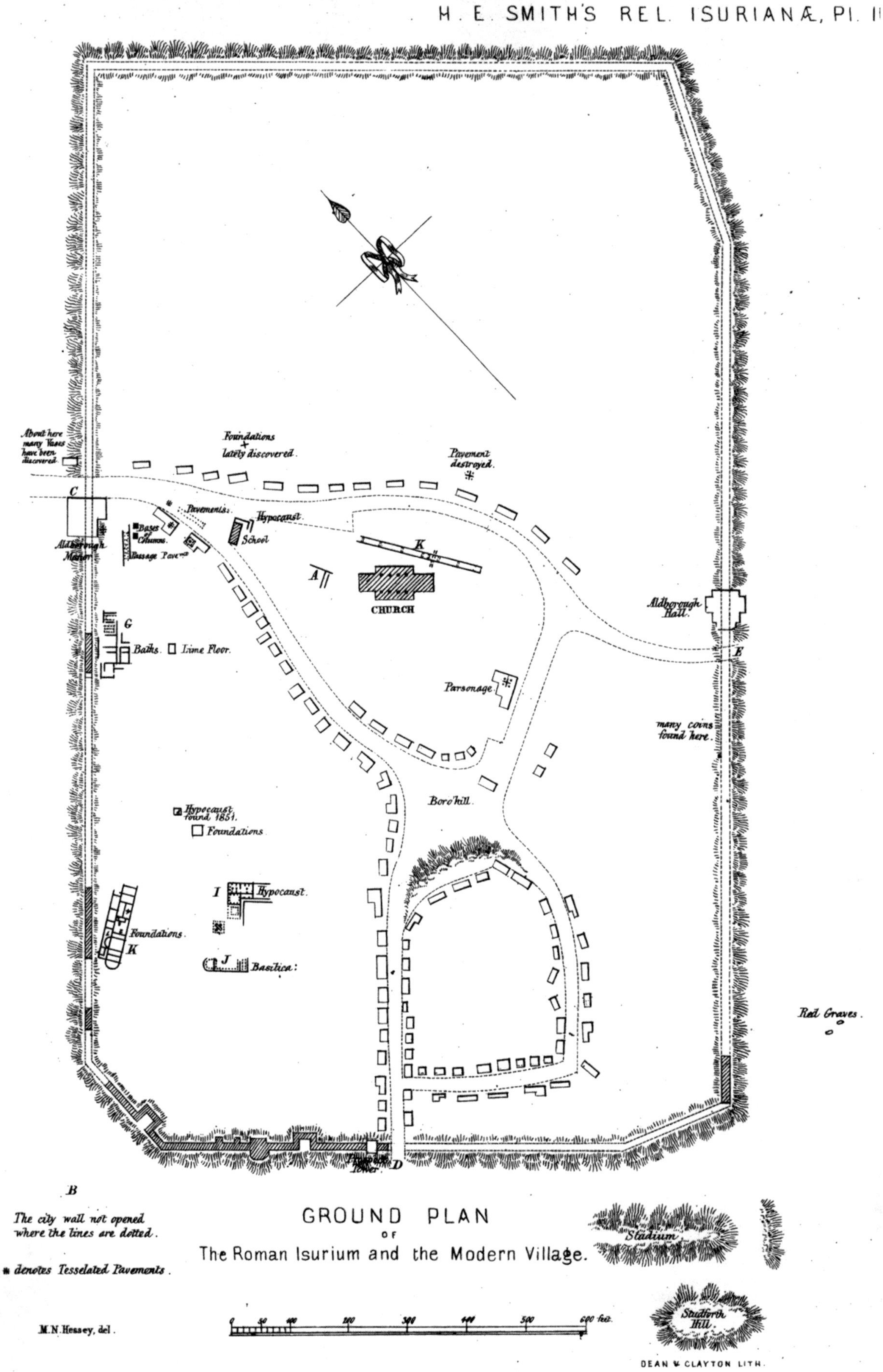

Fig 2.8 Plan of Aldborough from Ecroyd Smith 1852. Original illustration by M N Hessey

evaluated, the evidence presented is of very high quality. It also provides the earliest accurate plan of the town showing the location of most past discoveries[57] (fig 2.8). Broader discussion is limited to a descriptive account of what was found, but in passing it may be noted that although working within a framework dominated by the idea of Roman immigrants, he used the term 'Romanization' (quoting from Charles Roach Smith),[58] thus prefiguring a concept that has dominated the subject ever since.

Andrew Lawson's 'Museum Isurianum' displayed the material found in his excavations. It was initially housed in his house in Boroughbridge,[59] but was opened at Aldborough before 1853,[60] at first in a building situated over the excavated corridor mosaic (**G20**) just behind the Manor.[61] The purpose-built museum adjacent to the prospect tower at the culmination of the path through the garden was opened later, on the occasion of the British Archaeological Association's visit to the site in October 1863 (fig 2.9).[62] It may be noted in passing that the floor of this building incorporated the re-laid and restored panels from the corridor mosaic (**G20**) along its southern side. The mosaics on its northern side appear to have been created afresh but using ancient materials.

In many ways, Ecroyd Smith's volume[63] continued the antiquarian tradition of the previous century of providing a compilation of previous knowledge supplemented by new discoveries, but in having a single-site focus it also prefigures many later accounts of individual sites. However, although it illustrates a series of excavations, it lacks significant description or discussion of what had been found, and in this sense is antiquarian rather than archaeological. This is not the place to provide a detailed assessment of the book, rather the intention here is to draw out the new information provided by the investigations of this period.

The book works its way around the Roman town topographically, beginning at the Manor and then moving clockwise, first through the garden, then around the rest of the defensive circuit, before moving on to discuss the evidence of the mosaics and other discoveries within. Although not always easy to follow, the text provides a wealth of new information relating to discoveries between the 1770s and its date of publication (1852). Details are reviewed systematically in this volume's gazetteer (pp. 127–58), but it is worth summarising the extent of this knowledge. It includes information about the town walls (**G9** and **G13**), with additional detail about finds from the West Gate (**G8**) and East Gate (**G16**). An unpublished contemporary plan (fig 2.10), provides further details of the West Gate and its environs. The book then looks at the Roman buildings excavated in the south-western quarter of the town, within the Manor Garden (**G10**, **G11**, **G19**, **G20**, **G22**, **G23**, and **G24**) (fig 2.11). In aggregate, this represents probably the largest number of urban domestic buildings explored on a single site in Britain at that date. It is clear that these were excavated over a period of at least twenty years, whilst the inclusion

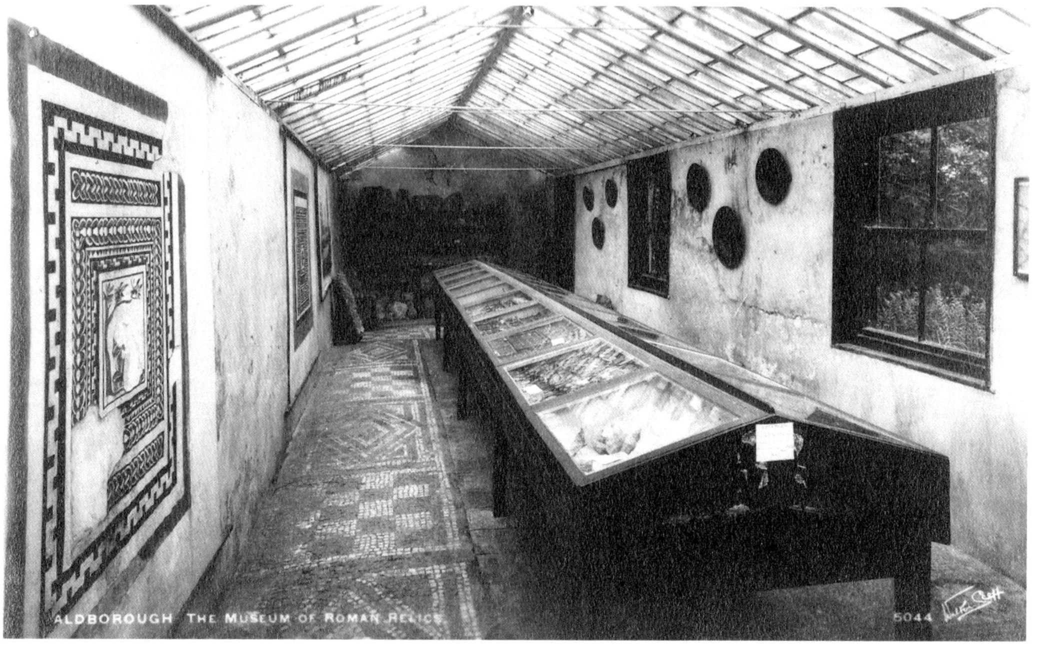

Fig 2.9 Photograph showing the interior of the museum in the mid twentieth century (looking west). Postcard by an unknown photographer. Reproduced by courtesy of Sir Andrew Lawson-Tancred

Fig 2.10 Unpublished plan of the West Gate (**G8**) and finds of adjacent Roman buildings (**G2**, **G19**, **G20**, **G21**). From an album of drawings by M N Hessey now in the collection of English Heritage. Reproduced by courtesy of English Heritage

on Ecroyd Smith's plan[64] (see fig 2.8) of a hypocaust (**G28**) and a floor (**G27**) not described in the text, but labelled as being 'found in 1851', indicates that Andrew Lawson's work was continued up to the time of his death in 1853. Beyond the Manor Garden, Ecroyd Smith also provides some evidence about other domestic buildings that had previously been discovered (**G2**, **G5**, **G21**, **G24**, **G25** and **G26**), as well as recounting earlier information about the *forum* (**G6**). He also notes finds beyond the walls, providing information on the cemetery at Chapel Hill (**G7**), and illustrations of probable funerary remains to the south west (**G12**), on the Redhills to the east (**G14**), as well as near the West Gate (**G18**). His discussion of the features on Studforth Hill (**G15**) recounts past debates, but he gives new information on a sculpture found there, as well as a statue of Mercury found in the grounds of Aldborough Hall (**G17**).[65] Finally, he notes the quarry outside the walls to the south west (**G30**), although expressing the view that it is not Roman.[66] One may also note that he deliberately excluded from this account the well-known (but probably fake) Romulus and Remus mosaic (**G31**), noting his own doubts in a later publication.[67] This confirms the view that his volume is thorough and authoritative, if at times poorly organised. As such, it provides a landmark piece of work of this type, as well as a key source for our present understanding of the Roman town.

2.4 From the 1850s to the 1920s

Although it appears that exploration of the site continued into 1851, significant work seems to have halted after the death of Andrew Lawson in 1853. His son, Andrew S Lawson, is noted as having 'carried-out excavations at intervals up to 1913',[68] but there is no systematic record of

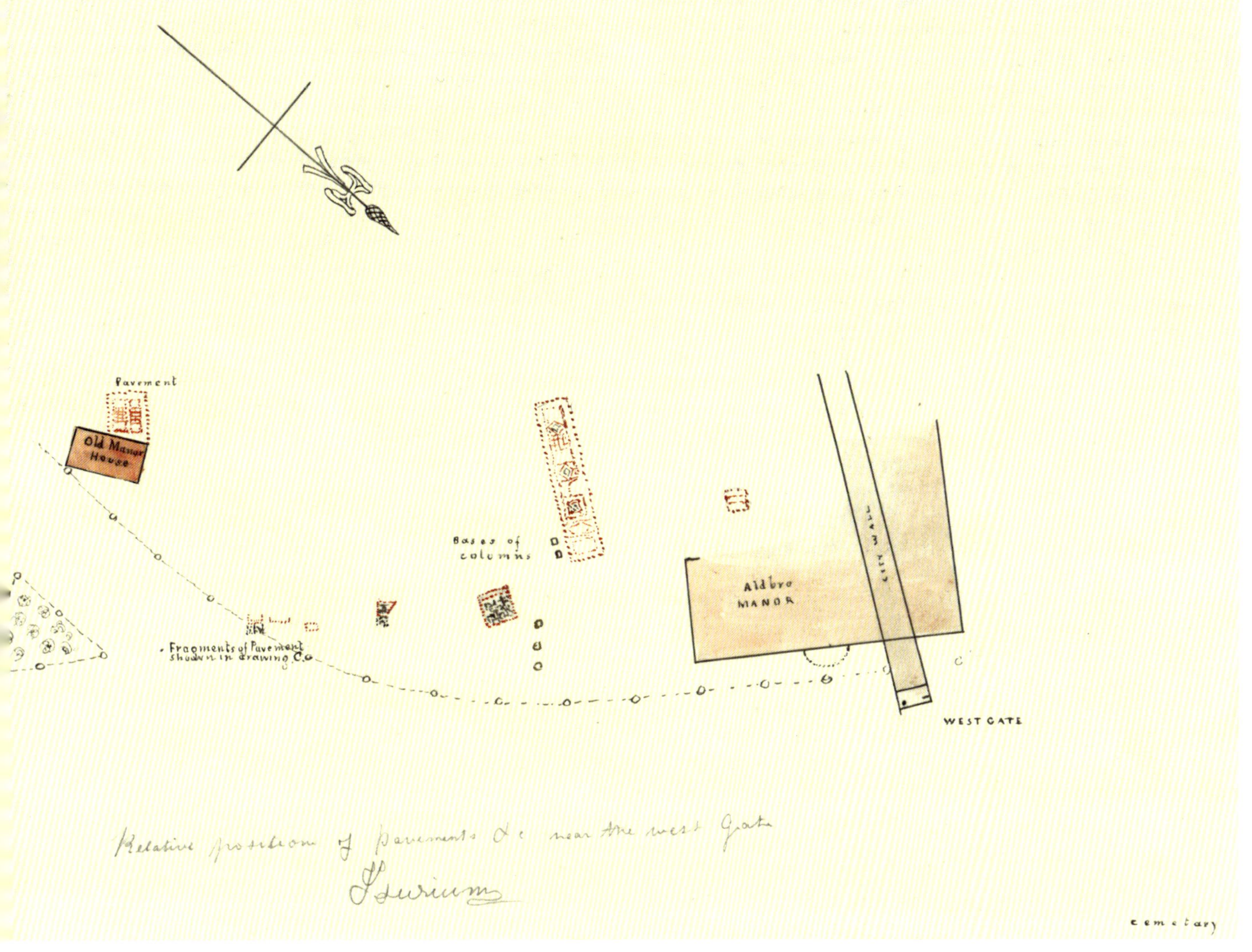

these. It is very likely that a photograph showing a hypocaust under excavation in the Manor Garden (**G32**) dates to this period, but the authors can locate no further details about this excavation. It is known that Francis Haverfield visited Aldborough Manor in 1906 and recorded the inscriptions, but there is no record of any excavations at this date.[69]

Despite this, the site became well known to those interested in the Roman past and was widely visited by individuals and organised groups (fig 2.12). Though these visits resulted in a series of publications, the publications provided no new information about the town. The earliest of these – the product of a visit of the Archaeological Institute in 1848[70] – provides a short discussion of the site, whilst Turner's *History and Aldborough and Boroughbridge*[71] includes a well-written and concise explanation of the site. The paper read by Andrew S Lawson on the occasion of the visit of the British Archaeological Association in 1863[72] is interesting as it explicitly celebrates the opening of the new site museum and provides detail of items displayed there. Finally, a systematic account of the town was published by Leadman,[73] reproducing past knowledge, while including for the very first time photographs of some of the mosaics. These contributions all attest to the continued importance of the site without helping to further its understanding.

2.5 Excavations of the 1920s and 1930s

The next excavations for which there is any evidence were undertaken over two campaigns in 1924 and 1934–8. Between the two, a short new synthesis of the site was provided by R G Collingwood (fig 2.13),[74] whilst a guidebook to the site, written by Lady Margery Lawson-Tancred, first appeared in 1922, thereafter going through a series of editions.[75]

The excavations of 1924 were led by S C Barber,

Fig 2.11 Drawing of the lion mosaic (**G22**) from Ecroyd Smith 1852. Original illustration by W Booman

Fig 2.12 Photograph of a visit by the Society of Naturalists to the site on 7 August 1867. They are shown standing in front of the 'prospect tower' and museum. Unknown photographer. Reproduced by courtesy of Sir Andrew Lawson-Tancred

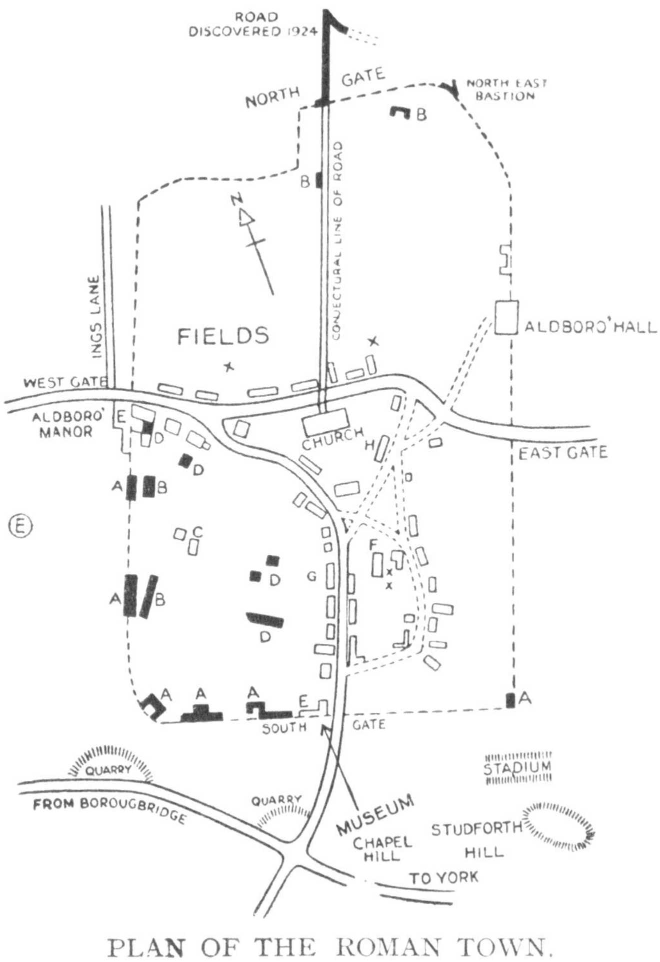

PLAN OF THE ROMAN TOWN.

C A Ridley and G F Dimmock, assisted by volunteers (fig 2.14). The full report on their work was never published, although the results were included within the account of the 1930s excavations.[76] However, a copy of the typescript of their report survives in the archive of Sir Andrew Lawson-Tancred.[77] It is clear from this that whilst the excavations were well designed to address some key issues, they were not executed to a very high standard, which probably accounts for the decision of the 1930s excavators to prècis the results rather than publish them in full. The illustrations included some very detailed plans (figs A9–A20), from which more detailed information can be gleaned. The work was concerned with exploring the northern part of the town, with a sequence of trenches examining the road leading to the river crossing (**G33**), exploring the North Gate (**G34**) and

Fig 2.13 Plan of Aldborough from Collingwood 1927. Note the erroneous line of the Roman Town Wall to the west of the North Gate. Unknown draughtsman

Fig 2.14 Photograph of the excavations just inside the North Gate by Barber *et al* in 1924 (**G34/3**). Viewed from the south east. Unknown photographer. Reproduced by courtesy of Sir Andrew Lawson-Tancred

North Wall (**G35–G36**), and investigating two buildings close to the town wall in the north-eastern part of the town (**G37–G38**). The work on the road and the North Gate was successful in providing confirmation of their plans, and a milestone[78] was found near to the North Gate. The other excavations provided some new information, but the results are very difficult to evaluate. Furthermore, the poor quality of the work led to some false conclusions being drawn, especially the idea that there was a road by-passing the town to the north east, cutting across from the bridge approach to the York road (below, p. 74).

R G Collingwood's brief synthesis of the site written as an excursion handbook for the visit of the British Association for the Advancement of Science meeting in Leeds in 1927,[79] is interesting for its succinct summary of archaeological knowledge (see fig 2.13). His emphasis on a purely civic origin for the town – perhaps under Agricola – is novel and prefigures ideas developed much more recently.

Excavations resumed in 1934, with Sir Thomas Lawson-Tancred inviting a distinguished group of young archaeologists to lead the work. One objective of these excavations was to resolve uncertainty over the course of the town wall to the west of the North Gate. Its course here seems to have been disputed, with that shown on the first edition Ordnance Survey map (1852) following a property boundary shown on the 1708 map and thus having a re-entrant near the North Gate. This course, shown on R G Collingwood's plan (see fig 2.13), differs from that shown by Ecroyd Smith (see fig 2.8) and was tested in the first season. The team – J N L Myres, K A Steer and Mary Kitson Clark (later Mrs Mary Chitty) – did some outstanding work in the years between 1934 and 1938, going on to publish their results in full only after the Second World War.[80] The circumstances of the work were described much later by Mrs Chitty.[81] Their excavations focused on the town walls, examining the north-western corner in 1934–5 (**G39–G40**), the south-eastern corner in 1936 (**G41**), the North Gate (**G34**) and North Wall (**G42**), both in 1938 (fig 2.15). The threat of war meant that no further work was undertaken – a great pity considering the evident quality of their excavations and analysis.

2.6 From the 1940s to the 1980s

Research-focused excavations did not resume immediately in peacetime, and when work was undertaken it was generally in response to the threat of re-development. In the absence of any organised system for dealing with rescue sites, *ad hoc* arrangements were made. In the case of Aldborough, since the site was a Scheduled Ancient Monument, such interventions were mostly dealt with by the Inspectorate of Ancient Monuments. The key person responsible for the site for much of this period was Dorothy Charlesworth. She undertook some of these excavations herself (**G49**, **G53**), but otherwise found other people to run them (**G43–G48**, **G51**, **G52**). In addition, that part of the site now controlled by Historic England (then the Ministry of Public Buildings and Works) was put into the guardianship of the state in the 1950s, and so was also overseen by Charlesworth. As part of this arrangement, a series of small excavations was organised to clarify

Fig 2.15 Section 1 shown cut across the defences near the south-eastern corner of the Town Wall by Myres *et al* in 1937 (**G42**). Viewed from the south east. Unknown photographer. Reproduced by courtesy of Sir Andrew Lawson-Tancred

Fig 2.16 Margaret Jones on her 1964 excavation. Unknown photographer. Reproduced by courtesy of English Heritage

knowledge of this part of the site and to help in its management (**G13**, **G23**). As with so much of the archaeological work of this period, the lack of provision for post-excavation work and analysis meant that these excavations were not published by their excavators. The single exception was the work conducted by Margaret Jones in 1964 (**G51** and **G52**), which was fully published (fig 2.16).[82] Other work was drawn together for publication much later, despite some major gaps in the archive.[83] Some of the missing archive material has now come to light and has been used in the gazetteer in this volume to complement the published information. As part of the same programme of research on unpublished material from the site, various of the finds from Aldborough were also studied. Mike Bishop thus published a catalogue of the small finds from the site as a monograph,[84] whilst Richard Brickstock produced a complete coin list for the site which has recently been published.[85]

Towards the end of this period, a series of syntheses of the evidence from Aldborough were published. John Wacher[86] produced a comprehensive review of the town in his work on the *Towns of Roman Britain*. This account reflects his view that urban development in Roman Britain was largely a product of Roman intervention and he was strongly inclined to link developments to documented historical events. It should be noted that some of his conclusions about particular excavated features have not stood the test of time.[87] Colin Dobinson later brought together all information from the site in a carefully constructed and critical review that took account of the general state of research on Romano-British towns at that date. Although unpublished, his manuscript was nonetheless widely circulated,[88] whilst a résumé was also published.[89] The content of his work clearly informed Wacher's second edition of his *Towns*.[90] Important new information collated by Dobinson included the suggestion that a levelling operation had been involved in the creation of the early Roman town; he also incorporated the results of aerial photography that revealed part of the street grid in the northern area, which allowed him to provide a new plan of the town (fig 2.17).[91]

Against the background of this research, Colin Dobinson also initiated a programme of fieldwork, including some limited geophysics, trial excavations (**G57**), and an extensive and innovative programme of field-walking in the environs of the town. The field-walking, which followed on from limited work by Jennifer Price, has recently been brought to publication, and provides key information that is drawn upon in this volume.[92] Alongside this there were a number of other excavations undertaken in advance of development and other watching-briefs on building sites.

2.7 The 1990s onwards

As a result of changes in the way that archaeological work in advance of development has been organised and become systematic, there have been more than thirty

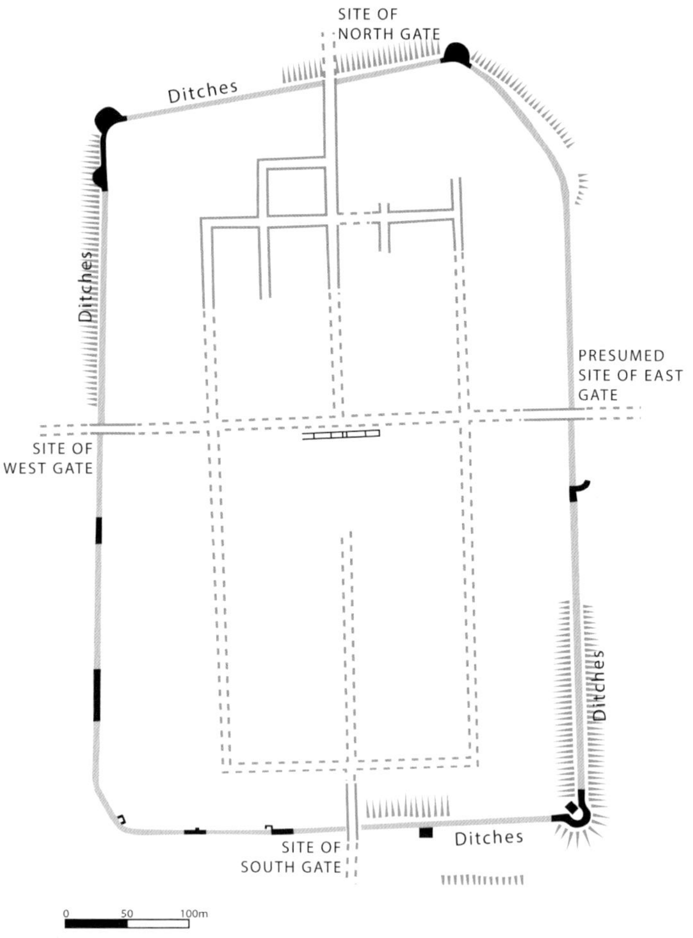

Fig 2.17 Colin Dobinson's plan of Aldborough. *Drawing:* Rose Ferraby after Dobinson 2012

small-scale excavations or observations at Aldborough since 1990. Alongside these, various small-scale geophysical surveys were also undertaken during the 1980s and 1990s, but none provided significant information. These are noted in a University of York MA dissertation, which also summarised evidence from various developer-funded excavations.[93] Given the small scale of these interventions and the extent of post-Roman landscaping, the information that they have added to knowledge of the Roman town is comparatively limited, although some have provided some key information. Individual excavators, such as Kevin Cale, who have worked on a number of these interventions have accumulated an important understanding on, in particular, post-Roman re-modelling of the landscape. A full listing of these has been included in the gazetteer (pp. 127–58), whilst figures in Chapter 3 locate all work to March 2018. Where appropriate, details from these interventions is used in the survey here (see Chapter 3).

The geophysical surveys

3

Incorporating contributions from Jason Lucas, James Lyall, Jess Ogden, Dominic Powlesland and Lieven Verdonck

3.1 Introduction

Methodology

The geophysical surveys presented in this study deployed two techniques and a variety of instruments. The main technique – fluxgate gradiometry survey – was initially undertaken using a Geoscan Research FM256 instrument in 30m grids (set out with a Leica Total Station) following 1m traverses with readings taken every 0.25m. Subsequently, work within the town mostly used Bartington Instruments Grad 601 dual sensor fluxgate gradiometers (fig 3.1), again within a 30m grid (laid out with a Leica Total Station and Leica GPS). With this instrument, measurements were taken at 0.25m intervals on 0.5m traverses, with data collected in a zig-zag fashion. Data from both these instruments were processed using Geoplot 3.0 software. In limited areas within the Roman walled town, and in all the areas outside the walls, survey was undertaken by James Lyall using a Foerster Ferex 4.032 DLG Karto belonging to the Landscape Research Centre. This comprises a two-wheel cart carrying four fluxgate gradiometers mounted 0.5m apart, giving a resolution of 0.2nT. A Leica GPS interface was connected to SMARTnet for real-time kinematic data georeferencing (RTK). The data were processed by the Landscape Research Centre using its in-house software G-Sys specifically designed to process the irregular but precisely located data generated by the Foerster instrument with a ground resolution of 0.10m by 0.50m and a location precision of <2.5cm. The georeferenced raster images of all the fluxgate gradiometry were exported to Adobe Illustrator. Interpretation was then carried out. Signal types were identified as positive, negative and dipolar, and strengths shown by levels of transparency (opaque being the strongest). The strength of the signals as represented on the interpretative illustration was assessed visually, with the threshold for the strongest signals at *c* 5nT. The resulting interpretative image thus visualises the features whilst maintaining some of the complexity of response. Features that have been labelled as modern are those where we have independent evidence of this.

Fig 3.1 Rose Ferraby undertaking gradiometry (magnetometry) survey on site using a Bartington Instruments Grad 601 dual sensor fluxgate gradiometer. *Photograph:* Tom Ferraby

Fig 3.2 Rose Ferraby and Jess Ogden undertaking GPR survey on site using a Noggin Plus System with rugged terrain cart and 500 MHz antenna. *Photograph:* Martin Millett

Ground-Penetrating Radar (GPR) survey was the other technique employed, again using a range of instruments. In 2011 and 2012, GPR was carried out by Jessica Ogden (L-P Archaeology) in St Andrew's churchyard using a Noggin Plus System with a rugged terrain cart and a 500MHz antenna (fig 3.2). A local survey grid was established for each on a north–south bearing, with the grid origin (0,0) used to rectify the start and end points of each profile. A setting of four stacks was used for ungained data collection with a total time window of 156 nanoseconds, with 781 points collected per trace. Data was collected at a 0.25m line separation in zig-zag mode. The radargrams were recorded in real time directly to the digital video logger, whilst the starting and ending coordinates were recorded manually for each traverse and subsequently converted in the GPR software format. The radargrams were imported in GPR-Slice for signal and image processing before being exported to the GIS for interpretation. The survey was followed in 2013 by work in Aldborough Manor and on the village green, using the same methods, with a GSSI SIR-3000 and its 400MHz antenna pulled by hand.

In 2015 and 2017 larger areas within the Roman walled town were surveyed by Dr Lieven Verdonck of Ghent University using an array of multiple 500MHz ground-penetrating radar (GPR) antennae mounted on a cart towed behind an all-terrain vehicle (a quadbike).[1] Data was gathered at 0.0625m or 0.125m intervals and locations recorded at high precision using a tracking total station in combination with a real-time kinematic (RTK) GPS allowing high-resolution data capture. Data processing included the application of a gain function to the radargrams (that is, the vertical sections that result from the measurements) to enhance reflections with later arrival times and a lower amplitude. Moreover, very low (< 100MHz) and very high frequencies (> 1000MHz) were removed, and background removal was applied (subtracting an average trace from all individual traces, to eliminate horizontal bands in the radargrams). Subsequently, horizontal time-slices were extracted from the vertical radargrams, by mapping the GPR measurements onto a regular 0.05m × 0.05m grid. In order to suppress the remaining variations in the amplitudes recorded by the different antennae (visible as stripes in the time-slices), the average of the measurements recorded by each antenna in the array was calculated, and these averages were equalised. Finally, the velocity of the GPR waves in the soil was calculated, and arrival times were converted to depths.

The GPR data from all seasons were georeferenced and added to the project GIS. They were interpreted by Rose Ferraby, and interpretation layers created in GIS. Features in time-slices were collated to create one single layer of interpretation, categorised into walls (strong), walls (weak), surfaces, and modern.

In addition to the geophysical survey, the project also sought to enhance the topographical record for the site. In addition to the processing of the LiDAR data (see fig 1.4) for the area, two further exercises were also undertaken. First, spot heights were recorded across all the areas where the geophysical survey was undertaken. These heights were collected automatically when survey was undertaken using the Foerster gradiometer and the Ghent GPR array, with height recorded for each data point. Elsewhere, spot heights were collected either with a GPS or a Total Station at approximately 5m centres. Spot heights were also collected wherever possible across the rest of the walled town in order to create the best possible digital terrain model of the site. Contours based on this are shown on the maps used in this chapter. It will be noted that where there was insufficient good data to provide reliable contours (for example, in some private gardens) these have been omitted. Second, in order to facilitate the accurate mapping of past archaeological work within the Roman town, the coordinates were recorded of a number of buildings and other structures that had been used to locate features and excavations. This detailed work has informed the georeferencing of features on the maps within this volume, but is not otherwise shown in the results.

Presentation of the results

The results of the different geophysical surveys are presented here integrated with the evidence from previous archaeological investigations. In order to do this, the site has been divided into a series of areas, each of which is mapped and discussed separately. The layout of these areas is shown in fig 3.3, with a key to the conventions used being shown in fig 3.4. For ease of use, these maps are reproduced here at natural scales (either 1:1500 inside the Town Walls, or 1:3000 outside), presenting the fluxgate gradiometry and GPR survey results separately, alongside an integrated interpretative plan of each dataset.

On the interpretative images where information on past excavations and finds has been included, these have been labelled using the gazetteer numbers (**G1**, etc). Buildings identified through the authors' geophysical surveys have been allocated numbers sequentially by area (hence, Building 1.1, Building 1.2). As with the gazetteer numbers, these are used for cross-referencing and in discussion within the text. The survey revealed a number of streets on the cardinal axes that the authors have labelled and numbered sequentially as North–South (NS1, NS2, etc.) and East–West (EW1, EW2, etc).

3.2 Area 1: North-western intra-mural area (figs 3.5, 3.6 and 3.7)

This area abuts Area 2 to the east, Area 9 to the north and Area 12 to the west, and overlaps with Area 3 to the south. The Town Walls defining this area to the north and west are visible in the surface topography. The ground within the walled area is comparatively flat, albeit sloping gently to the north. Beyond the line of the Town Wall the ground falls away steeply, whilst on the west side

Fig 3.3 Map showing the area numbers used in this chapter in relation to the extent of the fluxgate gradiometer (magnetometer) and GPR surveys. *Drawing:* Rose Ferraby. © Crown copyright and database rights 2018 Ordnance Survey (100025252)

Fig 3.4 Key to the conventions used in the geophysical survey illustrations. *Drawing:* Rose Ferraby

the line of the Wall itself is marked by a distinct ridge. The West Gate, which lies beneath the Low Road in Area 3, at the south-western corner of this area, was exposed in the 1840s (**G8**), whilst the North Gate, located just outside Area 1 to the north east, was excavated in 1924 and 1938 (**G33/K** and **G34**). Excavations in the 1930s examined the north-western corner of the defences, exposing the Wall foundation and an external tower (**G39** and **G41**). A second such tower was also located *c* 30m further south along the West Wall (**G39/3**). The line of the North Wall is comparatively clear, running along the present field boundary. References to the robbing of stone from the West Wall during the nineteenth century[2] and observations of similar robbing in the 1934–5 pipeline (**G40**) probably explain the complexity of the features revealed in the geophysical survey, although the Wall line is generally clear.

The area is bounded to the east and south by two of the principal streets within the walled town. The Principal North–South Street enters via the North Gate and lies on the central axis of the walled area. It was partially exposed there in the 1924 and 1938 excavations (**G33/K** and **G34**). It was also recorded in excavations behind the Ship Inn in 1996 (**G71**). Its course runs beneath modern boundaries, so it is not always visible in the survey within the town. The course of the Principal East–West Street can be clearly traced from the East Gate and runs to the north of the *forum* (below, Area 3). Within Area 1, the fluxgate gradiometry survey does not provide any direct evidence for its course as the survey stopped short of Low Road because of a metal fence. The GPR survey here does provide evidence for it (below Area 3), whilst excavations at Dominies Lodge in 1960 (**G47**) revealed a building that must have flanked its south side.

The geophysical survey of this area comprised principally fluxgate gradiometry (figs 3.5 and 3.6), with only a small area of GPR at the south west (fig 3.7). The fluxgate gradiometry results are exceptionally clear in those parts that remain as pasture. Towards the centre of the village (in Area 3), the presence of houses and agricultural buildings meant that survey was impossible. The north–south streets revealed regularity, dividing the part that is most fully surveyed into a series of north–south blocks. The regularity of these streets clearly indicates some overall planning, the principles of which are evaluated below (pp. 100–2). There is less obvious regularity in the east–west streets, which may be due to the lack of any overarching plan, or perhaps later modification to the original layout. Thus, here the descriptions of the intra-mural areas have been ordered according to the layout of the blocks defined by the north–south streets, progressing from west to east, then north to south.

Beginning in the north west, the area between street NS1 and the West Wall is clearly defined. At the northern end, there is no evidence for the continuation of street EW1, which is visible further east. However, its line defines the northern limit of buildings within the grid. The absence of street EW1 here may perhaps be the result of a lack of metalling, or later encroachment; it may also indicate that the road never extended this far. Along the west side, immediately behind the Town Wall, there is no convincing evidence for an intra-mural street. The area between NS1 and the Town Wall forms a strip *c* 50m wide, densely occupied by buildings that form three distinct compounds. To their south is a strong east–west linear anomaly, that coincides with the edge of a marked rise in the ground and seems to represent a medieval or post-medieval boundary that is recorded on the 1708 map (see fig 2.2).[3] The structures between this and the modern road are discussed alongside the GPR results (below, p. 37).

The northernmost compound, west of NS1, appears as a clearly defined L-shaped structure (Building 1.1), with a series of rooms visible in its south and east ranges that appear to open onto a courtyard to the north.[4] The more complex geophysical anomalies to the west may represent a continuation of Building 1.11 to the north, set at a slight angle (see below). To the south, there may be a street separating Buildings 1.1 and 1.2, although the

Fig 3.5 Area 1: results of the gradiometry survey in relation to modern topography. For the location, see fig 3.3. Scale 1:1500. *Drawing:* Rose Ferraby. © Crown copyright and database rights 2018 Ordnance Survey (100025252)

evidence is ambiguous. Building 1.2 has two clear elements: to the west is a structure *c* 17.5m by 11m, divided into two well-defined rooms, plus an annexe to the west, set within an open courtyard. Its form arguably suggests a twin-celled temple oriented east–west, with substantial foundations and possible steps at the east end.[5] To the east, a series of fainter anomalies form a range of rooms fronting onto street NS1, although their relationship to the structures further west is obscured by a modern field boundary. The compound occupied by Building 1.2 is defined to the south by a pair of features that indicate a side-street (EW2). Another pair of walls lies perpendicular, connecting it to Building 1.2 perhaps defines an access road, although they may equally

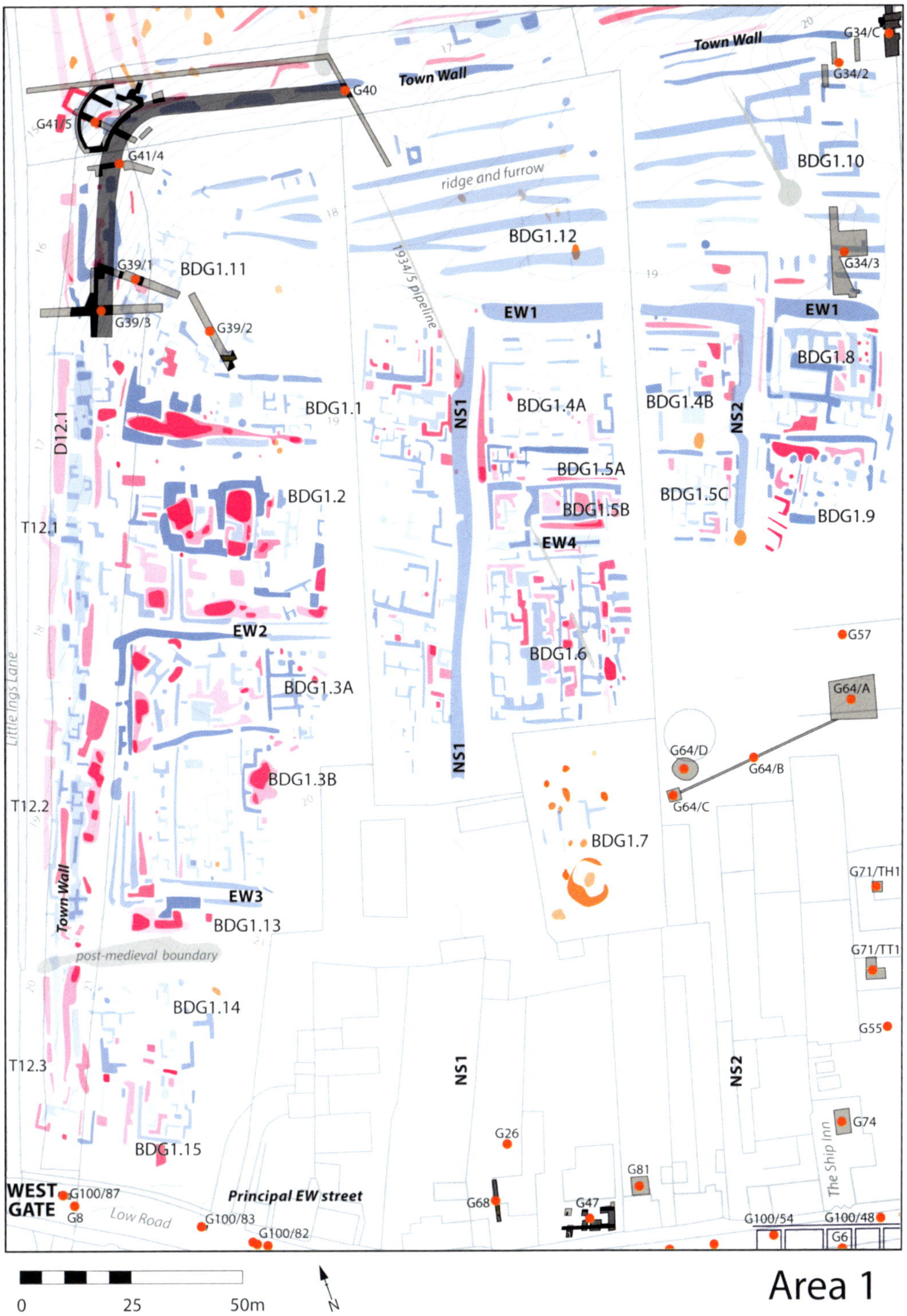

Fig 3.6 Area 1: interpretation of the gradiometry survey results in the context of the other archaeological evidence. For the location, see fig 3.3. Scale 1:1500. *Drawing:* Rose Ferraby. © Crown copyright and database rights 2018 Ordnance Survey (100025252)

represent a portico beside the courtyard.

The third compound is partially obscured by modern boundaries. It is enclosed by walls on all four sides, with perhaps a double wall to the west. It is cut by a slightly curving linear east–west feature, presumably later in date. The whole of the western part of the compound is occupied by structures on a north–south orientation that form a block of rooms (Building 1.3A). The walls of this building are closely aligned with those of Building 1.2 to the north. To the north east, there appears to be a separate house (Building 1.3B) facing onto street NS1. To its south, there was insufficient surveyed for certainty, but there may be a further house (Building 1.3C) in a similar position. It is unclear whether these three buildings were

Fig 3.7 Area 1: interpretation of the GPR survey results in the context of the other archaeological evidence. For the location, see fig 3.3. Scale 1:1500. *Drawing:* Rose Ferraby. © Crown copyright and database rights 2018 Ordnance Survey (100025252)

part of a single complex. Marking the southern boundary of this plot is a further east–west street (EW3). The area between this and the modern road is discussed below in the context of the GPR results.

The next block to the east is clearly defined by streets EW1, EW4, NS1 and NS2, which form a strip *c* 59m wide. To the south, modern buildings restricted access, and the results from the adjacent zone were obscured by a spread of modern farmyard debris. Clearly defined buildings cover the whole of the area surveyed, but the presence of a modern boundary down the centre makes it difficult fully to understand the layout. There are strong indications that the block was divided down the axis with separate properties facing onto both north–south streets. To the north, there are two buildings (Buildings 1.4A and 1.4B) that perhaps form a single complex. To the west, a courtyard (Building 1.4A) is flanked by porticoes with evidence of some internal features. To the east, Building 1.4B is probably a house oriented east–west, although details of its layout are obscured. Adjacent to the south is a courtyard perhaps associated with this house. Further south at the western end are two narrow strip buildings (Building 1.5A and 1.5B) clearly defined with rooms facing onto street NS1.[6] The layout to the east is less clear, but it appears that there was a single house (Building 1.5C) facing onto street NS2. The final structure in this sequence, separated from Building 1.5B by a side-street (EW4), is Building 1.6. This is a large rectangular courtyard house surrounded by ranges of rooms and built side-on to street NS1.[7] There is further evidence for walls of a building in the area to the south (Building 1.7), although the evidence is too fragmentary to understand its plan.

The next block to the east, *c* 34m wide, lies between street NS2 and the Principal North–South Street, and is defined at the north by street EW1. Only the northernmost part was available for survey. Facing end on to the Principal North-South Street, Buildings 1.8 and 1.9 are clearly defined, separated by a possible yard containing outbuildings. Building 1.8 is formed of a block of rooms, whilst Building 1.9 is an aisled hall with both sets of aisle posts clearly visible, implying the use of stone post bases.[8] An aerial photograph taken in 1976 shows that street EW4 continues to join the Principal North–South Street just to the south of Building 1.9.[9]

The remaining part of Area 1 comprises the ground between the end of the street grid (represented by street EW1) and the Town Wall. This forms a wedge-shaped zone, widening to the east. A series of structures (Building 1.10), not very clearly defined, face onto the Principal North-South Street just inside the North Gate. These are probably strip buildings built gable-end on to the street, and must relate to the street frontage explored in the 1924 excavations (**G34/2** and **G34/3**), where there was possibly a colonnade. Ridge and furrow across this area obscures much of the detail of the Roman features. Another cluster of structures is evident at the west end (Building 1.11) running at an angle to the Town Wall and street grid. These walls were cut by trenches in 1934 (**G39/1** and **G39/2**) and were shown to be later Roman in date. At the southern end of one of these trenches (**G39/2**) they also located a 3m wide late Roman ditch that had been cut through a wall of Building 1.11.[10] This ditch appears to be parallel with Building 1.1.[11] This has been interpreted by Wacher as a possible late Roman defence, but the authors' survey offers no support for this speculation.

There are vestiges of further structures and linear features in this area, but most do not reveal any obvious patterning. The exception is a pair of parallel walls running north–south (Building 1.12) to the north of Building 1.4A. Although these only show faintly, they form part of a long structure (*c* 20m) and appear on the same alignment as Building 2.17 further to the east. There is also a series of five substantial linear features parallel with the Town Wall. The LiDAR evidence (see fig 1.4) shows that these form a small block of medieval ridge-and-furrow cultivation.

Trial GPR survey in 2016 covered part of the south-western part of Area 1, overlapping with the fluxgate gradiometry survey (see fig 3.7). The results provide clear evidence for the line of the Town Wall as well as the post-medieval boundary that cuts across from west to east. To the north of this, the area covered by the GPR survey includes a small part of Building 1.3B and the walls bounding street EW3 are clearly very defined. Immediately to the south of this are walls that define a building (1.13), aligned east–west, that is not clearly visible in the fluxgate gradiometry. Between the post-medieval boundary and the Low Road, the two survey methods both suggest the presence of a pair of buildings. Building 1.14 is set back from the street, and shows up as a series of walls defining small rooms: those to the east (including floors) are best visible in the GPR, those to the west clearest in the fluxgate gradiometry. The overall form of the building is uncertain, but it does seem to occupy a broad area backing onto the Town Wall. Separating these buildings from the Town Wall is possible evidence for a surface that perhaps indicates an intra-mural street. This is perhaps confirmed by an anomaly in the fluxgate gradiometry results slightly further to the north. Another strip of surface material in the GPR results perhaps represents a lane linking this building to the Principal East–West Street further south. To the west of this, Building 1.15 is clearly defined in both surveys and faces onto the Principal East–West Street. It is on a slightly different alignment to the other buildings, but does seem to be Roman in date. The line of the Principal East–West Street is clearly visible in the GPR at the edge of the field.

3.3 Area 2: North-eastern intra-mural area (figs 3.8 and 3.9)

The Town Wall defines this area to the north and east, with the North Wall itself lying just beyond the limit in Area 9. The East Wall runs beneath the buildings of Aldborough Hall, which appear to have been constructed

Fig 3.8 Area 2: results of the gradiometry survey in relation to modern topography. For the location, see fig 3.3. Scale 1:1500. Drawing: Rose Ferraby. © Crown copyright and database rights 2018 Ordnance Survey (100025252)

to take advantage of it, paralleling the situation of Aldborough Manor, which was built on top of the West Wall. The partially excavated North Gate (**G34**) lies at the very north-western corner of the area. Further sections were cut across the North Wall in the 1920s and 1930s (below, Area 9). To the north east, the defences show clearly in the surface topography. In the fluxgate gradiometry survey the line of the Wall shows only as a series of slight negative anomalies, but a series of dipolar anomalies lie on the slope to the east of the Wall, with the ditches beyond showing as three bands of positive readings. However, the interpretation of these is made more complicated as the medieval ridge and furrow shares the same alignment (Area 9, below). At the south

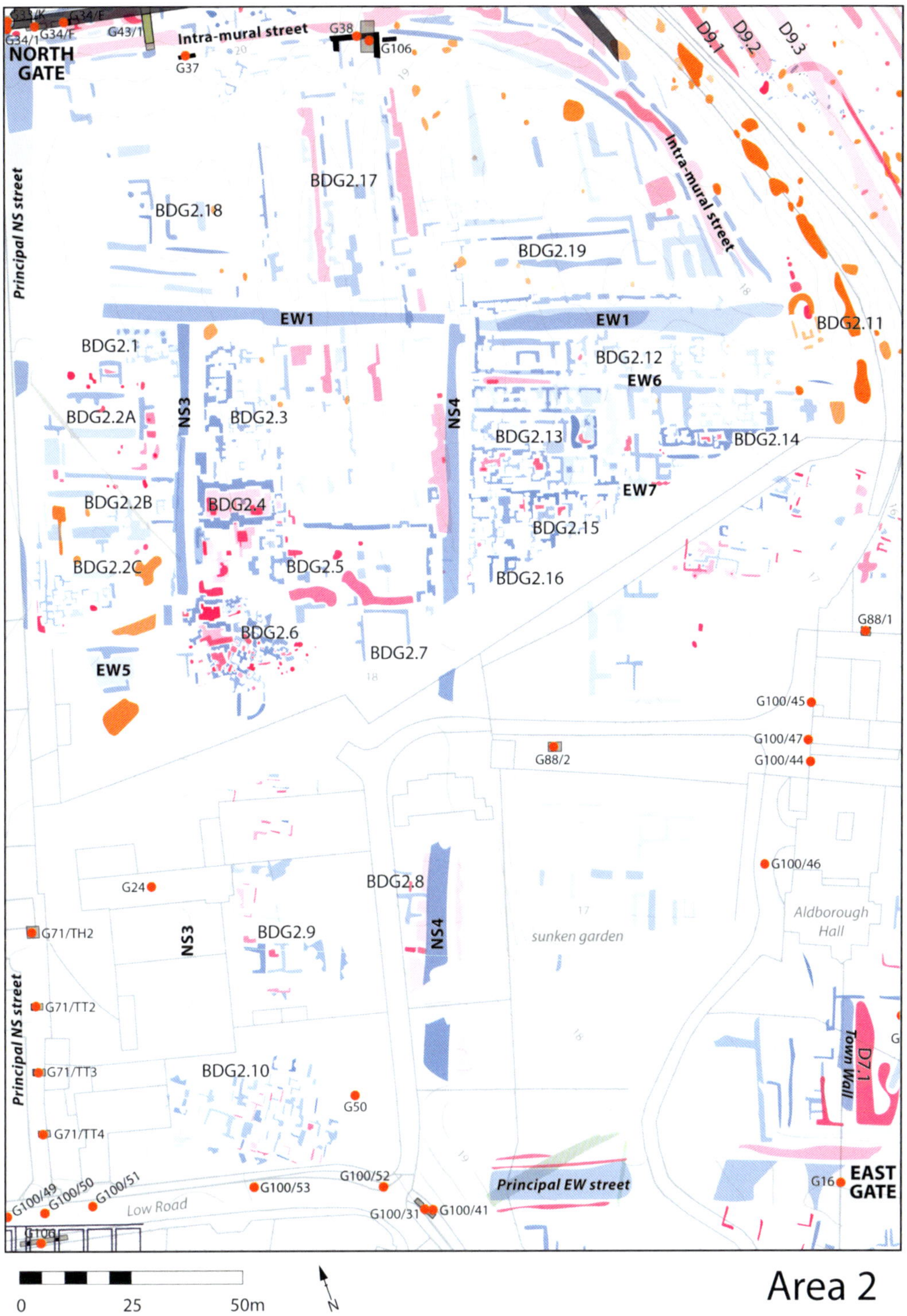

Fig 3.9 Area 2: interpretation of the gradiometry survey results in the context of the other archaeological evidence. For the location, see fig 3.3. Scale 1:1500. Drawing: Rose Ferraby. © Crown copyright and database rights 2018 Ordnance Survey (100025252)

east of the area, the line of the Wall shows clearly. The East Gate lies within the area surveyed, its location confirmed by the line of the Principal East–West Street, which is clearly defined just to the west and is visible passing through the Wall. It should be noted that the present line of the Dunsforth Road here was moved southwards in the nineteenth century to pass further from Aldborough Hall.[12] The road features in the survey thus relate to its earlier course (as shown on the 1708 map; see fig 2.2), which the authors presume follows the line of its Roman predecessor. The survey does not provide any clear evidence for the plan of the East Gate which, although known from antiquarian sources, was not planned (**G16**).

The Principal East–West Street is clearly visible at the southern edge of this area, and the other streets conform to the grid that was noted in Area 1. The Principal North–South Street is visible running along the western side of the area. The 1924 and 1938 trenches exposed its surface visible just inside the North Gate (**G33/K**, **G34/1** and **G34/F**), and it was also recorded in excavations behind the Ship Inn, located at the south-western edge of this area (**G71**). Area 2 is divided into two by street EW1.The area to the south lies within the planned grid while that to the north forms a continuation from the west of the wedge-shaped zone behind the Town Wall (above, Area 1).

The first block of buildings within the gridded area, *c* 33m wide, faces on to the Principal North–South Street, and is defined to the north by street EW1 and to the east by street NS3. There are no clearly defined east–west streets that sub-divide the whole surveyed area, EW5–7 being represented only in short stretches. Building 2.1 occupies the northern part of the block. Its overall plan is unclear, although a series of rooms can be discerned. Its northern and eastern walls are punctuated by a series of regular stronger signals, perhaps indicating columns. To its south is a series of three buildings aligned east–west which are perhaps a single property (Building 2.2). To the north, Building 2.2A appears as a rectangular structure, although its western and southern walls are less clear, and it is perhaps an aisled hall, the timber roof supports of which are not visible (cf Building 1.9). Building 2.2B is a rectangular structure, the internal plan of which is unclear, although there is perhaps a corridor along its northern side.[13] Building 2.2C, to the south, is poorly defined, although a series of small rooms are faintly discernible on its western side. Over part of this building, as well as street EW5 and the area to its south, the presence of surface rubble obscures the plan.[14] Further south, survey was not possible because of later buildings.

To the east, the next block is also defined by street EW1 at the north (with streets NS3 and NS4 to either side), and is *c* 57m wide. It is notable that the buildings within it are primarily focused on the frontage on street NS3, with less evidence for the importance of street NS4, although this is partly due to the presence of ridge and furrow obscuring the Roman deposits. Faint traces of walls in this area appear to be on the same alignment as Building 2.17 to the north.

Facing the northern stretch of street NS3 are two buildings (2.3 and 2.4). An east–west boundary continuing the southern wall of Building 2.4 effectively defines the southern part of the block. Building 2.3 comprises a series of rooms, although its overall plan is uncertain. The rooms at its north-western extremity are more clearly defined, suggesting more substantial walls on that frontage. Building 2.4 is also strongly defined, and comprises a simple rectangular building aligned east–west with an apparent annexe to the east. This may again represent an aisled hall (cf Buildings 1.9 and 2.2A), although the stepped plan of its perimeter wall resembles the buttresses used in granaries.[15] However, this apparent stepping may result from the spread of material from the walls having been cut by the ridge and furrow. The zone to the east of these buildings is less clearly defined, and has been cut by unusually deep ridge-and-furrow cultivation as seen in the LiDAR (see fig 1.4) and as reflected in the contours. Damage caused to the buried structures is shown here by the presence of rubble signals.

Further south, a strongly defined boundary – presumably a substantial wall – de-limits a plot (Building 2.5) that extends between the two north–south streets (NS3 and NS4). A very substantial block of buildings is indicated, with evidence for a series of rooms, but its overall plan remains uncertain. Building 2.6 lies to the south, facing onto street NS3. Despite surface rubble, the walls are clearly visible and the signals very strong. A range of three large rooms faces onto the street, with further smaller rooms and strong magnetic signals in the area behind it to the east. The strength of the signals and the plan perhaps suggest that Building 2.6 was a bath-house.[16] In this context, may be noted the presence of early Roman hypocaust tiles found in the field-walking survey just to the north.[17] It is confined to the western part of the plot, with a contrasting quiet zone to the east. A possible rectangular feature (Building 2.7) occupies the eastern part of this area. If Building 2.6 is a bath-house, this area may perhaps represent the *palaestra* behind. The central part of Building 2.6 also reveals a set of walls on a north-east to south-west alignment, perhaps indicating a later structure.

To the south, three further areas were surveyed within domestic gardens that have been landscaped. In one, street NS4 is well defined, probably as landscaping has reduced the soil depth. To the west of this stretch of street, faint traces of walls confirm the presence of buildings (2.8 and 2.9), although their full plans are not discernible. To the north east of Building 2.9 a mosaic was recorded in the nineteenth century (**G24**). At the southern edge of the survey, just north of the Principal East–West Street, further faint traces of buildings (2.10) were recorded. The character of these structures and their lack of alignment with the streets suggests that they are probably medieval or later, although excavation to the east (**G50**) revealed Roman deposits.

The next block to the east is defined at the north by street EW1, to the west by NS4, and by the defences to the east, forming a strip *c* 76m in width. South of the East Gate in Area 5, excavation (**G53**) revealed a street running along the back of the Town Wall (NS5). This road possibly continued to the north beside the East Gate (below, p. 104). If so, it may connect with the intra-mural street inside the Town Wall at its curving north-eastern corner (below, this page).

It is notable that to the east of its junction with street NS4, street EW1 appears to change character, widening slightly to the north. Where this street meets the Town Wall, on a prominence, there is diffuse dipolar anomaly, apparently a shallowly buried structure (Building 2.11).

Immediately to the south of street EW1 is a clearly defined strip with a narrow street (EW6) to its south. At its western end, perhaps separated from the street by a portico, is a strip building (2.12), with strongly defined walls. To the east, buildings continue, although it is unclear whether or not they form a single structure. The length of the complex, and the fainter signals to the east, imply that they probably formed separate buildings. To the south of street EW6, further buildings are very clearly defined. They appear to fill a block (*c* 20m wide), delimited to the south by a further narrow street (EW7). To the west, Building 2.13 is formed of a courtyard surrounded by ranges of rooms on three sides, opening onto Street NS4 on the fourth. There is a suggestion that the courtyard may be surrounded by a colonnaded portico.[18] To its east, is a range of rooms defined by very strong signals (Building 2.14), to the north of which are more faintly defined structures. Building 2.14 is of the winged-corridor or porticus-with-pavilion type, opening onto street EW7.[19] Its principal range of rooms forms a single series to the north, whilst the western pavilion is clearly visible. A presumed eastern pavilion lies beneath the hedge, perhaps just showing in the disturbed area to the south. To the north of the principal range of Building 2.14 there are clear but faint traces of a series of walls between it and the boundary wall beside street EW6. The stronger signals here, running north–south, result from the ridge and furrow, but the fainter ones suggest rooms of an associated structure.

To the south of street EW7, at the western end, there appear to be two separate buildings. Building 2.15 is a broad strip house, gable-on to street NS4. Only the north-western corner of Building 2.16 is visible; although its rooms are clearly defined, the character of its plan is unclear.

Further to the south, the survey covered areas of modern gardens where results are affected by disturbance. In the area immediately to the south of Buildings 2.15 and 2.16 there are faint traces of structures that align with the streets and are presumably Roman, although too little survives to discern their plans. To the east, south of Building 2.14, other faintly defined structures on a different orientation may be later and associated with Aldborough Hall. To the west of Aldborough Hall, the survey reveals part of the layout of a sunken garden. Faint traces of structures within this may relate to truncated Roman buildings.

At the south-eastern corner of Area 2, the survey shows a pair of clearly defined linear north–south features immediately inside the Town Wall. These may relate to later garden landscaping (as shown on the 1892 OS Map), but they define a strip that continues the line of street NS5 that was found to the south of the East Gate in 1965 (**G53**). This possibly continued to the north to link with the intra-mural street that runs around the north-eastern corner of the town, but evidence is lacking. Such a street would have provided direct access between the East and North Gates. To the west, there are traces of buildings to the north and south of the Principal East–West Street, although these are too fragmentary to interpret. The supposed findspot of the Wolf and Twins mosaic (**G31**) lies in this area or to the south in Area 3B. It is not precisely located, and there are very good reasons for doubting its authenticity.

Finally, to the north between street EW1 and the Town Wall, outside the regular street grid, the zone discussed in Area 1 continues (above, p. 37). It is wedge-shaped and has a curved boundary to the north east defined by the sweep of the Town Wall. Running immediately inside this, behind the rampart, is a clearly defined positive anomaly that represents a metalled surface, interpreted as an intra-mural street. Its existence has been confirmed by excavation (**G106**). It certainly connects North Gate to the eastern end of street NS1, and may possibly have linked to a continuation of street NS5 (see above).

Within this area, interpretation is made more complicated by the superimposition of ridge-and-furrow strips, which are cut deeply in places. It is notable that the alignment of this medieval cultivation appears to have been determined by earlier structures, most clearly in the centre of the area. Here, the excavations of 1924 revealed masonry walls in two areas (**G37** and **G38**). These structures both abut the intra-mural street. The survey shows that **G38** forms the northern part of a very much larger structure (Building 2.17) that continues for *c* 60m to the south, forming a very significant structure. Its alignment is different from that of the street grid, and its construction has been dated to *c* AD 250–300 (**G106**).

Building 2.17 is sharply defined by negative linear

anomalies that reveal a long north–south building comprising four walls defining three long narrow rooms with an overall width of *c* 28m. The north-eastern part of this building was dug in the 1920s (**G38**) and re-examined in 2018 (**G106**). The north wall, excavated in 2018, faced onto the intra-mural street. Further west, other walls (including **G37**) adjoin the intra-mural street, but it is unclear whether they represent a continuation of the same building. The size and character of these buildings suggests that they were warehouses.[20]

To the west, facing onto the Principal North–South Street, there are traces of structures just inside the North Gate. Between these and Building 2.17 is apparently an open area. Further south, facing street EW1, is a series of linear anomalies (Building 2.18) more nearly aligned with the main street grid. Their scale, and the absence of any visible internal divisions, may suggest a series of enclosures rather than a roofed building. Further similar structures (Building 2.19) continue to the east but on a different alignment, following that of the eastern extension of street EW1, and perpendicular to Building 2.17. It is possible that Building 2.19 forms part of the same complex as Building 2.17. In the angle between Buildings 2.17 and 2.19 there are faint traces of much smaller structures, but without any clearly defined overall form. In the remaining area inside the walls to the north east there are no discernible features beneath the ridge and furrow, suggesting an open area.

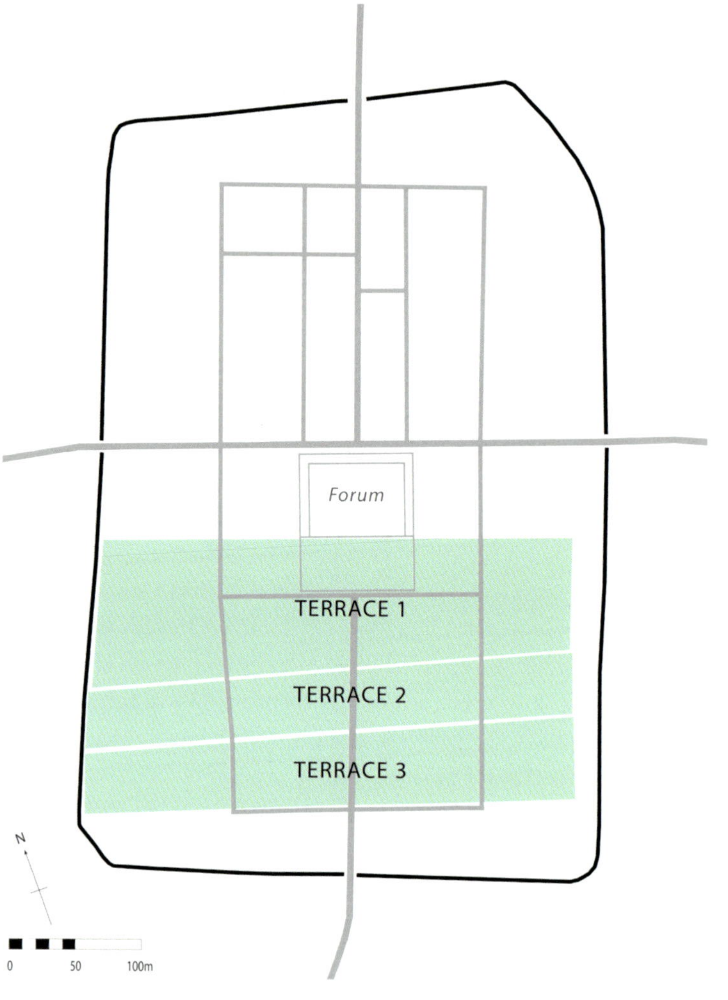

Fig 3.10 Map showing the location and numbering of the terraces in the southern part of the town. *Drawing:* Rose Ferraby

Note on terracing in the southern half of the town (fig 3.10)

As detailed in the descriptions of Areas 3–5 below, the survey has tentatively identified a series of three Roman terraces cut into the slope across the southern half of the Roman town. The layout of these, together with that cut to accommodate the *forum*, are shown schematically in fig 3.10. The extent of the terracing is also indicated by a grey tone on the detailed plans of Areas 3–5.

3.4 Area 3: Central intra-mural strip (figs 3.11, 3.12, 3.13 and 3.14)

Area 3 is sub-divided into two (Area 3A and 3B) and extends across the centre of the walled town between the East and West Gates, overlapping with Areas 1 and 2 to the north, and 4 and 5 to the south. The survey results are discussed in the descriptions of those areas. Very little fluxgate gradiometry was possible within this strip as the area was largely occupied by houses and gardens in use.

However, the parts of Area 3 surveyed using GPR but not included within the description of these other areas, are presented here (fig 3.11).

Lying as it does along the main east–west axis of the Roman and later settlement, this area has seen a number of previous discoveries, especially in and around Aldborough Manor. The West Gate of the town is known from nineteenth-century sources (**G8**) (see fig 2.10) and lies beneath the Low Road immediately to the north of the Manor. The GPR survey of the modern road in front of the Manor (fig 3.11) shows a feature in this location that almost certainly represents the south side of the gate. It is on the alignment of the Town Wall, but offset slightly behind, with a narrower feature continuing further north. This may suggest a gatehouse set back, perhaps with a later blocking across the road. A utilities trench here (**G100/87**) did not record any structure, presumably because it is on the line of the Roman street.

The line of the Town Wall to the north is visible as an earthwork (Area 1, above), and has been exposed in two excavations to the south (**G9** and **G46**). The route of the Principal East–West Street running westwards through the town is seen in the results of the GPR survey just inside the Gate. It was also recorded in two commercial excavations (**G68** and **G81**) further to the west. The line here confirms that the Roman building excavated at Dominies Lodge in 1960 (**G47**) faced onto its south side. Similarly, at the centre of the town, the north range of the *forum* (**G6**) planned in 1770 (discussed below) lies set back on its southern side.

Just inside the Gate to the south, a series of antiquarian records provide evidence for substantial town-houses with mosaics (**G1–2**, **G4** and **G19–20**). These represent at least one major courtyard building, a corridor of which was excavated in the nineteenth century (**G20**) with mosaics dated to the fourth century (fig 3.13). (The precise alignment of the corridor, **G20**, cannot be reliably assessed.) This was located some distance back from the line of the Principal East–West Street. If, as seems likely, the house did open onto this street, it would have been very substantial, perhaps with the courtyard set behind a main range of rooms.[21] Several of the other mosaics from this area probably relate to the same building, although that found under the Old Globe Alehouse (**G19**) arguably relates to another building further east. The building with a bath suite (Building 4.1, **G10** and **G46**) could perhaps form part of the same complex, but is more likely to represent another house. There is a notable contrast between these monumental buildings to the south of the street, and the smaller ones visible in the geophysics to its north (Area 1, above).

To the west, there is evidence from the nineteenth century for two further domestic buildings: one with a hypocaust, beside the village hall (**G21**), the other less well understood in the extension to the churchyard (**G25**). The published drawing of this shows stone gutters, suggesting a probable courtyard (fig A7). Although the precise character of these two buildings is uncertain, both appear to be domestic, supporting the idea that there was a row of substantial town-houses facing onto the Principal East–West street in this area. The results of the GPR survey in the churchyard do not provide any evidence for these buildings, but the area has been very intensively disturbed by burials. To the north, on the opposite side of Low Road, part of another house was explored in 1960 (**G47**), with a corridor flanking the Principal East–West Street. A wall on the same alignment in the gas main trench a little to the east may relate to the same building (**G100/58**).

At the centre of the town, the Principal North–South Street intersects with the Principal East–West Street. The line of the former, coming in from the North Gate, has been traced on excavations in the car park of the Ship Inn (**G71**). This places the intersection in front of St Andrew's church. On the street frontage here excavations in 1770 revealed the foundations of a substantial range of rooms interpreted as part of the *forum* (**G6**). Two sets of plans of these remains survive (see figs 2.4 and 2.5) along with a narrative description (Chapter 2, above). A central entrance through this range, with a north–south drain, opened onto the street intersection.

The *forum* has been investigated with GPR survey and limited re-excavation (**G105**). The GPR survey was carried out in two parts, the first in the churchyard and the second over the road to the north. The churchyard was heavily disturbed by graves. The original burial ground around the church shows an irregular pattern of burials, but the nineteenth-century extension (to the west) contains regular rows of graves. To the west of the church, the GPR revealed a pair of parallel north–south walls that seem likely to represent the west range of the *forum*, overlain by the old churchyard boundary wall. To the south of the church, a single wall perpendicular to the others probably indicates the south side of the *forum* square.

The GPR survey of the road to the north of the church located a series of north–south features that were tentatively interpreted as the walls separating the rooms of the range examined in 1770 (**G6**). A small excavation in 2017 (**G105**) confirmed the accuracy of the eighteenth-century plans and description (fig 3.14).[22] It also allowed the eighteenth-century finds to be accurately georeferenced. Given the confirmed location of the *forum* in relation to the Principal East–West Street, it seems likely that it was set back from the street frontage, perhaps behind a colonnade. It should be noted that the gas pipeline trench in the road to the north (**G100/54**) presumably lay within one of the rooms.

The general arrangement of the *forum* is thus clear, with its courtyard, measuring *c* 72m east–west by *c* 54m north–south, occupied by the medieval church and the north, west and south sides of the square approximating to the boundaries of the original churchyard. Furthermore, the west and north sides appear to have comprised ranges of rooms *c* 7m in width (below, p. 106). As noted above, the eighteenth-century plans provide clear evidence for an entrance in the middle of the northern range facing the street onto the North Gate, and arguably a colonnade fronting the street. The wall in the GPR to the south of the church seems likely to represent the boundary of the *forum* square. It is situated at the foot of the slope that defines the southern side of the Roman terrace, cut to house the *forum*, and related to the

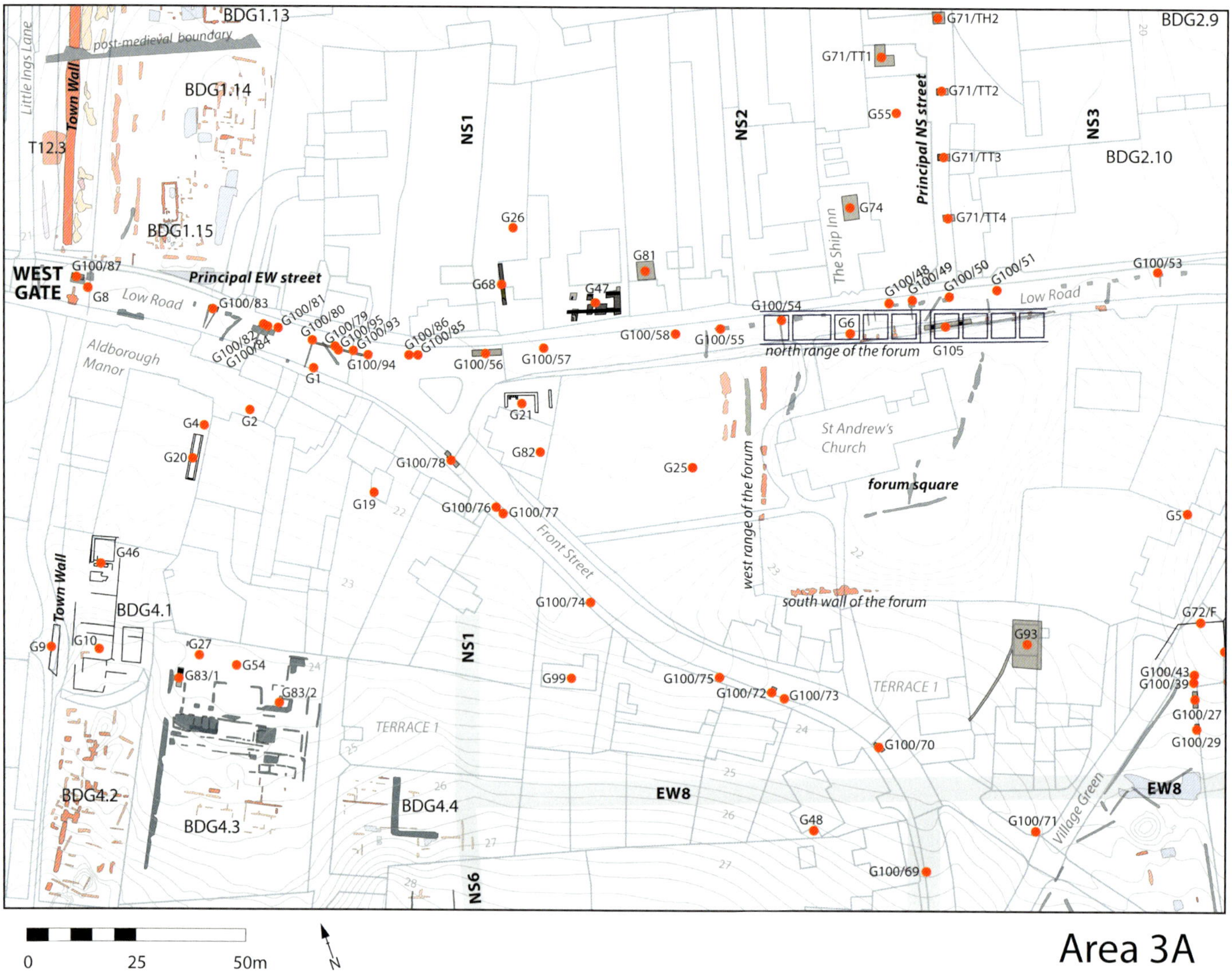

Fig 3.11 Area 3A: interpretation of the GPR survey results in the context of the other archaeological evidence. For the location, see fig 3.3. Scale 1:1500. *Drawing:* Rose Ferraby. © Crown copyright and database rights 2018 Ordnance Survey (100025252)

terracing higher up the slope. As discussed below (p. 106), it is likely that the *basilica* was located to the south of this wall. (A watching brief at Hazeldene (**G93**) was insufficiently deep to provide any evidence of this.) The GPR results do not provide any clear evidence for the east side of the *forum* because of disturbance. On the assumption that the entrance in the north range was central, the west range would lie just beyond the churchyard boundary to the west. It is interesting to note that the medieval tithe barn was located here (see fig 2.2), perhaps re-using part of the *forum* structure. The ground levels here have been significantly altered by post-medieval and modern building. It appears that the vicarage garden has been raised to form a terrace, with that to the north (now occupied by the modern house adjacent to the churchyard) apparently previously lowered to create a bowling green. Fluxgate gradiometry in the southern part of this area, in the vicarage garden, revealed faint traces of walls whose orientation suggests a later date (Building 3.1).

Further to the south of the church, poorly recorded excavations in 1960 (**G48**) identified a substantial east–west sewer of Roman date. The surviving records show that this lay towards the southern boundary of the development site, although its precise course cannot now be established. The sewer was of such a size that it probably lay beneath a main street. In this position, it would be a good candidate for the street that ran behind the *forum*, allowing traffic entering via the South Gate to pass around it by linking it with north–south streets located to its east and west. Two further pieces of evidence support the identification of this street (EW8). First, a length of possible road is visible in the GPR a little to the east under the Village Green in Area 5 (see fig

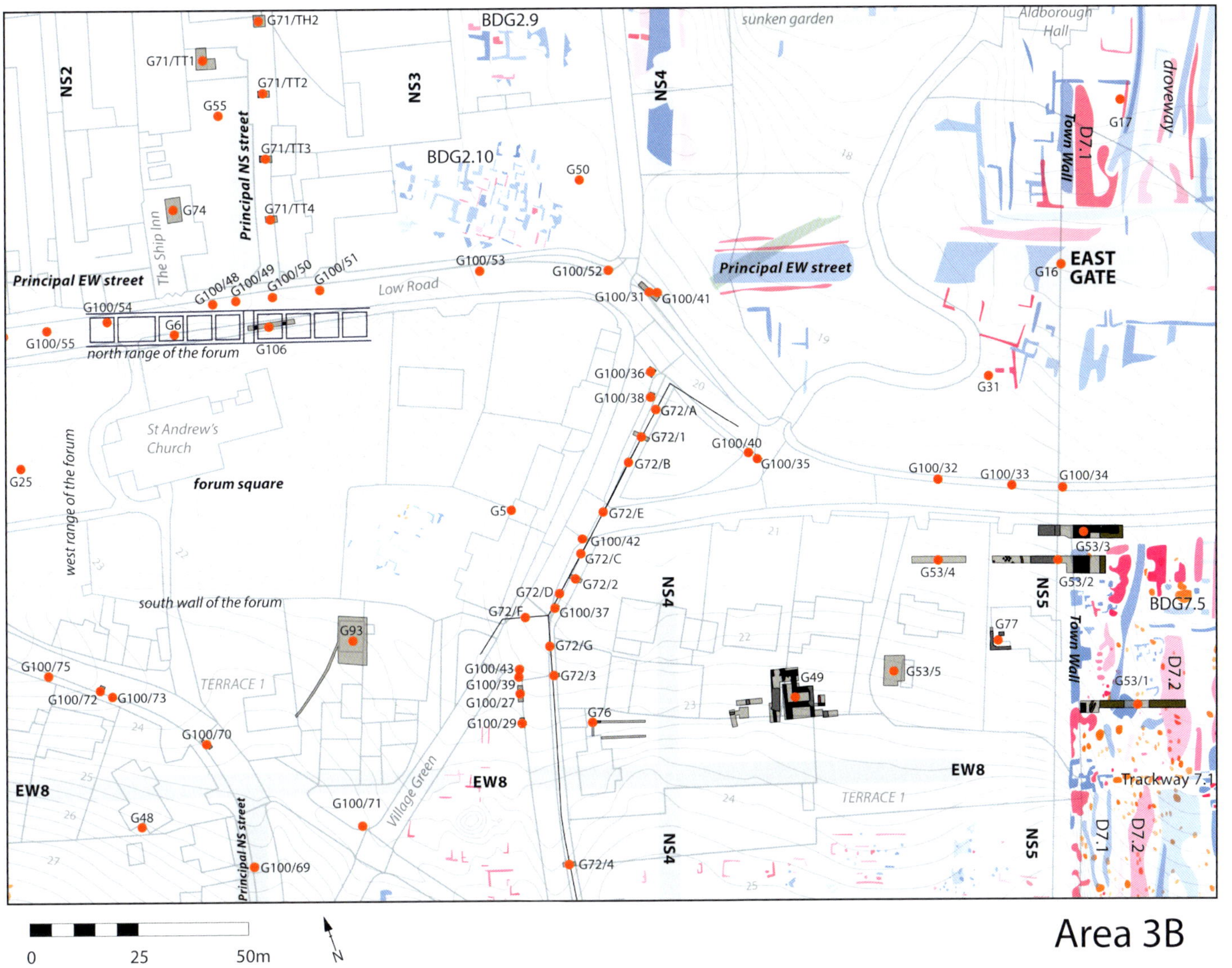

Fig 3.12 Area 3B: interpretation of the gradiometry survey results in the context of the other archaeological evidence. For the location, see fig 3.3. Scale 1:1500. *Drawing:* Rose Ferraby. © Crown copyright and database rights 2018 Ordnance Survey (100025252)

3.23). Second, its line coincides with a change in the orientation of the medieval property boundaries (see figs 2.2 and 4.14), which are preserved in the modern property divisions. This street is discussed further (below, p. 100).

To the north of the *forum* two excavations are recorded (**G50** and **G55**), but neither provides any topographically useful information. Between the *forum* and the East Gate (Area 3B) there is comparatively little survey evidence, although there have been a series of past excavations (see fig 3.12). (An area of GPR survey on the Village Green is discussed under Area 5, below, p. 59.) The line of the Principal East-West street shows in the fluxgate gradiometry survey (see figs 3.8 and 3.9), whilst the location of the East Gate is known from nineteenth-century observations (**G16**). A statue of Mercury was found close to the East Gate (**G17**), whilst the claimed findspot of the famous 'Wolf and Twins' mosaic also lies hereabouts (**G31**).

To the east of the churchyard a mosaic recorded as having been found at the vicarage (**G5**) seems likely to imply the presence of a house adjacent to the *forum*. Finds of loose *tesserae* from a trench in the road to the east (**G72/E**) would be consistent with this. Further east, excavations in 1961 (**G49**) examined part of a substantial house with rooms arranged along a north–south corridor. This appears to be second century in date and overlay two earlier phases of timber building that were started in the later first century. The stone-phase presumably formed part of a courtyard building that seems most likely to have faced onto a street either to the south (the eastward continuation of EW8), or to the west (the southward continuation of NS4). Timber buildings, most likely of second-century date, were also located just to the

Fig 3.13 Area 3A: drawing of the corridor mosaic (**G20**) from Ecroyd Smith 1852. Original illustration by M N Hessey

Fig 3.14 Areas 3A and 3B: photograph showing the foundations of the walls of the *forum* re-excavated in 2017 (**G105**). Viewed from the west. *Photograph:* Rose Ferraby

east of this in the excavation of the defences in 1965 (**G53**), a site that also revealed the line of an intra-mural street (NS5). A late Roman building was also recorded a little to the south (**G77**), presumably facing onto street NS5.

3.5 Area 4: South-western intra-mural area (figs 3.15, 3.16, 3.17, 3.18, 3.19 and 3.20)

This area lies largely within the gardens of Aldborough Manor and includes the English Heritage Guardianship site. To the north and east, the survey was constrained by houses and their gardens, whilst woodland skirting the area between the Manor and the English Heritage site also limited coverage. This southern half of the walled Roman town occupies a north-facing slope, the topography of which has been modified by terracing and by the landscaping of the Manor gardens. It should be noted that the modern land-use and the fragmented character of the gardens in Area 4 mean that the survey in its north part are harder to interpret than those elsewhere within the walled town. In order to address this problem, the authors combined a substantial amount of GPR survey (fig 3.17) with the full fluxgate gradiometry coverage (figs 3.15 and 3.16).

Area 4 is defined to the east by the line of the Principal North-South Street (which runs beneath Front

Street) and to the south and west by the Town Wall (which mostly lies just to the west in Area 12). The South Wall was extensively excavated in the nineteenth century and re-examined by Charlesworth (**G13**). These excavations and the creation of the garden walk, now within the English Heritage site, have resulted in considerable alterations to the topography, removing the front of the rampart and creating a new bank to the south of the Town Wall over the original, inner ditch (fig 3.18). Exposed sections of the Wall footings, including internal towers, remain on display. Along the West Wall, two further short sections were exposed in the early nineteenth-century excavations and incorporated into the display in the gardens (**G9** and **G11**).

In contrast to the relatively flat topography in the north of the town, this southern area is built upon a north-facing hillside (see fig 3.16). Evidence from both the geophysics, topographic survey and excavated remains suggests that this was terraced in the Roman period. The legibility of this terracing is made complicated by the superimposition of medieval tofts along the same orientation, some of which follow the Roman terraces (see fig 4.8). These appear regular in layout, aligned broadly east–west (about 105° East of North), and parallel to one another. There are three of them, although all may not extend fully between the east and west Town Walls. The slope becomes gentler close to the West Wall, and the evidence is less well preserved behind the East Wall. The terraces are numbered from 1 to 3, from north to south. Despite uncertainties about their extent, they are shown schematically and separated by gaps within the illustrations in this volume to allow the reader to appreciate their general extent (see figs 3.16–3.17, 3.21–3.22). The orientation of these terraces, and many of the features on them, differs slightly to the street grid of the town. The significance of this is discussed further below (p. 104).

The northern limit of Terrace 1 is visible to the south of the churchyard, defining the side of the *forum* square (above, p. 43). It is divided from Terrace 2 by the slope at the southern edge of the Village Green, and continues as property boundaries to the east and west. The step between Terraces 2 and 3 coincides with a medieval toft boundary that cuts the northern side of Building 4.10, visible across the western side of town but difficult to trace in the east. The southern limit of Terrace 3 is marked by a steepening of the slope. Terrace 1 is *c* 85m wide, whilst Terraces 2 and 3 are each *c* 60m across, echoing the steepening gradient of the hill.

Across the southern part of the town, evidence for the street grid is more fragmentary than that in the north. However, using evidence from the geophysical survey along with the toft boundaries, it is possible to reconstruct at least part of the grid. The location of the South Gate is known from Jones's excavations in 1964 (**G51**) (just beyond the south-western corner of Area 4). The Principal North–South Street is presumed to have accessed the South Gate and followed the line of the present Front Street northwards towards the *forum* (above Area 3). As noted above (pp. 44–5), an east–west street

Fig 3.15 Area 4: results of the gradiometry survey in relation to modern topography. For the location, see fig 3.3. Scale 1:1500. *Drawing:* Rose Ferraby. © Crown copyright and database rights 2018 Ordnance Survey (100025252)

(EW8) would have allowed the movement of traffic around the *forum*. Street EW8 is centrally placed on Terrace 1 and can be traced in the boundary running through the properties in this area. At the southern edge of Terrace 3 is a second east–west street (EW9). This is visible in the GPR results close to the West Wall and runs east through the field. The authors presume it continued along the terrace edge to the Principal North–South Street, to the east of which its line is followed by modern Back Street, then by a toft boundary east of Studforth House.

Between EW8 and EW9 the street system is less clear. A north–south street (NS6) is visible in the GPR running along Terrace 3. This is along approximately the same line

Fig 3.16 Area 4: interpretation of the gradiometry survey results in the context of the other archaeological evidence. For the location, see fig 3.3. Scale 1:1500. *Drawing:* Rose Ferraby. © Crown copyright and database rights 2018 Ordnance Survey (100025252)

as street NS1 to the north. A less regular street (EW10) runs close to the southern boundary of Terrace 2 at its western end, curving to the north to join street NS7. Three stretches of this street are visible in the GPR, one on each of the terraces. Although fragmentary, this suggests a street that probably connected with street EW8, as it cannot be traced beyond it.

Turning now to the buildings, starting at the north-western corner on Terrace 1, the survey was limited to a strip of lawn immediately inside the West Wall. At the northern end, excavations in 1830 revealed a structure that included baths (**G10**), with fragments of two fourth-century mosaics. Other elements are revealed in the survey (Building 4.1). The available evidence from the

Fig 3.17 Area 4: interpretation of the GPR survey results in the context of the other archaeological evidence. For the location, see fig 3.3. Scale 1:1500. *Drawing:* Rose Ferraby. © Crown copyright and database rights 2018 Ordnance Survey (100025252)

excavation indicates a range of rooms running parallel with the Town Wall (**G9**), perhaps with a courtyard to the north east. The rooms at the north included a hypocaust. These excavated rooms in the northern part can be discerned in the results of the magnetometer survey. Further buildings visible in both the fluxgate gradiometry and GPR continue to the south, also backing onto the Town Wall, but along a slightly different alignment. Although still broadly parallel with the Town Wall, they represent a different building (Building 4.2). The GPR survey also suggests that there may be more than one structural phase, with earlier walls aligned more to the north east than the Town Wall. Although not on the same angle as the excavated buildings further south (**G11**), they

Fig 3.18 Area 4: the southern Town Wall in the English Heritage site, viewed from the west, showing the Wall foundations (**G13**) as displayed in the nineteenth-century antiquarian garden. *Photograph:* Rose Ferraby

Fig 3.19 Area 4: photograph showing the re-excavation of part of a domestic bath-house, part of Building 4.8 (**G22**) viewed from the north. The two buildings behind were constructed in the 1830s and 1840s to cover the mosaics discovered then. *Photograph:* Rose Ferraby

Fig 3.20 Area 4: drawing of the apsidal building with the 'Helicon' mosaic (**G23**), from Ecroyd Smith 1852. Original illustration by M N Hessey

may also represent a pre-Wall phase. There is too little evidence to gain a clear impression of the types of building.

In the walled garden immediately to the east, there has been substantial modern landscaping to create an outdoor auditorium, reflected in the curving features shown in the fluxgate gradiometry. Previously, the area was occupied by a series of buildings shown on Ordnance Survey maps to 1952, as well as a swimming pool built in the 1960s. These are clearly visible in the results of the GPR survey. In the northern part of this area, a Roman lime floor was recorded in the nineteenth century (**G27**). Small-scale excavations in the 1960s (**G54**) and 1998 (**G83**) revealed deep deposits and a probable Roman foundation wall aligned east–west. In the more southerly part of the walled garden other features possibly indicate foundations of a Roman building (Building 4.3) aligned with the later (north–south) phase of Building 4.2 to the west.

The small parcel of land further east shows less evidence of landscaping and the results of both surveys reveal fragmentary traces of buried features. The clearest of these lie on a north–south alignment, and probably relate to the boundaries of the medieval tofts. The east–west features represent parts of underlying Roman buildings (Building 4.4); they are similar to Buildings 4.2 and 4.3 further west and share the same orientation. However, too little survives to see any coherent plan. There is no evidence for the continuation of the Street EW8, but this may be because it runs under the modern boundary. To the south of the line of street EW8 on Terrace 1, we pass from an area of the medieval settlement in which the tofts were aligned north–south to one where they run east–west, with the strips stretching from Front Street west to the Town Wall.

A hypocaust and foundations were found in 1851 (**G28**) in the walled garden at the western end of the terrace, remaining open in the formal Manor gardens and hence are shown on early Ordnance Survey maps to 1952. The fluxgate gradiometry and GPR of this area reveal a series of walls (Building 4.5) that form part of the same structure. The layout suggests a complex with east–west ranges of rooms, perhaps facing onto a courtyard to the north. Just to the west of the excavated hypocaust (**G28/A**) the GPR shows an apse, perhaps suggesting a bath suite. Another apse is clearly visible at the southern end of the area of 'foundations' excavated in 1851 (**G28/B**) on the eastern side of the complex. The GPR results here also show surviving floors. It is not clear whether this structure comprises one or more houses, although the GPR suggests a single large building. It may be noted that a few of the walls visible in the GPR at the

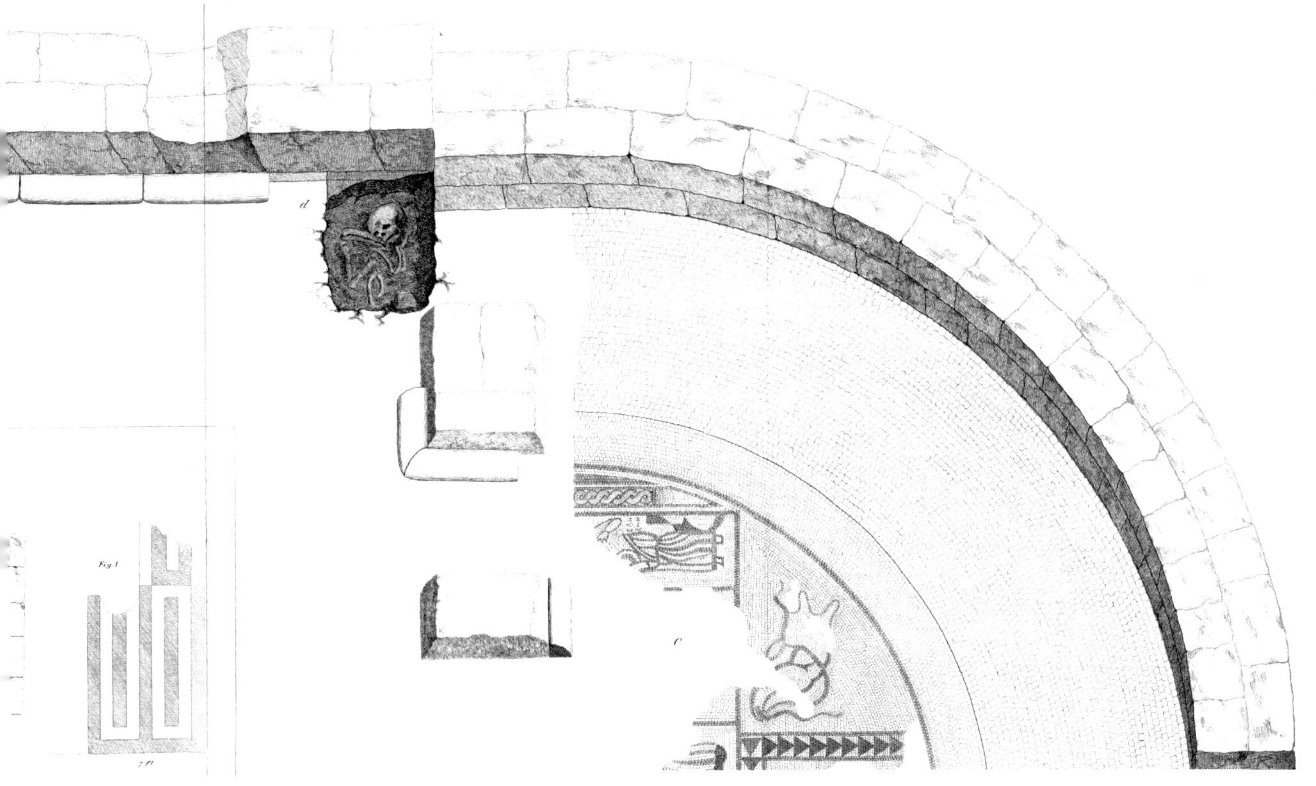

western limit of Building 4.5 are on a slightly different alignment: one that they share with the so-called 'barracks' to their south (**G11**). This suggests that they relate to an earlier phase, perhaps with the building continuing towards the West Wall. The greater depth of their appearance in the GPR results supports this idea.

The next garden to the east was also surveyed. In the area to the south of Building 4.4, the results are dominated by an east–west feature, probably a relatively modern garden wall. However, there are faint traces of a series of north–south walls, presumably of Roman date (Building 4.6). The garden just to the south was not included within the survey, but at its western end a hypocaust excavated before the First World War (**G32**) has been located using a photograph in the Manor archive (fig A8).

The largest area of the survey in this part of the town covered the field within which two mosaics are displayed in the Historic England site (**G22**). In the west, just within the Town Wall, the excavated remains of a Roman building dug in the nineteenth century are still visible in the Manor gardens (**G11**). Although Ecroyd Smith[23] described them as 'barracks', they are clearly domestic. The structure comprises a row-type building with two ranges of small rooms with two apses at the south. These presumably relate to a small bath suite and the published plan shows a furnace room (fig A2). It is also clear from the plan that several phases of development are represented.[24] It is notable that this building is on a slightly different alignment to both the Town Wall (exposed in the same excavation) and the surrounding buildings (see below). In this context, it may be noted that the hill slope is angled to the north west in this part of the town, perhaps influencing the building's layout. The building is placed to occupy the full width of Terrace 2, and commanded views both to the west and north. Its proximity to the Town Wall and its relationship with the enclosures to the west (Area 12) suggest that it pre-dates the construction of the Wall, which will have obscured its view to the west. A series of buildings on this side of the town are not aligned with the terracing (Buildings 4.2, 4.7 and the earlier phase of Building 4.5). The first two share exactly the same alignment as **G11** and are also regularly spaced on Terraces 1 and 3 respectively, suggesting a coherent scheme of planning. Building 4.7 was identified in the GPR survey (see fig 3.17) and is probably a row-type building, with three axial walls visible. A wall at its northern end appears to de-mark the end of the building, close to the terrace edge. It appears that this building was cut through by the Town Wall. A series of fragmentary walls at its southern end may relate to structures built against the back of the Wall. A surface just to its east probably represents a continuation of street EW9 (p. 48).

Moving across to the eastern part of the surveyed

area, there is a complex of structures that occupy the full width of Terrace 2, with further evidence provided by small developer-led excavations further towards Front Street (**G44**, **G59** and **G94**). There was also a series of major nineteenth-century excavations (**G22**) and continuing up onto the adjacent part of Terrace 3 (**G23**). Trial excavations in 2016 (**G104**) confirmed the accuracy of Ecroyd Smith's plan of **G22**.[25]

Although the exact arrangement of these buildings remains uncertain, their general outlines have been reconstructed here. Building 4.8, as excavated in the 1840s (**G22**), comprised a bath suite, two mosaics, and the corner of a courtyard. The two mosaics are dated to the late second century AD, and are displayed in purpose-built nineteenth-century structures which now form part of the English Heritage site (fig 3.19). At first sight, these rooms appear to represent the north-western corner of a large courtyard house that perhaps faced onto the Principal North–South Street.[26] In this reconstruction, the western range of rooms continued across the terrace with the Star mosaic and other room to the south projecting from its back wall. However, the geophysical survey also suggests that in its final form, this building was sub-divided to form a pair of houses (Buildings 4.8 and 4.9) separated by an east–west wall, which is also seen in excavations *c* 40m to the east (**G44**). This wall coincides with a change in level along the line of a medieval toft boundary. It also shows a series of rooms apparently built over the courtyard. A series of diagonal features with positive anomalies may represent pipes or later walls.

To the south on Terrace 3, Ecroyd Smith excavated a long room with an apsidal end and adjacent corridor, which he referred to as a 'basilica' (**G23**). It contained two early fourth-century mosaics, the larger of which depicts the muses and includes a Greek inscription, hence it is commonly referred to as the Helicon mosaic (see fig 3.20). These rooms, re-excavated in 1974 and 1979, had been truncated at the north by the edge of Terrace 3, which coincides with a medieval toft boundary. It is inferred that the missing north wall of the 'basilica' coincided with the original terrace edge and that the layout of the medieval tofts resulted in this being cut back. The apsidal room probably formed the north-western corner of a courtyard house facing onto the Principal North–South Street and, given its design, is best interpreted as a dining room (*triclinium*).[27] It may be noted that the situation of this room on the terrace edge at the north of the building will have afforded a clear view across the townscape to the north. The survey, just to the south east of the excavated room, adds a little to the understanding of this building (Building 4.10), but the ground here is disturbed, having been used as allotments with demolished farm buildings in the vicinity. A series of linear magnetic anomalies here relate to rooms continuing the line of the excavated structure to the east, although the strongest signal probably relates to the medieval toft boundary. A series of north–south features are probably Roman walls.

The main area of the geophysical surveys lay to the west and south west of these buildings, covering most of the south-western corner of the town and occupying Terraces 2 and 3. The results clearly show a complex of features that include the medieval toft boundaries and Roman terraces, as well as buildings. A comparison of the results with the 1708 map (see fig 2.2) allows the identification of a series of east–west features with the toft boundaries mapped at that time (see fig 4.14). However, some of the properties on that map represent amalgamations of original individual strips, the boundaries of which can also be tentatively identified. Certain of the north–south features in the survey also relate to these toft boundaries, so it can be inferred that these too are post-Roman in date. It should nevertheless be recognised that these medieval boundaries were influenced by the existing landscape, and so reflect the Roman layout (below, p. 121). Bearing these points in mind, it is possible to outline the authors' understanding of this part of the survey, starting from the north. Throughout the area surveyed, the evidence for Roman buildings is good, although the clarity of the fluxgate gradiometry and GPR both vary in different parts of it. Therefore, both will be integrated in the description here.

Immediately to the west of Building 4.8, a clearly defined range of rooms visible in the GPR continues along the northern edge Terrace 2 (Building 4.11). It is not clear whether this represents a single structure or a series of separate buildings running along the terrace edge. The continuation of this line with buildings further to the west (Building 4.12) perhaps supports the latter suggestion.

Immediately to the south of Building 4.11, and to the west of 4.9, there seems to have been a space, perhaps a courtyard, although the traces of several walls may suggest a more complex pattern. Flanking the western side of this area is one of the most clearly defined buildings in the GPR survey (Building 4.13). This is on a slightly different orientation to the buildings to the west, but is aligned with Building 4.14 to the south. Its western frontage comprises a north–south block of three rooms with wings comprising three rooms extending to the west at each end. Each of these wings has an apsidal room at its western end. The building therefore forms three sides of a courtyard, on the fourth side of which is a further structure. This may form a free-standing square room, but the absence of an eastern wall leaves open the possibility that it simply extended an enclosed courtyard. The whole complex is cut by the toft boundary, but the GPR shows surfaces within most of the interior that are likely to be surviving floors. There is no obvious parallel for what is clearly a well-planned and elaborate building, presumably a house. It is set in the centre of Terrace 2. Street EW10 runs to its south, separated by a series of minor structures on a slightly different alignment.

Between this and the so-called 'barracks' (**G11**), the fluxgate gradiometry suggests further structures (Building 4.12), but the GPR shows little, and the form of the buildings is difficult to discern. These features are generally on the same alignment as the Building 4.11 to the east, but different from **G11** to the west and Building 4.13 to the south east. Building 4.12 lies to the east of the line of street NS7, although it is not detected in the survey here. To its south, between it and street EW10, the fluxgate gradiometry shows a concentration of walls and highly magnetic features, while no discernible building plans are visible. Different wall orientations here suggest a number of building phases.

On Terrace 3, in the southern part of the field, the GPR clearly shows a rectangular structure – Building 4.14 (*c* 15 × 6 m) – that is aligned with the front of Building 4.13 and is on the same alignment. To its east is street NS6, to which it is connected by a short stretch of east–west street. Building 4.14 is probably a temple with steps leading up to its northern end. This conclusion is reinforced by its setting facing onto an open area occupying the northern half of Terrace 3. In this position, the temple overlooks the town below.

The results of the fluxgate gradiometry show buildings flanking the temple. To the east, it is not possible to discern the individual buildings facing onto the side-street that connects street NS6. To the west, the survey shows a regularly planned lay-out, with a series of blocks measuring *c* 16 × 16 m echoing the length of the temple (including the steps). An east–west wall continues the line of the temple frontage westwards for *c* 70m. It intersects with a similar north–south wall, forming three blocks of building (Buildings 4.15, 4.16 and 4.17), flanking the open area in front of the temple. Building 4.16 sits on the northern edge of Terrace 3. The outer walls of each block are clearly defined, and each has evidence for a major east–west internal division. Smaller internal walls are visible in each, but it is not possible to identify clear room plans, and several phases may be represented. West of Buildings 4.16 and 4.17, the axial east–west wall continues up to street NS7. A series of walls in this area clearly indicate buildings, although individual structures cannot be discerned. To the west of street NS7 a similar pattern pertains.

To the south of Buildings 4.14, 4.15 and 4.17, a toft boundary cuts across fragments of walls and rooms from buildings that must face onto street EW9, although no clear building layouts are decipherable. Street EW9 defines the southern edge of Terrace 3, partly covered by a further medieval toft boundary. Unfortunately, the area between street EW9 and the southern Town Wall is covered in thick woodland and therefore was not covered by the geophysical survey. The gradient of the slope increases towards the Town Wall, suggesting the existence of a bank, especially towards the west. Although this may result from the dumping of spoil from the nineteenth-century excavations and landscaping for the garden, it is also possible that the embankment behind the Wall was heightened here, as seems to have been the case at the North Wall in the later Roman period (below, p. 117).

3.6 Area 5: South-eastern intra-mural area (figs 3.21, 3.22, and 3.23)

This area occupies the south-eastern part of the walled town and is largely occupied by houses and gardens of the present village, so access for geophysical survey was very limited (fig 3.21). The ground slopes to the north, and the area is defined to the south and east by the Town Wall, and to the west by the Principal North-South Street. (The defensive ditches at the south east and South Gate are discussed within the section for Area 6, and the eastern defensive ditches within the section for Area 7, below). The Town Wall itself is clearly visible at the south east and along its eastern side. The internal corner tower, an external tower, and part of the curtain wall at the south-eastern corner were excavated in 1937 (**G42**). The internal tower and the external tower are clearly visible in the geophysical survey, and the line of the Wall itself can be traced in either direction, although there is evidence for other complex adjacent features. Along the East Wall two rectangular internal towers, similar to that excavated in the south-western sector (above, p. 47), can also be identified (Towers 5.1 and 5.2).

The gradient of the hill is relatively steep near the southern defences, but decreases towards the centre of the town. Although later buildings make it difficult to see the Roman terracing, this can usually be identified by comparison with Area 4, the 1708 map and in the contours (see fig 4.8). However, since the hill slope is slightly gentler to the west, the lower terraces may peter

Fig 3.21 Area 5: results of the gradiometry survey in relation to modern topography. For the location, see fig 3.3. Scale 1:1500. *Drawing:* Rose Ferraby. © Crown copyright and database rights 2018 Ordnance Survey (100025252)

out towards the East Wall. The northern limit of Terrace 1 appears to respect the natural slope, while the southern edge is still clearly visible as a steep slope running across the Village Green. The boundary between Terraces 2 and 3 is more difficult to discern, appearing in the contours in a couple of places. The superimposition of a trackway connecting Village Farm to the fields to the east (see fig 2.2) has clearly altered the levels in this area. In contrast, the southern boundary of Terrace 3 is very clearly identifiable.

Similarly, there is limited evidence for the Roman streets. Front Street follows the line of the Principal North–South Street, whilst the eastern branch of Back Street is aligned with street NS4, as identified in Area 2,

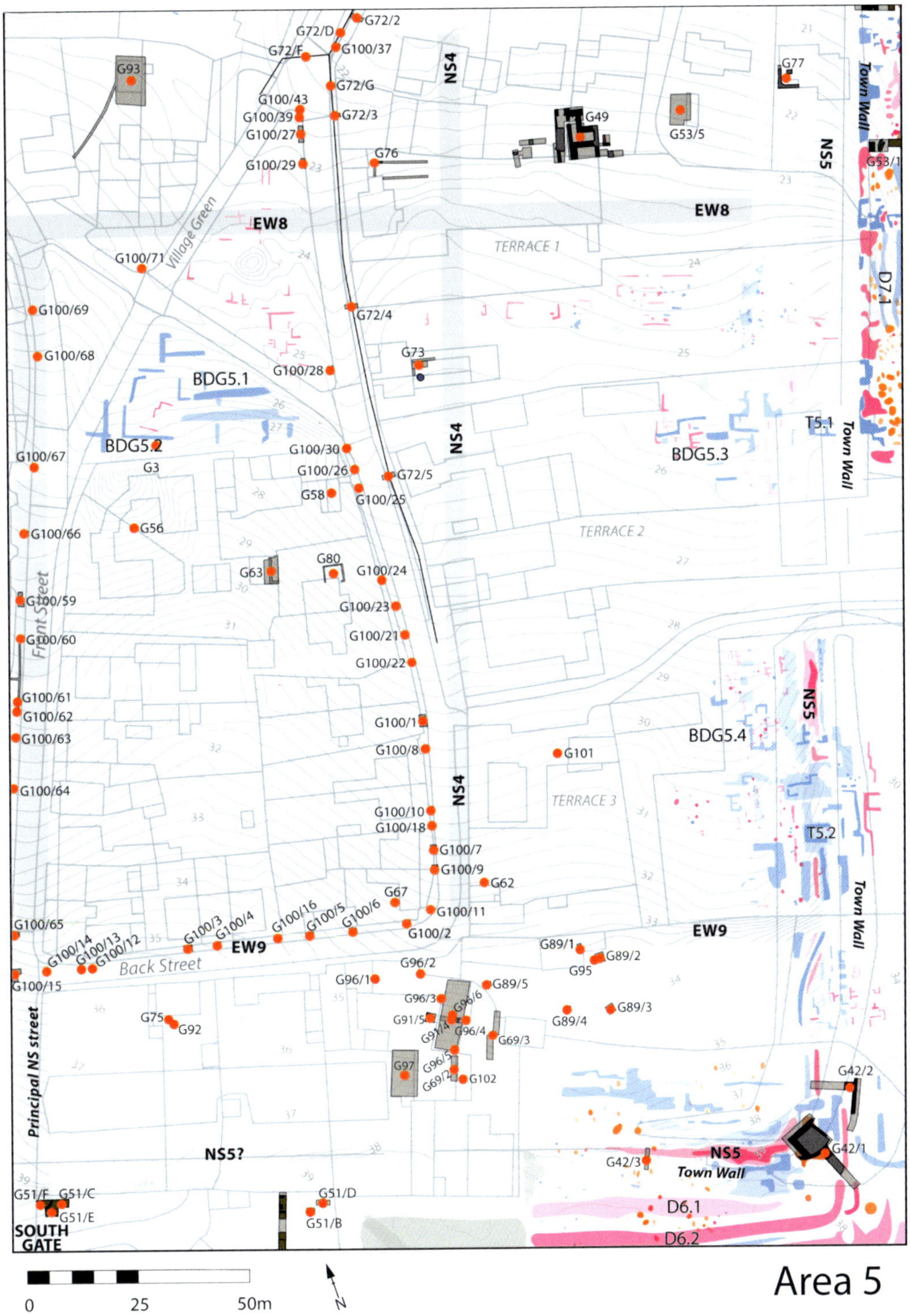

Fig 3.22 Area 5: interpretation of the gradiometry survey results in the context of the other archaeological evidence. For the location, see fig 3.3. Scale 1:1500. *Drawing:* Rose Ferraby. © Crown copyright and database rights 2018 Ordnance Survey (100025252)

and it seems reasonable to suppose that it continued. Further evidence for this hypothesis is provided by the symmetry this would accord with NS6 in Area 4, which is on the same line as street NS1. The GPR survey of the Village Green revealed another east–west street (EW8) that continued to the east, where a building (**G49**) faces onto it (above, p. 45). This route seems to have been extended beyond the wall in the later Roman period (below, p. 68). The implications of this are discussed in Chapter 4 (below, p. 121).

The southern branch of Back Street is broadly aligned with street EW9 in Area 4, which is assumed to continue. To the east, Street NS5 was identified by excavation to the south of the East Gate (**G53**) and can be seen continuing

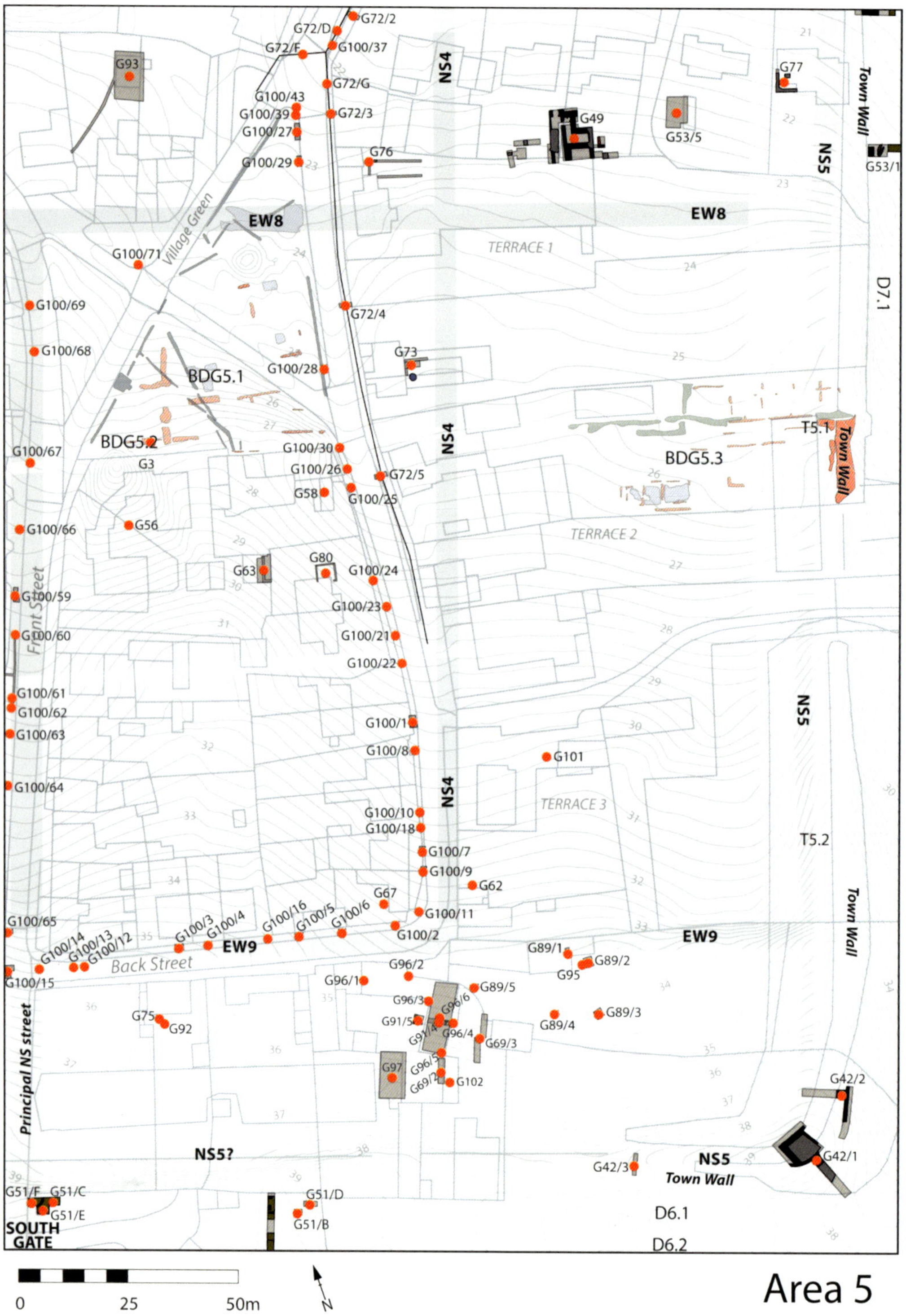

Fig 3.23 Area 5: interpretation of the GPR survey results in the context of the other archaeological evidence. For the location, see fig 3.3. Scale 1:1500. *Drawing:* Rose Ferraby. © Crown copyright and database rights 2018 Ordnance Survey (100025252)

further south, running just inside the Town Wall. The evidence is fragmentary, but it can be seen clearly on Terrace 3 and along within the south-eastern corner of the Wall, suggesting that it linked to the South Gate. Its absence on Terrace 2 is probably associated with later landscaping, which seems to have created a ha-ha over the Town Wall. Observations of building work just to the south of the Village Green (**G56**) recorded a 'metalled road', but it is difficult to understand the report or reconcile it with the other evidence.

The limited information on buildings in this area can be described working from north to south. The north-western corner of the area touches the corner of the *forum* with adjacent buildings discussed above (pp. 43–6).

On Terrace 1, the Village Green comprised the largest area surveyed, being fully covered by both fluxgate gradiometry and GPR. In addition to a stretch of street EW8, the survey revealed walls broadly aligned with the street grid. There is evidence for a building (Building 5.1) at the southern edge of Terrace 1. Both surveys suggest quite substantial walls, aligned with the terrace, but the plan of the building is unclear. Across the remainder of the Green, there is much later disturbance, and the 1708 map shows buildings here (see fig 2.2). This, together with evidence of a deep overburden, suggests that these features are probably relatively recent in origin. In the gardens immediately to the east, survey was limited in extent and complicated by restricted access. There are some traces of probable Roman structures; although these cannot be resolved in terms of any coherent plan, they follow the alignment shared by both the Roman town and the later toft boundaries.

At the southern limit of the Village Green, in the area known as Borough Hill, another building (Building 5.2) is visible on the northern edge of Terrace 2. The survey results here appear to include a retaining wall for the terrace, as well as the building. Mosaics were uncovered here in 1683 (**G3**). Drake describes a substantial building, whilst the mosaics indicate a fourth-century date. This can be identified with Building 5.2, which was probably a large and well-appointed house that faced onto the Principal North–South Street to its west. The GPR survey provides clear evidence for this. Observations during development work just to the south (**G56** and **G58**) do not provide any evidence for this building continuing in this direction.

Limited survey in the gardens to the east of street NS4 revealed structures in the area towards the Town Wall. Building 5.3 comprises a series of walls, including a range of three rooms with floors, presumably domestic, clearly visible in the GPR survey. The internal wall tower set against the back of the Town Wall noted above (Tower 5.1) is visible in both surveys. This was probably separated from Building 5.3 by street NS5.

To the south, on Terrace 3, only limited survey was undertaken. The area immediately inside the Town Wall beside Tower 5.2 shows evidence for a series of small buildings (Building 5.4) that are probably Roman in date, perhaps facing onto Street NS5. Excavations in 1937 (**G42**) explored an internal tower on the Town Wall and showed that part of the Wall had been rebuilt during the late Roman period. The course of the Wall is visible in the survey to the west of this tower. Finally, just inside the South Wall, and aligned with it, is a series of linear features that are not easily understood, but which may be associated with the medieval Studforth Farm.

3.7 Area 6: South-eastern extra-mural area (figs 3.24, 3.25, 3.26, 3.27 and 3.28)

This area covers the ridge top to the south of the walled town, together with parts of the slopes to both the south and north east. It includes the most prominent topographic feature in the area known as Studforth Hill, and has some very well-preserved earthworks (notably the town's defensive ditches). The limits of the geophysical survey to the south and east are arbitrary, and do not imply that the edges of the archaeology have been reached. There is very little overlap between the field-walking and geophysics coverage in this area (see fig 4.6).[28]

The Town Wall has been discussed above (see Area 5). The surviving earthworks of the ditches to its south are extremely well preserved, forming a sharply defined east–west trough. It was this that was previously identified as a stadium,[29] and an altar with a figured frieze was found here (fig 3.26).[30] Key to understanding the complex features revealed by the fluxgate gradiometry are Margaret Jones' excavations in 1964 a little further to the west. Her excavations revealed both the eastern tower of the South Gate (**G51/C, E, F**), and a sequence of four ditches parallel with the Town Wall (**G51/A**). Two inner ditches are interpreted as being contemporaneous with the Wall; the two outer ditches are seen as replacing these following the construction of an external tower, probably in the mid fourth century (below, p. 116). Although doubt has been cast on the existence of the outermost ditch,[31] Jones' identification is confirmed by the survey which shows four ditches (Ditches 6.1–6.4). The defences are discussed further below (pp. 108–11; 116–17).

An additional narrow bank (Bank 6.1), clearly visible in the topography, runs parallel, further to the south within the hollow created by the defensive ditches (fig 3.27). It connects with a curved bank to the east (Bank 6.2). Both are clearly much later in date and mark a field boundary shown on the first edition OS Map of 1852. The ditches on the eastern side of the Wall do not exactly match those to the south, although the broad pattern is similar (Ditches 6.5–6.7 below).

Immediately to the south of the ditches, the survey clearly shows an amphitheatre (**G15**). This occupies the highest point on the hill, providing clear long-distance views in every direction. The remains include a section of surviving earthwork from the seating bank to the south, together with geophysical signals revealing the extent of the arena (*c* 60m × 40m) and two further sections of seating bank to the north (fig 3.28). Two entrance passages to the arena are visible, to the north west and

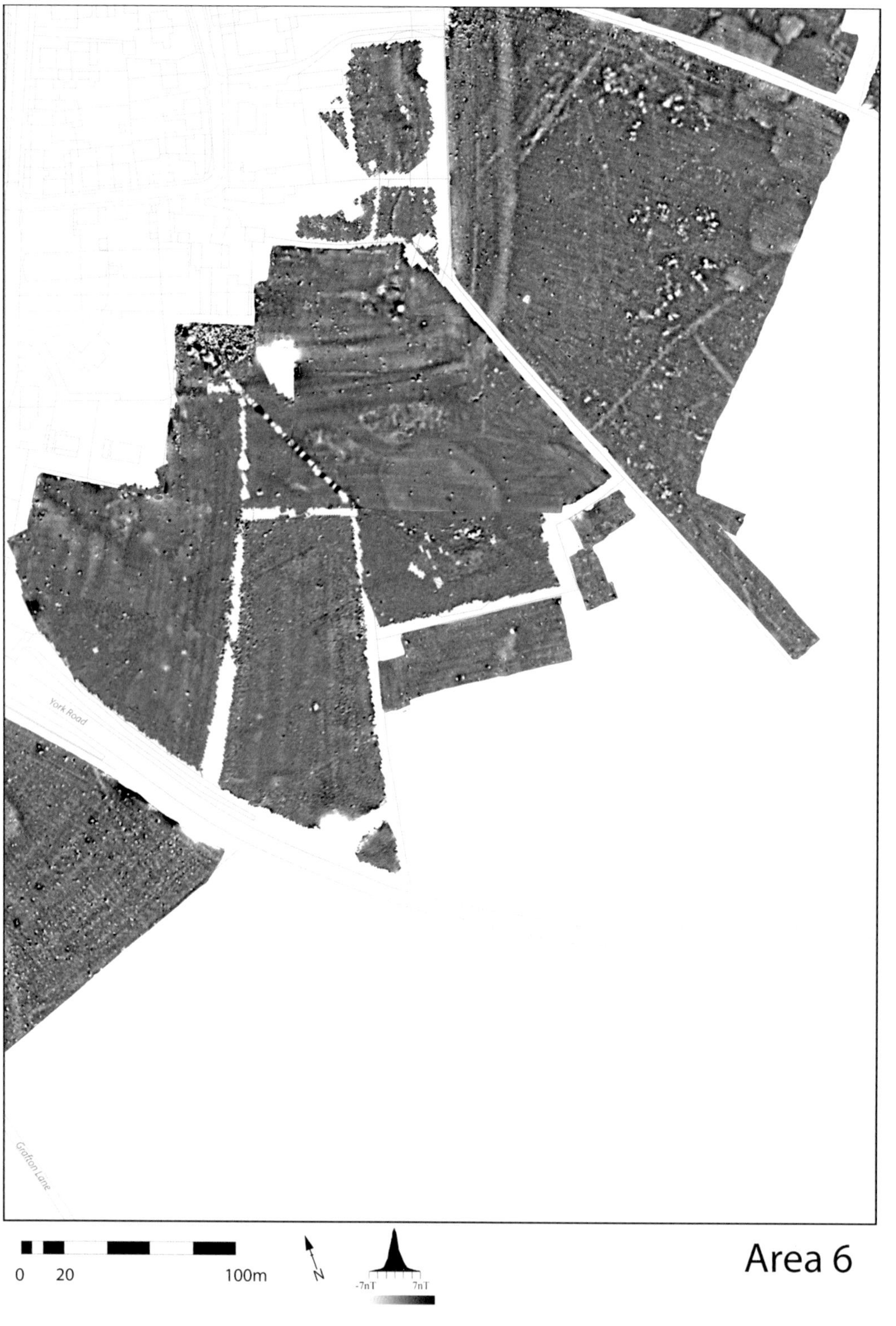

Fig 3.24 Area 6: results of the gradiometry survey in relation to modern topography. For the location, see fig 3.3. Scale 1:3000. *Drawing:* Rose Ferraby. © Crown copyright and database rights 2018 Ordnance Survey (100025252)

south east (although these are not exactly aligned). The arena itself is visible as an earthwork hollow, its perimeter defined by a narrow negative anomaly, probably a revetment wall. The surviving seating bank at the south shows possible signs of seating tiers, although it has been landscaped to create a knoll topped with trees.[32] This landscaping perhaps relates to the levelling of a supposed amphitheatre recorded in 1811.[33]

Earlier archaeologists have debated whether or not these earthworks formed part of an amphitheatre.[34] An unlocated trench on its northern side dug in 1935 suggested to the excavators that it was a natural feature.[35] It has also been concluded that it was a medieval ring-work,[36] perhaps to be identified with the castle known as

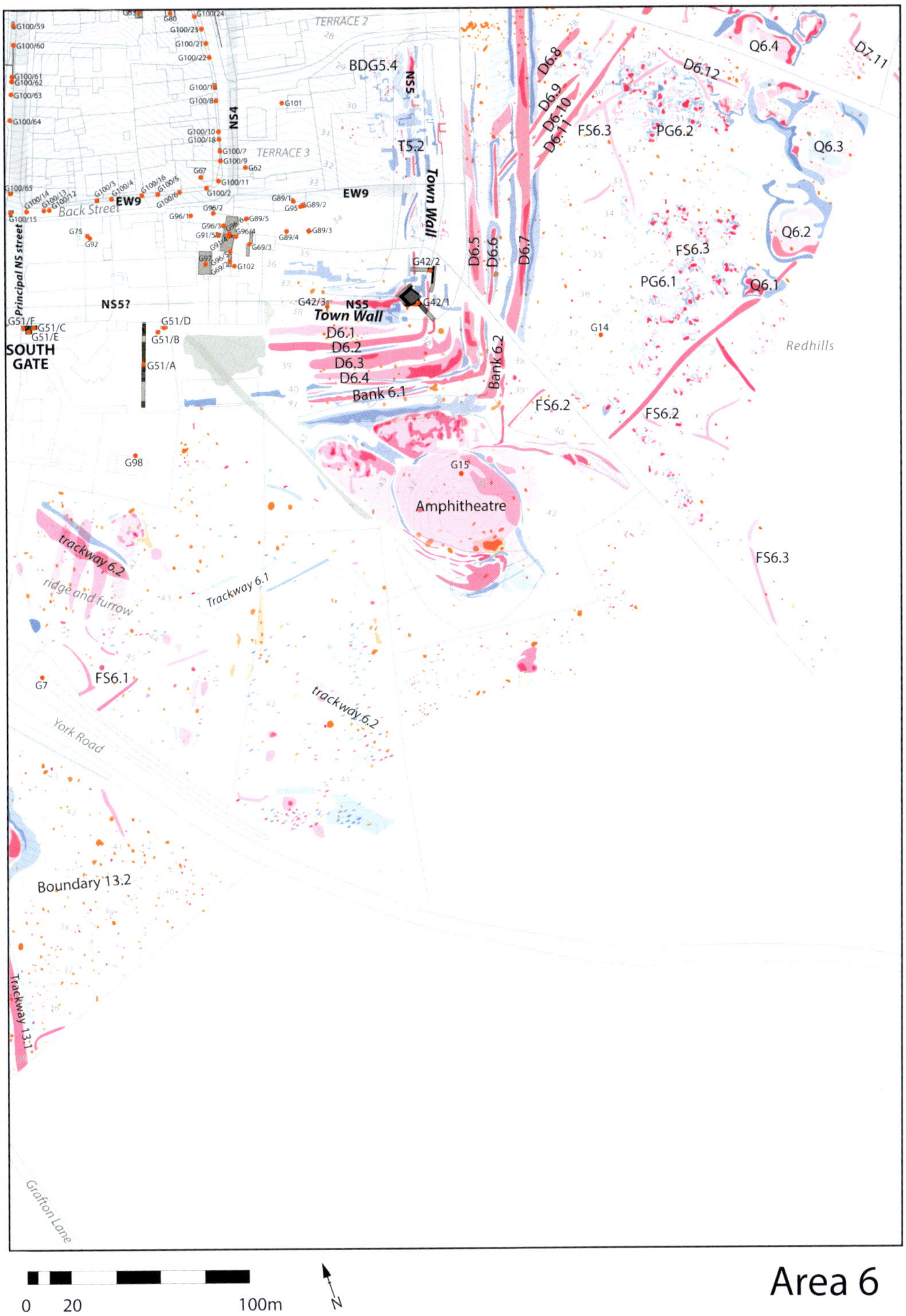

Fig 3.25 Area 6: interpretation of the gradiometry survey results in the context of the other archaeological evidence. For the location, see fig 3.3. Scale 1:3000. *Drawing:* Rose Ferraby. © Crown copyright and database rights 2018 Ordnance Survey (100025252)

'Stuteville', which was recorded between 1154 and 1205.[37] Aside from the name, this is an attractive hypothesis since it is situated to control the road from York approaching Boroughbridge, so it may well be that the amphitheatre was reused in this way during the medieval period.

The survey shows very clearly that the northern seating bank has been truncated by the cutting of the outermost defensive ditch (Ditch 6.4), which probably dates to the late fourth century. There is enough space to have accommodated the amphitheatre untouched by the earlier ditches (Ditches 6.1, 6.2 and perhaps 6.3). We cannot be sure about the date of the amphitheatre, although parallels with other sites shows that its size is comparable with larger examples from Britain, most of

Fig 3.26 Area 6: drawing of an altar with figures carved in relief, found at the amphitheatre (**G15**) and originally published by Ecroyd Smith 1852 (Appendix 5, no 4). Original illustration by M N Hessey

Fig 3.27 Area 6: photograph along the floor of the defensive ditches outside the southern Town Wall at Studforth Hill (**G15**), viewed from the west. The rise in the land in front of the trees to the left marks the Town Wall, that to the right (with standing figure) is where the defensive ditches cut through the amphitheatre. *Photograph:* Rose Ferraby

which date to the first or second century.[38] Access was probably via the road that passed through the South Gate, but it is difficult to see how this works. The only possible evidence is a track (Track 6.1) that runs south-westwards across the hill just to its south. However, it is not easy to see how this links with the town, and it may be later in date. A second trackway (Track 6.2) cuts in a south-easterly direction, possibly connecting with the South Gate. Other linear features in this area are mostly associated with later agriculture. The exception is a group of ditches that appear to be fragments of an ancient field system on either side of the York Road (Field System 6.1).

In the area to the south west of the amphitheatre, despite the visible ridge and furrow (see fig 4.13), there are also a large number of small, positive and negative magnetic anomalies. Indeed, these spread across much of the survey area outside the walls. A high density of dipolar anomalies in the area to the south of the York Road, which is regularly ploughed, is probably a result of modern debris. The positive and negative anomalies may indicate ancient features such as burials. It is notable that when the present York Road was cut through the ridge top in 1808, cremation and inhumation burials were found (**G7**). It may be noted in passing that the date of

Fig 3.28 Area 6: photograph showing the surviving seating bank from the amphitheatre at Studforth Hill (**G15**), viewed from the north west. *Photograph:* Rose Ferraby

discovery of the tombstone (*RIB* 710) perhaps suggests that this came from the same cemetery.[39] Ecroyd Smith[40] also notes graves found on the 'Redhills' (**G14**) – that is, in the area to the north east of the amphitheatre – although the two 'sarcophagi' he illustrates appear more likely to be pottery kilns (fig A4). Although none of the anomalies recorded in the survey provide the unambiguous evidence for cemeteries like those identified at Silchester,[41] these antiquarian finds confirm, as might be expected, that there were graves in the areas outside the Town Wall and around the amphitheatre.

To the north east of the amphitheatre arena, adjacent to the ditches, the ground has been cut away to form a curving slope. A boundary shown on the first edition OS Map follows this to join the line of the modern hedge. The character and dating of this feature remain uncertain, although they perhaps relate to the suggested medieval use of the site as a ring-work.[42]

Down the slope, further to the north east, the nature of the archaeology changes. The modern hedge boundary that crosses the town defences and runs north west to south east across the slope, follows a track that connects to Studforth Farm in the south-eastern corner of the walled town. Boundaries seen in the geophysics (Field System 6.2), although perpendicular to this, share an alignment with Roman features further to the north east (Areas 7 and 8). An extensive series of less clearly defined boundaries spread across the slope (Field System 6.3). They are principally on a north–south axis and appear to pre-date Field System 6.2. Ditch 6.12 is apparently later, and forms part of a field system to the north (below Area 7).

To the north, Field System 6.3 is cut by one of a series of parallel linear ditches (Ditches 6.8–6.11), which define an annexe to the defences (*c* 2.8ha in area), set around the road to York as it leaves the East Gate. These themselves intercut with the town defensive ditches (Ditches 6.5–6.7). It is not possible to be absolutely certain about all the relationships between these sets of ditches, but the general sequence seems to imply that Ditches 6.8–6.11 were cut sequentially from north to south, in concert with the development of the town defensive ditches. Furthermore, the latest of these (Ditch 6.11) is later than Field System 6.3, implying that this field system may pre-date the whole sequence. A tentative sequence for the main ditches is:

1. Ditch 6.5 [inner town defensive ditch]
2. Ditch 6.6 [middle town defensive ditch]

3. Ditch 6.8 [annexe boundary contemporaneous with, or later than Ditch 6.6, earlier than Ditch 6.7]
4. Ditch 6.9 [annexe boundary later than Ditch 6.6, earlier than Ditch 6.7]
5. Ditch 6.7 [outer town defensive ditch]
6. Ditch 6.10 [annexe boundary contemporaneous with, or later than Ditch 6.7]
7. Ditch 6.11 [annexe boundary contemporaneous with, or later than Ditch 6.7]

These ditches continue into Area 7 to the north, where their chronology and function is discussed in relation to the excavated evidence (below, this page).

The area to the east of these ditches and within the boundaries that define Field System 6.3 is peppered with other features. In addition to numerous small positive anomalies and pits, there are two principal zones of intercutting pits (Pit Groups 6.1 and 6.2), that seem to respect the ditches of the field system. This suggests a sequence of intercut pits, perhaps dug to obtain the clay that overlies the Sherwood Sandstone bedrock. This slope is known as Redhills, a name that may relate to pottery kilns, noting the comments above about Ecroyd Smith's possible illustration of kilns here (**G14**). There are no extensive magnetic features that look like kilns, but the possibility cannot be ruled out that kilns are represented by some of the smaller features. There is also evidence for pottery production a little further north (**G52**; below, Area 7).

Finally, at the north-eastern corner of the area, there are four larger sub-circular features, interpreted as quarries (Quarries 6.1–6.4), cut through the boulder clay to exploit the Sherwood Sandstone beneath. Each quarry covers a large area. One (6.3) cuts Field System 6.3. Quarries 6.1 and 6.2 overlie Field System 6.2, so they must be later in date. Evidence of the form of these quarries provides useful insights into their mode of operation, including the sequence of cutting.

3.8 Area 7: Eastern extra-mural area (figs 3.29, 3.30 and 3.31)

This area lies to the east of the walled town, and occupies the lower part of the Redhills, down to the Dunsforth Road, together with the more level land that runs northwards toward the River Ure (fig 3.31). The Roman road to York leaves the town via the East Gate, and can be clearly seen running east, although as noted above, the medieval road also followed this route until it was realigned to the south during the second half of the nineteenth century (above, p. 39). The road shows clearly in the geophysics as a major linear feature, flanked by ditches. At the present junction between the Dunsforth Road and Hall Arm Lane, the Roman road turns to the south east, running beneath the present road. It was recorded here during the construction of a new sewer in 1964 (**G52/A**). A significant proportion of this area was field-walked in the 1980s–90s.[43] The pottery collected shows a peak of deposition in the second century, tailing off through the third and fourth.[44] However, there is spatial variation, with areas to the north of the Roman road having a significant density of later Roman material, whilst that to the south of the junction between Hall Arm Lane and the Dunsforth Road producing very little of this period (see 4.6).[45]

The eastern Town Wall has been discussed above (Areas 2 and 5). The defensive ditches are clearly visible in the southern part of the area, continuing from Area 6, although further north they are less easy to understand, being overlain by ridge and furrow as well as an apparent accumulation of alluvium. Just south of the Dunsforth Road, close to the East Gate, three trenches were cut across these ditches in 1965 (**G53**). It is clear from the survey results that these excavations did not extend across all the ditches, but they do provide important chronological information. In contrast to the southern defences, there appear to be only three ditches. Closest to the town wall, Ditch 7.1 (= Ditch 6.5) is poorly defined due to its proximity to the modern boundary. This equates to the excavated 'inner ditch', contemporaneous with the construction of the Town Wall, and was overlain by the foundation for an external tower found in trench III (**G53/3**).[46] Its dating is considered below (p. 116). Ditch 7.2 (= Ditch 6.6), is more clearly defined. In the 1965 excavation (**G53/1**), this was labelled as the 'outer ditch',[47] constructed when the external tower was built, sometime after the late third century (below, p. 149). Ditch 7.3 (= Ditch 6.7), the outermost, is much more strongly defined, but lay beyond the extent of the 1965 excavation. It is also broader and straighter than the other ditches, and is presumed to be the latest in the sequence (pp. 116–17).

Although the correlation between the excavated ditches and the geophysical survey is relatively certain, there are a series of other linear features in the survey that were not recorded in the excavation. The significance of these is difficult to evaluate. Most obviously, a strong negative linear feature lies at a slight angle to the Wall, between Ditches 7.1 and 7.2. Although it possibly relates to the early post trenches seen in the 1965 excavation,[48] it is more likely to represent a boundary that is shown on the 1708 map (see fig 2.1).

To the north of the Roman road, the line of Ditch 7.3

may be preserved in some modern boundaries, but it is largely obscured by the course of a medieval droveway. This runs north from Dunsforth Road, curving out towards the flood meadows to the east. This route is respected by the ridge and furrow, most clearly to the south, and its course is seen in the boundaries on the 1708 map (see fig 2.1). Incidentally, the first edition OS map also labels a Drove Well beside it to the north of Aldborough Hall. In the north-eastern stretch, a pair of parallel dipolar linear features (most likely field drains) flank the droveway, connecting to those at a right angle to the north.

The area to the south of the Dunsforth Road contains a complex series of features within which can be identified a chronological sequence. Close to the road, there is clear evidence for ridge and furrow, which has been ploughed-out further up the slope to the south. The orientation of the furrows has been influenced by earlier features, which are predominantly set at right angles to the Roman road, and so change direction where the road turns towards the East Gate at Hall Arm Lane. The superimposition of this cultivation makes it difficult to distinguish earlier features in some places, so the description here begins at the south east.

There is a narrow strip of relatively flat land flanking the Dunsforth Road. This, and the foot of the slope to the south, is divided into a series of strips separated by boundaries set at right angles to the road. At the road frontage, these enclosures are occupied by a series of structures that seem most likely to represent funerary *mausolea*. These strongly resemble the type of cemetery that lined the approaches to a number of Roman cities across the empire.[49] Here, these have been labelled Funerary Enclosures 7.1–7.8 (east to west) lining the south side of the road. These vary in width and are separated by a combination of walls and ditches. Those to the west of Redhills Farm share a common southern boundary ditch (Ditch 7.9), whilst those to its east are a little longer, defined by a ditch that continues into Area 8 (Ditch 7.12). The line of rectangular *mausolea* creates a façade facing the road. To the west of Funerary Enclosure 7.8 is a much more extensive walled enclosure (Funerary Enclosure 7.9), which extends *c* 110m back from the road. Its trapezoidal shape is determined by the change in direction of the Roman road: the wall beside the road is visible to the east, but disappears beneath the modern road further west. Within the enclosure, parallel with its western wall, there is a series of substantial structures with very clearly defined walls. The three towards the road frontage are all rectangular (Buildings 7.1–7.3), whilst that at the south-western corner is circular (Building 7.4). All probably represent *mausolea,* although it is also possible that they are temples set within an extra-mural sanctuary. Towards the centre of the enclosure a large, circular anomaly may represent a large area of burning. The presence of other, similar signals by funerary enclosures and cremations to the east in Area 8 suggests that they all may be cremation pyres.[50] Otherwise, it is notable that the interior of this enclosure contains fewer features than the surrounding areas and that this area coincides with that noted above where very little third to fourth century pottery was found in the field-survey. However, there is evidence for walls that sub-divide the enclosure approximately east–west, resembling the narrower plots to the east.

A pair of parallel walls at the front of the enclosure, in its north-eastern corner, continue from Funerary Enclosure 7.8, and the curving wall to the south is apparently of the same phase. As the road frontage further towards the East Gate is obscured, it is not possible to tell whether such funerary encloses continued here.

Key evidence for the sequence of activity in Area 7 is provided by the relationship of Funerary Enclosure 7.9 to surrounding features. First, Ditch 7.4 (= Ditch 6.8) is clearly later than the western wall of the funerary enclosure, as it alters direction to run just outside of it. As noted in the discussion in Area 6 (above, pp. 63–4), this ditch connects with the sequence of urban defences, and must date to the fourth century. It is part of the defensive system, defining an annexe outside the East Gate (below, pp. 116–17). The course of Ditch 7.4 further to the north is obscured, but it is notable that it aligns with the eastern end of a pair of parallel ditches (7.7 and 7.8) in the field to the north of the Dunsforth Road (see below). The authors conclude that these defined the north-eastern side of the annexe. Two ditches (7.5 = 6.9 and 7.6 = 6.11), parallel to Ditch 7.4, to the south of Funerary Enclosure 7.9, also extend from the town ditches (above Area 6), representing a strengthening the circuit of the annexe. Both terminate at the southern wall of the funerary enclosure, confirming that they are later. The broader significance of this is discussed below (pp. 116–17).

Secondly, some boundary ditches can be phased in relation to Funerary Enclosure 7.9. Ditches 7.9 and 7.10 run south east from the enclosure and form part of a group of small fields (including those demarcated by Ditch 7.11 and 7.12), which continue along the slope into Area 8. These run at right angles to Field System 6.2 (above, p. 63), the line of which is continued in Ditch 7.13. These are part of a wider landscape of field systems in this area. The relationship of Ditches 7.9 and 7.10 to the eastern side of Funerary Enclosure 7.9 show that they must be later.

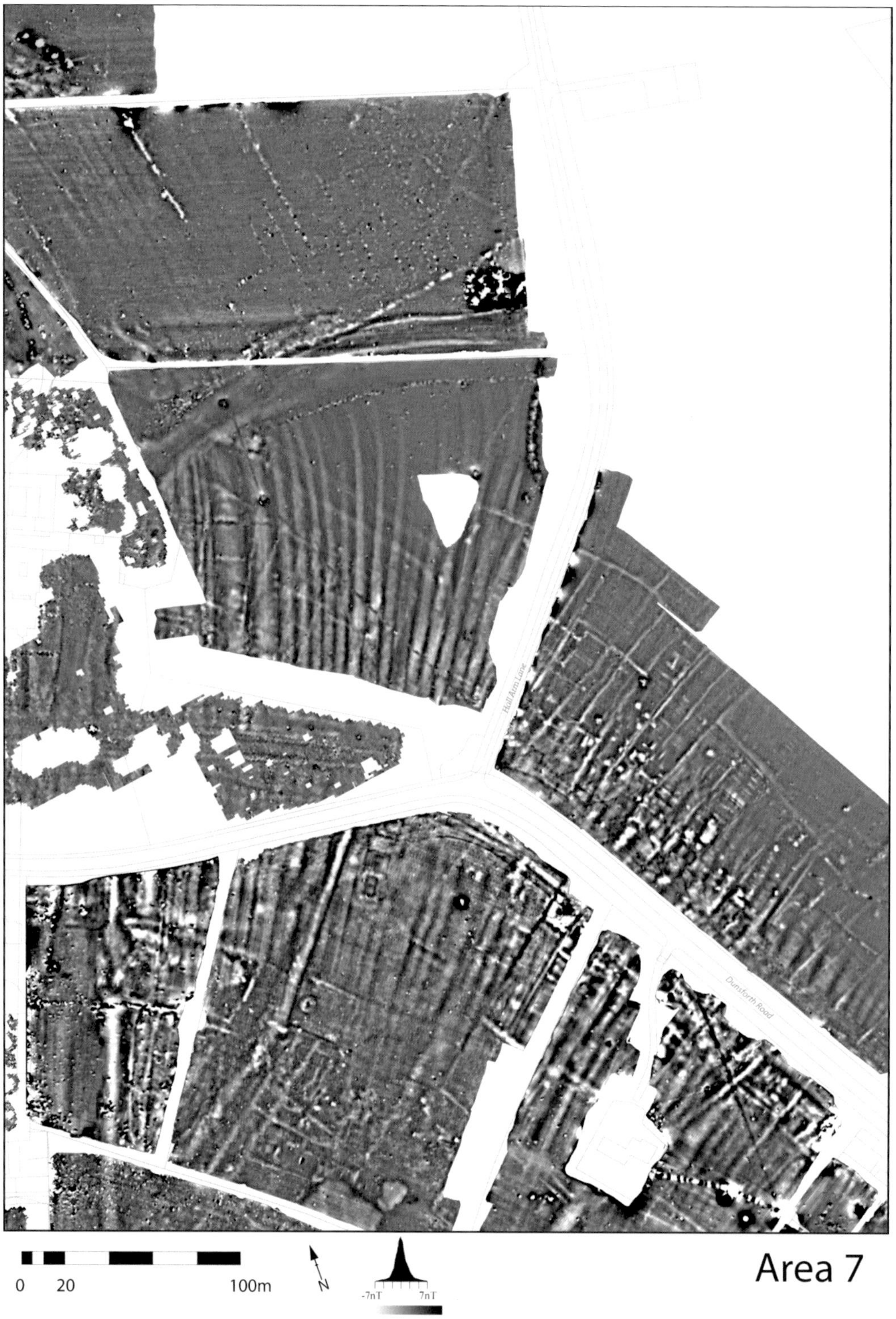

Fig 3.29 Area 7: results of the gradiometry survey in relation to modern topography. For the location, see fig 3.3. Scale 1:3000. *Drawing:* Rose Ferraby. © Crown copyright and database rights 2018 Ordnance Survey (100025252)

To the south west of the funerary enclosure there is a further system of ditches (Field System 7.1) that is later than both Funerary Enclosure 7.9 and the earliest phase of the annexe. Some of the boundaries are laid out with respect to Ditches 7.5 and 7.6, but none intersect with Ditch 7.4. The continuation of Ditch 7.11 forms part of this system, as does Ditch 6.12. One boundary stops at Quarry 6.4, but the chronology is unclear. This puts them very late in the Roman period or just beyond. Within this small group of fields there is evidence of pits and other earth-cut features which extend a little to the east.

Within the annexe defined by Ditch 7.4 there are a number of features, the interpretation of which is made difficult by the superimposition of the ridge and furrow.

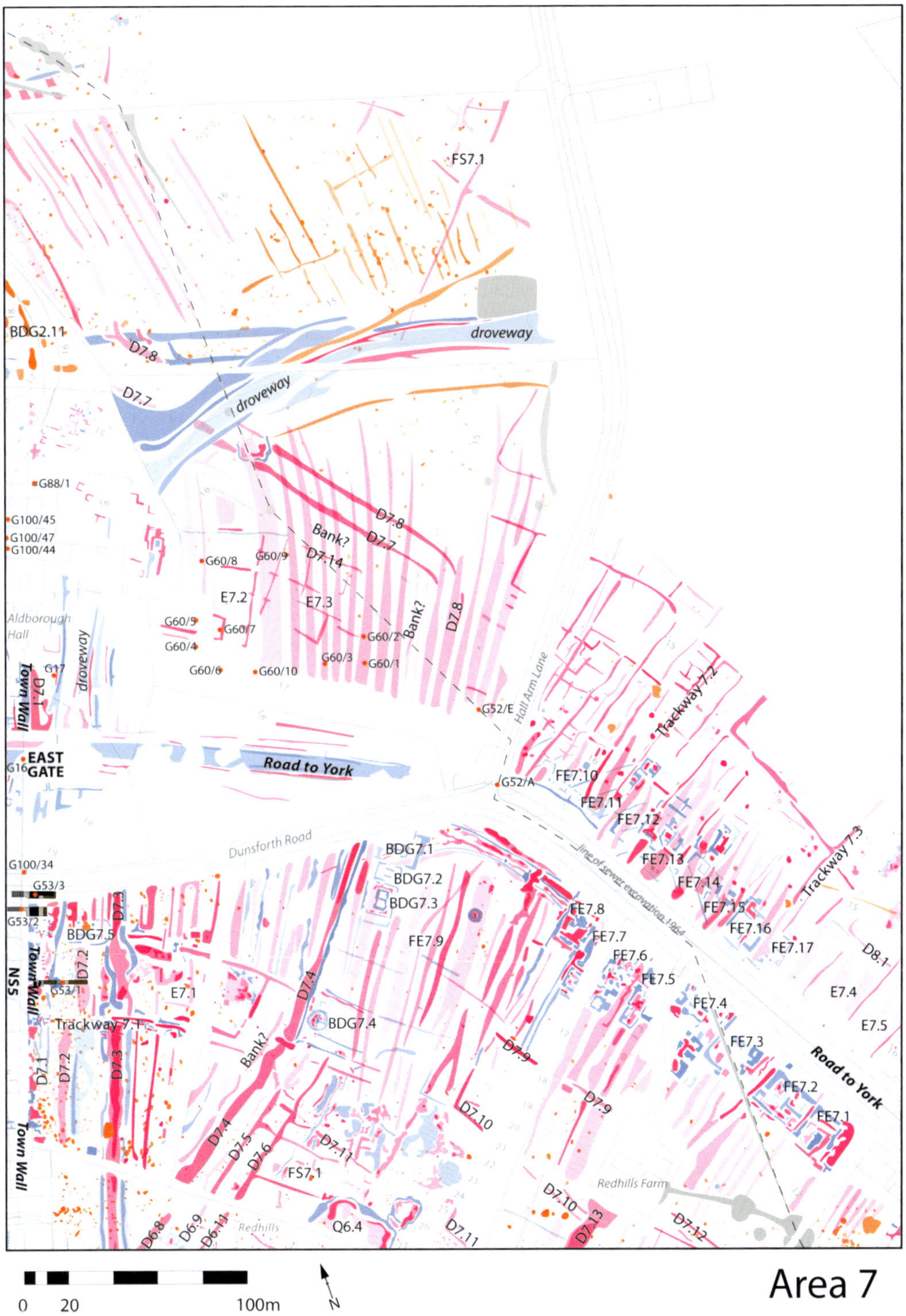

Fig 3.30 Area 7: interpretation of the gradiometry survey results in the context of the other archaeological evidence. For the location, see fig 3.3. Scale 1:3000. *Drawing:* Rose Ferraby. © Crown copyright and database rights 2018 Ordnance Survey (100025252)

This is much better preserved and thus more pronounced in the field adjacent to the Town Wall than in that to the east, which has been regularly ploughed in recent times. The ridge and furrow terminated at the modern field boundary to the south. Immediately to the west of Ditch 7.4, inside the annexe, there is a parallel strip relatively devoid of features, which is defined to the west by a narrow ditch. This zone, which is similar to that to the north of the Dunsforth Road, was presumably occupied by a defensive bank. Within the annexe, the only clear feature that pre-dates the ridge and furrow is Enclosure 7.1, which lies on an east–west axis stretching in a slight curve between the annexe bank and the Town Wall. At its eastern end, the ditches that define it cut through the

Fig 3.31 Aerial photograph of the extra-mural area to the east of the village viewed from the east. *Photograph:* Dominic Powlesland

boundary defining the bank. To the west, it clearly overlies the outer town ditch (Ditch 7.3) and seems to cut the inner ditches too. This is indicated by very different signals in the defensive ditches at this point, and it can be assumed that they have been filled in to create a flat area within Enclosure 7.1. On this basis, the enclosure appears to very late Roman or early post-Roman in date. Its northern boundary ditch is interrupted just to the west of Ditch 7.3 by what appears to be a curved wall that forms part of a building on the same alignment (Building 7.5). West of this, a linear anomaly marking a more recent field boundary runs oblique to the Town Wall (above, p. 64). Where most clearly visible, the southern boundary of Enclosure 7.1 is marked by a pair of ditches with a narrow surface between, whilst at the west end it is less clearly defined over the line of the earlier defensive ditches. To the east, the pair of ditches terminate towards the bank defining the annexe. This appears to be a trackway (Trackway 7.1), which continues the line of street EW8 within the walled town, connecting it to the annexe. As such, it must have required the creation of a gap in the Town Wall and dates very late in the sequence, as shown by its relationship with Ditch 7.3. Its significance is discussed below (p. 121). It is difficult to see any features within the enclosure, except for what appears to an area of later pits at the east end.

To the north of the Dunsforth Road, the remainder of the annexe is overlain by well-preserved ridge and furrow, whilst the medieval droveway discussed above obscures the town ditches to the west. Ditches 7.7 and 7.8, with an adjacent internal bank, define the north-eastern side of the annexe, the bank of which is partly de-limited to the south by a narrow ditch (Ditch 7.14). At the north west, the relationship between the annexe ditches and the Town Wall are obscured, although it is notable that the northern side of the droveway flares at the line of the annexe bank. Furthermore, it may be noted that the annexe joins the Town Wall at the point where it changes direction to curve to the north west. The eastern side of the annexe in this field is entirely obscured as it shares the same alignment as the superimposed ridge and furrow. However, a small fragment of Ditch 7.8 can be seen, whilst the field systems to the east appear to stop at the line of the annexe ditches (below, p. 69).

Within the annexe there are faint traces of a series of ditches underlying the ridge and furrow which define two series of enclosures (Enclosures 7.2 and 7.3) on slightly different alignments. That to the west is orientated north–south conforming with the Roman road, whilst to the east Enclosure 7.3 is on an axis slightly offset, echoing the curve in orientation seen in Enclosure 7.1. Both run back *c* 90m from the Roman road, bounded at the north by Ditch 7.14, so they resemble the funerary enclosures that line the road further from the East Gate. It is not, however, clear whether there were tombs on the frontage here. Enclosure 7.3 is bounded by Ditch 7.14, suggesting that the field system may have determined the layout of the annexe. The ditches just to the west of Hall Arm Lane appear to continue the same enclosure system, and are also cut by the annexe ditches. Margaret Jones recorded a dump of wasters from a kiln producing *mortaria* dated to the AD 95–140 in the area immediately to the west of Hall Arm Lane at this point (**G52/E**). This is just outside the annexe, to the east of the line of Ditch 7.8. This implies production nearby, but there is no clear evidence of kilns in the survey. Pottery production here would make sense in the context of these extra-mural enclosures.

In the field to the north of the annexe the survey results are less clear, partly because of ridge and furrow, but also because flooding has apparently led to an accumulation of alluvium. Immediately to the north of the droveway is a pair of substantial linear features representing banks, running parallel with the modern boundary. These pre-date the ridge and furrow as well as the droveway, and seem to have influenced its course. They are broadly aligned with street EW1 within the walled town, and meet the Wall close to Building 2.11. At the western end, these are cut by a ditch which appears to be a continuation of Ditch 7.8, the outer annexe ditch. However, the identification of this as a continuation of Ditch 7.8 is questionable, as it is aligned slightly to the north and may link to the ridge and furrow. It is not clear what these features represent or whether their alignment with the street grid in the town is significant. It can be concluded that the two banks are broadly contemporaneous, in which case they may de-limit a routeway from the town towards the riverside. If this is the case, they presumably pre-date the Town Wall. Alternatively, given the topography, they may represent embankments to prevent flooding. There is also evidence for land drains following the medieval furrows, showing as dipolar linear anomalies as well as the ditches of a field system (Field System 7.2) to the north east. This shares the same orientation as the Roman enclosures beside the road to York.

To the east of Hall Arm Lane and north of Dunsforth Road, there is clear evidence for a complex of enclosures underlying the ridge and furrow. These line the Roman road to York and mirror those on its southern side, although it is notable that there are fewer buildings, especially to the east. The enclosures represent a complex evolution, with some larger blocks apparently later sub-divided, and the continuation of certain boundaries into field systems can be seen further from the road. The Roman road itself was recorded underneath the present road at the junction between the Dunsforth Road and Hall Arm Lane (**G52/A**). A curved length of wall immediately to the east of the modern junction is perhaps associated with the edge of the road. It can be traced west beside the stretch of road visible towards the East Gate, and also to the south east where it is intermittently visible along the edge of the road.

Eastwards from Hall Arm Lane there is a series of enclosures containing buildings identified as *mausolea* (Funerary Enclosures 7.10–7.17). Beyond these are two enclosures lacking visible buildings (Enclosures 7.4–7.5), which contain few magnetic anomalies. This contrasts with some enclosures further east (below Area 8) and indicates that they were agricultural. Away from the road in Funerary Enclosure 7.11 there are two distinct dipolar anomalies, and there is also a series of large positive magnetic features behind other of the buildings. These are possibly ovens, kilns or funerary pyres. Two trackways (7.2 and 7.3) can be identified connecting the fields behind the enclosures with the road. These presumably provided access to farmland behind the enclosures. The enclosures closest to Hall Arm Lane show a series of sub-divisions, which may be linked to stock control.

3.9 Area 8: South-eastern extra-mural area (figs 3.31, 3.32 and 3.33)

There is considerable overlap between Areas 7 and 8, and labels for the features already discussed are thus duplicated on fig 3.33. Area 8 is dominated by the line of the Roman road to York that runs beneath the Dunsforth Road. There was no 1980s–90s field-walking in this area.

The fairly regular sequence of enclosures to the north of the road continues for a further *c* 175m (Enclosures 8.1–8.10). It is notable that those to the east share a common rear boundary (Ditch 8.1), which is parallel with a further boundary to the north (Ditch 8.2), suggesting a regular system of land division. The lack of magnetic features within these enclosures probably indicates

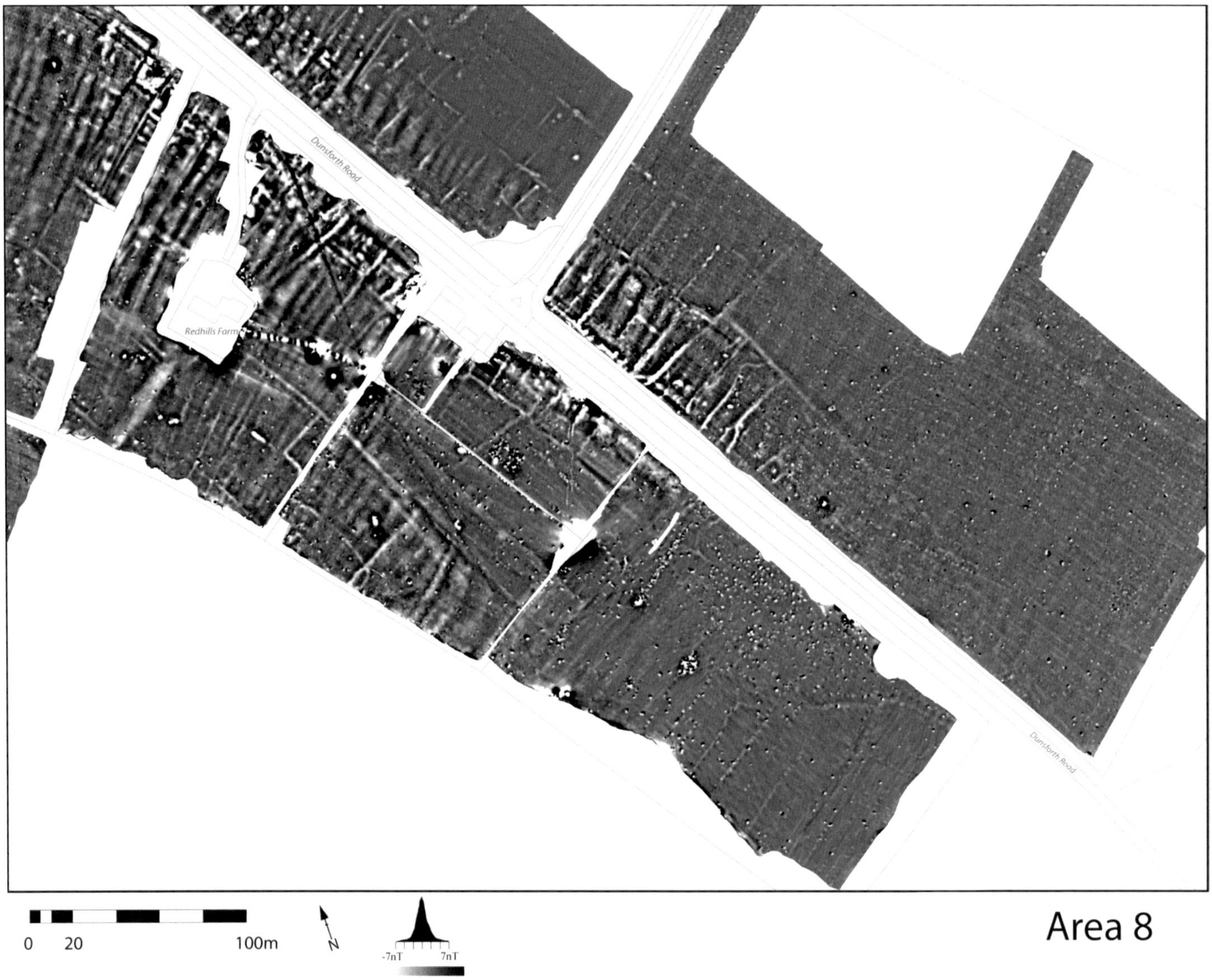

Fig 3.32 Area 8: results of the gradiometry survey in relation to modern topography. For the location, see fig 3.3. Scale 1:3000. *Drawing:* Rose Ferraby.

agricultural use. The boundary separating Enclosures 8.7 and 8.8 continues back from the road and marks a change in orientation, with the roadside enclosures beyond delimited to the north by Ditch 8.3. The road frontage in this stretch is defined by a wall and adjacent ditch. There are possible traces of buildings in Enclosures 8.3, 8.4 and 8.8 – most likely funerary. To the east of Enclosure 8.10, there is no visible evidence for the continuation of the enclosures, but Ditch 8.3 continues, converging with the road and joining it at the edge of the survey. Between Ditch 8.3 and the road, there are two possible square barrows (Barrows 8.1 and 8.2), which seem to overlie earlier features. The barrows are surrounded by small positive anomalies that might be cremation burials, as well as a dipolar anomaly suggesting burning. Ditch 8.3 has other boundary ditches joining it that define fields to the north. This area has alluvial cover that seems to deepen to the north and east, and also shows evidence for both ridge and furrow and more recent ploughing.

To the south of the road, the sequence of funerary enclosures continues from Area 7. Although partly overlain by beneath modern barns, five enclosures containing building can be discerned (Funerary Enclosures 8.1–8.5), but the area of buildings is confined to a narrower strip than in those further west. To the south these enclosures share a common boundary (Ditch 8.4), which forms one side of a rectangular enclosure (Enclosure 8.11) that covers the flat area before the ground rises to the south. The 1708 map (see fig 2.1) shows what appear to be springs feeding a channel that runs south-eastwards across this enclosure. A trackway (Trackway 8.1) cuts across it on a north–south trajectory heading towards the corner of Funerary Enclosure 8.3. On the slope to the south, Ditch 8.5 (= Ditch 7.12)

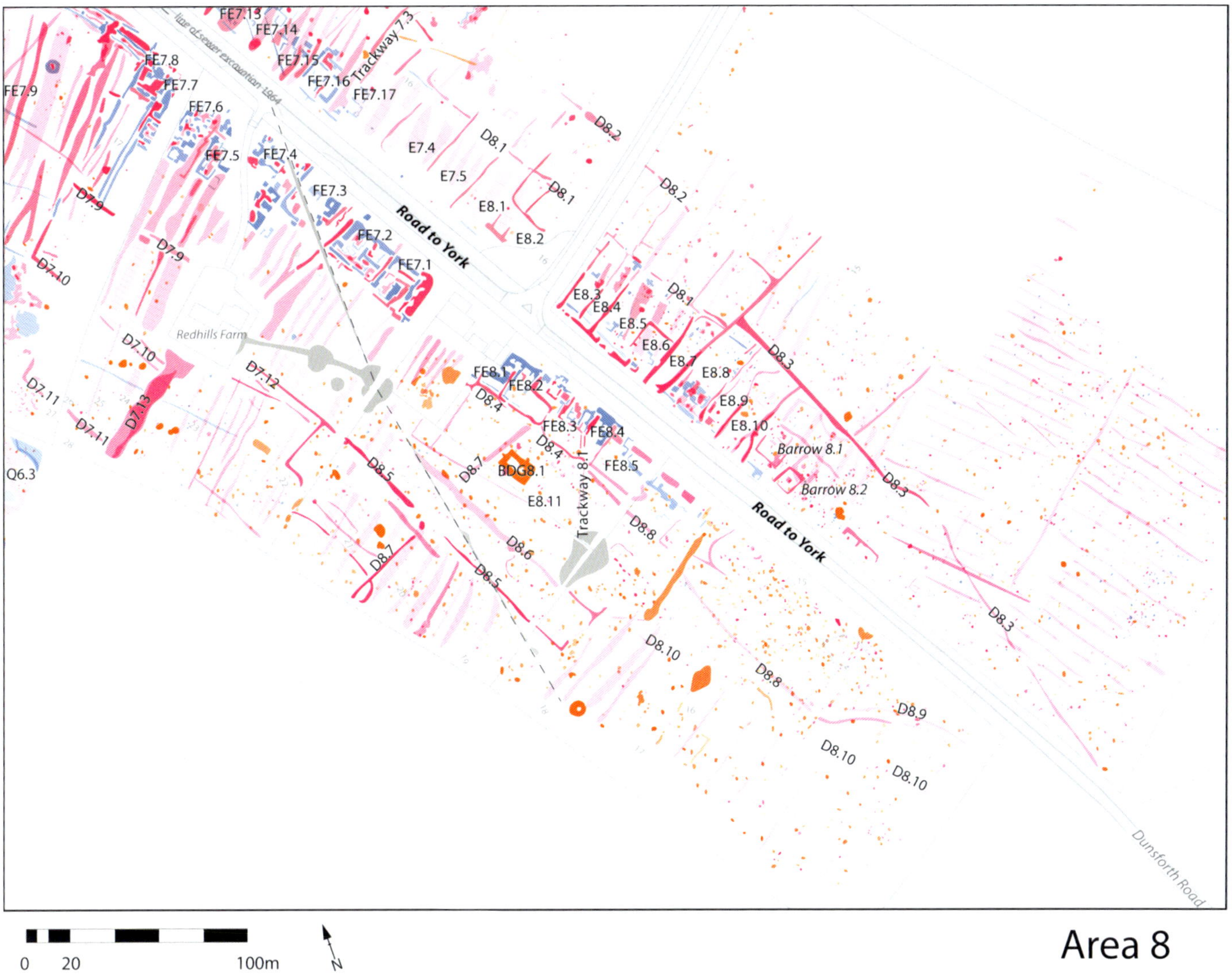

Fig 3.33 Area 8: interpretation of the gradiometry survey results in the context of the other archaeological evidence. For the location, see fig 3.3. Scale 1:3000. *Drawing:* Rose Ferraby. © Crown copyright and database rights 2018 Ordnance Survey (100025252)

defines the northern limit of a series of fields like those in Area 7. Ditch 8.5 also seems to define the southern extent of Enclosure 8.11, which is sub-divided by Ditch 8.6 a little to the north along the foot of the slope. The two ends of this enclosure are less crisply defined with ditches on the same orientation as the ridge and furrow. A series of dipolar readings indicate a substantial rectangular building at the centre of the enclosure (Building 8.1). Although the enclosure overlies an earlier field boundary (Ditch 8.7), it is integral with the system of Roman enclosures and probably represents a large funerary enclosure with a centrally placed *mausoleum*. It should be noted that the enclosure remained as a significant landscape feature, and is shown clearly on the 1708 map (see fig 2.1).

To the east, the sequence of funerary enclosures ends. Traces of a ditch (Ditch 8.8) can be seen following the foot of the slope from Enclosure 8.11 before curving in towards the Roman road where it is flanked by a parallel ditch (Ditch 8.9), their path echoing the contours in this area. These ditches mirror Ditch 8.3 to the north, forming a funnel around the road. Within the area defined by these ditches there is a large number of small dipolar and positive anomalies that are best interpreted as cremation burials. Some of these extend beyond the ditches to the south, up to the faint traces of a ditch (Ditch 8.10) which continues the approximate line of Ditch 8.6 to the west. It appears that the cemeteries of the town begin at this point on the road, opposite the square barrows on the northern side. Finally, on the slope to the south west of Ditch 8.10, in the field beyond the edge of the magnetometry survey, aerial photographs taken by Dominic Powlesland show faint traces of an enclosure system that probably represents an Iron Age farmstead.

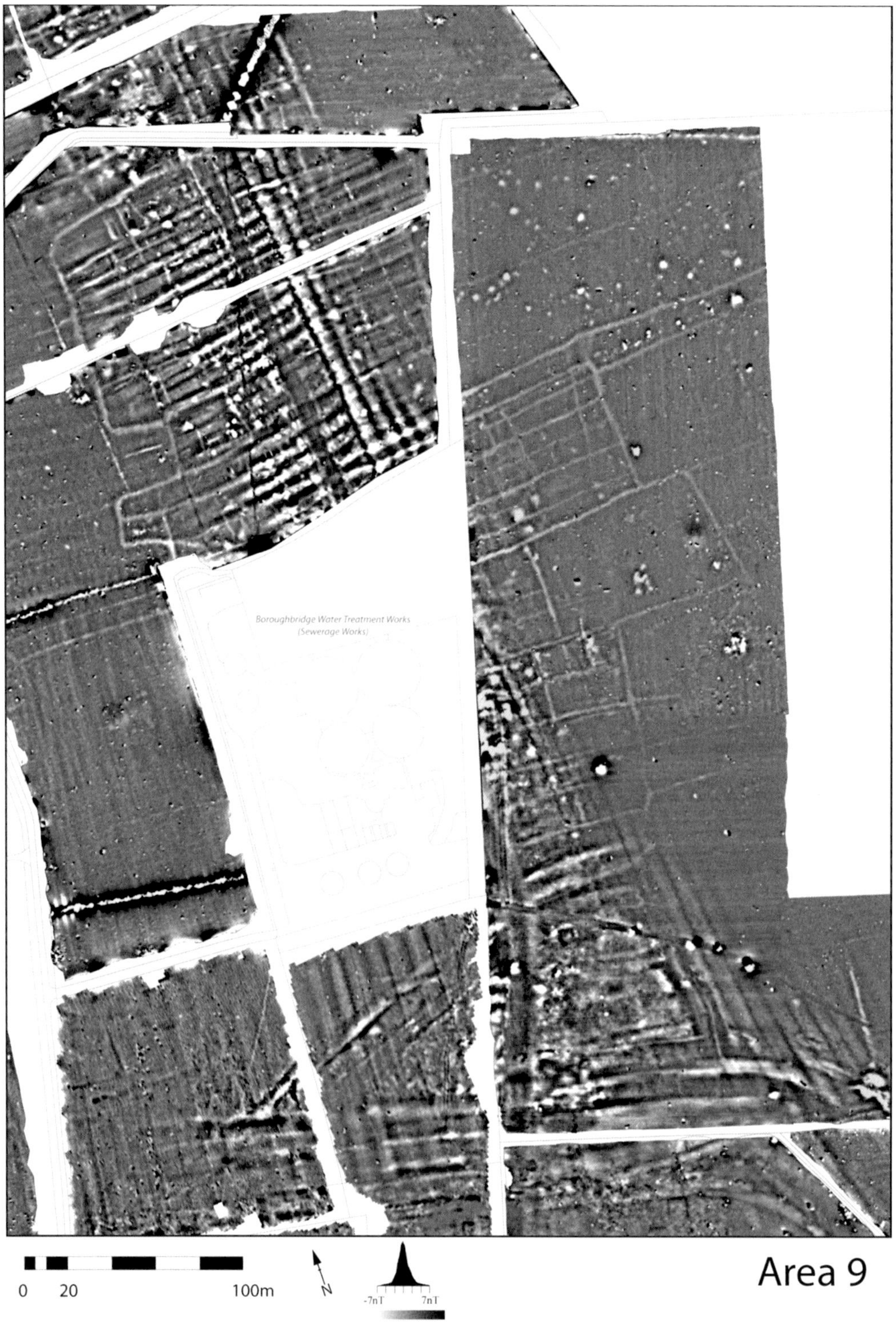

Fig 3.34 Area 9: results of the gradiometry survey in relation to modern topography. For the location, see fig 3.3. Scale 1:3000. *Drawing:* Rose Ferraby. © Crown copyright and database rights 2018 Ordnance Survey (100025252)

3.10 Area 9: Northern extra-mural area (figs 3.34, 3.35 and 3.36

This area lies immediately north of the walled town and covers features on either side of the road that runs from the North Gate towards the River Ure. Previous archaeological work has been focused on this area, which has seen three campaigns of excavation as well as field-walking (see 4.6). The field immediately to the north of the North Wall to the east of the road was covered most intensively, but fields further north on either side of the road were also examined.[51] The pottery recovered from this work shows significant activity from the *c* AD 80–100

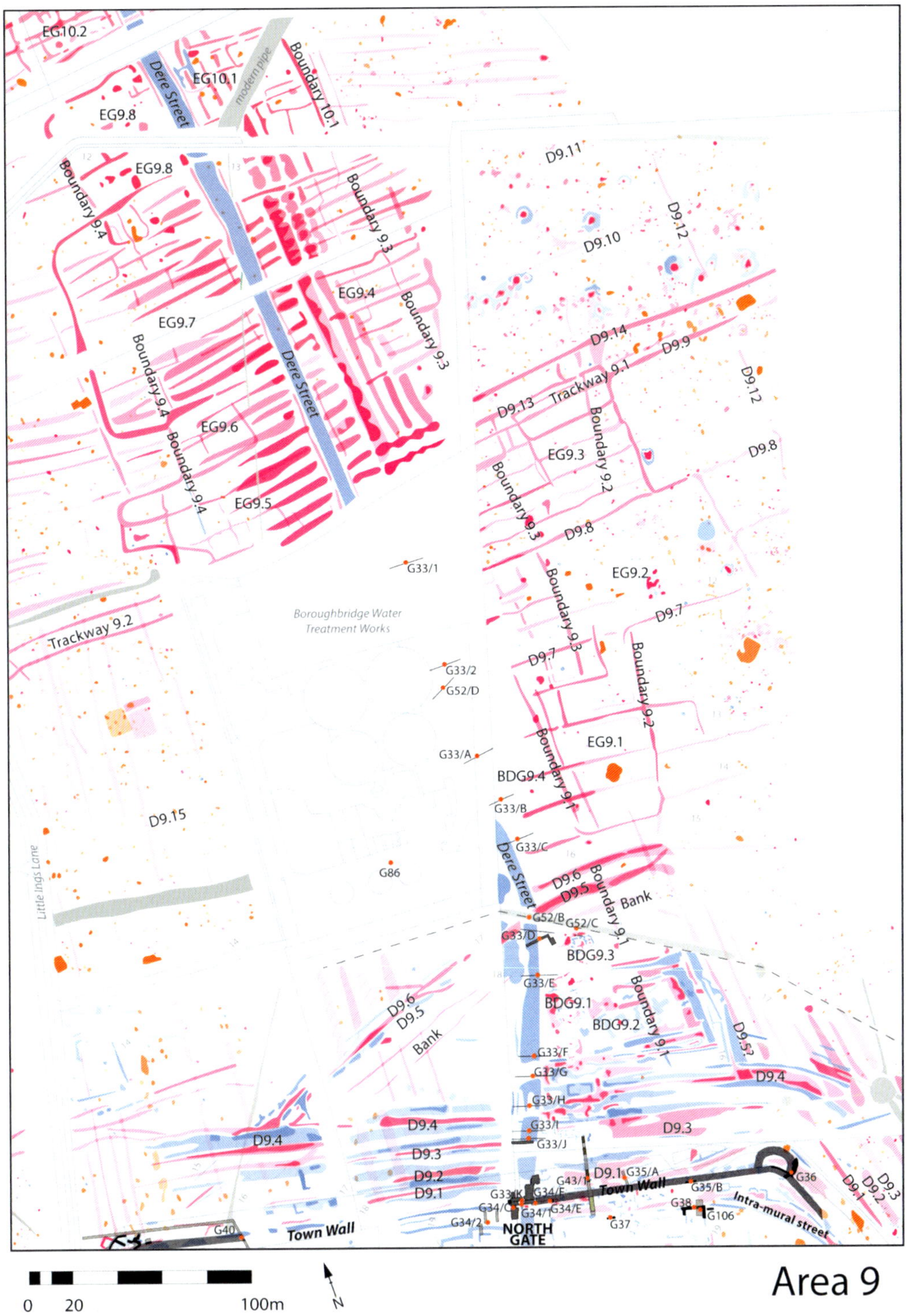

Fig 3.35 Area 9: interpretation of the gradiometry survey results in the context of the other archaeological evidence. For the location, see fig 3.3. Scale 1:3000. *Drawing:* Rose Ferraby. © Crown copyright and database rights 2018 Ordnance Survey (100025252)

with peaks in the second and fourth centuries.[52] Excavations have focused on the defences and the Roman road, and their results contribute to the interpretation of the geophysical survey. The excavations of 1924 investigated the North Gate, which was re-excavated in 1938 (**G34**). The 1924 excavation also revealed part of the Town Wall (**G35/B**) and an external tower at the north-eastern corner of the defences (**G36**), whilst the 1930s excavations on this stretch of the Wall included a major trench – Section I (**G43/1**). This cutting examined the Town Wall and three ditches to its north, as well as a series of beam slots at the southern end of the trench which pre-date the Wall, and date to the later first century AD. This trench aids in the interpretation of the defensive sequence seen in the geophysics.

The general line of the Town Wall is clear in the survey, even though the superimposition of later boundaries and probable robbing means that details of its line are obscured in places. Outside the Wall, there is a complex series of linear anomalies that relate to the defensive ditches, similar to those seen on the eastern and southern sides of the town. However, the precise details are difficult to distinguish, and are complicated further by probable filling in during the use of the defensive annexe here (below, this page). To the west of the Roman road the pattern is relatively clear with four parallel ditches (Ditches 9.1–9.4), though these become harder to distinguish in the magnetometer survey towards the north-western corner of the town's defensive circuit. To its east, they are less clear, but it would appear that Ditches 9.1 and 9.3 were recorded in the 1938 trench (**G43/1**). A smaller ditch between these two, not necessarily defensive, was shown to pre-date the Town Wall. This does not show up in the geophysical survey (because it lay beneath the modern fence). At the north-eastern corner, the detail of the layout is uncertain, but it seems clear that the inner ditches were affected by the construction of the external corner tower, whilst ploughing right up to the modern field boundary has cut into the underlying deposits. A possible trackway or ditch seems to cross the inner ditch, avoiding the external tower, so it can be presumed that this is a later feature. It can be inferred that Ditch 9.4 represents the outer ditch seen in other areas (below, pp. 116–17) and is, therefore, the latest in the sequence.

The 1924 excavations focused on the Roman road, with a series of sections cut to trace its route northwards from the North Gate (**G33**). These trenches successfully identified its course, whilst a watching-brief during the extension of the sewage works in 1964 also recorded the road line (**G52**). The overall route of the Roman road is very clearly visible on the survey, running due north for *c* 140m from the North Gate, then turning through *c* 25° to the west, and continuing on a straight course. At the point where the road changes direction, the 1924 excavators (**G33/D**) identified an area of gravel on its east side, which they interpreted as another road running south-eastwards to bypass the town and join the road to York outside the East Gate (fig A10). Margaret Jones' observations in the same area during the construction the sewer in 1964 led her to conclude that she had also seen this road.[53] However, the geophysical survey results show no evidence for any such road, and it is concluded that the gravel represents a roadside yard or compound. It is worth noting that the east end of the 1924 trench (**G33/D**) was located close to a building (Building 9.3), around which there appears to be a surface. It seems likely this is what the excavators mistook as a road.

Just outside the North Gate, a series of ditches define a triangular annexe comparable to that outside the East Gate (above, pp. 63; 68–9), although enclosing a smaller area (*c* 0.9ha). It is defined to the north west by a pair of ditches (Ditches 9.5 and 9.6), with a bank on the inside. On the eastern side of the Roman road, these ditches appear to respect the layout of enclosures that flank the road, indicating that these were in existence when it was created. It should also be noted that the northern limit of the annexe lies at the point where Dere Street alters direction.

The annexe ditches are cut by Ditch 9.4 and faint traces further south show that the annexe was contemporaneous with Ditch 9.2. Ditches 9.5 and 9.6 respect the Roman road, but in their continuation to its east they are more strongly defined. There is no visible evidence for any gate structure where the road exits the annexe, although this location is partly obscured by features along the modern field boundary and it is also cut by the 1964 sewerage trench (**G52**). About 60m to the east of the road, the geophysical evidence shows the ditches beginning to turn towards the south, but they then disappear, partly as a result of the superimposition of ridge and furrow on a north–south alignment. To the south, at the corner of the defences, there is a stretch of ditch running north from the outer defensive ditch – Ditch 9.4 – which seems likely to represent a continuation of Ditch 9.5. This identification is confirmed by an aerial photograph (fig 3.36) taken by Dominic Powlesland, which clearly shows the north-western corner of the annexe and both ditches (Ditches 9.5 and 9.6) on its western side, as well as the internal bank. This confirms that the annexe was constructed to join the north-eastern corner of the town's defences. It also confirms that the annexe ditches were cut by the outer town ditch (Ditch 9.4), although the relationship with the inner ditches is not clear. It is also notable that this annexe is clearly visible in the contours.

Within the annexe, the geophysical survey shows evidence for a line of buildings facing the road on its eastern side. These structures (Building 9.1), have been plough-damaged and are thus difficult to distinguish. Similar buildings probably flank to the road to the west, although this area is largely obscured by the modern field boundary. Between these buildings and the bank defining the annexe to the west, the geophysical evidence suggests the presence of building material, although no plans can be distinguished. Within the eastern part of the annexe, further from the road, strong magnetic signals indicate a

Fig 3.36 Area 9: aerial photograph showing crop marks revealing the north-eastern side of the northern annexe to the defences, viewed from the north west. *Photograph:* Dominic Powlesland

more substantial building (Building 9.2) with clearly visible walls. These form a rectangular structure flanked to the north and south by ranges of rooms. Although the details of the plan are indistinct, the evidence indicates a large compound with very substantial buildings. This appears to overlie Boundary 9.1 which is aligned with the Roman road further to the north (below, p. 76), and the buildings appear to share this orientation. Finally, adjoining the bank set back slightly to the east of the road, is a clearly defined square building with a separate room to the east (Building 9.3). Its prominent location may suggest that it was built on the back of the bank, perhaps to oversee the road to the north.

The area to the north of the annexe has a different character. The Roman road follows a natural ridge towards the river, with the ground falling away to either side and liable to seasonal flooding (see figs 1.3 and 1.4). Alluvial deposition thus obscures some features on the lower land, such as the defensive ditches towards the north-western corner of the town and some of the ridge and furrow to the west. In these lower lying areas, the magnetic features tend to be less strong. It is not always clear the extent to which this reflects lower intensities of activity or burial beneath alluvium. Along the ridge, the evidence for ridge and furrow is clear, with especially strong signals in the area to the north of the sewerage works. As elsewhere, the layout of the medieval fields is clearly influenced by the Roman topography, although it is notable that the junction between two areas of ridge and furrow is offset to the east of the road, perhaps influenced by a continuation of Boundary 9.1 (below, p. 121).

The Roman features in this area are dominated by blocks of enclosures facing onto the road, with fields continuing onto the lower ground beyond (and are therefore labelled as Enclosure Groups). In contrast to the area outside the East Gate, which was occupied by cemeteries, the overall impression is of domestic occupation with buildings and agricultural enclosures, perhaps for penning stock, lining the road. The enclosures appear to have been laid out in separate blocks which have varying characteristics, and there is evidence for their development through time. The earliest phase appears to have comprised a regular layout of fields and enclosures, oriented with the stretch of road to the north of the annexe. The key features defining this are Boundaries 9.1, 9.3, 9.4, 10.1 and 10.2 and Ditches 9.7, 9.8, 9.9, 9.10, 9.11 and 9.12.

Boundary 9.1 underlies the enclosures on the eastern side of the Roman road and is set back *c* 33m from it. It can be traced beneath the annexe to the south and appears to have influenced the layout of the ridge and furrow in the northern part of Area 9. Enclosure Group 9.1 lies to the east of the road between the annexe and Enclosure Group 9.2, but much of its road frontage lies beneath the sewage works and modern field edge. Ditch 9.7 marks its boundary with Enclosure Group 9.2. Its boundaries are set perpendicular to the road, although it is not clear whether they were laid out with respect to the annexe ditches or vice versa. Its eastern boundary (Boundary 9.2) is not parallel with the road, but rather connects to the corner of the annexe at the south, which it seems to pre-date. After a gap, Boundary 9.2 continues north to intersect with Ditch 9.14 and appears to be cut by ditches in Enclosure Group 9.3, suggesting that it is also earlier than them. Within Enclosure Group 9.3 there are six compounds of similar width running east–west. Adjacent to the sewerage works boundary to the north, there is evidence for buildings in the magnetometer survey, but their layout is not distinguishable (Building 9.4). Field boundaries extend beyond the enclosures to the east, although apparently disappearing beneath alluvium towards the edge of the survey. Within one of these fields a cluster of dipolar anomalies may indicate industrial activity.

Only the back part of Enclosure Group 9.2 lies within the survey. It is formed of a single large enclosure sub-divided towards the road, and with possible evidence for industrial features to the east. It also links to a field to the east. Enclosure Group 9.2 appears to overlie Boundary 9.3, which runs parallel to the road, continuing north beneath Enclosure Groups 9.3 and 9.4 into Area 10 (below, p. 77).

The area to the north is more complex, with possible evidence for several phases of layout. The boundary between Enclosure Groups 9.2 and 9.3 (Ditch 9.8) forms the southern limit of a rectilinear layout that stretches well back from the road frontage. Three parallel ditches (Ditches 9.9–9.11) continue the layout to the north beyond Enclosure Group 9.3, and one perpendicular (Ditch 9.12) sub-divides the system to the east. These ditches appear to form part of the primary layout of this area noted above. Enclosure Group 9.3 is later, and its northern boundary (Ditch 9.13) is aligned with a series of five evenly spaced dipolar anomalies which continue to the east. Ditch 9.14 seems to have been laid out to parallel this alignment, and defines the northern edge of a trackway (Trackway 9.1) that perhaps connects the road with the bend in the river to the east beyond the limit of the survey.

To the north of Trackway 9.1, Enclosure Group 9.4 comprises a sequence of shorter enclosures with evidence for buildings on the road frontage, although these are heavily obscured by the ridge and furrow. They lack a clear common rear boundary, extending just to the east of Boundary 9.3. The fields to the east between Ditches 9.14 and 9.11 are pock-marked with large positive anomalies, perhaps indicating an area of industrial activity. (The area further north is described under Area 10 below.)

Most of the frontage on the western side of the road lies beneath the sewerage works. In the northern part of the remaining area there are four Enclosure Groups (9.5–9.8), all with evidence of buildings along the road frontage. All these enclosures appear to overlie Boundary 9.4, which lies approximately the same distance from the road as Boundary 9.3 on its eastern side. As noted above, this appears to represent an early landscape layout that included the fields to the east of the road (above, this page). Enclosure Group 9.5 appears to be the earliest in the sequence of enclosures with Enclosure Group 9.6 constructed against its northern side. To its south, Trackway 9.2 runs onto the floodplain, but its relationship with the enclosure is unknown. It underlies the ridge and furrow and aligns with the boundaries of Enclosure Group 9.5, so it is concluded that it is probably Roman in date. It is notable that its intersection with the Roman road would lie almost opposite Trackway 9.1. Enclosure Group 9.6 is defined to the west by Boundary 9.3 and is comparatively small. Enclosure Group 9.7 is much more extensive and contains a number of subdivisions, both north–south and east–west. Its southern side seems to have been constructed against the ditch defining Enclosure Group 9.6, suggesting that its layout came later. Enclosure Group 9.8 also backs onto Boundary 9.4. It is bisected by the modern boundary and continues into Area 10. It comprises a rectangular enclosure, with probable evidence for a building beside the road. Looked at in a broader context, it is notable that the Enclosure Groups in the northern part of this area show regularity, with strong evidence the previously noted primary layout defined by boundaries (9.3 and 9.4) parallel with the road and both set back *c* 56m from it, with associated fields to the east.

Finally, it may be noted that at the south west of the area there is strong evidence for the burial of deposits beneath later alluvium. A single field boundary (Ditch 9.15) is probably Roman. Further south linear features and a trackway (Trackway 9.3), which continues into Area 12 (= Trackway 12.3), seem to be associated with the medieval or later landscape.

3.11 Area 10: Northern extra-mural area beside the river (figs 3.37 and 3.38)

This area lies between Area 9 and the River Ure and was partly covered in the 1980s–90s field-walking.[54] The Roman road continues its course for *c* 120m, before turning through *c* 25° to the east. At this point, there are two banks (Banks 10.1 and 10.2) that define the ancient river bank. These form the shape of a funnel, linking to features beside the Roman road further to the south. The road itself broadens out slightly with a stronger signal at this point, with an apparent access to the river to the east. The positive signal representing the line of the Roman road further north is interpreted as the stone foundation pavement for a bridge, on the basis of parallels with the excavated example from Piercebridge.[55] There, the Roman bridge was founded on a stone platform that crossed the river bed, with the stone bridge piers constructed on it. Here, the geophysics suggest a similar type of structure, preserved beneath the alluvium on the inside of the bend where the river has apparently migrated northwards since the Roman period.

Settlement features lining the road continue from Area 9 and are confined to the higher ground defined by the riverside embankment (Banks 10.1 and 10.2). To the east of the road, the line of Boundary 9.3 continues (Boundary 10.1), connecting to Bank 10.2 with a curve to the east. At this point, it also intersects with a ditch perpendicular to the road. This forms the northern limit of Enclosure Group 10.1, which abuts Enclosure Group 9.4 to the south. This group is subdivided into three main rectangular enclosures, each of which is also sub-divided although details are obscured by the overlying ridge and furrow.

To the west of the road, the line of Boundary 9.4 is also continued towards the river (Boundary 10.2), although its precise extent is unclear. It does, however, appear to terminate at the edge of Trackway 10.1 (see below). Enclosure Group 9.8 continues into Area 10, but its relationship with features immediately to the north is obscured by the modern drainage cut. In this area, there are three sets of enclosures (Enclosure Groups 10.2–10.4). The most coherent is Enclosure Group 10.3 through which Trackway 10.1 passes. This connects the Roman road near to the bridge with the lower ground to the west. The trackway splits into two, creating two routes through Enclosure Group 10.3. From this bifurcation, a further trackway (Trackway 10.2) leads north, along the western edge of the enclosures towards a gap in Bank 10.1 beside the river. This trackway appears to be cut by the ditch of Enclosure Group 10.3 at a later date. The west end of Trackway 10.1 terminates in a funnel-like opening close to the relict channel of a stream that runs north towards the river. This may suggest that the area beside the stream was used for pasture.

Within Enclosure Group 10.3 there are sub-divisions that may have been associated with stock control. In this enclosure and that to the north, there is little to suggest the presence of buildings. Enclosure Group 10.2 by contrast is formed of a series of narrow strips, with faint traces of buildings along the road frontage. A ditch parallel with the edge of the road and close to it (Boundary 10.3) runs through both Enclosure Group 10.2, 10.3 and 10.4, perhaps representing an early boundary. Enclosure Group 10.4 fills the irregular corner beside the river, and as with the area to the east of the road, it is apparently a paddock. At its north Ditch 10.1 defines a boundary with the river which coincides with end of the ditches defining Trackway 10.2. The ditch line is continued to the west by Ditch 10.2. The relationship of this boundary to Bank 10.1 is unclear. Where Trackway 10.2 accesses the river bank there are larger positive anomalies visible, perhaps representing quays.

Finally, we may note a pair of faintly defined curved positive features (Boundaries 10.4 and 10.5) that appear to underlie the enclosures to the west of the road. Interpretation is uncertain, but as Boundary 10.4 appears to have influenced the route of Trackway 10.1, they would seem to be early in date.

3.12 Area 11: Northern bridgehead (figs 3.39 and 3.40)

In the light of the discovery of the bridge in Area 10, a limited area was surveyed beside the presumed northern bridgehead on the other side of the river. Here, the northward migration of the river, on the outside of the bend, has meant that the bank is steep and has been eroded since the Roman period. This is reflected in the results of the survey, in which archaeological features are limited to the more level ground above the river. Even here, there is evidence that heavy ploughing has cut into the underlying deposits.

The area surveyed lay in two fields, separated by a strip occupying a slight hollow that approaches the river bank just to the west of the bridge. In the field to the west, a pair of parallel ditches *c* 20m apart define the line of the Roman road. There are various other features in this area, including a ditch that crosses the line of the road, but too small an area was covered to offer any firm interpretation. Two circular features on the line of the road may date from the period after the road had gone out of use. Projecting the line of the road south-eastwards suggests that the northern bridgehead lay roughly in the middle of the present river, and a feature close to the present northern bank may represent a boundary relating to the intersection between the bridge and road. The line running north west picks up the present route to Kirby Hill from Milby along Church Lane, where the Roman road rejoins the route of the old A1.[56]

In the eastern area, there is further evidence of the road network. A pair of linear ditches *c* 7m apart is aligned precisely on the site of the northern bridgehead based on the projected intersection of the bridge and

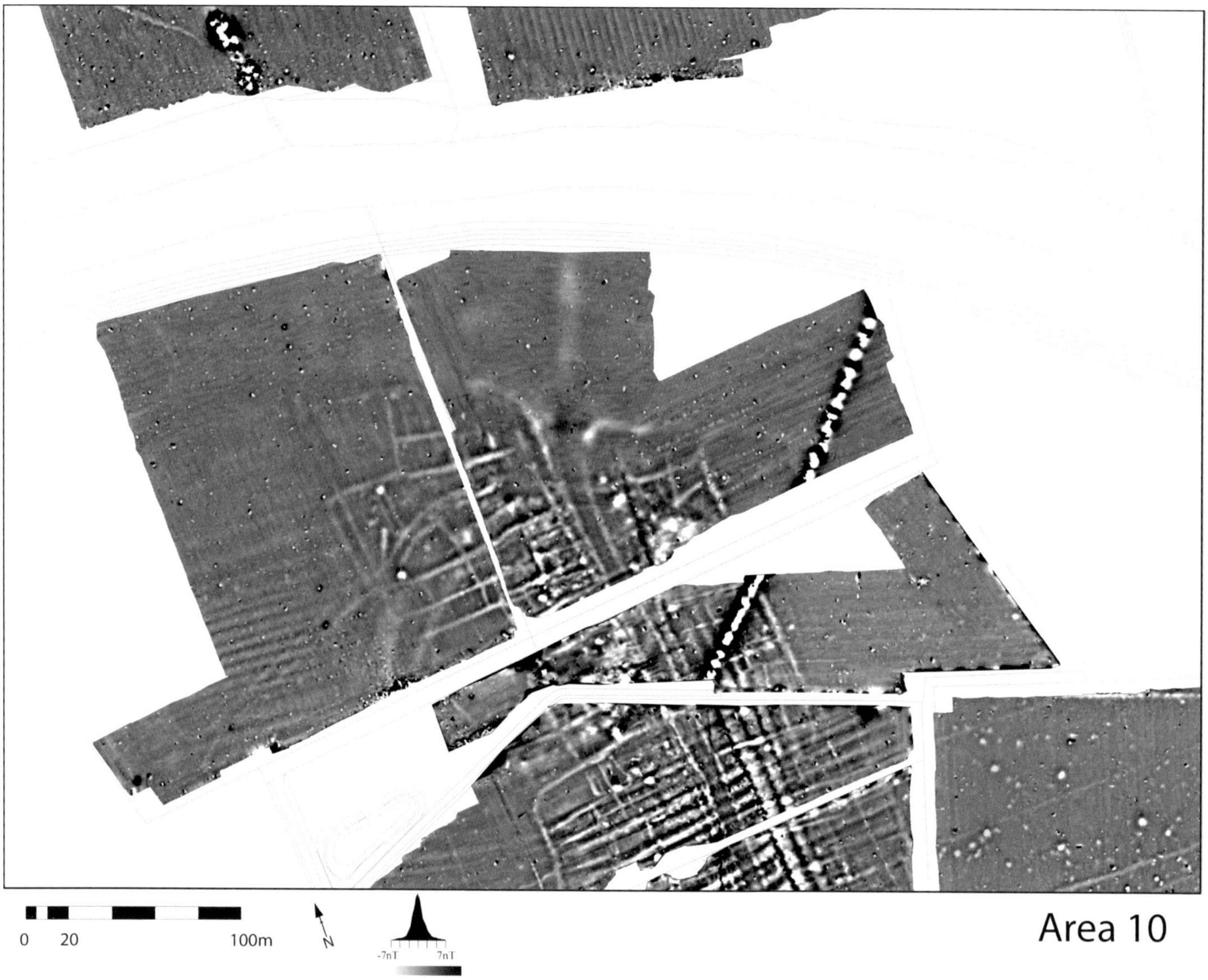

Fig 3.37 Area 10: results of the gradiometry survey in relation to modern topography. For the location, see fig 3.3. Scale 1:3000. *Drawing:* Rose Ferraby. © Crown copyright and database rights 2018 Ordnance Survey (100025252)

main Roman road. This supports the idea that the ditches define a second Roman road, that probably led to Malton. A section of Roman road that heads west out of Malton via Castle Howard may represent the other end of this road.[57] To the south of this road, a series of enclosures is visible, the orientation of which is more closely aligned with the river than with the road. Although the area examined is limited, there seems to be evidence for two trackways (Trackways 11.1 and 11.2) and a series of strips running parallel to them. Two east–west ditches appear to overlie the strip enclosures, modifying them to create a complex of enclosures with internal subdivisions. There is no clear evidence for buildings, perhaps due to plough damage, and whilst some of the smaller features may represent post-holes. The relationship between the road and the enclosures is difficult to assess in such a small area.

3.13 Area 12: Western extra-mural area (figs 3.41 and 3.42)

Area 12 lies to the west of the town, and the Town Wall along its eastern side has been described above (see Areas 1 and 4). Only a very small part of this area was covered in the 1980s–90s field-walking.[58] The ground here slopes steeply to the north and west away from a plateau at the south east. The northward slope is steepest to the south of Low Road, which crosses a more gently sloping area that sits above the flood plain. To the west of the plateau at the southern end of the area is another steep incline down to a more level area. Two Roman altars found in the eighteenth century may come from this area (**G29**), although it should be noted that those marked on various editions of the Ordnance

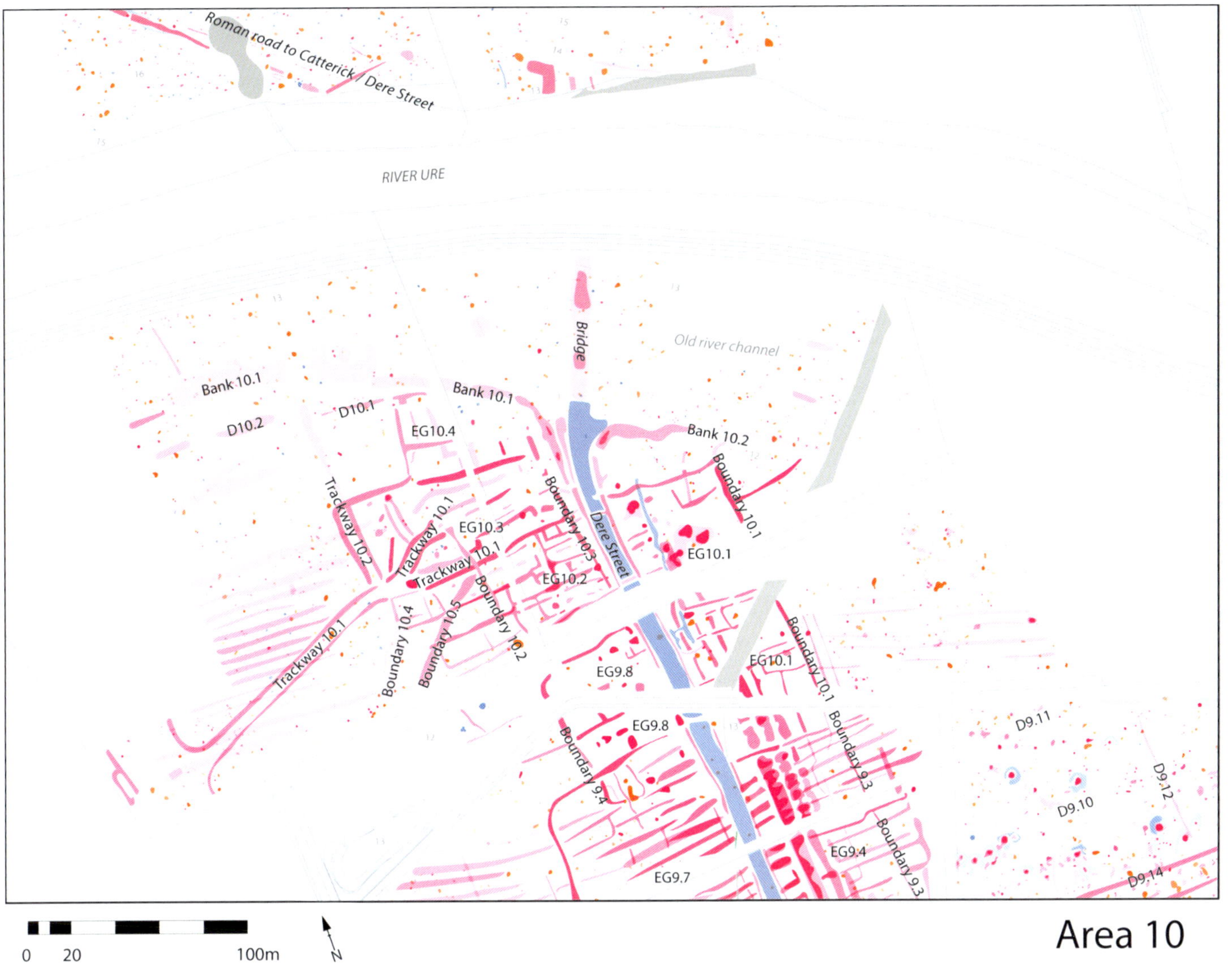

Fig 3.38 Area 10: interpretation of the gradiometry survey results in the context of the other archaeological evidence. For the location, see fig 3.3. Scale 1:3000. *Drawing:* Rose Ferraby. © Crown copyright and database rights 2018 Ordnance Survey (100025252)

Survey maps derive from the nineteenth-century formal gardens.

Along this side of the town, the multiple defensive ditches outside the Walls seen elsewhere are generally less visible, although their general location is indicated by property boundaries. Recent excavations outside the West Gate show that the ditches were filled prior to the eighteenth- to nineteenth-century building (**G61** and **G79**). To the north of Low Road, a stretch of the inner ditch (Ditch 12.1) is visible towards the north-western corner of the Town Wall. It appears to be cut by the corner tower identified in 1935 (**G41/5**), and another possible external tower (Tower 12.1) *c* 78m further south. To the south, two further towers (Towers 12.2 and 12.3) are visible in the GPR results at intervals of *c* 53m. The construction of external towers over the inner ditch has also been noted in Areas 6 and 7 (above, pp. 59 and 64). The outer defensive ditches are overlain by both ridge and furrow and a former walled garden. Further north, by the corner of the walled town, they are buried under later alluvium. To the south of the modern road, landscaping in the grounds of Aldborough Manor has also obscured the ditches for much of their length. Possible signs of them may be visible beneath the terraced lawns on the lower part of the slope (Ditch 12.2). Towards the southern limit of the area, to the west of exposed section of wall (**G11**), they survive as clearly defined earthworks in the woodland, with the western side marked by a slope up to the field boundary.

The location of the West Gate is known from antiquarian sources (**G8**), but the course of the Roman road outside the town is less certain. The general arrangement of enclosures to the west of the gate must indicate that the Roman road runs more or less along the

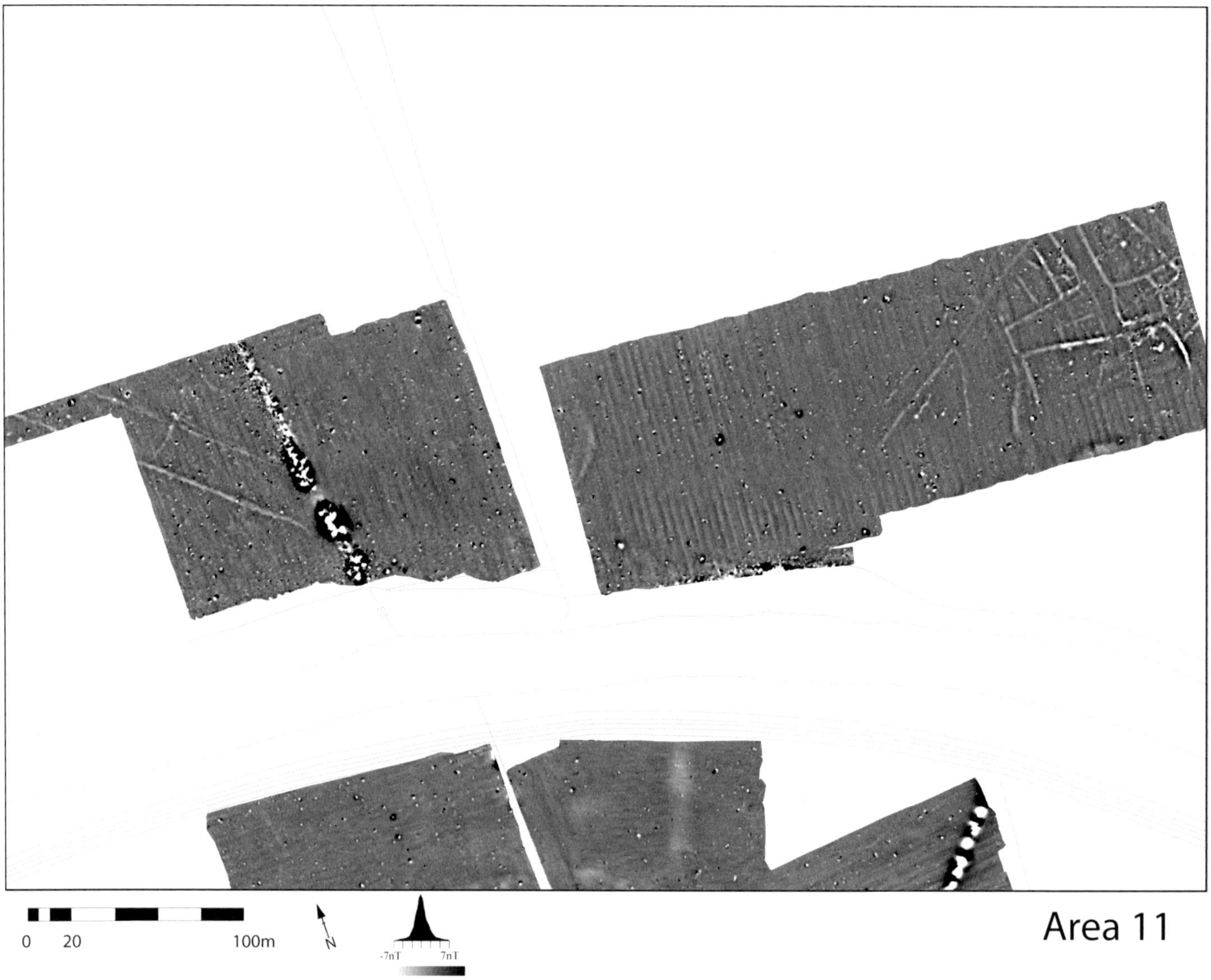

Fig 3.39 Area 11: results of the gradiometry survey in relation to modern topography. For the location, see fig 3.3. Scale 1:3000. *Drawing:* Rose Ferraby. © Crown copyright and database rights 2018 Ordnance Survey (100025252)

line of the modern road, diverging slightly to its south. The destination of this road is also unclear. It must head broadly up the valley through what is now Boroughbridge, and it probably links with a route recorded to the north of the Flavian fort at Roecliffe,[59] a route that appears to be heading for a crossing over the River Ure a little further upstream. On this basis, it is argued that this was the original route northwards (below, p. 98).

In the area to the south of Low Road, there is much clearer evidence for two further routeways leading away from the West Gate.[60] Trackway 12.1 is clearly visible in the survey, flanked by ditches, on the plateau at the south of the area where it also survives as an earthwork. It is apparently aligned directly on the West Gate, and its straight course continues into Area 13 to the south west. This, together with its size may suggest that it formed another significant long-distance road, leading up the valley to the south of the River Ure. If it continued in this direction it may have connected to the supposed route that connected Aldbrough to the fort at Ilkley,[61] crossing the valley of the river Nidd en route (see fig 1.1). In the area close to the West Gate, evidence for Trackway 12.1 is obscured by more recent landscaping, but it is inferred that its course will have been altered when the outer defensive ditches were constructed. In this area, lies the junction between Trackways 12.1 and 12.2, the latter cutting west across the slope before following the hill around to run south west. Its route through the woodland to the south is uncertain, but it seems most likely that it cuts down the slope to lead to the terrace below.

A regular series of enclosures flank Trackway 12.1 in the southern part of the area. To its east, these comprise a series of narrow strips that run towards the Town Wall where they appear to overlie a north–south feature right

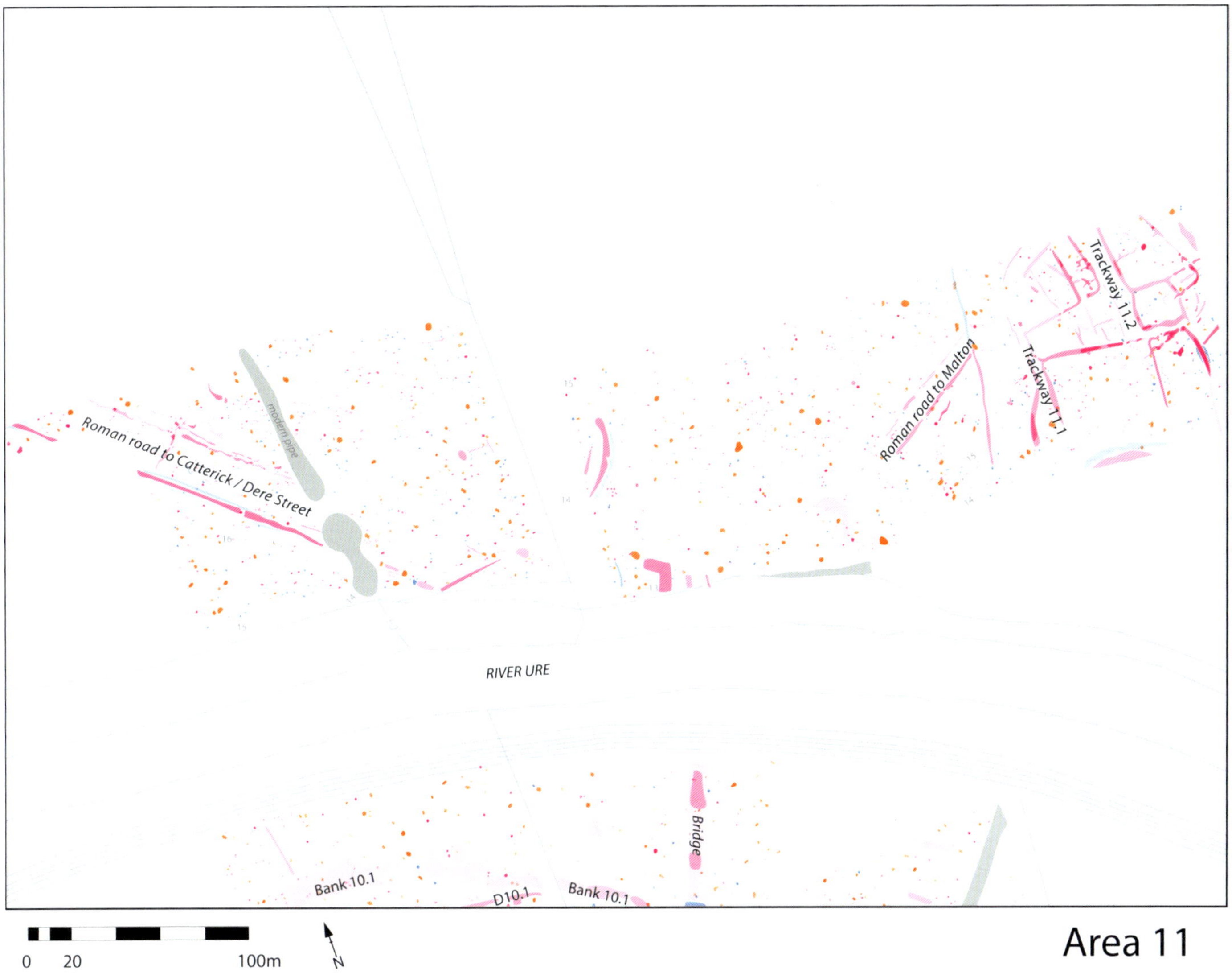

Fig 3.40 Area 11: interpretation of the gradiometry survey results in the context of the other archaeological evidence. For the location, see fig 3.3. Scale 1:3000. *Drawing:* Rose Ferraby.

at the edge of the survey (Boundary 12.1). Parallel with this, *c* 23m to the west is further ditch (Boundary 12.2), also overlain by the enclosures, west of which lies a later subdivision of the strips (Boundary 12.3). The boundaries between the strips mostly comprise pairs of ditches, which may suggest narrow pathways, a characteristic not seen elsewhere in the survey. Within these enclosures there is possible evidence for a stone building as well as features suggestive of industrial activity. It is notable that the alignment of the enclosures is similar to that of the adjacent excavated building (**G11**) within the walled town to the east. It seems likely that they formed part of the same complex, and thus pre-date the construction of the Town Wall, which probably dates to the later second century (below, p. 110).

To the west of Trackway 12.1, there is a series of wider enclosures aligned with those to the east but broadening out down the slope. There is evidence for a complex sequence here, partly overlain by the remains of ridge and furrow. At the south, a closely spaced pair of ditches resembles the paths between the enclosures seen to the east. On the slopes, the ditches defining the enclosures diverge, apparently because they have been set to run directly downslope. Part-way down the slope they apparently incorporate an existing enclosure (Enclosure 12.1), which may be cut by Trackway 12.2. This is defined to the south and east by double ditches, perhaps with a trackway between. A small building (Building 12.1) is set beside Trackway 12.2, just inside the enclosure. A ditch on a similar orientation to the eastern side continues north of Trackway 12.2. This runs perpendicular to the likely line of the main Roman road, suggesting it may have been laid out contemporaneously.

On the top of the plateau and on the slope below, lie

Fig 3.41 Area 12: results of the gradiometry survey in relation to modern topography. For the location, see fig 3.3. Scale 1:3000. *Drawing:* Rose Ferraby. © Crown copyright and database rights 2018 Ordnance Survey (100025252)

Building 12.2 (with a substantial hall-type plan) and Enclosure 12.2. Building 12.2 appears to have been deliberately centrally placed on top of one of the enclosure ditches. A concentration of small anomalies within Enclosure 12.2 may indicate pits, while dipolar anomalies suggest industrial activity. A circular arrangement of post-holes looks like a roundhouse.

On the lower ground to the west, there is evidence for a continuation of the enclosure alignment in a single boundary (Boundary 12.4). To the north on the lower ground a limited area of survey suggests the layout following the slope continues. Between Trackway 12.2 and Low Road a similar pattern can be detected with some evidence for enclosures flanking the line of the

Fig 3.42 Area 12: interpretation of the gradiometry survey results in the context of the other archaeological evidence. For the location, see fig 3.3. Scale 1:3000. *Drawing:* Rose Ferraby. © Crown copyright and database rights 2018 Ordnance Survey (100025252)

postulated Roman road.

To the north of the modern road, further enclosures boundaries are confined to the ground above the flood plain. These suggest larger enclosures, the orientation of which is largely determined by the slope. The character of the enclosures here is very different from those seen beside the roads outside the North and East Gates, suggesting a different type of use, although evidence from the road frontage is lacking. They are overlain by ridge and furrow, and it is notable how ploughing has apparently dragged highly magnetic material northwards from the ditch at the corner of the westernmost enclosure (Ditch 12.3). Beyond this area to the north, the Roman landscape seems to be buried beneath later alluvium.

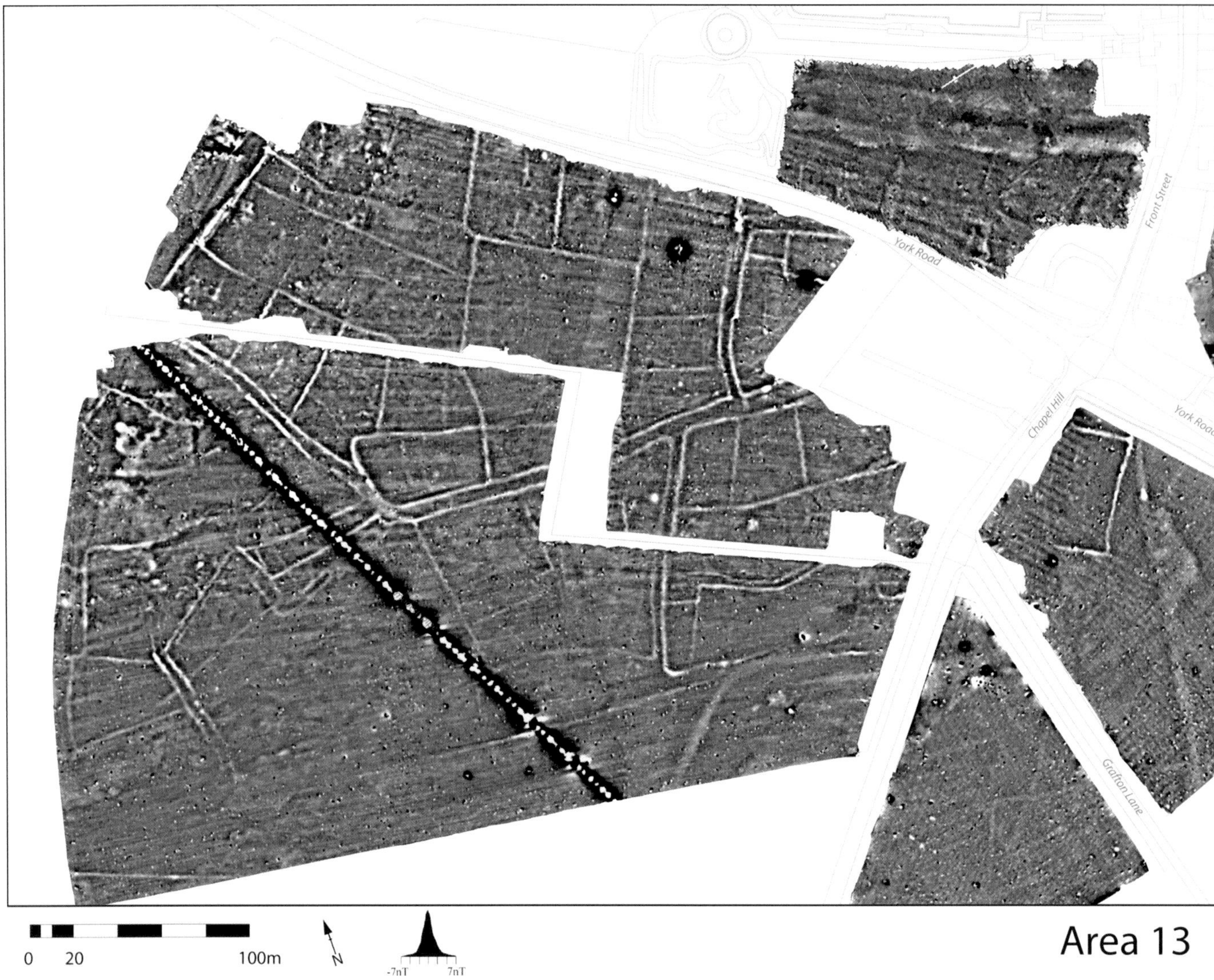

Fig 3.43 Area 13: results of the gradiometry survey in relation to modern topography. For the location, see fig 3.3. Scale 1:3000. *Drawing:* Rose Ferraby. © Crown copyright and database rights 2018 Ordnance Survey (100025252)

Trackway 12.3 (which continues the line of Trackway 9.3) seems to be medieval or later.

Looking at this area in perspective, it is clear that the postulated Roman road running westwards has had less influence on the settlement topography than Trackway 12.1 that runs south west from the gate. This may have significance for understanding the comparative importance of the routes approaching the town (below, p. 105).

3.14 Area 13: South-western extra-mural area (figs 3.43, 3.44, 3.45 and 3.46)

This area lies to the south and south west of the walled town, with the Town Wall (discussed in Area 4, above) to the north east. The partly excavated projecting tower of the South Gate (**G51/C, F, G**) lies at the north east (above, p. 59). The highest ground lies just outside the South Gate at the modern crossroads, known as Chapel Hill. It is notable how this topography blocks the view south from the defences. From here the ground slopes to the south and west, reaching a relatively level terrace in the south-western corner of the area. Burials were found in this area in the early nineeenth century (**G7**). A significant part of this area was included in the field-walking survey of the 1980s–90s.[62] The pottery recovered shows that there was activity from the *c* 80–100, continuing to the end of the fourth century. However, unlike most of the rest of the survey, the strongest representation of finds dates to the second half of the fourth century.[63]

The town's defensive ditches are partly obscured by the landscaping of the gardens now within the Historic

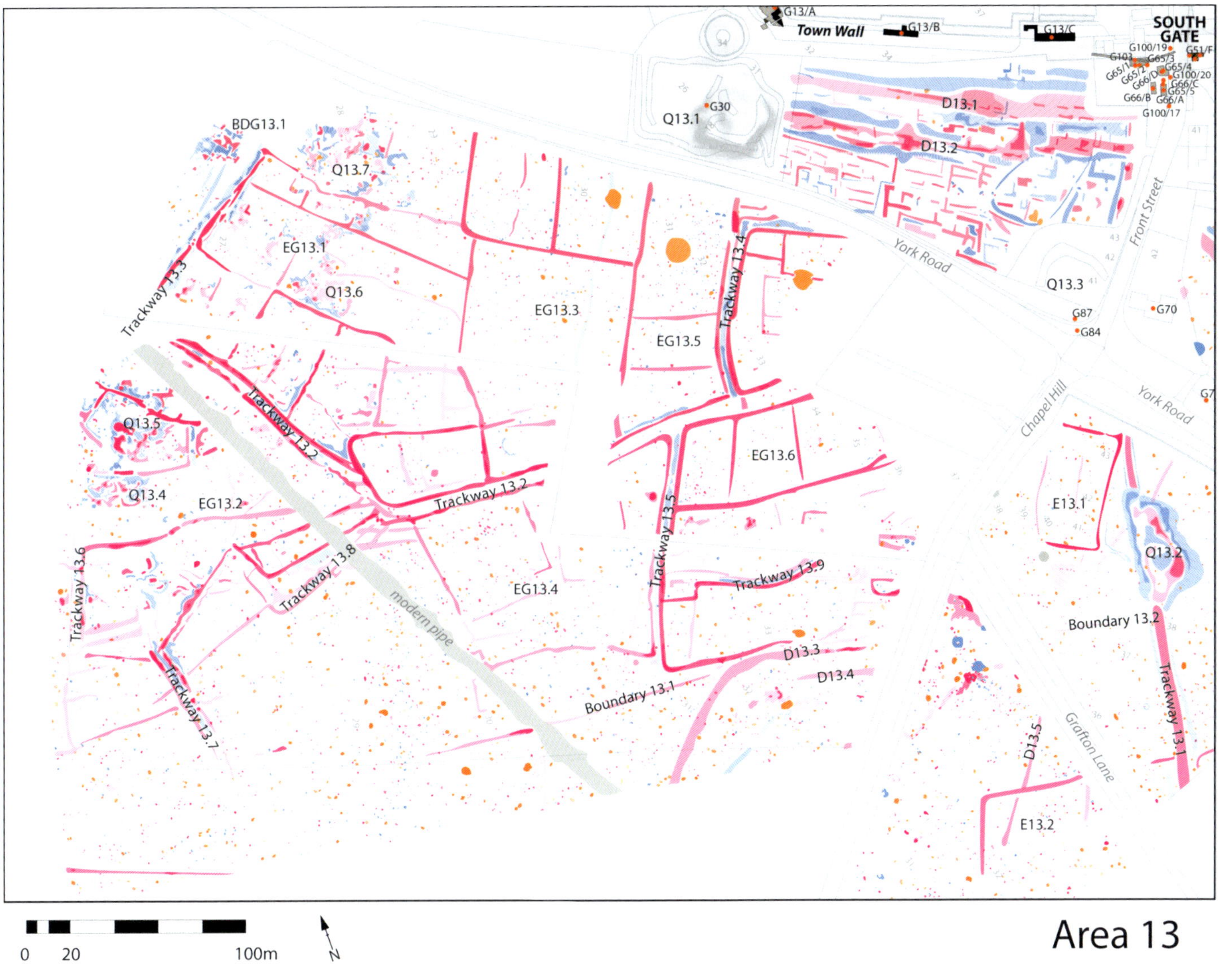

Fig 3.44 Area 13: interpretation of the gradiometry survey results in the context of the other archaeological evidence. For the location, see fig 3.3. Scale 1:3000. *Drawing:* Rose Ferraby. © Crown copyright and database rights 2018 Ordnance Survey (100025252)

England site (**G13**; above, pp. 46–7), which has probably obscured the inner ditch (see fig 3.18). The survey of the field to the south shows the two outermost ditches (Ditch 13.1 and 13.2) that correlate with Ditches 6.3 and 6.4 to the east. It is notable how these survive as a substantial hollow running across the field. The exact relationship of the defensive ditches to the road out of the South Gate is unknown. Outside the south-western corner of the town wall lies a substantial stone quarry (**G30** = Quarry 13.1) partly re-designed as a garden feature (figs 3.45 and 3.46). It is notable that this quarry lies on the line of the defensive ditches at their south-western corner. Although also worked in the post-medieval period, recent work suggests that the quarry is Roman in origin.[64]

Understanding the roads leading out from the South Gate presents a problem as there is no clear evidence for any substantial route running south, and there is little evidence for a Roman road beneath the modern road. The area immediately outside the gate was unavailable for survey, but further out there is a linear feature that probably represents a cutting for trackway (Trackway 13.1), itself cut by a later quarry (Quarry 13.2). However, both its scale and the absence of major features along it show that it cannot have been a major Roman road. Indeed, it may even be later in date. The character of this feature also contrasts with those revealed outside the other gates and in the survey to the west within this area.

A more obvious route (Trackway 13.2) runs south-westwards from the area of the gate, before turning to the north west and meeting Trackway 13.3 (the continuation of Trackway 12.1 leading to the West Gate). The route of Trackway 13.2 is uncertain closer to the

Fig 3.45 Area 13: photograph of the quarry (**G30**) showing the north-facing worked surface and ramp, taken from the north. *Photograph:* Rose Ferraby.

South Gate, but there seems to be no doubt that it must have led there. Given the importance of Trackway 12.1 (= 13.3) in relation to the West Gate, it seems most likely that the main route out of the South Gate is Trackway 13.2, which allows this major access point to link to the route further up the valley. As noted above, this may equate to Margary route 720b, leading to Ilkley.[65]

The importance of Trackway 13.2 is emphasised by its intersection with other secondary trackways. Trackway 13.4 runs to its north, apparently both connecting with Quarry 13.1 and also turning to run alongside the defensive ditches. It may have continued to connect back to Trackway 13.2 just outside the South Gate where a later quarry lies (Quarry 13.3), although the date of this quarry is not clear, and may be associated with building the wall along the York Road in the early nineteenth century. In the stretch beside the town ditches Trackway 13.2 seems to have been flanked by a series of buildings, although their plans are difficult to decipher. Slightly further west, Trackway 13.5 leads to the south off Trackway 13.2, apparently opening into fields beyond an area of smaller enclosures. The final major trackway (Trackway 13.6) lies at the western edge of the survey. This appears to join Trackway 13.3, although the suggestion that it represents a continuation of that main route turning to the south (although it is different in character) cannot be precluded. It is notable that the enclosures flanking Trackway 13.3 show a much higher density of anomalies, suggesting more intensive use, than any elsewhere in this area. The character of these suggests that some of these are quarries (Quarries 13.4 to 13.7), as seen in Area 6 on the eastern side of the town (above, p. 64). This would make sense, as the outcrop of Sherwood Sandstone seems of particularly good quality in this locale and runs closer to the surface. West of Trackway 13.3, and away from the quarries, there is a possible building (Building 13.1) fronting onto the track and aligning with the enclosures opposite. There are further short stretches of trackway (Trackways 13.7, 13.8 and 13.9) across the area which appear to have served local agricultural needs.

The area connected by these routeways is covered by a patchwork of small enclosures, which generally appear agricultural. They show up less clearly to the south, probably due to geological conditions or increased soil depth. In broad terms the enclosures can be divided into a series of topographical groups. Those beside Trackway 13.3 (Enclosure Group 13.1) are generally aligned with it, and continue the more or less regular arrangement seen beside it in Area 12. To the south, the arrangement is

Fig 3.46 Area 13: photograph of the Victorian niches in the quarry face (**G30**) with the statues remaining in all three of them. Unknown photographer. Reproduced by courtesy of Sir Andrew Lawson-Tancred

altered where Trackway 13.6 diverges, and the enclosures fill the irregular area at the junction (Enclosure Group 13.2), and include areas of quarrying noted above. A third block (Enclosure Group 13.3) to the east are aligned with the town defences and street grid, although their layout clearly suggests piecemeal development. Several dipolar anomalies within these enclosures may relate to industrial use, but it is also possible they may be funerary pyres relating to the burials found further east (**G7**). To the south, Enclosure Group 13.4 is aligned with Trackway 13.2 although clearly made up from a variety of different arrangements. Towards the South Gate, two groups of enclosures (Enclosure Groups 13.5 and 13.6) appear to have been designed around the axis of Trackway 13.2, 13.4 and 13.5. Both sets of enclosures extend *c* 40m back from the trackways, and have regular subdivisions.

To the south, a large ditch (Ditch 13.3), seems to represent the corner of a major enclosure, possibly of pre-Roman date. Ditch 13.4 may be related, although its identification is less certain, and it is possible that Ditch 13.5 to the east represents the other side of this enclosure, although plough damage in this area is severe. The enclosure can be traced across an area previously surveyed by West Yorkshire Archaeological Service further south. This major feature seems to have influenced the subsequent topography. A major linear boundary (Boundary 13.1) appears to have been constructed in line with its north-western corner, and this boundary perhaps continues to the east (Boundary 13.2). The small enclosures to the north appear to finish at this boundary, and the southernmost part of Enclosure Group 13.4 also respects its line.

Finally, to the west of the modern road there is an isolated rectilinear enclosure (Enclosure 13.1), with part of another further to the south (Enclosure 13.2) set perpendicular to Trackway 13.1. These appear different in character to the features further west and, given the evidence of the cemeteries found when the York Road was cut through the hill in the early nineteenth century, it is possible that they too may be funerary (**G7**). Other major isolated anomalies between these enclosures could also be burials. It should also be noted that this part of the survey is peppered with small anomalies that are unevenly distributed. Whilst some probably result from the presence of magnetic pebbles, etc, where others are clustered especially within enclosures, they may relate to burials, pits or post-holes. Enclosure 13.2 cuts Ditch 13.5, and another fragment of this ditch may be visible within Enclosure 13.1 to the north. The alignment of Ditch 13.5 with the modern road might support the idea that a Roman road lies beneath it.

Re-evaluating the history of *Isurium Brigantum*

4

The information presented in this volume has wide significance for the interpretation of the Roman period in northern Britain. The results of the survey, together with a re-evaluation of earlier finds, provide the foundations for a new understanding of the Roman town, while acknowledging that further work is required to test some of the ideas presented. The following discussion is structured around the development of the town as the authors now understand it, linking this synthesis with broader historical issues.

4.1 The Iron Age background

Any discussion of the Roman town must begin with a consideration of the Iron Age landscape in which it was established. This is problematic since there is comparatively little evidence from the immediate area, and what does exist is open to a range of interpretations. In general, evidence for Iron Age settlement in this part of the Vale of York is sparse, with published site distribution maps showing a gap, perhaps a result of the generally heavy soils.[1] This contrasts with areas nearby to the south west where there is now a rich archive of sites known on the Magnesian Limestone, and also to the east on the edge of the Vale and the Wolds and Howardian Hills beyond.[2] However, on the equally intractable soils of the lower Tees Valley, recent research has provided substantial evidence for a developed arable economy in the later Iron Age.[3] It is debatable the extent to which the lack of evidence around Aldborough represents a real pattern, or is the product of difficulties in identifying sites due to the absence of soils that produce good crop marks and/or the extent of pasture, along with the low density of the type of modern large-scale development that has revealed hidden rural sites elsewhere. A recent review of the Ure and Swale valleys suggests that the Vale of York was more heavily exploited through the later Iron Age than has hitherto been assumed (fig 4.1). Based on palaeoenvironmental research, including the analysis of three pollen cores from the Ripon area, just to the north west of Aldborough, it is concluded that arable cultivation expanded in the late Iron Age, leaving little woodland and good evidence of a mixed farming economy.[4] While the published distribution of querns of Iron Age date seems to suggest that this part of the Vale of York was not heavily exploited prior to the Roman conquest, Vyner has recently noted that this may result from the different character of settlement in the region rather than an absence of occupation.[5] Furthermore, the very dry weather conditions in the summer of 2018 resulted in the identification of crop marks of further Iron Age farms across the broader area (see fig 4.1). These are mostly enclosure complexes, without the extensive associated field systems noted in the York area.[6] There is some evidence that they may have been more common close to rivers (with a cluster beside the River Nidd to the south of the Aldborough area), but this evidence may have resulted from soil conditions differentially favouring the development of crop marks.

The broader settlement context within which the Roman settlement at Aldborough developed is thus becoming clearer. Even so, despite the extensive geophysical survey, there is no evidence for the presence of any substantial pre-Roman focus at the site. Given the

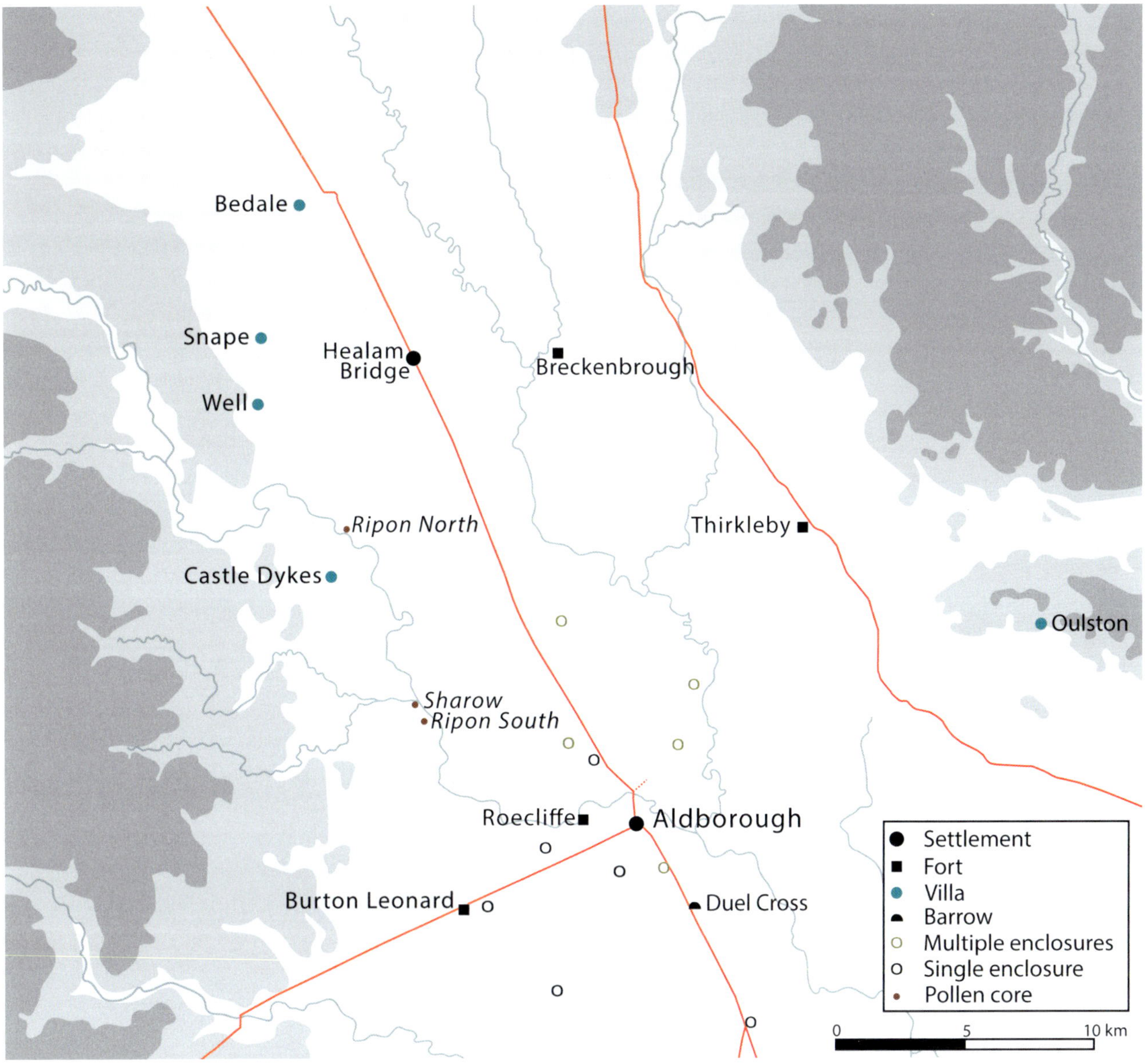

Fig 4.1 Map showing key Roman sites in the area around Aldborough. Note: enclosure sites are plotted from 2018 aerial photographic coverage and are likely to be Iron Age–Roman in date. *Drawing:* Rose Ferraby

intensity of work within area surveyed, this can probably be relied upon. In the immediate area, the only possible candidate for a pre-Roman Iron Age settlement lies a little to the south of the walled town (Area 13, Ditches 13.3–13.5). The dating of this feature is far from certain, and relies solely on its morphology, which is consistent with that known from Iron Age enclosed farmsteads.[7] Given the widespread general distribution of such farms, there is nothing to suggest that this was any more than an ordinary settlement. Another possible enclosed farmstead is also recorded from aerial photography on the slope overlooking the road to York in Area 8 (above, p. 71), but this remains unexplored and undated.[8] There is thus no evidence for the type of regional focus that might be expected if the Roman settlement had been sited here to succeed a centre of indigenous power. On this basis, the presence of any such centre in the area of the later Roman town can be ruled out.

A little further from the site of the later Roman town there are several landscape features that might have been foci in the immediately pre-Roman period, although firm evidence is lacking for this at present. The first is the alignment of three (of four) surviving standing stones (each *c* 6–7m tall) known as the Devil's Arrows, which lie on the south side of the River Ure, 1.5km west of Aldborough (incidentally close to the site of the early Roman fort at Roecliffe, discussed below) (fig 4.2). They are undated, but are associated with Late Neolithic pits,[9] and arguably mark a crossing point on the river. Although they would have been about 3,000 years old by the late Iron Age, they clearly remained highly visible and are unlikely not to have attracted attention during the Iron Age and Roman periods. They may perhaps have provided a reference point in the landscape, acting as a focus for periodic gatherings in much the same way as the Iron Age Ferry Fryston barrow (in West Yorkshire) seems to have done. There, the placement of cattle bones from large-scale feasting indicates significant activity down to the fourth century AD, perhaps associated with a shrine, where the animals were brought to the site for slaughter from very substantial distances.[10] Whilst such conjectured activity cannot be equated with the presence of a settlement focus at the Devil's Arrows, continued activity at such a monument drawing people from a broader region may go some way to account for subsequent development nearby.

Close to the northern bank of the River Ure slightly to the west, the LiDAR image (see fig 1.4) reveals a substantial sub-circular enclosure *c* 500m across, cut by the modern A1(M) road. This site was not investigated during road building, but had it been artefact-rich, it would surely have been noticed during construction.[11] Since it is untested and undated, it is pointless to speculate about its function, although it should be observed that its scale indicates a significance that may perhaps be relevant to the period under discussion here.

Finally, at Grafton, about 5km south-south-east of the Roman town, an enclosed hill-top site was destroyed by quarrying in the middle of the twentieth century.[12] This site has sometimes been described as a hillfort, and as such treated as a potential Iron Age predecessor to Aldborough. However, the pottery from it dates to the late Bronze Age–early Iron Age,[13] about 500 years before the Roman conquest, so it cannot be related to the later town. Interestingly, pottery of similar date has recently been found *c* 1km to its east at Hundayfield Farm,[14] perhaps suggesting a significant earlier Iron Age focus in the area. As in the case of the other places just discussed, it remains possible that this part of the landscape continued to attract attention through later periods. This idea is supported near Grafton by the presence of a substantial Roman tumulus at Duel Cross and an adjacent burial *mausoleum*.[15]

In the absence of convincing evidence for a significant pre-Roman focus in the vicinity, it seems most likely that the siting of the Roman town was a result of decisions made after Rome's arrival in the region.[16] It is worth noting here that one analysis of the etymology of the Celtic place name *Isurium* suggests that it means 'place in the region on this side of the River **Uria* ['the clean one'].[17] On this basis, Breeze argues that this places *Isurium* on a 'Celtic boundary', going on to argue that 'The toponym's very form may imply that there was no particular community at Aldborough in pre-Roman times.'[18]

In this context, it is worth pausing to reconsider the pre-Roman Iron Age geography of the broader region. As noted above, Classical sources discuss the people known as the Brigantes in the context of Rome's relations with Queen Cartimandua in the period between AD 57 and 71 (above, p. 3). The character and extent of their territory is contested,[19] but it seems unlikely that they comprised a single coherent social group, and they may well have been a loose confederation, perhaps temporarily brought together in the context of Rome's expansion in Britain. At one extreme, the name of the Brigantes has sometimes been applied to a huge territory stretching from the Humber, across the Pennines and up to the River Tyne. At the other, its use has been confined either to the vale between York and the River Tees, or even just to the lower Tees Valley itself.[20] Although the principal focus of activity evidenced in the ancient texts lies around Stanwick in the lower Tees Valley, the later ascription of the tribal name to the *civitas* centred at Aldborough surely implies that this area was included within any broader pre-Roman confederation. However, it would be a mistake to assume either that the Roman political geography simply reflected earlier social organisation, or that such structures would have been stable, so attempts to map Iron Age groupings through later material culture are probably misguided.[21] The extent of the Roman *civitas* is considered below (pp. 113–14).

4.2 The Roecliffe fort

The earliest evidence for Roman activity in the Aldborough area comes from the fort at Roecliffe that was partially examined during the widening of the A1(M) in 1993–5. This fort was located *c* 2km west of the later Roman town, beside the River Ure, on a slight terrace just above the highest navigable point on the river. It seems to have controlled a river crossing immediately to its west, where there is marginally higher ground on either side of the river (see fig 1.4). The 2.5–3ha fort (figs 4.2–4.3) was dated by its excavators to *c* AD 71–85,[22] but a recent re-evaluation of the coinage suggests that the presence of Claudian copies might place it marginally earlier, perhaps starting in the late 60s.[23] Whatever the exact chronology, it is clear that its establishment relates to the conquest of the region that developed during the Flavian period. The date of its abandonment as proposed by Bishop was based on the argument that a fort was established to replace it at Aldborough itself around AD 85–88,[24] so we should be wary of getting involved in a circular argument and

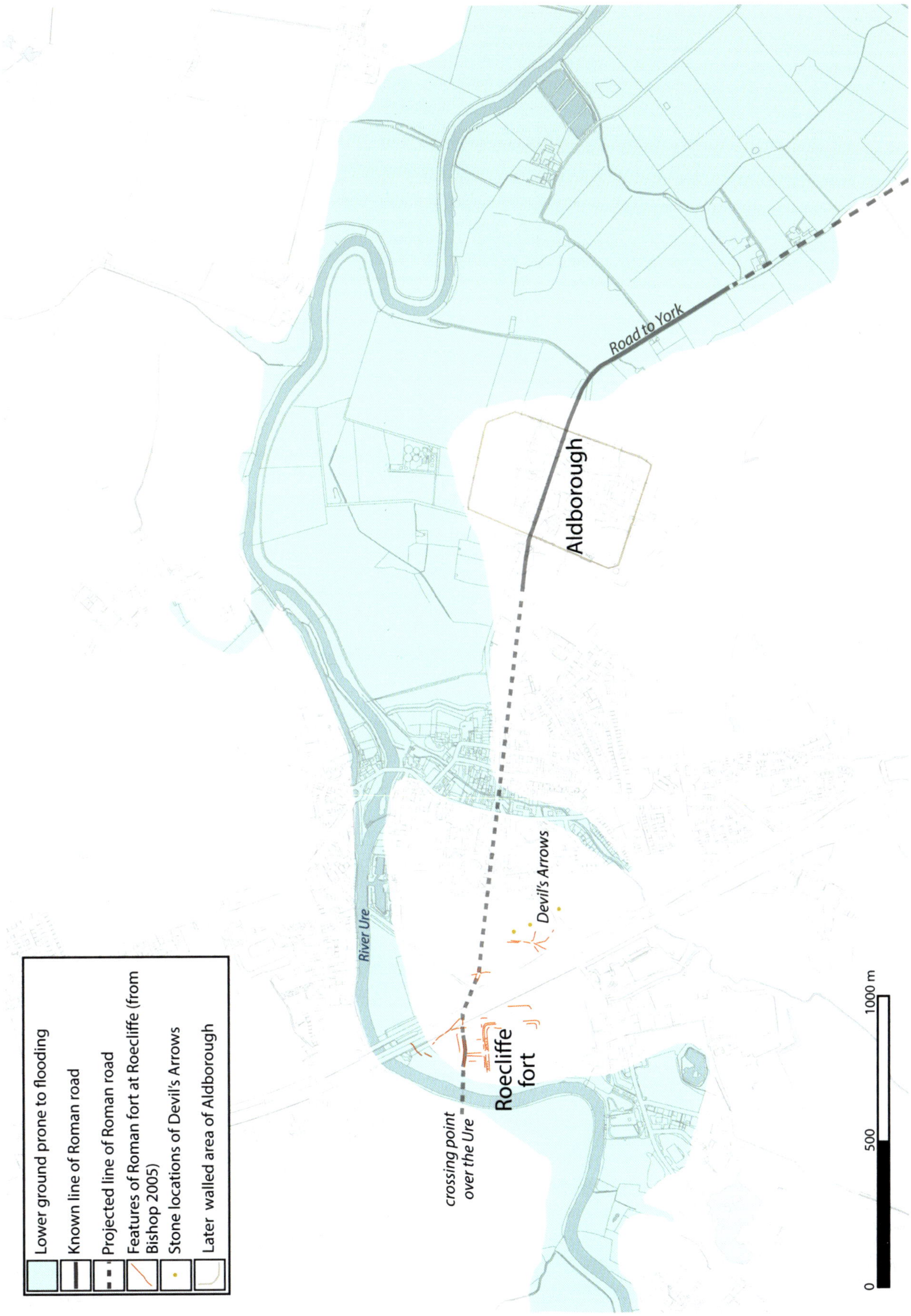

Fig 4.2 Map showing the location of the Roecliffe Roman fort. *Drawing:* Rose Ferraby. © Crown copyright and database rights 2018 Ordnance Survey (100025252)

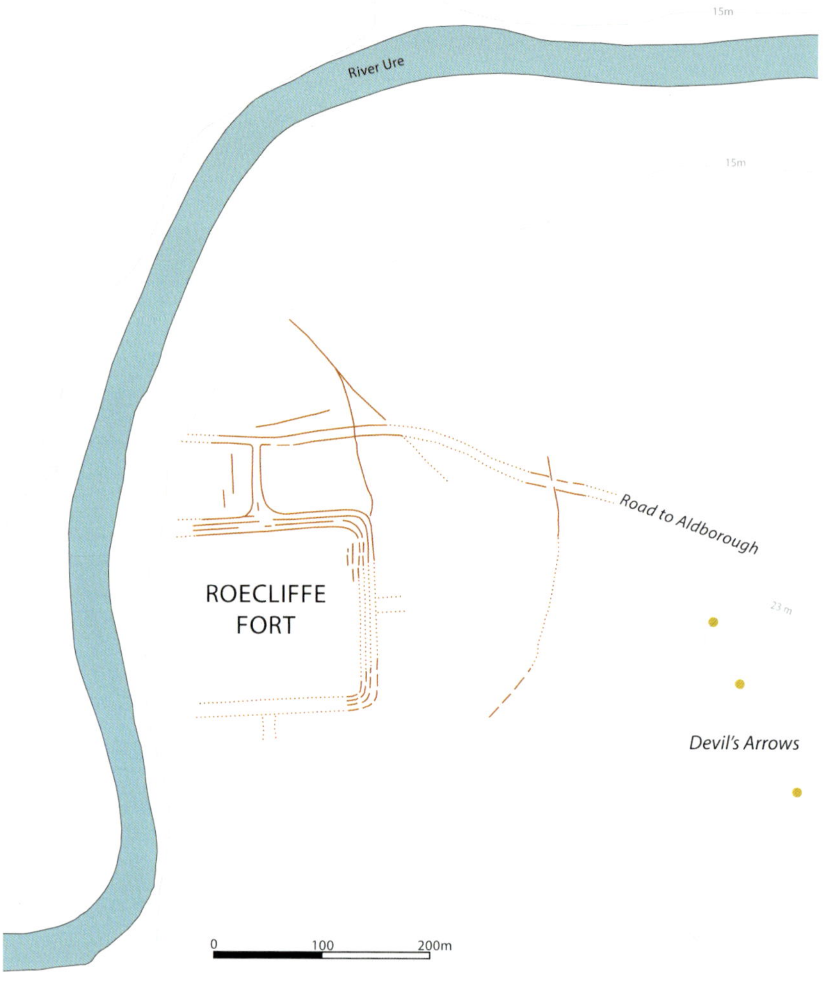

Fig 4.3 Plan showing the Roecliffe Roman fort.
Drawing: Rose Ferraby after Bishop 1995

instead focus on the available evidence from the site. None of the coins found at Roecliffe dates to later than the reign of Vespasian. There are known peaks in the supply of coins to Britain during the Flavian period in AD 71/2, 77/8, 86, 87 and 97.[25] Against this background, there is a preponderance of issues of 71/2 in the Roecliffe assemblage, but a scarcity of those of 77/8, and an absence of issues of 86 and later. This suggests that the fort ceased occupation earlier than Bishop suggests – certainly before 86, and perhaps around 77/8. This might arguably relate to the re-deployment of troops for the Agricolan campaigns.

Aerial photography has recently revealed further detail of another probable fort at Burton Leonard, 6km south west of that at Roecliffe.[26] Although undated, this fort, with a probable annexe to its south, seems likely to be first century in date. The Roecliffe fort itself has generally been considered in the context of the progressive annexation of the Roman North (fig 4.4). This model has explained the pattern of known forts in terms of a move up to the Humber and south Yorkshire by the Neronian period,[27] then with the campaigns of Petilius Cerialis in AD 71–74, extending a frontier into the North East, before Agricola's successful annexation and occupation of much of Scotland in the period AD 77–83.

Such a progressive and linear process of territorial expansion is based on a model of Roman military action that should perhaps be questioned, both on the basis of newly available evidence, and because it largely ignores the human geography of the areas conquered. It was long ago stressed that Roman military strategy in the south and east of Britain was based on the control of social groups rather than simply control of territory.[28] Although the social geography of the Iron Age peoples of this region differs from that of those further south, and is more difficult to evaluate, it is worth reconsidering the evidence for how the region was annexed.

There are several strands of new evidence from the broader area. The publication of the research project at Stanwick has confirmed the long-standing links between that site and the Roman world, with significant volumes of imports arriving at least from the period of the Claudian conquest of southern Britain.[29] Very close by, at Scotch Corner, a newly discovered and very substantial

Fig 4.4 Map showing sites related to the Roman conquest of North-East England in the first century AD as mentioned in the text. *Drawing:* Rose Ferraby (using data from Digital Atlas of the Roman Empire, CC BY-SA 3.0)

settlement with an impressive array of imported goods was established by the turn of the millennium, receiving consignments of Roman imports from *c* AD 15. There was a period of abandonment from *c* AD 85–90, followed by diminished occupation until *c* 135–150.[30] Its earliest phases must be linked to the role of Stanwick (to which it was connected by a trackway), and it may well have been related in part to the presence of Roman troops that are historically attested there in the Neronian period.[31] If this is correct, it would undermine the traditional notion that Roman military annexation progressed gradually from south to north, thus requiring a fundamental re-thinking of current narratives. In this context, we should also take into consideration the evidence that, across the Pennines from Stanwick, the earliest fort at Carlisle can now be securely dated by dendrochronology to the winter of AD 72–73,[32] significantly earlier than in the conventional reading of Tacitus' narrative,[33] in which the Carlisle area was only reached in the second or third year of Agricola's campaigns (AD 78/79 or 79/80).[34] The evidence from York may also indicate that there was a fort here before the conventionally accepted foundation date of fortress of *Legio* IX in AD 71.[35]

By contrast, recent work on the site at Healam Bridge has disproved the previous idea that there was an early Flavian fort there that formed part of a chain of installations leading up the line of the later A1 road through the Vale of York.[36] This model for the period of Roman conquest is also called into question by the evidence from Catterick, which, although a key military centre, seems not to have been occupied by a fort until the 80s.[37] Although other possible sites for a fort nearby have been suggested by Ottaway,[38] none seems convincing if one questions the idea that Roman annexation simply involved progress northwards through the Vale of York.[39] It remains unclear how an undated marching camp at Breckenborough[40] might relate to the conquest of the region.

Instead of seeing conquest moving steadily northwards, we should perhaps follow the evidence that surely shows Rome approaching initially via the coast rather than overland. Contacts between the Roman province and Stanwick in the pre-Flavian period will thus have come directly via the Tees estuary. In this context, a move across the Pennines to Carlisle in the early 70s might make good sense in the wake of an assault on the region via an already known route using the riverine access. Similarly, the establishment of a base at York before the arrival of *Legio* IX in AD 71 would have used the Humber as its entry point, allowing the establishment of a base that could be supplied by sea. A move into the Vale of York thus became secondary, and may have taken place by expansion southwards from the Tees as well as northwards, potentially at different times. The establishment of the fort at Roecliffe, possibly in the late 60s, supports the idea of piecemeal expansion, not a steady progression. In this model, forts like that at Roecliffe, Castleford[41] and perhaps Newton Kyme[42] were initially placed to control the valleys and routes leading into the Pennines.[43]

The recent discovery of a Flavian fort at Thirkleby,[44] on the eastern margin of the Vale of York, supports the idea that the control of east–west routes was key at this date. Equally, so does the probable early fort at Burton Leonard.[45] Thus, Dere Street was a secondary construction, linking existing valley-controlling forts and controlled zones to provide a secure corridor. In this context it may be noted that Poulter's observation that the section of Dere Street between York and Dishforth to the north of Aldborough does not conform to a system of long-distance alignments that he identifies further north.[46] His suggestion[47] that its route in the Aldborough area represents a deviation from an original (hypothetical) alignment is unconvincing, and it seems more likely that it represents the original route to Roecliffe that was only later extended northwards. This is most likely to have been created in the context of consolidation in the wake of Agricola's successful move into Scotland. Its later construction, around AD 80, required an additional fort at Catterick. If Roecliffe is viewed in this way, it provides a better context for understanding the subsequent development of Aldborough.

4.3 Earliest activity on the site of Aldborough

There is considerable evidence for activity on the site of the later town at Aldborough during the Flavian period, and which has generally been thought to represent a military fort, either replacing that at Roecliffe or sitting alongside it.[48] The date, scale and character of this occupation now suggests that this proposition requires careful review. It is best to start by drawing together the strands of evidence for the dating and distribution of the activity before debating its interpretation. Evidence for the chronology is provided by the coins and pottery, particularly the samian ware, whilst further information about the character of the site comes from the published discussion of the small finds,[49] as well as data from past excavations. A broader analysis of these finds provides information about the spatial extent of first-century activity, while some clues about its buildings and layout are provided by certain excavations as well as the authors' survey. In addition to this archaeological evidence, we also need to consider the information provided by textual sources and broader parallels that open up discussion about the origins of the Roman site.

Considering first the chronology, although there are comparatively few stratified coins from past excavations, the combination of older collections, excavated items, and more recent metal-detected finds has allowed Richard Brickstock to provide a comprehensive reassessment.[50] He notes that there is a significant Flavian assemblage, suggesting that occupation began at this period. It may also be noted that in contrast to the assemblage from Roecliffe, the coin assemblage from Aldborough includes a strong representation of coins from both the Vespasianic and Domitianic peaks in coin supply (AD 71–3, 77–8 and 86–7).[51] Although we should be cautious about this (given the uncertainties about coin circulation), it does imply that there was activity at Aldborough throughout the Flavian period, overlapping with the activity at Roecliffe.

The pottery from previous excavations is difficult to assess since the quality of the surviving archives means that it is generally impossible to isolate stratified assemblages. However, analysis of the material from the mid-twentieth-century excavations and the authors' own recent work (**G105** and **G106**) provides some sound evidence about the site's overall chronology.[52] In his study of the samian ware from the mid-twentieth-century work, Steven Willis noted that the assemblage includes Flavian material that, although principally later Flavian in emphasis, contains some Neronian fragments. He also shows that the ratio of plain to decorated sherds is similar to that generally found on military sites.[53] The assemblage of *mortaria* studied by Mrs K F Hartley includes Flavian material as well as the occasional Claudian piece.[54] Other pottery similarly includes a few pre-Flavian sherds, with *Terra Nigra*, Pompeiian Red ware and Lyon ware represented – all of which have possible military associations.[55]

The same general impression is given by the less comprehensive discussion of the pottery from the 1930s excavations.[56] These strands of evidence support the conclusion based on the coinage that activity at Aldborough began around AD 70, not significantly later (and possibly even a little earlier). This implies that, whatever the nature of the activity on the site, it was occupied at the same time as the fort at Roecliffe: there is thus no convincing case to support Bishop's belief[57] that any fort at Aldborough was a successor to that at Roecliffe.

The spatial distribution of first-century pottery shows a reasonably clear pattern. Previously excavated sites with securely Flavian material are confined to the northern part of the later walled area (**G39**, **G41**, **G43**, **G49** and **G50**). It may also be noted that when a sewer trench was cut across the northern part of the town in 1934–5 (**G40**), 'it was only in the farmyard and in the village street, near the centre of the town in fact, that first-century pottery was thrown out of the trench in any appreciable quantities'.[58] The material from the authors' own re-excavation of old trenches has also produced Flavian material (fig 4.5) both from the *forum* (**G105**) and the north-eastern corner of the walled town (**G106**). In these

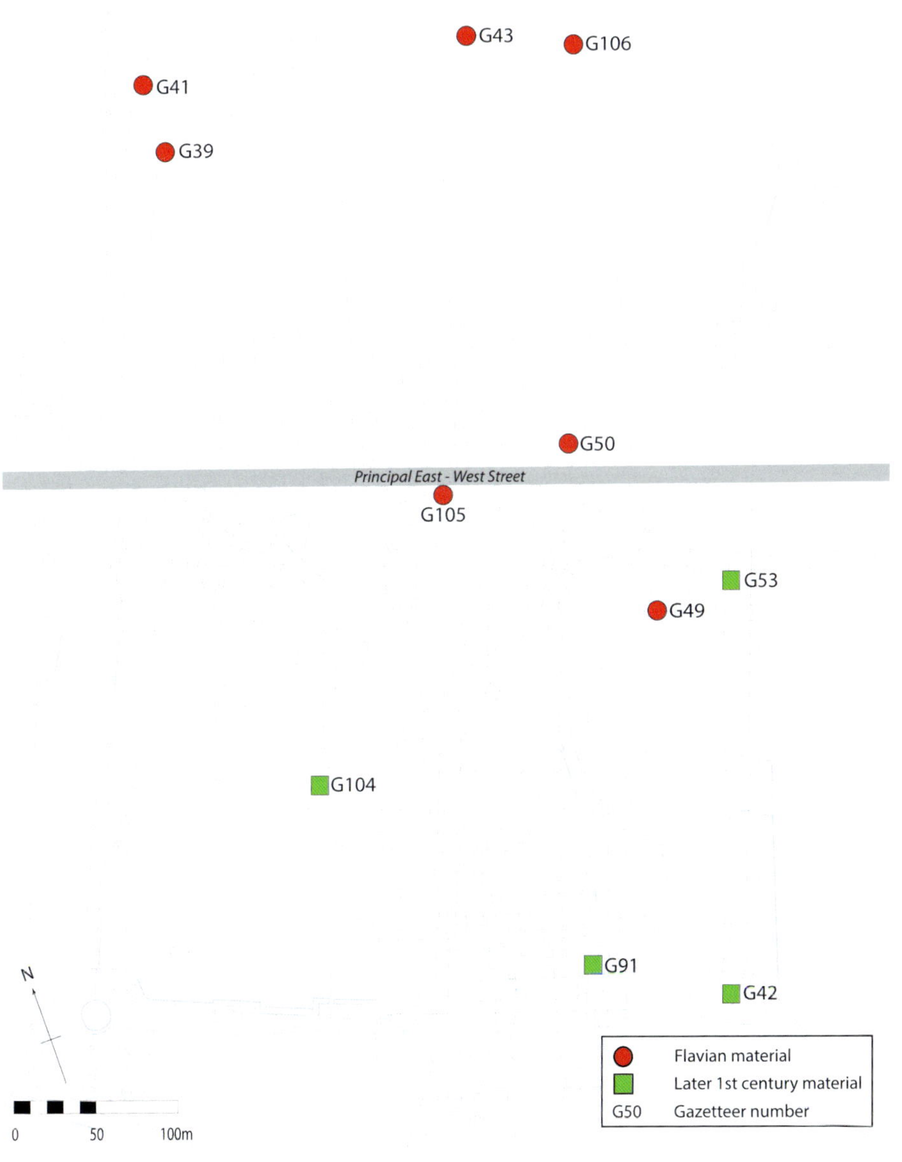

Fig 4.5 Map showing the distribution of Flavian finds at Aldborough. *Drawing:* Rose Ferraby. © Crown copyright and database rights 2018 Ordnance Survey (100025252)

most recently examined areas, the quantity and variety of excavated finds is substantial. Elsewhere, excavated finds of first-century pottery have a later emphasis (**G42**, **G52**, **G53**, **G91**, **G104**), as does the pottery from field-walking,[59] suggesting activity only in the last decade or so of the first century. This makes it clear that the original focus of activity covered an area of *c* 10ha, on the level ground in the northern part of the later town (fig 4.5), expanding northwards towards the river, and southwards across the rest of the later town by the end of the first century AD. It is at this stage, too, that we see a light scatter of material spreading across the field-walked areas in the environs of the town (fig 4.6).[60]

The character of the pottery assemblage suggests that the earliest phase at Aldborough had military associations. This resonates with Bishop's analysis of the small finds from various excavations at Aldborough. His discussion of the assemblage draws attention to the wide range of military material, seven items of which can be dated to the first to early second century AD.[61] He suggests that this may be related to the presence of a fort, although his discussion of the larger assemblage of later military material (20 items) indicates that they may be accounted for by other factors. It is not entirely clear why this should not also be the case with the earlier items. This, like the nature of the pottery assemblage, highlights a broader interpretative problem: given the widespread presence of the army in this part of Britain during the first century AD, with supplies to them swamping the local economy, is it really possible to distinguish a military from a civilian occupation? Furthermore, the intermixing of soldiers and civilians in the region at this period may make such a distinction inappropriate anyway.

Finally regarding finds, we should consider the significance of a number of military stamped tiles found at Aldborough. These represent three different units: *Legio* IX *Hispana*,[62] *Legio* VI *Victrix*,[63] and *Cohors* IIII *Breucorum*.[64] Both the legions were based at York: IX *Hispana c* 71–122, with VI *Victrix* then replacing it after 122.[65] The tile stamps of *Legio* VI *Victrix* are all from dies associated with York, rather than from those linked to the north Pennines and Hadrian's Wall, implying a later rather than earlier date.[66] The *Cohors* IIII *Breucorum*, raised in Pannonia, is first attested in Britain in AD 122, probably having arrived in connection with the building of Hadrian's Wall.[67] Stamped tiles naming this unit come from a cluster of fort sites in Yorkshire, with the die recorded from Aldborough also being found at a tilery at Grimescar, close to the fort at Slack, which also implies a post-Hadrianic date.[68] Thus, only the *Legio* IX *Hispana* stamps relate to first-century or early second-century activity at the Aldborough; the other stamps certainly date to a period after which there is unlikely to have been a formal military presence at the site.

Such tiles certainly cannot be used on their own as evidence for military activity and, although it is unlikely that there was a trade in tiles in their own right, they are probably best understood in the context of the general spread of military material in a region with a substantial army presence. However, as items with a known origin, they are useful in mapping the contacts of Aldborough in the first and second centuries, and are also relevant to its role in broader supply networks. Furthermore, if river transport was important for Aldborough, the possibility that the tiles were used as ballast for returning empty river vessels should not be overlooked (below, pp. 99–100).

The earliest textual references to *Isurium* in the Vindolanda tablets are also of significance for this period.[69] The two references demonstrate that around the end of the first century, Aldborough was a stopping point on the military route to the North, supplying goods to meet the requirements of travellers. The omnipresence of such passing soldiers might well account for the finds of military equipment noted above, but this does not help clarify the nature of the settlement here at that time. It is interesting to note that the other settlements on this route also mentioned in the tablets are *Vinovia* (Binchester), *Cataractonium* (Catterick) and *Bremesio* (perhaps Piercebridge).[70] Binchester and Catterick were principally military centres, although Catterick subsequently had a substantial civil settlement attached. The nature of activity at Piercebridge at this date remains uncertain, but on the evidence of extensive excavation a fort now seems unlikely.[71] Interestingly, *Eboracum* (York), the key military centre for the Romans in this region, is omitted from the tablets. Although perhaps an accident of survival, this may be a result of the nature of the communications routes discussed below (pp. 99–100).

If we turn now to the structural evidence from excavations for the earliest phases of Aldborough, the only useful information comes from sites dug in the 1930s and the authors' recent re-investigation of old trenches. A pair of beam slots was also excavated in 1965 immediately outside defences on eastern side of the town (**G53**),[72] but these are not well dated, with the most likely date being the second century AD. Given this uncertainty, they will not be considered further here in the context of first-century occupation.

The 1930s evidence comes from three areas. At the north-western corner of the later Town Wall, two trenches provide useful information. The 1935 Section III (**G39/3**) revealed an enormous backfilled sand-quarry behind the Town Wall that contained a deposit dated to

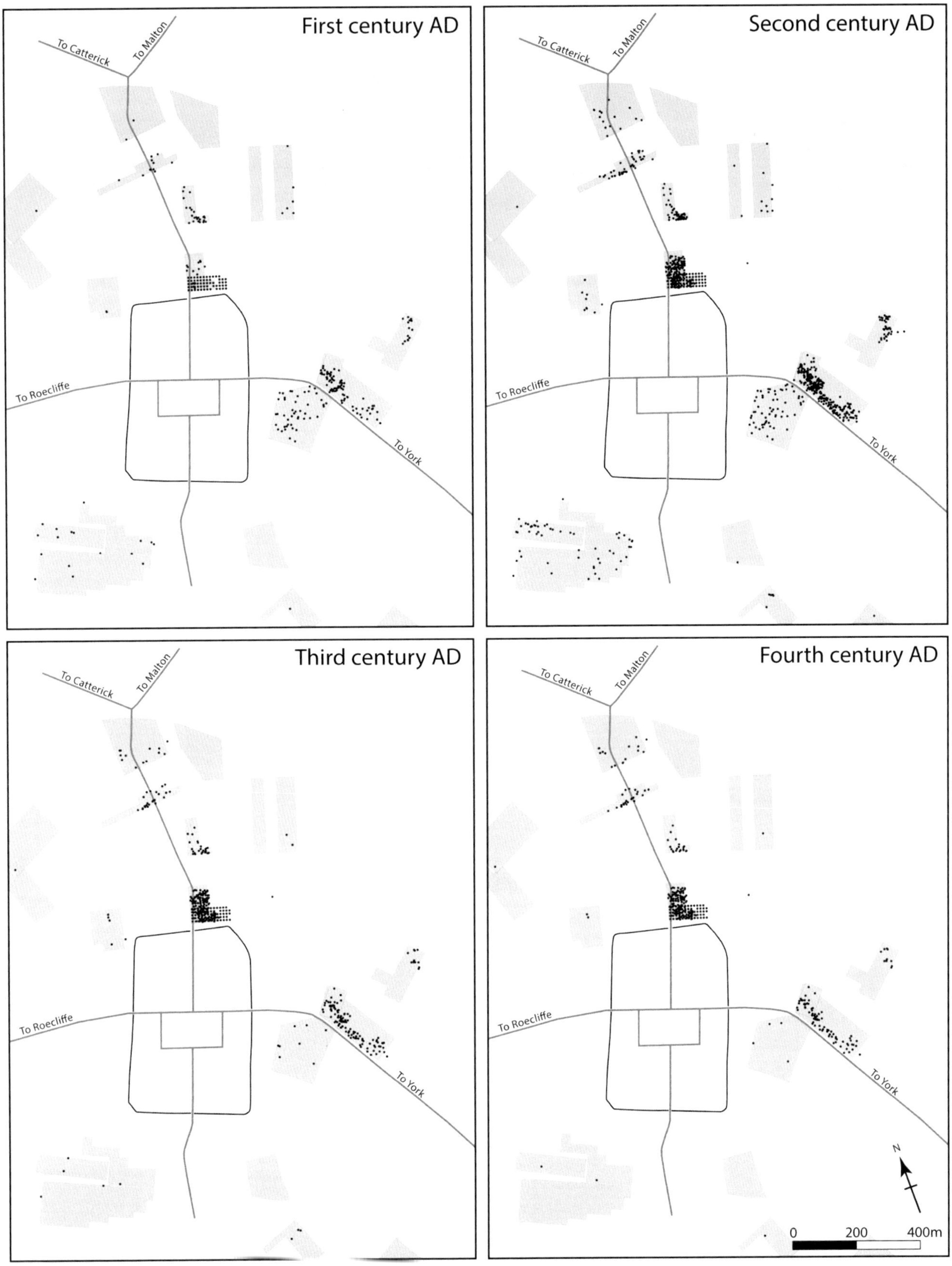

Fig 4.6 Summary plans showing the distribution of dated pottery sherds from field-walking in the vicinity of the Roman town. *Drawing:* Rose Ferraby after Dobinson *et al* 2018. © Crown copyright and database rights 2018 Ordnance Survey (100025252)

the Flavian period, and there were also contemporaneous deposits just outside the Town Wall to the west.[73] Nearby, 1935 Section V (**G41/5**) also revealed a beam slot of probable Flavian date.[74]

On the northern defences, between the North Gate and the north-eastern corner of the later Town Wall, 1938 Section I (**G43**) uncovered both a U-shaped foundation trench with two parallel features described as eaves drip gullies in the southern part of the cutting, and a beam slot slightly further north.[75] The stratigraphy was disturbed by the construction of the later wall, but the associated samian ware is Flavian and includes some material dated by Oswald to 'not later than AD 70'.[76] Further north in the same section was a ditch 2.6m wide that pre-dates the Town Wall, and was infilled during the second century AD.[77] This does not seem sufficiently large or of the right profile to represent a fort defence,[78] and cannot be traced further in the geophysics. The authors' trench on the site of the later *forum* (**G105**) also provided evidence for structural features of the early Flavian period, although too small an area was excavated to see any coherent plan.

Of these features, only those found in 1938 Section I (**G43**) provide any indication of building type, and here the excavators noted that the structural form was reminiscent of early military architecture (but see below, this page).[79] The orientation of the foundation trenches and eaves drip gully lie at *c* 26° east of North, significantly different to the later orientation of the planned town. Too little was uncovered to be sure, but if each of the three longer slots represent foundations, then they resemble a type of timber granary known from early sites elsewhere in Roman Britain.[80] If this is the case, then the orientation of the beam slots in comparable examples would seem to indicate that the building ran east–west, allowing for the beam slot further north in the trench to represent another structure, albeit on a different alignment (97° east of North).

Turning to the broader pattern of evidence, the geophysical survey and past excavations together potentially provide key information about the layout of this earliest phase of the site, which is fundamental to understanding subsequent phases of the town's development. The principal road that runs east–west through the later town is broadly aligned with a trackway identified in the work at Roecliffe that runs east–west slightly to the north of the fort, and leads to the suggested crossing over the River Ure near the fort (see fig 4.2). The authors conclude that this probably represents the original route from York to the river crossing at Roecliffe from *c* AD 70. Its direction up the valley is consistent with the suggestion made above that it pre-dates the establishment of Dere Street. This east–west route seems to have determined the subsequent layout of the settlement at Aldborough, although the excavated first-century features discussed above are on a different alignment, except beneath the later *forum* (**G105**). Although the evidence is severely limited, this implies that there was no overarching plan to the earliest activity.

In summary, there was clearly intensive activity, including buildings, from *c* AD 70 and continuing thereafter, located along and to the north of the route that ran from York to a crossing over the River Ure at Roecliffe. What remains uncertain is the character of this occupation. The conventional answer was first to identify the site as a fort, with an attached civilian settlement or *vicus*, then to surmise that the later town grew out of the civilian settlement after military occupation had ended.[81] However, both general considerations and the accumulated evidence from the site perhaps suggest a more complex and interesting explanation.

The presence of a fort here cannot be ruled out,[82] and the buildings uncovered in 1938 (**G43**) noted above perhaps support a military role, although the evidence is far from certain. Such first-century sleeper-beam granaries are only paralleled in military contexts in northern Britain, although they do occur on civilian sites in the south.[83] This may be an accident of survival, but given the general absence of rectilinear buildings on early Roman indigenous sites in the north, the evidence might be taken to support a military presence here. On the other hand, a newly established community at the site may well have adopted such a building type for themselves. The dating evidence shows that any such fort existed – at least for a period – alongside that at Roecliffe. However, the evidence does raise certain issues. First, the area of confirmed early Flavian activity at Aldborough is extensive, covering an estimated *c* 10ha on the level ground between edge of the river terrace and the road from York to Roecliffe (see fig 4.5). This provides much more space than required for an auxiliary fort of comparable size to those known of similar date at, for example, Roecliffe (2.5ha),[84] Hayton (1.5ha)[85] or Elginhaugh (1.6ha).[86] The available area is too small to allow the possibility that there was a full legionary base here (with that at York extending to *c* 26ha),[87] although one might consider the possibility of there having been a *vexillation* fort, like that at Rossington Bridge (*c* 9.3ha)[88] or Longthorpe (*c* 11 ha).[89] However, it is very difficult to see a plausible historical context into which any legionary presence might fit, certainly after the 70s. On this basis, the extent of early Flavian activity must surely imply a significant civil settlement, whether an adjunct to an auxiliary fort (for which there is no incontestable evidence) or existing independently.

There has been little discussion of possible models of settlement development in the Roman North beyond the purely military, and the scale of early activity evident at Aldborough should prompt a wider discussion. Such consideration must draw on some general considerations as well as a broad assessment of evidence beyond the site itself. This discussion needs to be set in the context of two wider debates. First, elsewhere in Roman Britain it is becoming increasingly clear that a clear binary distinction between military and civilian sites is problematic, and this must prompt some consideration of how sites like Aldborough are understood. Second, whilst there has been much discussion of the movement of armies during the annexation of Britain, there has been much less consideration of the logistic requirements behind this, and how they were met.

Drawing these issues together, it is clear that the period from around AD 71 onwards saw a massive military movement into the North, culminating in the campaigns under the governor Agricola. The provisioning and support of these campaigns will have required a substantial mobilisation of supplies and resources, not least for food. Firstly, it may be noted that the distribution of military sites shows that the Roman army commonly relied upon sea and river transport to supply its campaigns, as shown by the location of many major military bases on navigable rivers. Secondly, it is revealing that after the initial Claudian campaigns (which seem to have been supported by military stores bases like those at Richborough and perhaps Fishbourne),[90] there is comparatively little evidence for a specifically military supply infrastructure (at least until the second–third centuries AD). This might fit in with a model of economic development best exemplified by *Londinium*, which can be argued to have been developed as a trading settlement to service the new province. This was largely populated by traders from Gaul and other nearby provinces, attracted by the opportunities for profit in the new province.[91] Such a model seems consistent with the evidence that military supply was dominated by *ad hoc* arrangements rather than systematic 'military contracts'.

Applying these general ideas to the Aldborough context in the period after AD 70, the significance of the intersection between the Roman road and the navigable river is surely key, allowing transhipment of bulky goods like grain and creating a communications hub.[92] Furthermore, after the development of the Dere Street to the north, perhaps *c* AD 80, its location became crucial as a crossroads where the key north–south route intersected with those routes leading into the Pennines. Within the local context, the development of Aldborough rather than Roecliffe thus results from two factors: first, assuming a similar river regime, Aldborough lies downstream of the shallows at Milby and Boroughbridge that impede navigation; second, the proximity to the river of flat ground above the flood-plain makes Aldborough an attractive point for development as a river port. It is tempting to see this development coming in to its own with the Agricolan advance that will have required the establishment of a sustained supply infrastructure. On the chronology suggested above, this may be connected to the abandonment of the fort at Roecliffe in *c* AD 80 – although this is perhaps more likely to represent an independent decision when the unit based there was moved north in the wake of the Agricolan campaigns. The establishment of a river port at Aldborough may be directly linked with the military, but on the basis of parallels with *Londinium*, we should also consider the possibility that its development was driven by traders moving in from adjacent regions and provinces. For comparison, the pre-Flavian settlement on Cornhill (in London) covered approximately 18ha,[93] about twice the size of Flavian Aldborough. In this context, a further parallel may be observed with *Londinium*, which seems to have been deliberately founded away from centres of indigenous power (perhaps to provide a better opportunity for incomers to create a new settlement beyond the networks of established political control). A similar context may have pertained at Aldborough, as suggested by the place-name evidence noted above (p. 90).

There is one further factor that may have been influential in the growth of Aldborough at this period, and that is the development of lead and silver mining in the Pennines. This is attested in the Pateley Bridge and Heyshaw Moor areas from the Flavian period onwards. Evidence from this comes from two lead pigs dated to AD 81 (fig 4.7), and another of AD 98.[94] These are very likely to be the by-product of the extraction of silver, which was a key state interest (although there is considerable debate about how imperial control was exercised).[95] It is of interest that in the early eighteenth century there were two important cargo wharfs at Aldborough that were used, amongst other things, for the transport downriver of lead from the mines in the same area of the Pennine foothills.[96] Although it would be a mistake to press this eighteenth-century parallel too far, this does suggest another reason why a river port may have developed here in the first century AD.

Returning to the issue of military links, it has been noted elsewhere in Roman Britain that, whether or not the exploitation of bullion was under direct state control, it was often overseen by the military.[97] This may provide

Fig 4.7 Lead pig found at Heyshaw Moor (in Nidderdale), dated to AD 81 (*RIB* 2404.62). The inscribed face is 508mm × 140mm. Photograph reproduced by courtesy of Bonhams, London

a context for a continued military presence after the establishment of a river port at Aldborough, whether or not it was largely controlled by traders.

Once established at such a communications intersection on a now vital route to the frontier, it seems likely that Aldborough would have continued to develop, with its economic growth intertwined with the military economy of the North as well as increasing local development. In the context of the omission of any mention of York in the Vindolanda tablets, this does perhaps leave open the possibility that river traffic could bypass York travelling to and from the Humber and the sea lanes beyond. Indeed, at this period, there may have been little beyond the legionary base at York,[98] and hence little reason to stop there.

Such a hybrid model of development offers a possible new perspective on the development of Aldborough, but may also help us to understand other key settlements in the area – for example, at Catterick and Piercebridge – where the question of early military occupation remains open. It may also perhaps help us to understand better frontier centres at Corbridge and Carlisle.

4.4 Town planning

The geophysical survey has provided very clear evidence for a planned street grid in the northern part of the walled town, in the area now occupied by open fields (fig 4.8). Here, in Areas 1 and 2, it has been possible to identify a series of streets running parallel to the principal North–South Street leading up to the North Gate. These streets are aligned at about 20° east of North. This grid layout in the northern part of the town was previously partially identified by Colin Dobinson on the basis of aerial photography.[99] He also argued that the Front Street and Back Street in the southern part of the Roman town formed a continuation of the same grid. This grid clearly also informed the layout of the later Town Walls, which lie on the same orientation (except on the northern side).

Although this phase of planning is preceded by a variety of features dated to the first and early second centuries on slightly different alignments (above, p. 98), there does not appear to be any evidence for any systematic earlier planning. As noted above, the Principal East–West Street, which runs between the later East and West Gates, seems to follow the route of an early road from York to a river crossing beside the fort at Roecliffe. The exact line of this primary route cannot be known with certainty, but it appears that this broadly determined location of the town and its later plan.

The street grid was clearly laid out in relation to the *forum*, which as argued in this volume was constructed as part of the same project (below, pp. 103–5). The *forum* was situated on the south side of the route from York to Roecliffe, probably set back behind a colonnade (fig 4.9). The Principal North–South Street was laid out to intersect with the Principal East–West Street opposite the northern entrance to the *forum*. The distance from this junction to Street EW1, which marks the northern limit of the grid, is *c* 202m (*c* 680 Roman ft).[100] The northern entrance to the *forum* is equidistant from the later East and West Gates (at *c* 190m, *c* 640 Roman ft), which were presumably situated on the *pomerium* or town boundary. Street EW8, which, it is argued, flanked the south side of the *forum/basilica*, lies *c* 160m (*c* 540 Roman ft) from the edge of the street grid at Street EW9, inside the later South Gate. The Principal North–South Street is presumed to continue beneath Front Street, running south from the *forum/basilica*. On the basis of this, the *forum* was integral to the grid, set a few degrees off the cardinal points.

As the *forum* interrupted the Principal North–South Street, it was necessary for streets to carry traffic around it. Street EW8 will have allowed traffic to turn in either direction on reaching the *forum/basilica* from the south and must have connected with a pair of north–south streets that skirted the east and west sides of the *forum*. There is no clear evidence for these, but there are two alternative positions. They may have run close beside the

Fig 4.8 Summary plan showing the layout of the known streets and terracing in the Roman town. *Drawing:* Rose Ferraby. © Crown copyright and database rights 2018 Ordnance Survey (100025252)

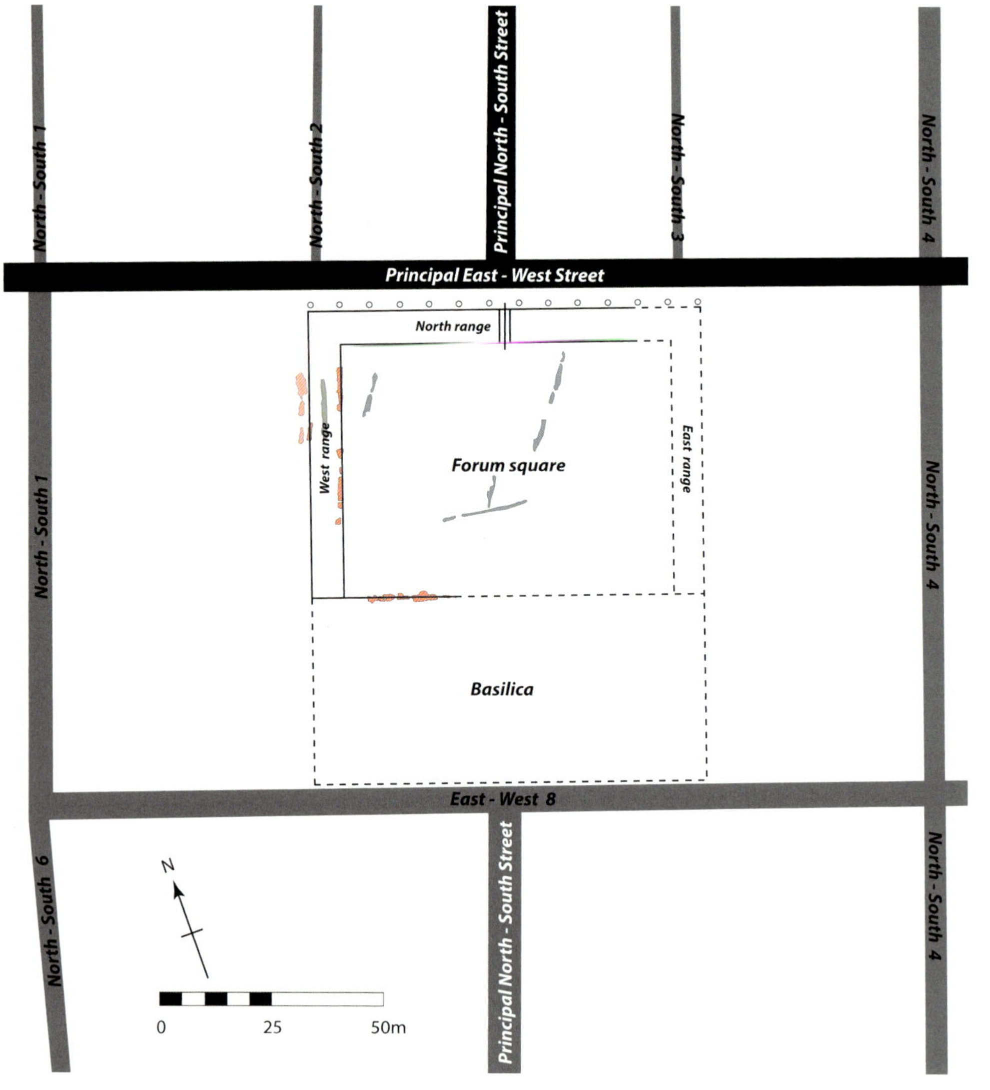

Fig 4.9 Suggested plan of the Roman *forum* and *basilica* at Aldborough based on the GPR survey evidence, the 2017 excavation trench and the plan of the 1770 excavations. *Drawing:* Rose Ferraby

forum, perhaps aligned with streets NS2 and NS3 in the northern part of the town. Against this is the lack of any evidence for such a street in the GPR survey of the western part of the churchyard, whilst the alignment would also have made a very tight fit given the suggested dimensions of the *forum* (below, p. 106). It is more likely that these streets were further apart, continuing the lines of streets NS1 and NS4 to the south of the Principal East–West Street. The later topography of the town supports this idea, with the two modern roads that continue Front Street and Back Street to the north of the Village Green, passing to north west and north east of the churchyard, following the same basic route, with both meeting Low Road at the positions of the suggested Roman street intersections (fig 4.10).

The layout of streets within this grid is only partially known, with the east–west streets generally less clear than those running north–south. The survey shows that the north–south streets in the northern half of the town form a regular pattern – although precise measurement is impossible given the nature of the survey evidence and the difficulty in defining where to measure from (see fig 4.8). Four north–south streets (NS1, NS2, NS3 and NS4) are between *c* 60m (*c* 200 Roman ft) and *c* 70m (*c* 240 Roman ft) apart, with the strip between the centre two (NS2 and NS3) bisected longitudinally by the Principal North–South Street. This spacing possibly suggests that this layout was based on the Roman *actus* (120 Roman ft). The northern limit of the grid is defined by street EW1 but there is no detectable regularity in the other east–west streets in the northern part of the town. It also appears that the side streets to the west of NS1 and to the east of NS4 might be later additions.

To the south, the evidence is much less clear. As noted above, Back Street aligns with street NS4, which is presumed to continue across this area. The southern limit

Fig 4.10 Summary plan showing the development of the modern street plan of Aldborough in relation to the Roman layout. *Drawing:* Rose Ferraby.

of the grid is marked by street EW9, which runs beneath the continuation of Back Street where it turns to the west and is also visible in the geophysical survey in the south-western quadrant of the town. The intra-mural street known from the eastern side of the town (NS5) lies about 80m from NS4, but on analogy with the area to the north, this may be a secondary addition. Elsewhere there is little evidence for regularly laid-out streets, with only short stretches of streets NS6, NS7 and EW10 having been mapped. This is probably because of the terracing of the slope, which itself reflects a major part of the planned layout of the town. Street NS6 on the southernmost terrace is imprecisely aligned with street NS1, mirroring street NS4 and suggesting that the overall grid layout may originally have extended across this area.

The above interpretation sees the town grid as having been planned in a single principal phase with the *forum* set at its heart, designed to face the street leading north to the river. Such a regular and unified plan would be unusual in Roman Britain, where the layouts of most towns seem to have evolved through the addition of secondary blocks of streets. An alternative interpretation of the Aldborough evidence would see the *forum* and northern part of the grid as primary, but the southern section added at a later date.[101] This would explain the misalignment of street NS6. In the absence of further evidence, it is difficult to distinguish between the two hypotheses, although the authors prefer the former.

The construction of the *forum* involved cutting into the foot of the hill-slope to make a level platform the width of the *forum* square, as now preserved in the churchyard. This artificial terrace more or less aligns with the foot of the natural slope at the eastern edge of the town. Post-medieval landscaping in the area of the vicarage (above, pp. 44–5) means that it is now difficult to assess whether the *forum* terrace continued to the east to link these two areas. The upper part of the hill-slope in the southern part of the town seems to have been cut to create three further terraces which stretch most of the way across its width (see figs 3.10 and 4.8). They are approximately parallel to each other (at about 105° east of North) and are respectively *c* 85m (*c* 290 Roman ft), *c* 60m (*c* 200 Roman ft) and *c* 60m wide (above, p. 47). Their orientation is slightly different (about 5°) from that of the street grid to the north, presumably owing to the shape of the natural slope. However, they clearly formed a carefully planned layout, and their construction must have required a substantial investment of resources. Economy of hypothesis suggests that these were part of a single overall project, but there is no evidence to support this suggestion.

The street grid as it finally existed therefore covers a block 370m by 475m (17.6ha), including the areas up to the later walls to the east and west. It is amongst the smallest *civitas* capitals in the province,[102] but there are few other towns in Roman Britain with hints of such a unified and planned layout. In contrast to the *de novo* foundation of Aldborough, most others result from a long evolution, with even the three veteran *coloniae* (Colchester, Gloucester and Lincoln) having been developed on the sites of previous legionary bases. In addition to the pre-AD 60 settlement at *Londinium*,[103] only Caerwent (*Venta Silurum*) appears to have had a similarly regular plan. It seems to have been a second-century foundation, although the grid was not completed until later.[104] Most of the other major towns of the province were laid out on comparatively level ground, so the construction of the terraces in the southern half of Aldborough is also difficult to parallel. Only the so-called lower walled city of the *colonia* at Lincoln shows similarity, although the hill there is steeper so at least one of the streets runs diagonally.[105] Given the evidence that Aldborough was deliberately planned, it must follow that the choice to include a terraced hill-slope was the result of a wish to create an architectural effect, somewhat reminiscent of some sites in the Mediterranean, and allowing commanding views across the landscape.[106]

Establishing an absolute chronology for the planned grid is difficult. The only associated evidence comes from the *forum*, notably a small sample of excavated pottery from the 2017 re-excavation (**G105**) and a coin from the 1770 excavation (**G6**). Limited excavation in 2017 beside the entrance in the north range provided evidence for minor structures from the early Flavian period, sealed by a major levelling-up, preparatory to the construction of the stone building. There was no evidence for the presence of any pre-existing piazza or major timber building on the site pre-dating the stone *forum* suggesting that it was constructed *de novo*.

Pottery from the levelling-up provides a sound *terminus post quem* of *c* AD 120 for the construction of the stone building. Support for such a date is provided by the gold *aureus* of Trajan, dated to AD 112–14, which was found in the building's foundations in 1770 and is precisely located on the plans (see fig 2.5), but its context is otherwise uncertain. Gold coins are extremely unusual as site finds, so it seems unlikely to have been a casual loss. If it is instead a deliberate deposit – perhaps marking the foundation of the building – it is unlikely to have been very old when deposited. This supports the authors' conclusion based on the stratified pottery that the construction of the stone *forum* most likely dates to the Hadrianic period and not significantly later (below, pp. 106–8). Although it is unusual for Romano-British *fora* to have been constructed *de novo* in stone, most of the available evidence comes from sites in the south where there was a long history of urban development before the second-century fashion for monumental stone-built *fora*. The absence of good comparative information from sites closer to the northern frontier makes it difficult to assess how unusual Aldborough might have been. The possibility that there was an open area here reserved for activities such as marketing prior to the construction of the stone *forum* certainly cannot be ruled out, but this is speculative.[107] It should also be noted that prior to the construction of the *forum*, this location lay on a hill-slope perhaps rendering this position inappropriate for such a facility.

Although the construction of the stone *forum* is not necessarily linked to the laying out of the street grid, the authors would argue that this was probably the case and hypothesise that both formed part of a larger re-planning that was linked to the re-alignment of the road to the frontier. As previously discussed, the road from York seems originally to have headed to cross the river close to the Flavian fort at Roecliffe, running across the site of the later town on the line that became the Principal East–West Street (above, p. 98). This road seems to head up the Ure Valley, and may only later have linked northwards up the Vale of York to form Dere Street, perhaps around AD 80. At some later stage, a new bridge was built to the north of the town (see Chapter 3, Area 10, fig 3.38). At its northern bridgehead the road bifurcated, with one road heading north east, probably towards Malton, and another, more major, road[108] heading north west, climbing past what is now Kirby Hill to join the line of the Dere Street heading north (figs 3.40 and 4.15). This new bridge was integral with the layout of the street grid and the construction of the stone *forum*.

Within the town, the Principal North–South Street is axial to the grid plan and intersects with the Principal East–West Street in front of the north entrance to the *forum*. It continues northwards to the river crossing, thence becoming the main route (Dere Street) leading to the northern frontier. Significantly, the new bridge over the river was laid out on a parallel alignment to the street grid slightly beyond the line of the later western Town Wall.[109] This road (via the later North Gate) first follows the grid axis northwards for about 200m (*c* 675 Roman ft) beyond the edge of the street grid. This distance is the same as that from the crossroads in front of the *forum* to the edge of the grid at Street EW1, suggesting a consistency of planning. At this point, the road turns through about 23° to the north west continuing for about 500m (*c* 1690 Roman ft), before returning to the original orientation (20° east of North) to approach the bridge. This must surely indicate that the layout of the grid was integral with the construction of the new bridge and hence the re-alignment of the road to the frontier. Such a grand scheme of development is difficult to parallel in Roman Britain, and the authors would argue that the scale of planning involved indicates a very major initiative, thereby strengthening the case for considering the construction of the stone *forum* and the terracing of the southern half of the town to be part of the same scheme.

Previous studies of Dere Street have commented upon the unusual provision of a series of bridges along the route up to Hadrian's Wall,[110] reflecting the strategic importance of the road. Given this, and the significance of the bridge at Aldborough, there must surely have been a provincial government interest in the development of the route, although there is little evidence to support the idea that the bridges were constructed simultaneously.[111] The only structurally similar example to Aldborough is that at Piercebridge, which is only insecurely dated to the late second or early third century,[112] rather later than the Aldborough bridge.

Finally, it may be noted that the grid plan can be shown to pre-date the construction of the Town Wall as excavation at the North Gate showed that the road there was earlier, with several road surfaces dating to prior its construction.[113] Unfortunately, there is no dating evidence for these layers, but the clear chronological separation means that the planned town was not designed to be surrounded by walls when first established.

There are two other issues relevant to this period of the town's development. The date of the amphitheatre, which as noted above is likely to be first or second century AD in date on the basis of parallels with other towns (above, pp. 61–2). Although it is aligned differently to the town grid, consideration of how it was accessed suggests that it pre-dated the construction of the Town Wall. The orientation, which is anyway difficult to measure precisely, does not seem to relate to any other features in the survey, and is perhaps most likely to have been determined by the topography of the hill that was modified by its construction. Whilst we cannot rule out the possibility that its origin is related to an earlier military phase, given that the idea of the amphitheatre has a military origin[114] and in Britain some were related to forts,[115] its position at a considerable distance from the focus of first-century activity makes this very unlikely. Indeed, the provision of such an amenity fits well within a context in which the newly established *civitas* centre was being planned and developed.

Finally, in some past discussions of the planned town it has been suggested that there was a process of large-scale levelling-up of the northern part of the town associated with its planning.[116] This seems unlikely as the scale of any project to raise the level over a substantial area in the northern part of the town would have been a massive undertaking, even allowing for the movement of earth resulting from the construction of the terraces in the southern part of the town. The idea seems to result from a misreading of the topographic evidence. Although there is some localised levelling associated with the early town,[117] the townscape seems to have taken advantage of the natural edge of the river terrace. However, along the North Wall there is an exceptional depth of deposits recorded in some previous excavations,[118] all of which (with the exception of **G40**) lie very close to the Town Wall. The authors' work in 2018 indicates that the enhanced depth of deposits here results from the addition of an embankment behind the Town Wall, probably in the very late Roman period (**G106**). It appears that previous observations that led to the idea of levelling had failed to note this heightening.

4.5 The *forum* and the establishment of the *civitas*

Before moving on to discuss the next phase of the town's development, it is worth pausing to consider the stone *forum* as well as the implications of its construction at this period. The proposed Hadrianic date is comparable with that of many other *fora* in Roman Britain.[119] However, it is first worth laying out the evidence that this structure does actually represent a *forum*, as has been assumed since 1959.[120] The scale of the excavated structure (with the north range (**G6**) recorded in 1770 as being 220 ft (*c* 66m) long by 18 ft (*c* 5.4m) wide) and the courtyard plan as confirmed by the GPR survey, shows that it is similar in size to other Romano-British *fora*.[121] On the basis of these parallels, it is assumed that the *forum* square was flanked by a *basilica*, which seems most likely to have been placed to the south (see below). This plan-type would thus be typical of most others from Britain, and different to most continental examples.[122] Aside from *fora*, the only other courtyard structure that bears possible comparison is the uncompleted building on Site XI at Corbridge,[123] which, although comparable in size, is later in date (*c* AD 160–80), and its interpretation is itself debatable.

If, as seems most likely, the north range were symmetrically laid out around the entrance (fig 4.9), then the *forum*'s overall width would have been *c* 90m (*c* 304 Roman ft). The GPR evidence from the churchyard, suggests that the *forum* piazza itself was *c* 72m (*c* 243 Roman ft) across internally and *c* 54m (*c* 182 Roman ft) long, with the west range being *c* 7m (*c* 24 Roman ft) wide, and a matching range to the east should be assumed. The GPR survey shows only a single wall to the south of the *forum* square, sitting at the foot of the slope in the present churchyard that defines the back of the Roman terrace. Allowing for erosion of this slope (and hence a greater depth of deposits to the south), it is possible that there was also a range of rooms flanking this side of the square (see fig 4.9). However, if the *basilica* stood on this side of the square, a range of rooms is unlikely as in all the other excavated examples in Britain the *basilica* is separated from the square, whether by a single wall or a wall and colonnade.[124] The location of Street EW8 defines the limit of the area available to accommodate a *basilica*. This space is *c* 40m (*c* 135 Roman ft) wide, allowing plenty of room for a *basilica* if it were similar in type and scale to others in Roman Britain (for example, Caerwent, Caistor-by-Norwich, Exeter, or Silchester).[125] The one difference between Aldborough and other examples is that here such a location for the *basilica* would have meant that it was set *c* 2m above the level of the *forum* square, on the edge of Terrace 1 above. This would have created an impressive architectural feature. An alternative reconstruction, with a temple set on terrace edge, as though on a podium above the *forum*, would work well within the canons of Roman architecture, but is not paralleled in Roman Britain. Finally, it is worth noting that in this unusually formal urban layout, the *forum* is clearly designed to face the road approaching from the north, that is from the frontier, and not that from York.

Whatever the exact form of the buildings, their construction necessitated the terracing of the hillside to form a platform. This implies a major infrastructure project, an impression reinforced by the evidence that its construction was preceded by the insertion of a major drain. This was noted in 1770 running beneath the entrance in the north range. It would seem likely that a system of drains was required at an early stage in construction, when the terrace to accommodate the building was created. The known drain beneath the northern entrance was presumably linked to a system running beneath the road beyond the building, arguably continuing towards the river (below, p. 111).

In previous discussions of *fora*, it has often been assumed that they represent a key symbol of municipal self-government.[126] In the case of Aldborough, such a connection might imply that its construction was associated with the formal creation of the *civitas Brigantum*. It is a mistake to be rigid in making assumptions about the relationship between administrative buildings and civic status in the Roman world, but as there are reasonable grounds to conclude that at Aldborough the construction of the stone *forum* formed part of a bigger scheme, it is worth exploring whether this might have related to the establishment of the town as a major centre of local self-government, arguably around the Hadrianic period.

Two aspects of this question are perhaps best explored separately. First, we need to consider the issue of self-government, and second the relationship between this and the provision of a *forum*. In 1927 R G Collingwood speculated that Aldborough was founded as a Roman town by Agricola in the 70/80s, no doubt reflecting on the well-known passage of Tacitus that praised the governor's patronage of urban building.[127] More recent commentators have tended to move away from associating town-building with particular governors and historical horizons, whilst there has been an increasing recognition that in the early stages of their development, Roman towns in Britain were neither entirely planned nor replete with a full range of Roman-style public buildings. Even in the case of Verulamium, where the epigraphic evidence links Agricola with the construction of a *forum*, the extent of the planned urban core at this period was very limited.[128] Similarly, there has been an increasing awareness that the establishment of self-governing urban communities in the province may not have been as straightforward as some have previously assumed, with urban communities established in their wake as the army of conquest progressed through the landscape. In the absence of sound textual evidence much current interpretation is based on assumption and extrapolation from individual instances, with the better-documented situations most commonly in the south and east of the province. Here, although messy, the picture appears to show that pre-existing nucleated centres serving local communities, like those at Silchester and Verulamium, were transformed into self-governing urban communities not long after their conquest.[129] Alongside this, new urban foundations comprised veteran colonies (Colchester, Gloucester and Lincoln)[130] formed on the sites of disused legionary fortresses and the trading settlement that was founded at London.[131] Further north and west, in the absence of indigenous centres, some military sites were transformed into towns at Exeter and Wroxeter.[132] What this demonstrates is that there was no single model of establishing urban centres. Furthermore, there remains serious doubt about the extent to which *civitates* were based on the transformation of indigenous social groupings,[133] and the extent to which they were *de novo* creations of the imperial system.

Against this background, there are two distinct explanations for the emergence of the self-governing community of *Isurium Brigantum*. At one extreme, one could argue that after the Roman defeat and annexation of the Brigantes in AD 71, the former client kingdom was rapidly left to self-government as happened around the same time with the kingdom of Togidubnus in the south.[134] The problem with this parallel is that the kingdom of Togidubnus never revolted against Rome in the way that the Brigantes had done. However, there is equally now nothing from *Venta Icenorum* to support the notion that the Boudiccan revolt led to any unusual delay its development.[135] This model is thus perfectly possible and would be consistent with the chronological evidence for the growth of Aldborough in the AD 70s. However, there are two objections to this reconstruction. First, since Aldborough was developed on a new site, it is not clear what the mechanism for its foundation would have been.[136] Second, although one might envisage a co-existence between a military occupation and the establishment of self-governing civil community,[137] it is perhaps stretching credulity to suggest that they came into existence together close to the same date in the 70s at Aldborough.

The other extreme of explanation would see the establishment of a system of civic self-government delayed until the demilitarisation of the region, arguably in the Trajanic or Hadrianic periods.[138] In this scenario, the region will have remained under some form of direct military control, which raises the question of how the nascent settlement at Aldborough, which (as argued here was associated with traders) would have been governed in the period through from the 70s onwards. It seems implausible that it did not have some form of self-determination and a parallel might be drawn with the early trading community at London[139] or the government of fort *vici*.[140]

Whilst this is not impossible, it may be preferable to seek some middle ground, adopting the view that self-government as a *civitas* was granted to a community that had already established itself at Aldborough, but after the withdrawal of the nearby garrison at Roecliffe, arguably around AD 80 (above, p. 92). Support for such a chronology would be provided if Fulford's suggestion that the building stones recording the presence of corvées from various *civitates* can be dated to the original period of construction of Hadrian's Wall (and if the identification of one these as being from the *civitas* of the Brigantes is correct).[141] Paradoxically, this takes us back closer to the suggestion made by Collingwood (this page, above), although we would not now expect there to have been anything like a developed Roman urban centre at this date. This also takes us to the second part of the problem: the relationship between the civic status and the *forum*. Again, we are limited by the available evidence. It is neither clear that there was a connection between self-government and having a *forum*, nor whether an open space will have sufficed as a *forum*. Furthermore, at Aldborough, we do not know whether or not there was any open space in the area later developed as the *forum* (above, p. 105).

As elaborated above, the case can be made that when the stone *forum* was built it was part of a plan that made it integral with the street grid and new road to the north, and which involved a large-scale engineering project creating terraces in the southern half of the town. It is difficult to imagine that this could have resulted from anything other than a provincial government initiative, although the extent of collaboration with the local *civitas* authorities is a matter for debate. Finally, there are some indications that the area flanking the new road to the north of the town was organised into a regular series of plots, presumably at or very soon after the road was realigned (below, p. 115). This again would seem to suggest actions that were part of a broader plan, arguably involving the provincial government.

The broader context for this may be the re-organisation of the province connected with the establishment of Hadrian's Wall from AD 122.[142] We know surprisingly little about the wider changes associated with this, but it seems reasonable to conclude that with the establishment of what was intended to be a permanent frontier, it would have been appropriate to regularise the organisation of the hinterland. If the suggestion made above that there was not yet an existing system of *civitates* in the region, it would not be surprising if the provincial governor chose to establish a new *civitas* centre on the site of the thriving commercial hub at Aldborough at this time. If one were already in existence, as seems most likely, then the realignment of the road to the new frontier will have provided an excellent opportunity for it to have displayed its urban status through this re-planning and redevelopment.

Although this planning was large in scale, it probably cannot be related to imperial benefaction, and is more likely to be the product of an administrative decision more locally. Although Hadrian is known to have visited Britain in AD 122[143] in association with the establishment of Hadrian's Wall, this would surely have been too soon for any consideration of the establishment of cities in the hinterland. Furthermore, the scale of this foundation is too small and, as it was not a *colonia*, of the wrong status, to suggest an imperial benefaction. Furthermore, Hadrian is known to have been rather less active in city foundation than some of his predecessors.[144] Nevertheless, in comparison with other cities in Roman Britain, the nature and extent of formal planning seen in this phase at Aldborough is unusual and it is tempting to relate this to cosmopolitan ideas mediated through someone on the staff of the governor.

4.6 The Town Wall

The construction of the Town Wall followed sometime after the development of the street grid, when there had already been building in the areas beyond the planned town. This is most clearly shown in the field-walking survey of the area outside the North and East Gates (see fig 4.6),[145] whilst excavations in 1965 on the East Wall (**G53**) provide evidence of earlier timber buildings beneath it. It is only on the western side of the town that a series of structures, the so-called barracks (**G11**) and Buildings 4.2 and 4.7 seem to represent a major phase of building that pre-dates the wall. These buildings are, unfortunately, not dated.

A number of excavations have examined the walls of Aldborough, although these have provided little clarity about their development and date. The Wall encloses an area of 21.6ha and follows a broadly rectangular circuit that bounds the main street grid on the western, southern and eastern sides, although the south-western corner is cut across at an angle (fig 4.11). The North Wall does not respect the rectangle created by the street grid, but instead runs straight from the north-western corner following an alignment at about 15° north of that of the grid, before turning at the north east to follow a broad curve to join the line of the East Wall at the line of Street EW1. This creates an irregular extension to the walled *enceinte*, the reason for which remains uncertain (below, p.111).

All four principal gates have seen some archaeological exploration, although none has been adequately explored. The West Gate (**G8**) is known from nineteenth-century observations (see fig 2.10), the find of a hinge block, and has also been located in the GPR survey. There is however too little information to reconstruct its plan. What has been identified as a projecting east tower of the South Gate was clipped by Margaret Jones' 1964 excavation (**G51**). The excavation was limited in extent, and the results are difficult to interpret, but suggest that the projecting tower had a rounded plan, perhaps like those at Verulamium.[146] The East Gate (**G16**) is only minimally known, however, its position is securely established on the basis of the roads located in the survey and a pivot block recovered in 1772. The North Gate was more fully explored in both 1924 and 1938 (**G34**), although its complete plan was not recovered. The

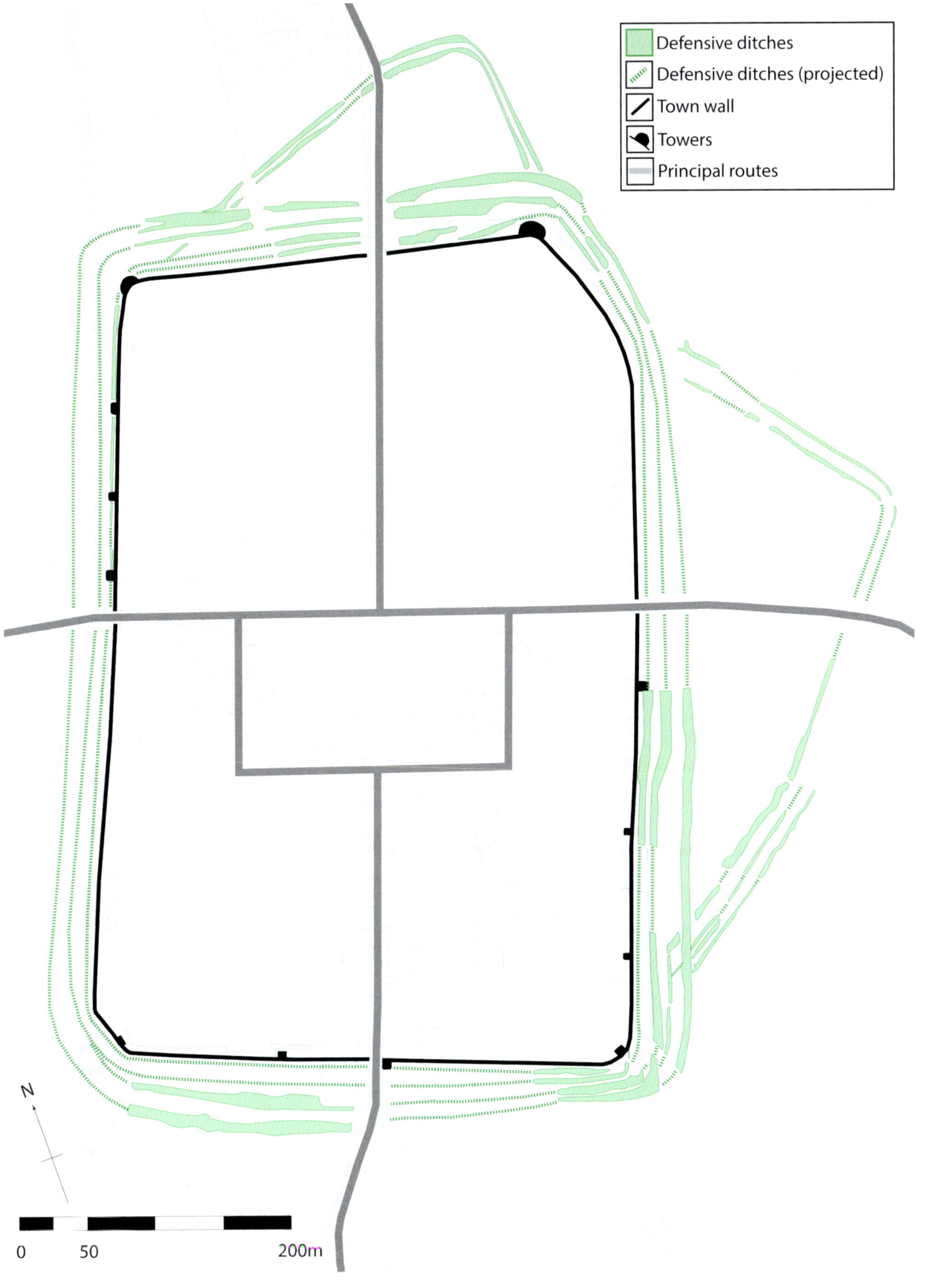

Fig 4.11 Summary plan showing the layout of the Roman defences of Aldborough. *Drawing:* Rose Ferraby. © Crown copyright and database rights 2018 Ordnance Survey (100025252)

fragmentary evidence shows a carriageway *c* 10m wide, and the presence of a central footing implies that it had a twin-portal, the eastern opening of which seems to have been blocked in the later Roman period. Set behind the gate on the west side, was a large stone water tank, partially encroaching on the road, presumably for watering animals (see Appendix 4, nos 47–8). A little further to the west, the 1924 excavation exposed a structure behind the line of the Town Wall that perhaps represents a guard chamber set back from the road. However, given its position, it is more likely to be an internal tower like those on the South Wall (**G13/C**), and at the south-western and south-eastern corners (**G13/A** and **G42/1**).

As far as it is possible to tell, the South Gate is positioned centrally in the South Wall. The North Gate is also centrally placed in relation to the street grid. The West and East Gates both lie approximately 315m from the South Wall, offset from mid-point of the plan, in order to accommodate the Principal East–West Street that runs to the north of the *forum*. This confirms that the gates were planned in relation to the existing street layout. The survey appears to provide evidence for a further gate that carried the line of Street EW8 out into the eastern annexe, where it is marked by the line of Trackway 7.1. As this overlies the outermost of the town's defensive ditches (Ditch 7.3), it must be very late Roman or later (below, p. 120).

The walls themselves were explored in the nineteenth century, trenched in the 1920s, then intensively examined in the excavations of the 1930s, with further work undertaken in the 1950s and 1960s (**G9**, **G11**, **G13**, **G35**, **G36**, **G39**, **G41**, **G42**, **G43**, **G46**, **G51**, **G53**). This evidence has been carefully reviewed by Snape *et al.*[147] They conclude that the Town Wall was first constructed with an integral embankment behind, and a ditch in front,[148] contradicting Charlesworth's conclusion that the stone wall had been added in front of a primary, free-standing, earthen bank.[149] A single phase of construction with integral bank and wall is certainly consistent with the published section drawings.[150] However, some slight doubt about this conclusion is raised by Margaret Jones' excavation of the east tower of the South Gate (**G51**). Her trench showed that this overlapped the inner ditch, and was dated by pottery and a coin to sometime later than the early third century AD, although the evidence appears questionable.[151] If Jones was correct in her identification of the feature as a gate tower, and this was contemporaneous with the Town Wall, her excavation might support Charlesworth's conclusions. The more likely alternative is that the tower represents a secondary modification to the gate. The balance of evidence supports the view that the Wall and internal bank were contemporaneous.

The dating of the construction of the Wall is problematic. In this context, it should be noted both that the dating of town defences in Britain is notoriously difficult, and that in the case of Aldborough, where the fabric of the walls has been heavily robbed, it is even more complex. On the basis of their careful excavations, Myres *et al* firmly concluded that the defences were built in the second half of the second century,[152] although they then became embroiled in a discussion about the possible historical context. In their review, Snape *et al* agree that past excavations generally provide a mid Antonine *terminus post quem* (perhaps *c* AD 170 on current pottery dating), but then conclude that the Wall is probably early–mid third century.[153] This was based on a key piece of archaeological evidence, placed alongside an historical discussion. A very worn and plated *denarius*, probably a copy of an issue of Julia Domna, was found in 1938 Section I on the northern defences (**G43**) 'embedded in the footings at the back of the wall'.[154] There is doubt about when such copies were produced, with George Boon (cited by Snape *et al*) having suggested the period *c* 238–49,[155] although more recent work may indicate an earlier date for some, perhaps beginning in the Severan period.[156] If the context is secure, then this coin must support a third-century date, but the evidence is slim, and it seems significant that the original excavators, who were generally judicious in their use of evidence, preferred a second-century date for the Wall, presumably believing that the coin's context was insecure. They comment that 'the footings did not occupy the entire width of the foundation-trench that had been dug for them, and the spaces on either side were packed with dirty sand'.[157] Even if produced earlier than Boon suggested, this coin seems unlikely to have been deposited much before the second quarter of the third century. On balance, the authors therefore prefer a date for the construction of the Town Walls in the second half of the second century, a view consistent with Jerry Evans' conclusions concerning the dating of the pottery collected in the field survey outside.[158] In accepting this, it is acknowledged that this places the Walls of Aldborough somewhat earlier than some other Romano-British towns.

With the Walls as early as this, it is tempting to suggest that they were constructed as part of the same scheme as street grid. However, this is clearly incompatible with the evidence noted above that three road surfaces pre-date the construction of the North Gate.[159] On this basis, it is concluded that there was a gap between the establishment of the street grid and the construction of the defences.

It is also worth observing that the Town Walls are somewhat curiously placed in terms of the local topography. Whilst clearly visible to those approaching from the north, the walls on the south and eastern sides were situated such that they were hidden by natural features for those approaching along the other roads (at least, until the very last moment). This also meant that those within the town could not see arriving travellers until they were almost at the gates. This does not suggest that the Walls were constructed out of fear of attack, and it is difficult to escape the conclusion that they were designed as an expression of civic status rather than for military reasons.

Returning to the issue of the odd position and layout of the North Wall, it seems most likely that this was the result of the builders' wish to include existing features within the circuit. The geophysical survey suggested that the very large buildings (2.17 and 2.19) in the north-eastern corner of the town might have been the cause, with their orientation determining that of the North Wall. However, the excavation (**G106**) that sampled Building 2.17 by re-opening a 1924 trench has shown that it was constructed *c* AD 250–300, long after the Town Wall. Whilst it is possible that Building 2.17 was reproducing a much earlier building alignment, it now seems more likely that its orientation was determined by that of the Town Wall. One possibility is that the Wall follows a significant earlier boundary. The only contender for this is the pre-Wall ditch dated to the second century, noted in 1938 (**G43**). This seems unlikely as it cannot be traced further in the geophysical survey, and was anyway comparatively slight. On this basis, it does not presently seem possible to provide an adequate explanation for the position of the North Wall.

4.7 The character of the early to mid Roman town

Having established a broad framework for the development of the town in the period from the first through to the third century AD, it is worth pausing to consider the character of the settlement at this period as understood in the context of recent work. There are limits to this understanding, given the meagre chronological evidence from past excavations, but this is counterbalanced by the excellent results of the survey. Whilst the survey results lack refined chronological differentiation, this is compensated for by their spatial coverage, so it is worth starting with the broad overview that this allows.

The planned town has comparatively few identified public buildings, and it is only the *forum* for which there is any dating evidence. As described above, it is probably Hadrianic and not significantly later. Similarly, the identification of the amphitheatre adds significantly to our knowledge of Aldborough's public buildings, and its construction at a similar period would be consistent with the development of the civic community. Its scale is notable, placing it in the larger range of known examples,[160] which raises interesting questions about the size of the community served. If it is civic in origin (as seems most likely), it must have been designed to serve a much larger population than lived in the town itself, which might make sense of its highly visible position on the most prominent hill in the local landscape.

The only other possible public buildings are two likely temples (Building 1.2 and 4.14), and a possible bath complex (Building 2.6). Neither of the two temples can be dated, although they are both of Classical rather than Romano-Celtic plan-type, perhaps implying an earlier rather than later Roman date. The possible baths are also undated, but a coherent assemblage of tile associated with a hypocaust and dated to *c* AD 100–80 came from field-walking in the adjacent field to the north and might well derive from this building.[161]

In addition, and as noted above, evidence from the *forum* and from Street EW8 (**G48**) confirm that a significant system of sewers existed within the town. This is almost certainly connected with the account given by Drake quoted in Chapter 2 (pp. 11–12), which describes tile-covered drains, one of which led towards the river.[162] This sewerage system appears to be associated with layout of the *forum* (above, p. 106) and the street system, and is by inference Hadrianic in date.

In the absence of better evidence from the southern part of the town it is impossible to draw any firm conclusions about the extent of provision of public buildings in the town. However, we may note that its tally now compares well with what is known of other Romano-British towns.[163] As with most other sites in Britain, the number of public buildings provided is not well reflected in the epigraphic record, with no inscriptions relating to them surviving. Indeed, the only related item is a statue base (*RIB* 3208) now in the nearby church at Kirby Hill, probably dedicated to the Emperor Caracalla after his death in AD 217. This presumably derived from a public building in Aldborough.

The only other monumental inscriptions from the town are part of an altar dedicated to Jupiter Optimus Maximus and the Mother Goddesses (*RIB* 708), which is a very finely cut piece, and two tombstones (*RIB* 709 and 710), the first of which found re-used in a wall in

Boroughbridge. The latter was perhaps found in the cemetery outside the South Gate (**G7**).[164] Alongside the dedication to Jupiter, there are also two published sculptural reliefs, each depicting Mercury.[165] One is built into the church wall, the other found near the East Gate (**G17**). These presumably indicate the presence of a sanctuary to this deity. The half life-size marble head from a Classical statue of a Graeco-Roman deity is attributed to Aldborough in *CSIR*, but has no recorded findspot and may well be a Grant Tour import.[166] There are also three unpublished sculptural fragments from the site listed in Appendix 3. An altar with figures in relief found near the amphitheatre (see fig 3.26) is difficult to interpret, as is a fragment of a relief perhaps showing drapery. Finally, there is a fragment from the left-hand side of a small relief, which depicts one of the Genii Cucullati,[167] which presumably relates to the practice of 'Celtic' religion at the town.

Finally, there is a substantial collection of architectural fragments from Aldborough, mostly unpublished and almost wholly unnoticed.[168] The pieces that have been traced are listed in Appendix 4. They include seven column capitals, nine bases, and twelve fragments of column drum as well as four cornice mouldings and assorted other pieces. There are several paired items, suggesting that they were from excavated buildings. It is a relatively large assemblage from a Roman town, and although only a few of the pieces can be related to particular buildings, as a group they provide some evidence for Classical-style architecture here.

They are almost exclusively cut from millstone grit, so the finer details of the mouldings tend to be eroded, but they are generally typologically consistent, with a predominance of capitals and bases of provincial Tuscan type as discussed by Blagg.[169] There are a couple of notable exceptions, including a foliate capital (Appendix 4, no. 1) which indicates a building loosely styled on the Corinthian order. There is also a fragment of a fine cornice moulding with a plain cyma recta, fillet and bead, above modillions and a coffered soffit (Appendix 4, no. 31). This comes from a more Classical façade, and its thickness suggests that it derives from a building with columns at least *c* 0.5m in diameter, thus perhaps a column height of *c* 3.5–4m, which implies a public building.

Most of column drums are 0.3–0.35m in diameter, with the largest being *c* 0.55m. Following Vitruvian conventions,[170] and depending on the architectural order, this suggests column heights of 2.1–2.8m and 3.85–4.4m respectively. Whilst it is clear from the empirical evidence of British examples that Vitruvian ideals were not always followed,[171] these figures indicate that most of these columns come from domestic structures, with only occasional pieces from public buildings (see below). This provides an interesting insight into the cultural aspirations of the inhabitants. Given the stylistic consistency of the capitals and bases as well as the homogeneity of the raw materials deployed, they may come from a locally based workshop.

One feature of Aldborough that is not paralleled in other comparable towns is the group of substantial *horrea* ('warehouses') inside the North Wall (Buildings 2.17 and 2.19), representing a major storage facility. The building, *c* 60m × 28m, comprising three long rooms is very substantially built. The excavated evidence (**G106**) suggests that it was constructed *c* 250–300, slightly earlier than continental examples of a similar scale that may have been associated with the *annona*.[172] There seem to be very good grounds for believing that these buildings continued a role that the site had played since the Flavian period (above, pp. 99–100). The monumental character of these *horrea* suggests that they were public rather than private buildings. If this was the case, then it would suggest that the town continued to play a significant and formal role in the provisioning of the army long after it had become a self-governing civic community.

Direct evidence for a significant state role in supplies at Aldborough is provided by three lead sealings from the site, all found in a field just outside the Walls to the north of these warehouses. Such sealings were used to seal the bindings around larger packages, bales or other merchandise in order to prevent interference during transit, so their findspots indicate a destination rather than an origin. Although it has been noted that provincial sealings like the first discussed below are almost exclusively found within their issuing province, this does not seem to contradict the idea that sealings were most likely to have been discarded when goods were being unpacked.[173] The first[174] shows a bull, and bears the legend [P](rovinicae)B(ritanniae)[I(nferioris)] – 'of the Province of Lower Britain' – and can be closely paralleled by examples from York, Felixstowe and Binchester.[175] It must date to after the division of the province in the early third century, but before its further sub-division around the end of the third century, when this provincial name was superseded.[176] Given the association of a comparable sealing with the imperial estate at Combe Down, Bath, the editors of the *Roman Inscriptions of Britain* speculate that this type may also be associated with procuratorial activity.[177] Furthermore, given that two of the close parallels come from Binchester and York, a connection with the supply route to the frontier via Dere Street seems certain.

The second[178] is inscribed 'BFV', which refers to a *beneficiarius consularis*, although the meaning of the 'V' remains obscure.[179] *Beneficiarii* were soldiers seconded to specialist duties (for example, with the procurator). Whatever the particular role represented here, this sealing confirms the town's link with military provisioning. Indeed, as Frere suggests, since *beneficiarii* were often posted to places on key roads, including Dere Street, they perhaps played a regular role in the supervision of supplies.[180] The date of this sealing remains uncertain as *beneficiarii* continued in the imperial service throughout the Roman period in Britain.[181]

The final example, which carries the text D(omini) N(ostri),[182] ('property of our lord [the emperor]') is closely paralleled by examples from Corbridge and South Shields.[183] At South Shields, one came from a third century context where it was concluded that 'DN' referred solely to the reign of Caracalla (AD 212–17). The imperial status of this sealing not only confirms the official connection, but also provides a specific link with the supply network to Hadrian's Wall. It is arguable that all three sealings relate to activity in the third century. Ensuring the security of such supplies provides a different perspective on the provision of the town's defences, which (should be noted) enclosed the *horrea* even though these lay outside the street grid (above, p. 111).

Such connections with the Roman state and army also provides a context for the scatter of Roman military equipment that has come from Aldborough.[184] The link with Hadrian's Wall and South Shields illustrated by these sealings also raises the possibility that, when the military supply network was enhanced during the Severan campaigns in Scotland, the role of *Isurium* was reinforced.[185]

Turning to domestic buildings, the overall pattern of housing shown in the survey in the northern part of the town is dominated by strip buildings of various varieties, alongside several aisled halls. There are fewer examples of larger houses (for example, Buildings 1.6 and 2.13), a pattern which contrasts with what is known from the southern part of the town. It is difficult to know how far this is a result of the selective nature of antiquarian reporting for the southern part of the town, but the evidence does indicate a genuine distinction. The pattern of very densely occupied areas in the northern section of the town, which presumably continues into the later Roman period, is comparable with other extensively explored Romano-British towns. This confirms the impression that Aldborough became a busy and crowded urban centre.

The only large town house that can certainly be dated to the earlier Roman period is the courtyard house (Building 4.8/4.9) facing onto the Principal North–South Street. This included the mosaics now in the English Heritage site (**G22**), which have been dated to the late second century on stylistic grounds.[186] Given that one of these is in a room that is clearly secondary to the original building, this must imply that the building is comparatively early.

In the southern half of the town, there are other, more modest, houses that can be confidently dated to the earlier Roman period. The first (the so-called barracks dug in the nineteenth century – **G11**), is earlier than the Town Wall (above, p. 53), and thus probably of second-century date. Like Building 4.8, this includes a bath suite, which implies elite status and a comparatively high level of cultural assimilation.

Further east, the part of a house excavated in 1965 (**G49**) has a well-understood sequence, with two phases of timber buildings that are probably Flavian–Trajanic, succeeded by three phases of a stone building (the first of which dates to after *c* AD 125). Development culminated in a plan with a corridor on its eastern side and a range of slightly irregular rooms to the west. This house probably faced on to Street EW8. Finally, almost opposite the *forum*, part of another house (**G47**) perhaps originated comparatively early in the life to the town. The character of the excavated building is not certain, but it had a corridor to the north and a wider room to the south, both with *opus signinum* floors.

The development of the Roman town at this period is clearly closely linked to its establishment as the administrative centre of the *civitas* of the Brigantes (above, pp. 106–8). As noted in Chapter 1, its identification as a *civitas* capital is based on a single textual reference in the Antonine Itinerary, which dates to the third century AD (above, p. 7). We may also note the presence of a contingent from the *civitas* recorded in a building stone from Hadrian's Wall usually associated with its late Roman restoration.[187]

The facilities offered by the town, as now witnessed by the archaeological evidence, show that it was comparable with other British *civitas* centres, although was comparatively modest in size. Estimating the extent of the *civitas* territory governed from Aldborough remains all but impossible, the issues being comparable to those discussed above in the context of the Iron Age social geography. In broad terms, interpretation depends on the extent to which one follows Mattingly[188] in his assumption that much of northern Britain remained under direct military control, or follow the alternative suggestion that the default option for the Roman administration was to pass land back to the control of local peoples.[189] The former assumption would allow the territory governed from Aldborough to be fairly modest in extent, perhaps extending to little more than the Vale of York;[190] the latter would allow us to envisage a much larger territory extending well up towards the northern frontier. There is little to enable us to distinguish between these two extremes, and with either scenario it seems that the territory contained comparatively few villas or similar settlements (below, p. 116),[191] implying that the social and economic system was different to that of other *civitates* further south, and was surely very closely linked to the military economy, which recent evidence suggests had an influence deep into the countryside.[192]

One set of information that is interesting but difficult to evaluate is the distribution of dedications to Brigantia, the eponymous goddess of the territory. There are seven inscriptions to her,[193] including one from Birrens in south-west Scotland with a fine sculptural relief depicting her.[194] The three from Yorkshire arguably come from within the *civitas*, and may help define its extent, but those from Hadrian's Wall and the Antonine Wall cannot be used in this way,[195] and instead relate to the pattern of adoption of a range of local deities by the army and those associated with them. Although there is evidence for a Brigantian serving in the Roman army,[196] it is not possible to relate such dedications specifically to such recruits. The tradition of appropriating local deities was clearly widespread, as witnessed by the Brampton example, dedicated by a *procurator Augusti*, who we have no reason to believe was a Brigantian.

Finally, in the context of the mid third century town it is notable that there are three milestones found in and around Aldborough dated to the reign of the emperor Trajan Decius (AD 249–51).[197] This concentration is exceptional, there being only eight milestones known from Britain dating to his short reign.[198] Whilst this might be taken to suggest a spate of road improvement around Aldborough in this period, Sauer has recently and plausibly suggested that milestones of this period represent a way in which local communities expressed loyalty to an emperor.[199] In the local context of Aldborough, one might raise the possibility that this emperor's name (Traianus) had a particular resonance with visible epigraphy in the town if we are correct in concluding that both town and *forum* were Hadrianic.[200]

4.8 The development of the extra-mural areas

One of the most remarkable results of the survey is the evidence it has provided for the different areas outside the Town Walls, both in their extent and in visible differences in their character. This provides an entirely new perspective on these areas, complementing the recently published results of the field-walking undertaken in the 1980s and 1990s (see fig 4.10).[201] This work showed that the spread of finds outside the area occupied by the Town Wall began around the end of the first century AD, with the bulk of the material collected dating to the latter part of the second century and a second peak in finds in the middle of the fourth (fig. 4.6). Spatially, the pattern shows the highest density of finds within *c* 500m of the East Gate on the route to York, and just outside the North Gate beside the road to the river crossing. The broader spread of pottery shows activity all around the town, with a slightly increasing density towards the river through time. The general density of finds overall tails off in the second half of the fourth century, but there are clear differences between areas. Activity to the east of the town seems to decline before other areas, with a low density of finds after the early third century. By comparison, fields to the north reveal a dip in the number of finds in the third century, but experience a recovery during the fourth. Only in the southern area do we see unusually high numbers of fourth-century finds.[202]

Standing back from the details of the various features mapped in the geophysical survey of these extra-mural areas discussed by area in Chapter 3, several key themes emerge. First (and most obvious) is the variation in the patterning between the different sides of the town, reflecting in part the importance of the roads approaching Aldborough. The so-called Dere Street from York, which approaches the East Gate and continues to Hadrian's Wall via the North Gate, is significantly more built up than the routes leading away out of the South and West Gates, a pattern also seen in the field-survey results. This is not surprising given the strategic importance of the road to the northern frontier and the connection to York. Although the routes from the South and West Gates were of importance in the regional communications network, they do not seem to have been arterial. Indeed, it is not entirely clear where these led (see below). This is reflected not only in the lower densities of activity along them, but also in the more organic layout and less ordered development of these suburbs, all of which imply a process of rather piecemeal development in these areas.

By contrast, the areas alongside the roads outside the East and North Gates are not only heavily developed, but there is considerable evidence both for larger scale planned layouts and some specialisation of functions. There is strong evidence for organised cemeteries flanking the road to York (Areas 7 and 8). These include both funerary enclosures with large *mausolea* (Funerary Enclosures 7.1–71.5, and 8.1–8.5), and areas further from the walls apparently given over to cremation burial in the south-eastern part of Area 8. The broad layout includes a series of boundary ditches parallel with the Roman road, with the enclosed strip sub-divided into enclosures that face onto it. The parallel ditches extend further from the road to the north east than to the south west (Ditches 7.9, 7.12, 8.1, 8.2 and 8.6), where the limit is probably determined by the local topography. Although these land divisions are a little too irregular to suggest any over-arching system of land allotment, they are sufficiently ordered to show how the land, including fields further from the road, were parcelled up, presumably indicating separate land-holdings. The evidence equally suggests that there was significant competition for funerary plots along the road frontage, confirming its prime significance. This can be paralleled in other Roman towns, where monuments to the ancestors were displayed beside the most important approach roads.[203]

Industrial activity is also attested in the area just outside the East Gate, most notably the wasters from a kiln producing *mortaria* and coarse wares close to the junction of Hall Arm Lane (**G52/E**), and dated to *c* 100–40,[204] arguably before the development of the funerary landscape. It is clear that the clays in this area were suitable for ceramic manufacture, as witnessed by the brickworks a little further from the town along the Dunsforth Road shown on the first edition OS map. There is evidence for stone quarries (Quarries 6.1–6.3) on the slope to the south of the Roman road. Across the whole area there are also various features in the fluxgate gradiometry survey that may represent ovens, kilns or other small-scale industrial features.

The land flanking the road between the North Gate and the bridge over the River Ure is just as heavily occupied, but the character of the activity there is different to that beside the road to York in two respects. First, there is no evidence for funerary activity, with the road frontage instead largely occupied by buildings and associated enclosures, arguably agricultural, pastoral and industrial in function. Secondly, although there is some evidence for primary land divisions running parallel with the road (see below), these were not all maintained as key boundaries. Instead, they were succeeded by a series of large but subdivided enclosure blocks that face onto the road (Enclosure Groups 9.1–9.8, 10.1–10.3). It seems most likely that these represent separate land-holdings. Predominantly agricultural functions are suggested by the integration of some with the field systems running back from the road.

The primary layout of the area between the town and the river appears to have been contemporaneous with the construction of the road, which arguably dates to the Hadrianic period. The boundaries, which extend back from the road into the fields behind the later roadside settlement, are sufficiently regular to suggest an organised system, but not regular enough to discern any standard sizes. What they do clearly imply is that the planning of the town street grid and the road also entailed broader-scale alterations to properties with all that this implies in terms of political power.

Although farming seems likely to have played a significant role in this area, it would be a mistake to think of the area as exclusively agrarian. The density of buildings along the frontage, and hints of intensive furnace use in areas away from the frontage to the east behind Enclosure Group 9.4, suggest that these properties were also engaged in industry and there was presumably commerce, too. In this sense, the landscape between the North Gate and the river crossing looks very similar to that seen in the roadside settlements like Shiptonthorpe,[205] Hayton,[206] or Stamford Bridge[207] elsewhere in the region. By analogy with such sites, this area was a booming economic zone, serving the needs of those passing along the road.

Given the suggested importance of the river for communication (above, pp. 99–100), it is notable that the survey provides only limited direct evidence for wharfs, with the only identified structures just to the west of the bridge where Trackway 10.2 meets the river bank. It is unlikely that vessels for regular water transportation would simply have been drawn up on the river bank, so we would expect there to have been jetties or quays against which boats could be moored. Such features would only show up in survey if they were made of stone (like those by Trackway 10.2), and we should observe the predominant use of timber for such structures elsewhere.[208] On this basis, where might other wharfs have been located? Both the topography of the site and the northward bend of the river make it most likely that the main quays were located on the south bank of the river rather than the north. Equally, the presence of the Roman bridge probably meant that the principal quays for moving goods further down the river would probably have been located to its east. Interestingly, as the Roman road approaches the bridge, there is a possible widening to the east which could indicate an access to quays on the river bank here. We may also note that one of the eighteenth-century quays was located at some distance to the east (see fig 2.1), and if there were Roman wharfs in a similar location, Trackway 9.1 may have connected them to the road. This eighteenth-century wharf lay off the slight ridge on which the road and settlement is built. The geomorphological history of this area is complex, with both the erosion and deposition of alluvial deposits, so any earlier remains may have been destroyed or masked by riverine clays (see fig 1.3). This will be explored in future fieldwork.

The landscape outside the West Gate is far less busy, with little evidence for enclosures or other features running west beside the presumed road that connects to Roecliffe. This implies that the route was of limited significance after the river crossing shifted, perhaps early in the second century AD. There is more evidence for activity beside the two trackways (12.1 and 12.2) that head to the south west just outside the gate, especially the more southerly one which headed up the Ure Valley and may have become a main route, linking with the road to Ilkley (see below). Trackway 12.1 is flanked by agricultural enclosures, with occasional buildings and possible burials and a few industrial furnaces or ovens. However, there is nothing to indicate any more general planning of this zone.

The area outside the South Gate is more varied, although again there is little evidence for activity focused along the presumed line of the road beyond the South Gate, which is likely to have led to Ilkley.[209] This may imply that the later Roman route had changed, perhaps to link with Trackway 12.1 from the West Gate. There is again no evidence of any overall planning in this part of the extra-mural area. To the south east, outside the gate, the landscape was dominated by the amphitheatre (**G15**), with possible pottery kilns further to its north east (**G14**) on the area known as Redhills. There is also good evidence for the presence of cemeteries immediately outside the South Gate (**G7**, **G12**, **G14**), although there is nothing to indicate how these were organised, and the impression is of a less formal cemetery than outside the East Gate. By contrast, the area to the south west of the gate is densely occupied by trackways and small enclosures, apparently mostly agricultural but with a few, probably industrial, furnaces or kilns. One of the trackways connects with the stone quarry outside the south-western corner of the Town Wall (**G30**), indicating that this was Roman in origin. This more varied and complex area lacks the coherence of the zones outside the North and East Gates, but the evidence suggests much activity.

Finally, looking further afield, it is notable that there are comparatively few known villas or other major rural settlements in the vicinity of Aldborough, and those known do not seem to cluster around the town. The nearest villas that we know of are at Castle Dykes[210] (North Stainley), Snape (Thorpe),[211] Well[212] and Bedale,[213] all of which are situated on the edge of the higher ground along the western side of the Vale and not far distant from the Dere Street. A further possible site in such a location may lay beneath Ripon,[214] and another seems likely to lie to the south of Aldborough in the vicinity of the burial monuments at Duel Cross.[215] This pattern seems unlikely to result from biases in the recovery of archaeological evidence, as villas in particular are generally archaeologically quite visible. Rather, the paucity of villas locally and the distinctive distribution of those known may be a feature of the social landscape of the region. On the one hand, some of the wealthy elites who were engaged in the business of supplying the military may have chosen to live in the town not the countryside. This contrasts with the tradition of a rurally resident governing class as seen in areas of southern Britain. On the other, the elites who elected to reside in the countryside lived in locations that facilitated interaction with the Dere Street, arguably also to engage with commerce.[216] If this is so, it implies a different relationship between local elites and the land, and may suggest that primary agricultural production may have been less dominated by these families.

4.9 The later Town Wall and annexes

Evidence for the development of Aldborough's Town Walls in the later Roman period has come from a series of past excavations, as recently reviewed by Snape *et al.*[217] They suggest that the construction of the external towers, and hence the excavation of the 'outer ditch', dates to sometime after the third quarter of the third century (see fig 4.12). This appears too early as the external tower at the north-western corner (**G39**, Section III) overlay pottery in backfilled ditch dated to the early fourth century, whereas in the 1938 excavation (**G43**), the refurbishment of the Wall is dated to the early fourth century whilst the outermost ditch excavated was respected by a fourth-century rubbish layer. This would indicate a date in, or after, the early fourth century for the addition of the external towers.

However, the survey has shown very clearly that the sequence of the defences in the later Roman period was more complex than previously assumed, largely because past excavations had missed the ditches furthest out from the Wall. The details of the sequence on the southern, eastern and northern sides have been discussed in detail above (pp. 63–4, 74) and, although it is clear that the sequence shows some variation between the different sides of the town, it does reveal a consistent pattern. First, we see the addition of external towers and the consequent cutting of a pair of new ditches further out from the wall (Ditches 6.2 and 6.3; 6.5 = 7.2 and 6.6; 9.2 and 9.3). This was followed by the addition of two annexes, on the northern and eastern sides. Finally, the Town Wall was strengthened with the addition of a substantial outer ditch (Ditch 6.4 = 6.7 = 7.3 = 9.4). This is probably contemporaneous with the strengthening of the annexe defences (Ditches 6.11 = 7.8 and 9.6). It is probable that these actions also coincided with the addition of a strengthening of the embankment behind the Town Wall, as recorded on the northern side (**G106**).[218]

The dating of the sequence remains uncertain, but the pattern of pottery deposition immediately outside the Walls suggests that activity declined after the mid fourth century.[219] This is compatible with the limited evidence from the heightening of the bank behind the North Wall, which dates to after *c* AD 350–400.[220] At some stage certain of the external towers examined in past excavations were also demolished, but the date and extent of this, and how it relates to the longer sequence of the defences also remains unclear.[221] Given the complexity of this defensive sequence, it seems likely that the latest strengthening was actually undertaken after AD 400, perhaps considerably later. If this is the case, the creation of an entrance through the Town Wall leading into the eastern annexe with Trackway 7.1, which follows the line of street EW8 must date to the fifth century. This has considerable potential implications for our understanding of Aldborough in the post-Roman period (below, p. 120).

The discovery of the annexes in the survey is one of its more surprising results. They have few obvious parallels in the defences of other Romano-British towns,[222] and their functions are not obvious. Indeed, we cannot be entirely certain that the two are contemporaneous, although this seems likely both in terms of the survey evidence and on the basis of their general similarity in plan and form. However, several strands of evidence are relevant. First, the location of the annexes is surely significant as they occur only outside the gates on the main arterial road, on the approach from York and from the northern frontier. Secondly, they are defined by substantial ditches that must presumably imply a genuinely defensive function, not simply a symbolic one. This, along with the evidence for the progressive strengthening of their defences and those of the town, suggest that they were of long-term importance rather than a simple response to a short-term problem. Thirdly, they must presumably have been designed to enclose that which could not be accommodated within the existing wall circuit, either due to a lack of space or for other reasons. This might indicate that they were provided to house people, animals or materials passing through – in other words, items not for the town's permanent residents. It should also be noted how they became part of the later landscape, with a series of fields de-limited by Ditch 7.11 laid out to respect the eastern annexe (above, p. 65).

The possibility that they were for the use of the Roman state (either for the army or the provincial government) is perhaps supported by the discovery in the area of the annexe outside the North Gate of three lead sealings discussed above (pp. 112–13), which have evident administrative associations, and one of which possibly dates to the fourth century.

Two complementary functions are worth considering. First, the annexes may have been used to provide secure storage for goods moving along the road and river in transit to the frontier. This would be consistent with the earlier evidence for the role of Aldborough within the state supplies system, implying a continuity of function, but with the addition of areas for secure storage outside the town itself. Second, with the emergence of a more organised system of taxation in kind in the later Roman period, and the suggestion that major towns may have played a key role as tax collection centres,[223] the annexes may have been created to provide for the collection, storage and transmission of the taxes in-kind collected in this way. This idea is attractive, and complements the first suggestion. It would also be consistent with the strengthening of the town's defences, which surely suggests that it was an important hub that potentially needed defending in the later Roman period. Furthermore, such functions for the town might explain the very substantial building (Building 9.2) seen in the geophysical survey within the northern annexe, that may have complemented or superseded the *horrea* just within the North Wall (Building 2.17). It is notable the pottery assemblage from the survey outside the North Gate, near the site of Building 9.2, contains much fourth-century material, with supplies only tailing off after *c* 380.[224]

4.10 The later Roman townscape

Given the evidence from the defences and the annexes, it is clear that later Roman Aldborough was a key location, so it is particularly frustrating that we have little good information about the interior of the town. As noted above, our evidence for the chronology of the buildings is comparatively slight, so there is little that we can draw out about the character of the later Roman phase.

What is clear is that it contained a very significant group of well-appointed town-houses, especially in its southern half. Most are only known from antiquarian exploration but these can be dated by their mosaics, although they may have been established in an earlier

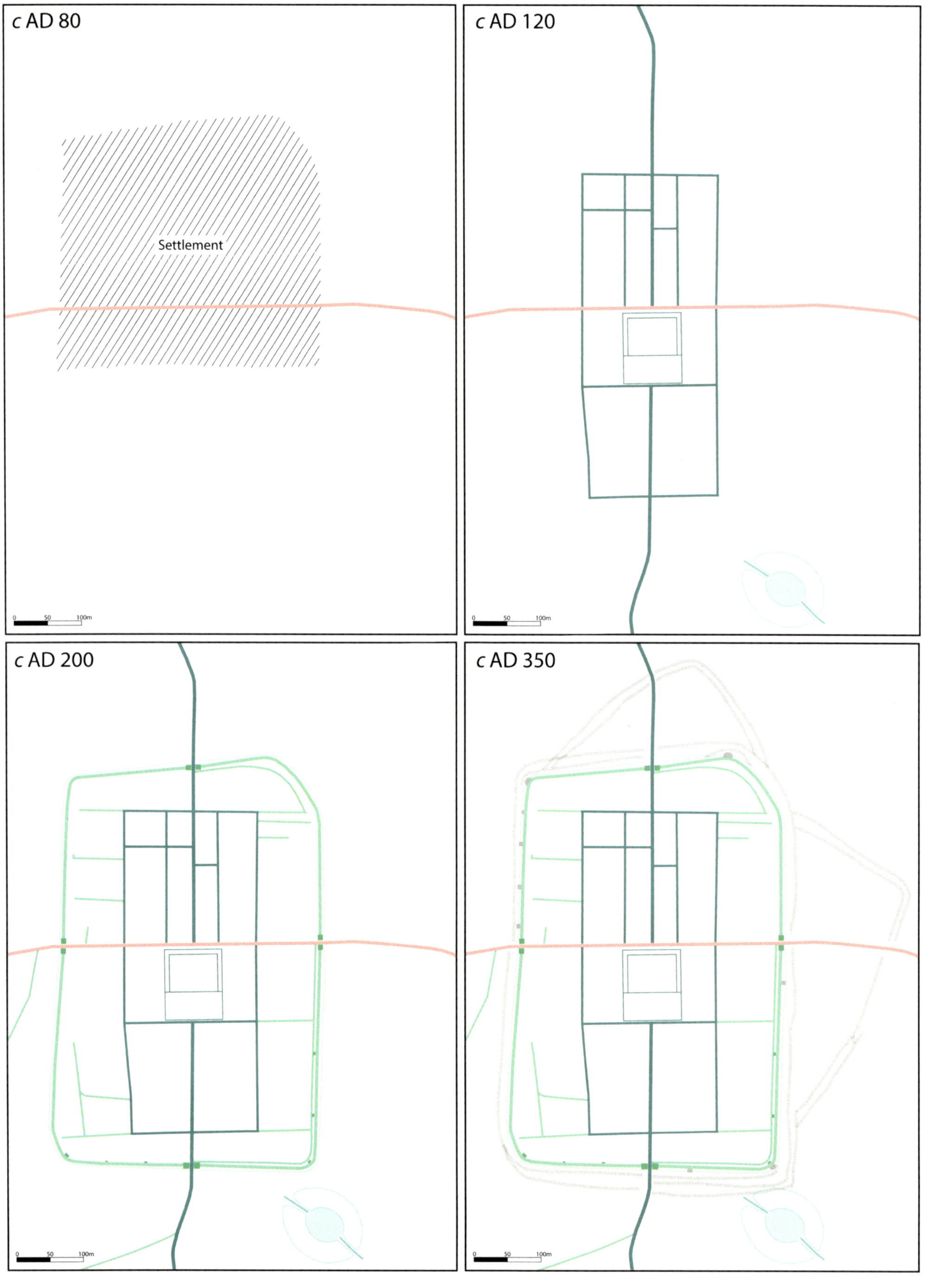

Fig 4.12 Summary plan showing the development of the Roman town and its defences. *Drawing:* Rose Ferraby.

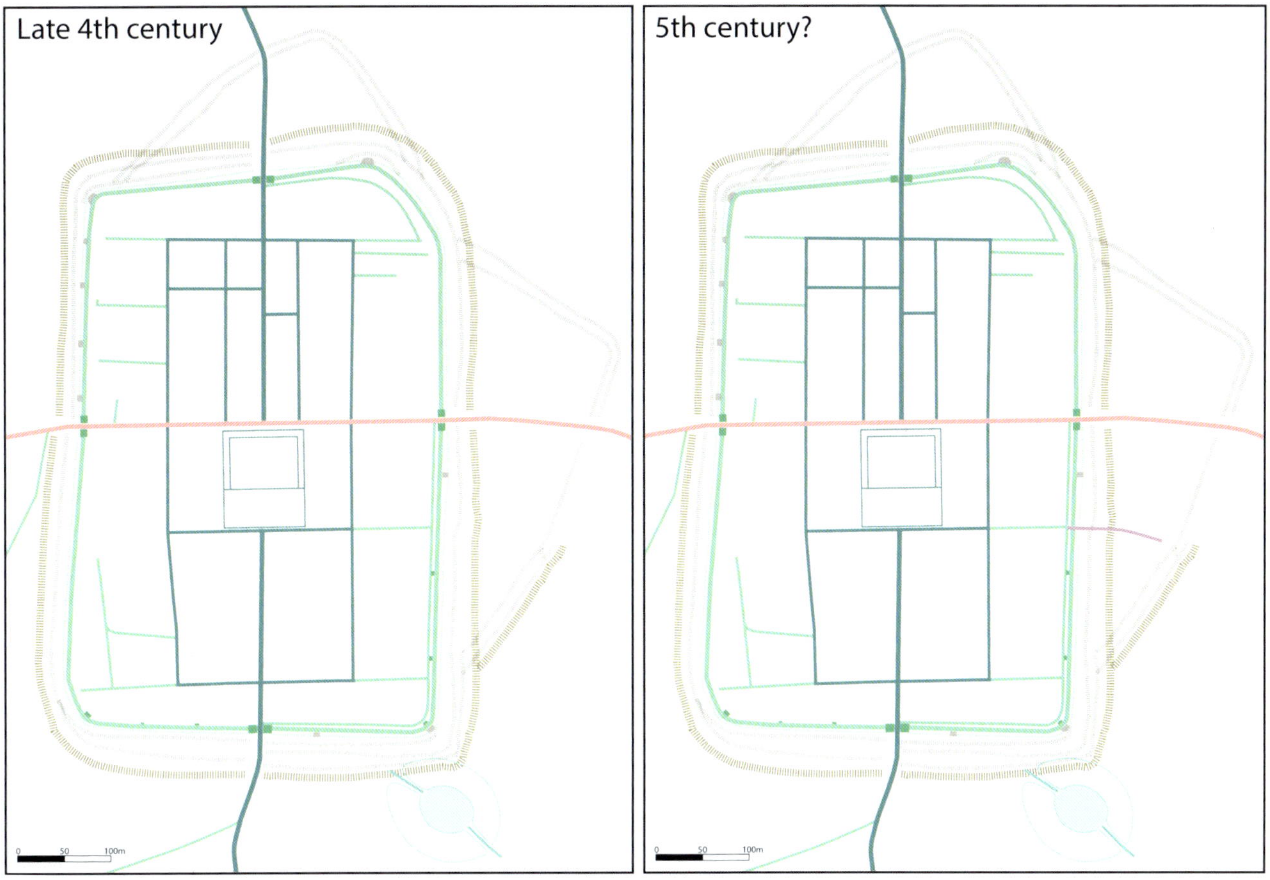

period. The most prominent (**G20**) faced the Principal East–West street and had a mosaic corridor more than 10m in length forming the west side of a colonnaded courtyard, the column bases from which are *c* 0.38m in diameter, implying a height of *c* 2.7m. Other substantial town-houses fronted the Principal North–South street. These include Building 4.10 (**G23**) with its Helicon mosaic flooring and apsidal dining room, and a courtyard house (Building 4.8/4.9 = **G22**) with late second-century mosaics, which was arguably later divided into two separate properties. Further mosaics (**G1**, **G2, G3**, **G5**, **G10**, **G19**) indicate other significant houses in the southern half of the town, but only a single pavement (**G24**) is known from the north. This reinforces the suggestion made above (p. 113) that the two halves of the town had distinct characteristics. But taken together, this represents an exceptional cluster of mosaics when compared with other Romano-British towns,[225] confirming that there was an unusual concentration of substantial town-houses and thus well-off residents in late Roman Aldborough. This must imply that *Isurium* was a very significant political centre during the fourth century. To place this in perspective, York, the civil settlement that covers *c* 40ha (about twice the size of Aldborough), has produced only eleven mosaics, although it should be noted that their quality is high.[226] Whilst there is considerable evidence for other forms of civic display in late Roman York,[227] the contrast does underline the importance of Aldborough at this period.

It is difficult to assess the size of the town's population, but the geophysical survey is very helpful for this, and it is useful to have an impression of its approximate size, even if it should be acknowledged that such estimates are inherently unreliable. Simply taking the area of the walled town and multiplying it by urban population densities that have previously been used for Roman Britain,[228] we obtain a range of between *c* 2950 and *c* 4650 people. However, recent work in Italy suggests that this overestimates Roman urban population densities, giving a range of *c* 2600–3250 people.[229] An alternative is to look at the number of buildings found in the areas covered by the geophysical survey, which covered *c* 8.85ha (or *c* 41 per cent of the walled area). Within this area the authors have identified a total of fifty-two buildings. Although not all are domestic, this would suggest a total of perhaps 125 buildings within the town. Taking an average household size (including children and servants or slaves) as twenty people, this suggests a population of *c* 2500. Although it should be emphasised that neither of these sets of calculations is very robust, together they would indicate that the resident population was unlikely to be outside the range of 2500–3000 people.

Alongside the evidence for prosperity and political power at this time, there are also suggestions of fundamental change. The survey evidence from outside the Walls, indicates a decline in activity from the middle of the fourth century,[230] perhaps associated with the strengthening of the defences and the movement of activity within the Walls. Disuse of one of the larger houses, Building 4.10 (**G23**), is evidenced by burials cut through the floor, some of the bone from which was radiocarbon dated to AD 250–420.[231] As in other towns, there is also evidence for the abandonment or re-use of public buildings. The excavation of the outer defensive ditch must have put the amphitheatre out of use as it cut through part of the northern seating bank (above, p. 61). This probably took place in the later fourth century, although as noted above, it may have been later. The contemporaneous heightening of the bank behind the Town Wall also seems to have followed the demolition of the *horrea* in the north-eastern corner of the town, and may have been the reason for the loss of these public buildings. Certainly, if they were associated with tax collection, their demolition has significant implications.

The authors' limited re-excavation of the *forum* (**G105**) also demonstrated a change of use. Although truncated in the eighteenth century, it would appear that the flooring was removed in the late Roman period. A hearth cut into the floor make-up seems to have been associated with iron-working. This is radiocarbon dated to AD 343–421, which fits into a broader pattern of the re-use of public buildings, especially *fora* for metal-working in fourth-century Britain.[232] A recent survey has identified such activity at nine other *fora*, suggesting a consistent pattern, although whether this is associated with state or military production seems more doubtful. In the case of Aldborough, it highlights a contrast between an apparent private prosperity and the loss of earlier public monuments. However, in the absence of more precise chronological evidence it is impossible to know whether or not these were synchronous.

4.11 The transition to the Middle Ages

Evidence for the ending of Roman Aldborough, and the transition to the Middle Ages, is even more scarce. The only good sequence is provided by the creation of a route (Trackway 7.1) through the Town Wall connecting the central area directly to the eastern annexe, and the creation of the adjacent enclosure (Enclosure 7.1). These are both later than the final defensive ditch, and arguably date to the fifth century (above, p. 117). Past excavations were insufficiently sophisticated for us to know whether or not they destroyed sub-Roman and early medieval deposits without noticing them. As with most Roman sites, finds continue down to the early fifth century, but after the cessation of regular coin supplies in AD 402, it becomes difficult to date artefacts, hence any occupation that was there is impossible to identify (at least, by conventional means).[233] The pottery from the Yorkshire Archaeological Society field-survey shows that supplies continued in the second half of the fourth century, although declining in volume.[234] The coin list from the site also remains comparatively strong down to last regular consignments of bronze coinage sent to the province in 388–402.[235] Furthermore, textual evidence is also thin on the ground until late in the Medieval period. It is not the intention here to trace the history of Aldborough in detail through this challenging period, but a few brief observations should be made.

From the perspective of the survey, there is very strong evidence for the continued importance of the town down to the end of the Roman period. Indeed, it is tempting to see the final strengthening of the defences of the town and annexes with a major ditch as indicating its continued value to the Roman state and those living within, perhaps even after the decline of the provincial administration in the early years of the fifth century. If, as has been suggested above, Aldborough was closely integrated into the Roman system of power fulfilling roles in military supply to the frontier and the collection of taxes, then it will have been particularly susceptible as imperial power collapsed or ebbed away. But equally, as it was also evidently a major centre of elite residence in the late Roman period and controlled a key communications route, it will have been an obvious location for the emergence of a sub-Roman centre of power under the control of local potentates. In this context, it is notable that Aldborough lies close to the western margin of the distribution of early Anglian cemeteries, and between the two documented British kingdoms of Rheged to the north and Elmet to the west, which existed down to the early seventh century.[236] As it has been argued that the Vale of York remained in the 'British' hands down to the later sixth or seventh century, [237] there are strong circumstantial reasons to indicate that Aldborough remained a key place. Indeed, Glanville Jones long ago suggested that Aldborough (rather than Catterick or York) might be the fortified town (*oppido municipio*) mentioned by Bede that was held by Caedualla of Gwynedd and besieged by the Northumbrian army in

AD 633–5.[238] This view has recently been revived by Breeze, although it is questioned by Woolf.[239]

Following the annexation of the area, now under Northumbrian control, St Wilfrid's monastery at Ripon, endowed in AD 671–8, became dominant, and likely eclipsed any surviving settlement at Aldborough. Re-used Roman stone in the monastic church of St Wilfrid at Ripon seems most likely to have derived from Aldborough, only *c* 10km to the south east.[240] This includes some very substantial slabs incorporated into the roof of the seventh-century ring-crypt.[241]

Much later, at Domesday, Aldborough is recorded as a major centre known as Burc, held by the Crown, and the chief manor in Burghshire.[242] Its widely spread land-holdings indicate that it was the centre of a significant pre-Domesday estate, so there is some temptation to assume its continued importance in the intervening period, although the evidence for this is lacking. However, it should also be noted that there is no evidence to support the frequently repeated suggestion that the Danes destroyed Aldborough around AD 870.[243] The tradition that York was burned by the Danes at this date was current in the early eighteenth century, appearing, for example, in Gibson's 1722 edition of Camden's *Britannia*.[244] Citing the fourteenth-century *Polychronicon* of Ranulf Higden, and noting black earth on the site at Aldborough, Richard Gough concluded in 1789 that Aldborough was destroyed at the same time as York.[245] York was not destroyed by the Danes at this time,[246] and the link to Aldborough is probably the result of a confusion over place names in Higden's text.[247]

Moving to the archaeological evidence, aside from items probably from a seventh-century grave[248] and some casual finds of Anglo-Scandinavian objects, there is little archaeological evidence of this period.[249] The finds mentioned all indicate activity in the area, but contribute nothing to an understanding of the character of the site during this period. However, some strands of the topographic evidence do, however, hint at the nature of its continued use.

First, the present church sits squarely in the centre of the *forum* square, and has a dedication to St Andrew that may indicate an early foundation.[250] The present building is primarily fourteenth century, but there may well have been an earlier structure on the site.[251] The location may have been chosen for a number of factors: its centrality; the ease of building in an already levelled area; the access to a ready supply of building stone; or for a combination of these.[252] Since the gates through the Town Walls will have determined the course of the later roads, even the central location could simply represent an intelligent re-use of a defended site rather than direct urban continuity. However, the evidence for the relationship between some of the internal streets of the Roman town and later village would seem to suggest more substantial continuity (fig 4.10).

Furthermore, there are clearer elements of land-boundary continuity across the survey area. First, as is clear from the geophysics, Roman-period boundaries strongly influenced the layout of the later ridge and furrow in several areas (fig 4.13). This is visible flanking the Roman roads in Areas 7 and 8, but is most pronounced just to the east of the road in Area 9 where the change in direction of the ridge and furrow follows Boundary 9.1.

Since current thinking generally places the origins of this form of cultivation in the ninth century, this seems to provide strong evidence for the continuance of the Roman boundaries as visible features down to this period. If we accept Rippon's argument that deserted land will have been rapidly overgrown, this would support his notion of settlement continuity applying to Aldborough.[253] Even this does not necessarily imply any continuity of ownership, and certainly not urban function, especially since the areas concerned mostly lie outside the Roman Town Walls. Indeed, against Rippon's argument, boundary banks and ditches may well have remained visible to later users of the land, even if it had reverted to secondary woodland. After all, woodlands act to preserve ancient earthworks, and some of the Roman features remain visible even today.

Equally tantalising is the evidence from within the walled town that suggests that the layout of the later landscape was informed by the Roman plan. In the northern part of the town the major east–west boundary shown on the 1708 map (see fig 2.2) seems to follow the edge of the Roman grid represented by street EW1. This is shown as an earthwork on the first edition Ordnance Survey map and was mistaken for the line of the Town Wall in the 1920s (see fig 2.13). More significantly, the 1708 map (see fig 2.2) shows that the surviving layout of the medieval tofts in the western half of the town follow two different axes: one in the southern part of the walled area, orientated east–west; the other, in the central part of the town, which runs broadly north–south (see fig 4.14). Those running east–west follow the alignment of the Roman terracing and some of the Roman buildings. Those running north–south cannot be linked to any Roman features, but it is surely significant that the change in orientation coincides with the line of a key Roman street (EW8) that carried traffic around the *forum* and the line of which is continued by Trackway 7.1, which probably dates to the fifth century (above, p. 68). These features may again simply indicate that significant topographic features remained visible at a period of

Fig 4.13 Map of Aldborough and its environs showing the extent of ridge and furrow cultivation as mapped from the authors' survey and the LiDAR (see fig 1.4). Field names taken from Lawson-Tancred 1937, 107. *Drawing:* Rose Ferraby. © Crown copyright and database rights 2018 Ordnance Survey (100025252)

re-colonising the site, but taken together there is a case to argue that there was some form of continued use of land-holdings long after the Roman period.

Of less relevance to the issue of continued occupation is the amphitheatre on Studforth Hill, which may have become a medieval fortification (**G15**). Its identification as a Norman ring-work, seems to have originated with E C Waight and S Moorhouse.[254] Such a castle may be

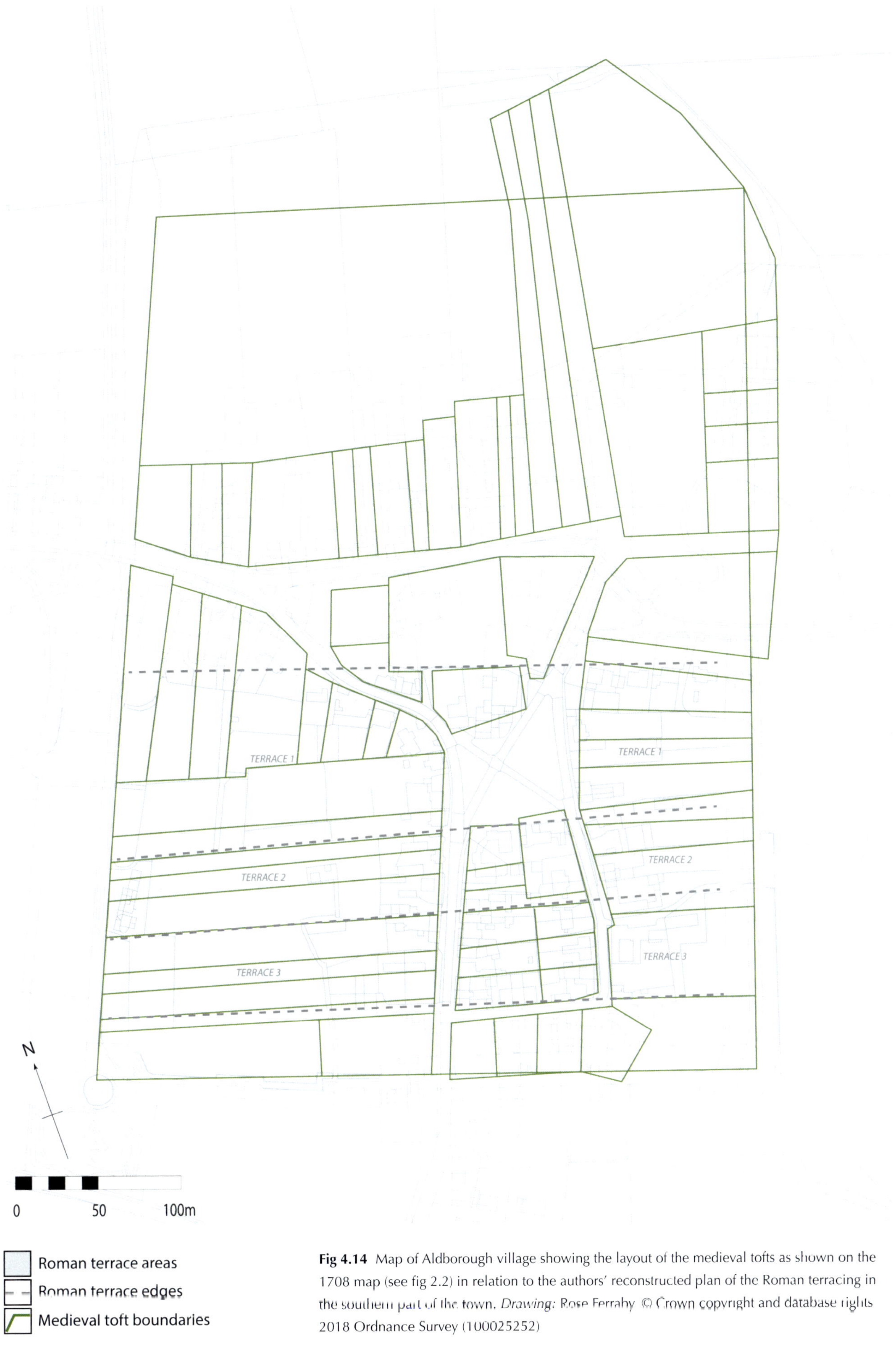

Fig 4.14 Map of Aldborough village showing the layout of the medieval tofts as shown on the 1708 map (see fig 2.2) in relation to the authors' reconstructed plan of the Roman terracing in the southern part of the town. *Drawing:* Rose Ferraby © Crown copyright and database rights 2018 Ordnance Survey (100025252)

identified with that known as Stuteville, which, along with Knaresborough, was held by William de Stuteville from 1173, and granted to him by Henry II in 1175.[255] It is documented variously from 1158 to 1205, when it was confiscated by the Crown.[256] This is surely evidence for re-use, and it is important to note how the location of Studforth Hill controls the present road from York that passes to the south of Aldborough on its way to Boroughbridge, where the new river crossing was established by the mid twelfth century when the town's charter was granted by Henry II.[257] The establishment of this as the key route that bypassed the Roman walled town, saw the beginning of the process that led to Boroughbridge becoming the principal population centre and market here.

4.12 Epilogue: history, antiquarian development and landscape

Finally, it is worth observing how the development of Aldborough in the eighteenth to twentieth centuries was linked to external historical events. Comparing the map of 1708, created soon after the acquisition of the manor by the Duke of Newcastle in 1701 (see fig 2.2), with the plan of the village published in Ecroyd Smith's *Reliquae Isurianae* in 1852 (see fig 2.8) and the aerial photo of it today (see fig 1.2) shows just how little the village has grown during over 300 years – a period of immense change over most of England. This was no coincidence, but began as the result of the political value of the borough, which had been given the right to return two Members of Parliament by Queen Mary in 1553, despite having only a handful of electors.[258] Hence, it was important for each successive duke, as landowner, to restrict its growth and limit the number of electors to ensure that he was able to control them, and hence who was elected as Aldborough's Members of Parliament.

That interest disappeared with the passing of the Great Reform Act of 1832, which removed the right of the borough to such parliamentary representation. The fourth duke of Newcastle-under-Lyme then moved to divest himself of the estate in 1834, providing the opportunity for Andrew Lawson to buy most of it. Lawson had already been in residence at the manor since about 1825, and came to acquire all but Aldborough Hall and its adjacent land. This continued unity of land-holding then ensured that settlement growth carried on being modest. Furthermore, by good luck, Andrew Lawson's great interest in the site's Roman history provided a stimulus for the exploration of the archaeology, the creation of a museum, and the development of the antiquarian garden behind the manor house. This interest in the heritage has been maintained by the family ever since, most notably with Lady Margery Lawson-Tancred in the mid twentieth century who not only encouraged research[259] and produced the first guidebook,[260] but also put that part of the site now displayed by English Heritage into the guardianship of the State in 1952. These events led to the creation of the landscape as we know it today, conserving much of the Roman town and forming the framework for understanding explored in this volume.

4.13 Retrospect and prospect

The preceding discussion has, we trust, provided a stimulating review with broad ramifications. If it has been successful, this provides a valuable illustration of the value of combining geophysical survey with systematic antiquarian research and the results of past excavation in order to create a new kind of site synthesis. Any aspect of archaeological work has its limitations, and it is only through combining different sources that we can attempt to compensate for these.

In the context of Roman Britain, where most of the evidence concerning larger urban centres has a distinct bias towards areas further south in the province, it can be argued that the evidence from Aldborough is especially valuable in indicating differing patterns of development. This complements current understanding of the urbanisation of the province, giving added weight to the evidence that processes were contextually varied. The key conclusions to emerge from this study of Aldborough may be summarised as follows. There is no evidence for any pre-Roman focus at or near the site of the Roman town, and there are reasons to believe that the settlement might have been founded in a neutral zone. Occupation began *c* AD 70, and in the settlement's initial stages the site was occupied alongside the Roman auxiliary fort at Roecliffe. It remains unclear whether there was an early military occupation beneath the later town but this now seems unlikely, and the authors suggest that the settlement may have been established by a community of traders, taking advantage of the location at the head of the navigable section of the River Ure. Early exploitation of lead and silver deposits in the hills nearby may have been key and, as the Roman road to the north was created, the intersection between river and road reinforced Aldborough's trading advantage.

It is debatable when the community became a self-governing Roman town and the centre of the Brigantian

Fig 4.15 Overall plan of the Roman town and its immediate environs summarising the results of the survey. *Drawing:* Rose Ferraby

civitas, but this is presumed to date to sometime between AD 70 and 120. Around AD 120 there seems to have been a large-scale re-planning of the settlement, creating a street grid and a *forum*, at the same time that a new bridge was built to carry Dere Street to the frontier. The early Roman town was furnished with other public amenities, including an amphitheatre, a sewerage system and public baths. Alongside these, there was a series of substantial private houses, some with mosaic floors. The Town Wall was added, probably in the late second century, undergoing a series of enhancements through the rest of the Roman period and probably into the fifth century. This included the construction of two annexes, outside the North and East gates. The settlement extended well beyond the Town Walls, where there is evidence for a wide variety of activities spread out along the approaches to the town. The mosaics from the town suggest that it prospered in the fourth century, and there are indications that the centre's importance may have continued into the post-Roman period.

This work not only provides a new synthesis of the evidence, but it also defines a series of questions for future research. Partly because of the nature of the present evidence, we currently lack a clear understanding of the economic roles that were central to the town, and this inhibits any deeper understanding of its functions in the broader region. Addressing this gap must be a key objective for future research. At a more specific level, we need better dating evidence both to test the sequence reconstructed here, and to refine our understanding of the relationship of Aldborough to other sites. Particular issues concern the dating of the street grid and bridge, and that of the latest defences. The former requires an improved understanding of the past local environment and, in particular, the relationship between the river and the town. More broadly, it would also be highly desirable to examine a more substantial contiguous area somewhere within the town to provide the kind of fuller understanding of it as a place, as has resulted from the excavations at Silchester.

Appendix 1
Gazetteer of archaeological interventions

This gazetteer is designed to provide a basic reference work on the site. It includes material available in the North Yorks Planning Office up to March 2018. In general, it is confined to records of work that have revealed structural remains of the Roman period, so individual stray finds have been omitted. Entries (referred to in the main text of this volume using the form **G1**, **G2**, etc) give the date of discovery, briefly summarise knowledge about the discovery, and provide a bibliography relating to the primary sources, omitting repetitions except where useful and appropriate (for example, with Ecroyd Smith's reporting of earlier finds). Plans are reproduced where helpful and otherwise difficult to access, and structures are cross-referenced to other investigations, including the Building numbers (Building 1.1, etc) used in the geophysical surveys published within this volume. Also included here are full cross-references to published inscriptions (*RIB* number), sculpture (*CSIR* number) and mosaics (citing the mosaic number from Neal and Cosh 2002). The authors have sought to locate all past discoveries as accurately as possible on their plans within Chapter 3. Where there is doubt about the precise location of a past findspot, the authors have evaluated the evidence and explained their conclusions within the text for each entry. Where possible, a National Grid Map Reference for the centre of the site has been included.

G1 Mosaics near the West Gate
SE 4048 6647
Before 1714
Mosaic described in the letter from the Reverend Edward Morris quoted by Gibson (1722). Its location is marked on Stephenson's map in the Stowe MS by the letter B (see fig 2.2). The mosaic was visited by antiquarians as early as 1692 (Lukis 1887, 281–2) and is described as being composed of 'stones of about an inch square; but within are little stones of a quarter that bigness, wrought into knots of flowers, after the mosaic fashion'. Since this description does not match any of the pavements in this part of the town identified from later sources and catalogued by Neal and Cosh (2002, nos 123.5–9), the authors have concluded that it is a separate pavement, although probably from same building as later finds (**G2, G19** and **G20** below).
Primary references: Stowe MS; Gibson 1722, 875; Lukis 1887, 281–2.
Location: recorded from Stephenson's map of 1708 (above, fig 2.2)

G2 Mosaics east of Aldborough Manor
SE 4047 6648
c 1732
Francis Drake's account of Aldborough (1736, 24–5) illustrates two mosaics found close together beneath a cottage. Later sources place these just to the east of Aldborough Manor where they presumably relate to the same building as **G1**, **G19** and **G20** (see fig 2.10). Neal and Cosh (2002) date the mosaics to the fourth century.
Primary references: Drake 1736, vol 1, 24–5, Pl opposite p 24, figs 1 and 2; Ecroyd Smith 1852, 35, Pl XII (bottom and top right).
Other key references: Neal and Cosh 2002, mosaic nos 123.4–5.
Location: shown on Ecroyd Smith 1852, Pl III.

G3 Mosaics on Borough Hill
SE 4059 6629
1683
Francis Drake's account also includes a description and illustrations of mosaics and other finds from Borough Hill in the centre of Aldborough (1736, 25–6, fig 2.3). His account notes the presence of substantial walls as well as three mosaics and a pair of column bases. For the column bases, see this volume, Appendix 4, nos 15–16. Moore-Jessop (1849) dates this to 1683; Neal and Cosh (2002) suggest that the mosaics are fourth century. These finds relate to Building 5.2 in the authors' survey.
Primary references: Drake 1736, vol 1, 24–5, Pl opposite p 24, figs 3 and 4; vol 2, xiii–xiv, Pl p xiii, nos 12–15; Moore-Jessop 1849, 74; Ecroyd Smith 1852, 42–3, mosaics Pl XIX and finds; Pl XX columns nos 4–5.
Other key references: Neal and Cosh 2002, mosaic nos 123.1–3.
Location: shown schematically on Drake 1736, vol 1, Pl p 22 (fig 2.3) but cannot be precisely located although buildings in this area are clearly revealed in the geophysical survey.

G4 Hypocaust near Aldborough Manor
SE 4046 6648
1762
Richard Gough notes in his edition of Camden's *Britannia* (1789) that four or five circular pillars from a hypocaust were found behind the Globe Alehouse '20 yards south or south-west from the pavements' (**G2**). It is presumably part of the same building.
Primary references: Gough 1789, 59; Ecroyd Smith 1852, 35.
Location: Not shown on Ecroyd Smith 1852, Pl III or elsewhere. Position on fig 3.11 is based on Gough's text on the understanding that he is referring to the mosaic described under **G2**.

G5 Mosaic beneath the vicarage of St Andrew's church
SE 4065 6637
Before 1789
Richard Gough (1789) also notes the discovery of a mosaic in the garden of the parsonage; Ecroyd Smith remarks that with rebuilding, this lay beneath the vicarage by 1852.
Primary references: Gough 1789, 59; Ecroyd Smith 1852, 43.
Location: shown on Ecroyd Smith 1852, Pl III. Comparison with the position of the garden on the 1708 map (fig 2.2), locates it fairly well but without precision.

G6 North Range of *Forum* to the north of St Andrew's church
SE 4060 6645
1770
William Stukeley's *Itinerarium Curiosum* (1776) notes that 'some very great buildings' were located in the street before the church, indicating that ruins were visible at the time of his visit in the earlier eighteenth century. Richard Gough's edition of Camden's *Britannia* (1789) records the excavation of these structures during work to rebuild the churchyard wall in 1770. There was 'discovered a double row of stone walls parallel to each other and joined by transverse ones. The side walls extend nearly from the south-east to north-west above 220 feet, at the distance of 18 feet. They are all strongly cemented, and three feet thick, and five feet below the present surface. A drain crossed them nearly about the middle, the top and sides composed of tiles 16 inches by 11 ½ and one inch and half thick… At **e** was found an urn, and at **a** a gold coin of Trajan, IMP. TRAIANO AVG. GER. DAC. P. M. TR. P. COS. VI. P.P. rev. a figure standing holding in its right hand a *patera*, in its left an ear of corn, S. P. Q. R. OPTIMO PRINCIPI.' This account is accompanied by an illustration (see fig 2.4) that shows the range of buildings in relation to the position of the church. However, the findspots noted are not shown on this published plan.

The find was reported in *The Oxford Times* for 28 July 1770, stating that the discovery took place around between 16 and 20 July.[1] An unpublished plan in one of the notebooks of William Hargrove shows the same features in relation to the buildings on the opposite side of the road, but omits the church (see fig 2.5). This is clearly related to the plan in Gough's publication as it shows the locations of the findspots he mentions. It is inferred that the unpublished drawing probably originated with William Hargrove's father, Ely Hargrove (above, p. 18).

Ground Penetrating Radar survey, followed by small scale re-excavation in 2017, confirmed the accuracy of the plans and the precise location of the walls (**G105**, see fig 3.14).
Primary references: Stukeley 1776, 73; Gough 1789, 59; Ecroyd Smith 1852, 47.
Location: Gough 1789, vol III, p 61, Pl III; Hargrove MS vol III, 90; Ecroyd Smith 1852, Pl III.

G7 Cemetery outside South Gate at Chapel Hill
SE 4047 6598
1808 and 1846
Cremation burials and eighteen skeletons were discovered during the widening of the road cutting at Chapel Hill. It is possible that a tombstone (*RIB* 710) comes from the same site (above, p. 18). Ecroyd Smith notes two further cremations having been found in 1846.
Primary references: Hargrove 1818, vol II, 359; Moore-Jessop 1849, 75; Ecroyd Smith 1852, 21; Turner 1853, 98.
Other key references: *RIB* 710.
Location: Described in Ecroyd Smith 1852, 21, but not located on his plan.

G8 West Gate of Town
SE 4045 6651
c 1840s
Ecroyd Smith (1852) notes the discovery of the West Gate and a substantial hinge-pivot block adjacent to the Manor House. He illustrates the block, but does not provide a plan. An unpublished sketch-plan, however, shows its location beneath the road to the north of the house (see fig 2.10), which has been confirmed in the authors' Ground Penetrating Radar survey (see fig 3.11). For hinge block, see Appendix 4, no 38.
Primary references: Ecroyd Smith 1852, Pl III C, p 13, Pl XXII, fig 1.
Location: Unpublished sketch plan (see fig 2.10).

G9 Town Wall to south of the West Gate
SE 4041 6644
1794
Stretch of the Town Wall opened in the garden of Aldborough Manor.
Primary reference: Ecroyd Smith 1852, 13–14.
Location: Ecroyd Smith 1852, Pl III, adjacent to G.

G10 Buildings, including baths, in garden of Aldborough Manor
SE 4041 6644
1830
Group of buildings, including a domestic bath-house, excavated adjacent to the Town Wall in the garden of Aldborough Manor (see fig 1.5). Two mosaics are dated to the fourth century by Neal and Cosh (2002).
Primary references: Ecroyd Smith 1852, Pl III (see fig 2.8); mosaics Pl XVII, 2 and 3; painted plaster Pl IV and pp 15–16. The plan of a bath-house shown on Pl XIV, b (fig A1) may represent part of this building but it is difficult to relate this to the small-scale published plans. These structures formed part of Building 4.2 in the authors' survey.
Other key references: Neal and Cosh 2002, mosaic nos 123.11–12.
Location: Ecroyd Smith 1852, Pl III, G, but no detailed plan provided. The excavation remained open into the twentieth century, and is shown on Ordnance Survey maps.

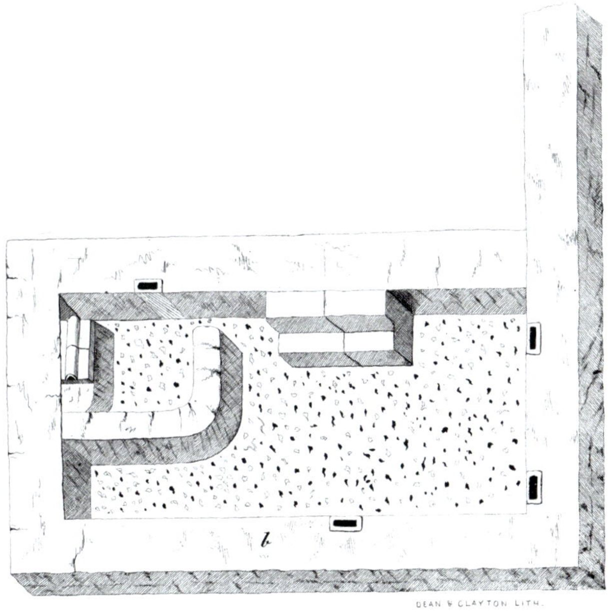

Fig A1 Plan of the baths (**G10**) from Ecroyd Smith 1852, Pl XIV. Original illustration by M N Hessey

---

G11 Buildings, including baths, and a stretch of the Town Wall in garden of Aldborough Manor
SE 4037 6632
c 1849
Range of buildings including a domestic bath-house beside a stretch of the town wall in the garden of Aldborough Manor (figs 2.6 and A2). This was identified by its excavators as a 'barracks' although it is evidently a range of domestic buildings.
Primary references: Ecroyd Smith 1852, 17–18 (where it is wrongly located at H on Pl III, rather than at K), Pl V (with vignette showing details).
Location: Ecroyd Smith 1852, Pl III K. The foundations are still visible so have been precisely georeferenced.

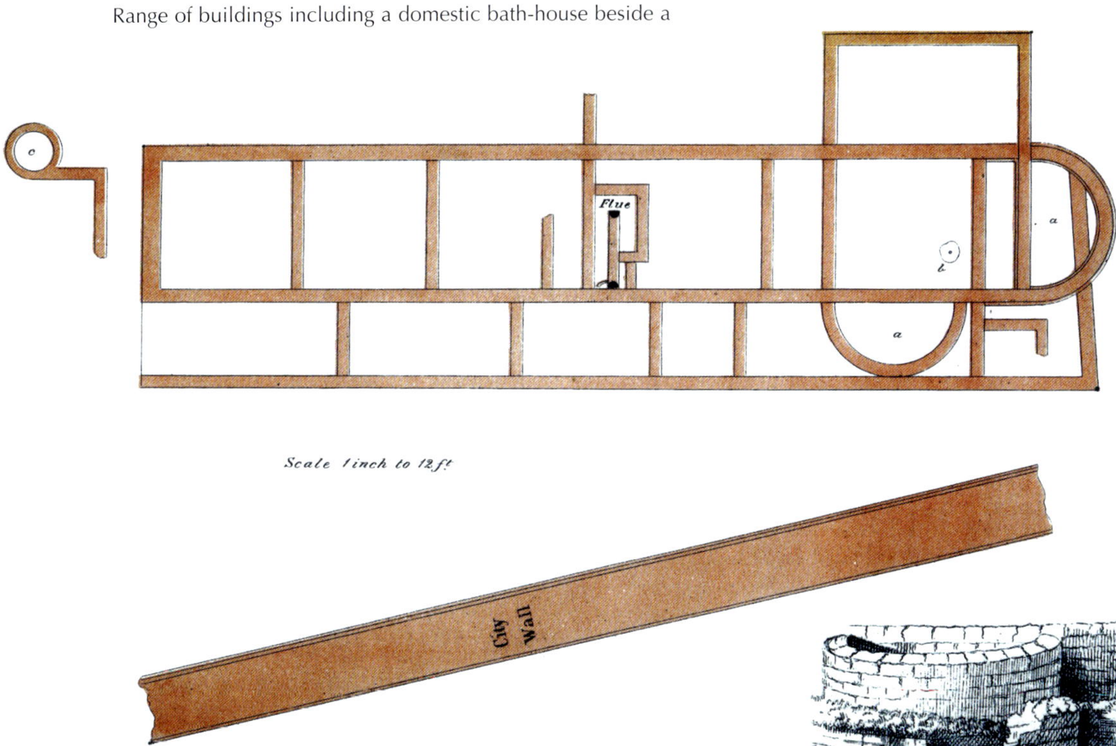

Fig A2 Plan and sketch of so-called barracks (**G11**) and adjacent stretch of the Town Wall from Ecroyd Smith 1852, Pl V. Original illustration by M N Hessey

G12 Burials outside south-west corner of Town Wall
SE 4029 6624
c 1840s
Cremation burials and supposed *bustum* excavated in Andrew Lawson's work in the 1840s.
Primary references: Ecroyd Smith 1852, 19 and Pl VII.
Location: Ecroyd Smith 1852, Pl III B.

G13 Southern stretch of Town Wall, western end
A: SE 4034 6622, B: SE 4039 6619, C: SE 4045 6617
c 1840s and 1967–73
Three stretches of the Town Wall, including the south-western corner and a length leading almost as far east as the South Gate, were excavated in the 1840s and laid out as part of the garden of Aldborough Manor (fig 3.18). These are illustrated by Ecroyd Smith, but without substantial description (fig A3). They were partially re-examined by Dorothy Charlesworth who published a discussion, with further reporting completed by Snape *et al.* Ecroyd Smith records the discovery of human burials in one of the wall towers. This stretch of wall includes two internal towers, rectangular in plan. Stone-by-stone drawings of the wall faces were completed by Alan Whitworth in 1991 for a condition survey. They are held in the Historic England archive at Helmsley.
Primary references: Ecroyd Smith 1852, 21, Pl VIII; Charlesworth 1971, 163; Snape *et al* 2002, 64–9.
Location: Ecroyd Smith 1852, Pl III; detail is also shown on OS maps.

G14 Burials or kilns outside the walls to the south east
SE 408 661
1846
Moore-Jessop notes the excavation of supposed graves at Redhills in 1846. Ecroyd Smith illustrates these, describing them as *sarcophagi*. However, neither description mentions human bones and Ecroyd Smith's illustrations suggest that they were pottery kilns, a conclusion supported by the records of ash and burning (fig A4).
Primary references: Moore-Jessop 1849, 75; Ecroyd Smith 1852, Pl III, 25–6, Pl X.
Location: Ecroyd Smith 1852, Pl III, labelled as 'Red Graves'.

G15 Studforth Hill earthworks
SE 4067 6600
c 1840s
Ecroyd Smith records earthworks on Studforth Hill, just outside the south-eastern corner of the Town Wall (figs 3.27, 3.28 and A5). He interpreted these as evidence for a stadium. It is clear that these features are, in fact, a well-preserved stretch of the defensive ditches surrounding the Town Wall, with a later field boundary on top. A tree-covered mound a little further to the south east was identified by R G Collingwood (1930, 106, fig 26, e) as part of an amphitheatre, a conclusion he himself had doubted in 1927 (p 10), but which is now confirmed by the authors' survey. Myres *et al* (1959, 5, n 4) note the excavation of a trench in 1935 on the northern bank, which suggested that it was apparently natural. The location of this trench is not recorded. An altar with a sculptural frieze is recorded as having been found here: it is not listed in *CSIR* (fig 3.26).
Primary references: Ecroyd Smith 1852, 23, Pl IX, 46, Pl XXI no 7 (altar = Appendix 5, no 4)
Location: Ecroyd Smith 1852, Pl III.

Fig A3 Illustration from Ecroyd Smith 1852 showing part of the southern stretch of the Town Wall (**G13**). Original illustration by M N Hessey

Fig A4 Illustration from Ecroyd Smith 1852 showing two probable kilns at Redhills (**G14**) originally interpreted as sarcophagi. Original illustration by M N Hessey

G16 East Gate of town
SE 4080 6640
1772
Ecroyd Smith identifies two hinge pivot blocks found at the location of the East Gate, but he does not provide further information on the circumstances. See this volume, Appendix 4, nos 39–40.
Primary references: Ecroyd Smith 1852, 13, 27 and Pl XXII nos 7 and 8.
Location: Ecroyd Smith 1852, 13, Pl III, F; this general position for the gate is confirmed by the survey in this volume.

G17 Garden of Aldborough Hall
SE 407 664
c 1840s
Statue of Mercury found within the grounds of Aldborough Hall.
Primary references: Ecroyd Smith 1852, 27 and Pl XI no 1.
Other key references: CSIR vol 1, Fasc 3, no 16, Pl 4.
Location: Not shown on Ecroyd Smith 1852, Pl III, but location marked on OS maps.

G18 Outside Town Wall to north of West Gate
SE 404 665
c 1840s
Ecroyd Smith notes the discovery of cremation urns and coins.
Primary references: Ecroyd Smith 1852, 27.
Location: Ecroyd Smith 1852, Pl III.

Fig A5 Illustration from Ecroyd Smith 1852 showing Studforth Hill, the amphitheatre (**G15**). Original illustration by M N Hessey

G19 Mosaics at Globe Alehouse, east of Aldborough Manor
SE 4049 6645
c 1780
Ecroyd Smith notes the discovery of mosaics that were displayed in a purpose-built structure behind the Globe Alehouse, the site of the original Manor House (fig 2.10). The principal pavement remains *in situ*, but is not now visible. They presumably relate to the same building as **G1**, **G2** and **G20**. Neal and Cosh (2002) date the main pavement to the fourth century.
Primary references: Ecroyd Smith 1852, 35, Pl XIII; photograph in Leadman 1893, Pl opposite p 420.
Other key references: Neal and Cosh 2002, mosaic nos 123.8, 123.9, and perhaps 123.10.
Location: Ecroyd Smith 1852, Pl III. The covered building is shown on Ordnance Survey maps.

G20 Corridor with mosaics behind Aldborough Manor
SE 4045 6647
c 1846
Ecroyd Smith describes and illustrates a corridor more than 30ft in length with mosaic floors and two *in situ* column bases set to the east, implying the presence of a courtyard (fig 3.13). For the column bases, see Appendix 4, nos 9 and 10. Neal and Cosh date the mosaic to the fourth century. This is probably part of the same building as **G1**, **G2** and **G19.**
Primary references: Ecroyd Smith 1852, 36, Pl XIV (mosaics and column bases).
Other key references: Neal and Cosh 2002, no 123.17.
Location: Ecroyd Smith 1852, Pl III shows the general position, as does an unpublished sketch plan (fig 2.10). The precise location is more problematic, but it is clear from Ecroyd Smith that these pavements were covered in and the room used as the first location for Andrew Lawson's Museum Isurianum (Lawson 1864, 45–9). Given the layout of the Manor House at this date, the authors have located the mosaics as precisely as is possible using this evidence and the sketch plan. It should be noted that the authors' conclusion about the position of these mosaics has changed since the publication of the English Heritage Guidebook (Millett and Ferraby 2016).

G21 Hypocaust beside the old School House (now the Village Hall)
SE 4052 6646
c 1840s
Ecroyd Smith illustrates a plan of a hypocaust found 'lately' adjacent to the School House.
Primary references: Ecroyd Smith 1852, 36–7, Pl XIV, a.
Location: Ecroyd Smith 1852, Pl III shows the location which the authors have georeferenced in relation to the standing building, now the Village Hall. The orientation of the structure shown by Ecroyd Smith is on the same alignment as the northern range of the *forum* (**G6**), although he recorded that inaccurately. The unpublished sketch plan of this area (fig 2.10) shows it at a more distinct angle to the School, aligned with other structures in this part of the town. This seems more likely to be correct.

G22 Mosaics behind the Aldburgh Arms
SE 4048 6630
1832 and 1848
The accidental discovery of a mosaic showing a lion (fig 2.11) during the burial of a calf in 1832, led to its excavation and display in a small brick-built structure. Later excavation revealed a further mosaic (fig A6) a little to the west as well as the corner of a courtyard building including a bath suite. The second mosaic was displayed in a stone-built structure. Both now form part of the English Heritage site display. Small-scale re-excavation of the bath-suite in 2016 (**G104**) confirmed the accuracy of Ecroyd Smith's plan (fig 3.19). Neal and Cosh date the mosaics to the later second century. These mosaics relate to Buildings 4.8 and 4.9 in the authors' survey.
Primary references: Ecroyd Smith 1852, 17–18, 37–41; Plan Pl XV (with vignettes), painted plaster P VI, mosaics Pls XVI and XVII; flue tile Pl XX no 3.
Other key references: Neal and Cosh 2002, mosaic nos 123.13 and 14.
Location: Ecroyd Smith 1852, Pl III, I. Location georeferenced during the authors' excavations in 2016 (**G104**).

G23 Building with apse and mosaic floors behind the Aldburgh Arms
SE 4047 6627
1846
Excavations revealed a substantial building with an apse at its western end, although the north side had been lost thorough later erosion (fig 3.20). This was identified at the time as a *basilica*, although it is most likely a dining room from a private house. The main mosaic features a scene of the muses, and includes an inscription in Greek, hence it is often referred to as the Helicon Mosaic. This was displayed *in situ* until the 1960s, when it was backfilled. Re-excavation in the 1970s, first by Dorothy Charlesworth in 1974, then by Stephen Johnson in 1979, was followed by the lifting of the surviving figural fragment which is now displayed in the English Heritage site museum. Neal and Cosh date the pavements to the fourth century. This building equates with Building 4.10 in the authors' survey.

Ecroyd Smith's plan shows a burial, and further human remains were uncovered by Charlesworth. These were radiocarbon dated and shown to be late Roman (above, Chapter 4, n 231).
Primary references: Ecroyd Smith 1852, 41–42, Pl XVIII; Re-excavation, Johnson and Neal 2002.
Other key references: Neal and Cosh 2002, mosaic nos 123.15 and 16; inscription *RIB* 2448.5, also discussed by Ling 2007, 71–4.
Location: Ecroyd Smith 1852, Pl III, J.

Fig A6 Illustration from Ecroyd Smith 1852 showing the star mosaic (**G22**) from Building 4.8. Original illustration by M N Hessey

G24 Mosaic to north of Low Road
SE 4068 6650
1827
Ecroyd Smith notes a mosaic found in 1827 to the north east of the church which, although then preserved and covered with a building, was later destroyed. The text shows that it was located on a farm, now identified as Hall Farm.

Primary references: Ecroyd Smith 1852, 43.
Other key references: Neal and Cosh 2002, mosaic no. 123.22.
Location: Ecroyd Smith 1852, Pl III, labelled as 'pavement destroyed'; a location is shown on a manuscript plan labelled 'Barber's Plan' in the English Heritage archive at Swindon (CHA01/02/01/003), the authority for which is uncertain, but it is used as the basis for the location shown here.

G25 Walls to the west of the church
SE 405 664
c 1840s
Ecroyd Smith notes the discovery of walls 'lately discovered a little west of the church' (fig A7). This includes a series of drainage gullies suggesting a courtyard (see this volume, Appendix 4, nos 41–4).
Primary references: Ecroyd Smith 1852, 47 plan p 44.
Location: Ecroyd Smith 1852, Pl III, A. This locates it within the area of the nineteenth-century churchyard extension, although it is not identifiable on the Ground Penetrating Radar survey of this area (above, p. 43). The orientation shown by Ecroyd Smith is suspect (cf **G21** above).

G26 Foundations north of Low Road
SE 405 664
c 1840s
Primary references: although marked on Ecroyd Smith's plan, there is no apparent mention of these remains within his text.
Location: Ecroyd Smith 1852, Pl III labelled 'foundations lately discovered'. The position must lie close to **G47**.

G27 Floor in Aldborough Manor Gardens
SE 4044 6642
c 1840s
Primary references: shown on Ecroyd Smith's plan, but not discussed in his text.
Location: Ecroyd Smith 1852, Pl III labelled 'lime floor'. The position is *c* 20m west of **G10** but cannot be precisely located. It may form part of Building 4.1.

G28 Hypocaust and foundations in Aldborough Manor Gardens
A: SE 4042 6636 (hypocaust), B: SE 4041 6635 (foundations)
1851
Both are shown close together on Ecroyd Smith's plan, but are not discussed in his text. It should be noted that this is shown 'as found in 1854 on Leadman's (1893) plan. These structures can be identified within Building 4.5 in the authors' survey.
Location: Shown on Ecroyd Smith 1852, Pl III. They have been precisely located using the authors' GPR survey (fig 3.17).

G29 Altars found between Boroughbridge and Aldborough
Approximately SE 3981 6661
Before 1779
Richard Gough provides two illustrations of uninscribed altars discovered 'betwixt the two towns'; Ecroyd Smith illustrates another (with an inscription, now known to be a modern fabrication) found 'near those just mentioned'.
Primary references: Gough 1789, 59, Pl II p 44, nos 7 and 8; Ecroyd Smith 1852, 45, Pl XXI, nos 1, 2 and 6.
Other key references: Kewley 1970, cat nos 618 & 619; *RIB* 2347*; Appendix 5, nos 2–3
Location: precise location uncertain. The grid reference given is that of the location shown on OS maps from the 1890s onwards, although the authority on which this is based is unknown. It should also be noted that the Roman altars shown on early OS maps in the ground just to the west of the Manor garden refer to features in the garden layout, not the original findspot of these altars.

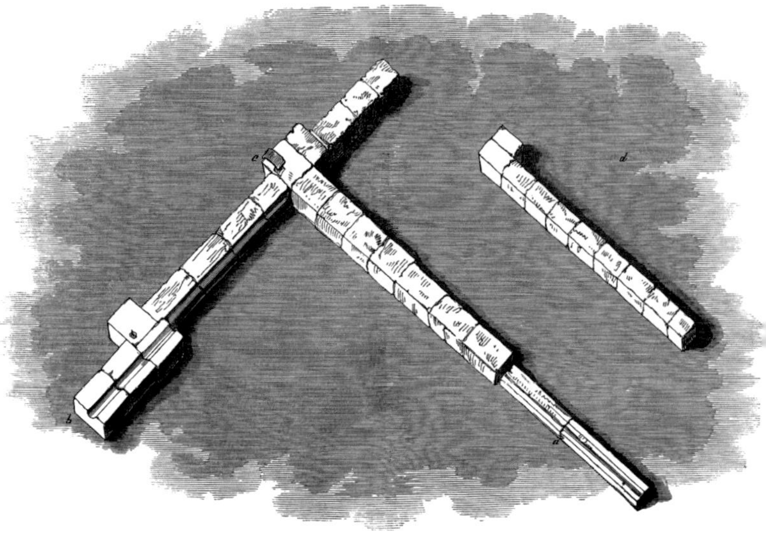

Fig A7 Illustration from Ecroyd Smith 1852 showing foundations excavated to the west of the church (**G25**). Original illustration by M N Hessey

G30 Quarry to the south west of the Town Wall
SE 4030 6618
Before 1852
This quarry (Quarry 13.1 in the authors' survey) lies just outside the corner of the Town Wall and was modified as part of the design of the nineteenth-century gardens. This included the addition of steps and specialist planting, as well as the construction of a viewing mound to its north (fig 3.45 and 3.46). Ecroyd Smith suggests that it is recent, but recent fieldwork indicates that its earlier phases were Roman, perhaps starting from a cutting through rock at the corner of the defensive ditches (above, p. 85).
Primary reference: Ecroyd Smith 1852, 61; Ferraby in preparation.
Location: still open and shown on OS maps.

G31 Romulus and Remus mosaic near East Gate
SE 407 663
c 1840
In a note published after the appearance of his book, Ecroyd Smith says that he was aware of this pavement but omitted it from his 1852 publication for good reasons. It is noted by Moore-Jessop (1862) that it was 'restored' by a local bricklayer. It is almost certainly a fake, made using genuine *tesserae* and based on the central square of the Lion mosaic (**G22**), a conclusion also reached recently by Larionov 2015.
Primary references: Moore-Jessop 1862, 164; Ecroyd Smith 1859–68.

Other key references: Neal and Cosh 2002, mosaic no 123.19.
Location: Ecroyd Smith 1859–68 places it imprecisely adjacent to Aldborough Hall and the East Gate, south of the (then) main road through the village.

G32 Hypocaust in the garden of 'Rose Mead', behind Aldborough Manor
SE 4045 6633
Early twentieth century
A photograph in the archive of the Lawson-Tancred family shows an excavated hypocaust with a man seated on the trench edge, and a distinctive brick wall behind (fig A8). The photograph has no annotation or date, but the photographer, T J Hanstock of York, was active from 1908. The photo mount matches another showing **G10** in an overgrown state, which is also probably of early twentieth-century date. This would tie in with a note in Lady Lawson-Tancred's guidebook (1948, 13), that excavations continued on the site down to 1913.
Primary reference: unpublished.
Location: The walling type is distinctive and typical of those in the Manor gardens. It can be identified as the southern garden wall at the south-western corner of the garden of 'Rose Mead'.

G33 Sections cut through the Roman road outside the North Gate
Section 1: SE 4075 6699, Section 2: SE 4075 6694, Section A: SE 4076 6689, Section B: SE 4076 6687, Section C: SE 4076 6685; Section D: SE 4075 6681, Section E: SE 4075 6679, Section F: SE 4074 6676, Section G: SE 4073 6675, Section H: SE 4072 6674, Section I: SE 4072 6673, Section J: SE 4072 6672, Section K: SE 4071 6670
1924
Excavations by S C Barber, C A Ridley and G F Dimmock in 1924 included the cutting of a series of sections to trace the route of the Roman road to the north of the North Gate (figs A9 and A10). A copy of the typescript of their unpublished report (Barber *et al* 1925) includes plans and photographs showing the results of these excavations. In addition to their work at the North Gate (**G34**), they cut twelve sections across the line of the road (labelled Sections 1–2, and A–J). Their conclusion (based on observations in Section D) that a second road cut across from this one to join that to York, by-passing the town walls, has now been disproved by the survey (Dobinson *et al* 2018, 32–3; above, p. 74). However, their observations on the general line of the road are accurate.
Primary references: Barber *et al* 1925.
Location: Barber *et al* 1925, plan A provides sound locational information. Accurately mapped in project archive.

Fig A8 Photograph showing the excavation of a hypocaust (**G32**), uncovered in the early twentieth century, viewed from the north west.
Photograph: T J Hanstock. Reproduced by courtesy of Sir Andrew Lawson-Tancred

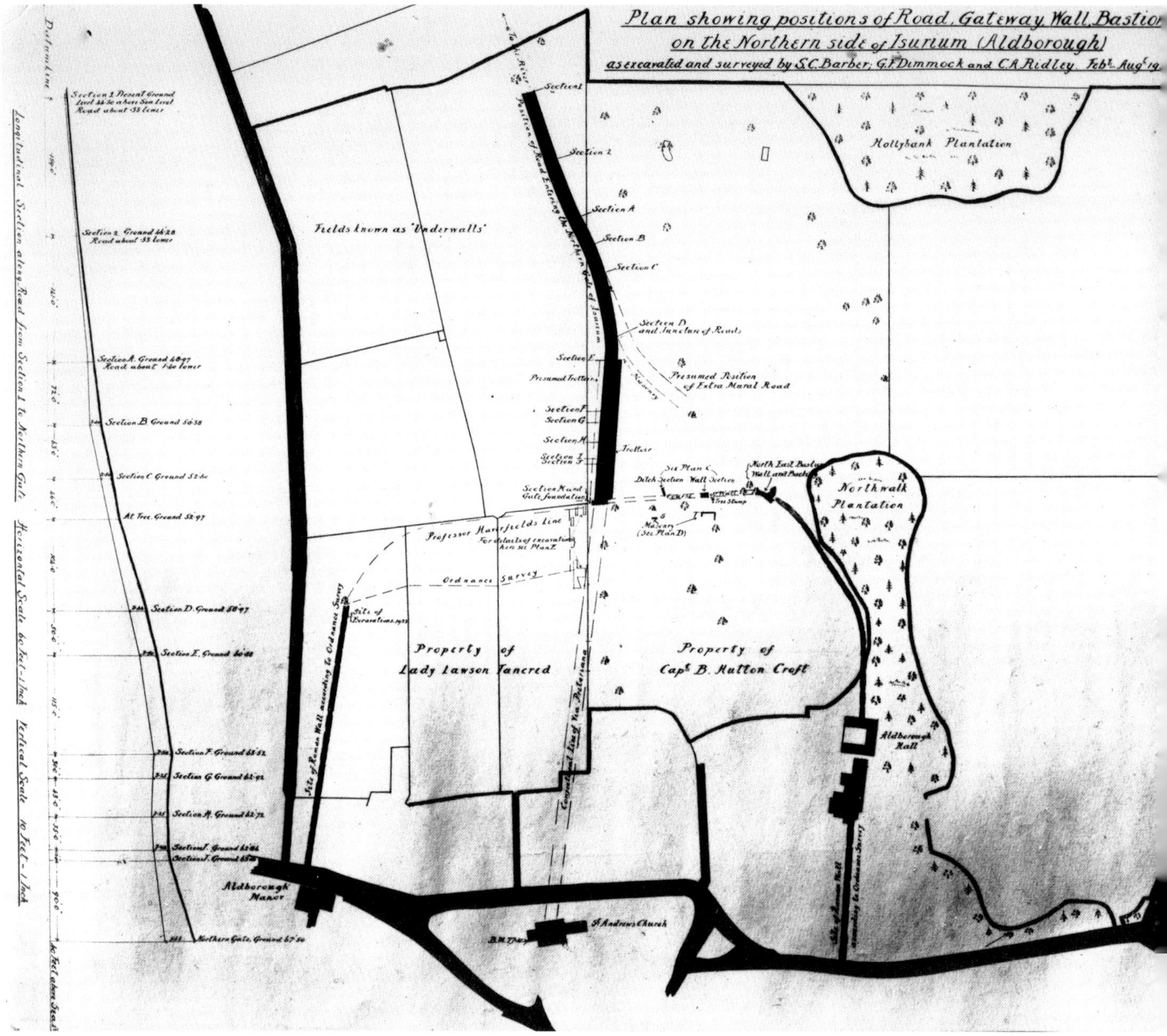

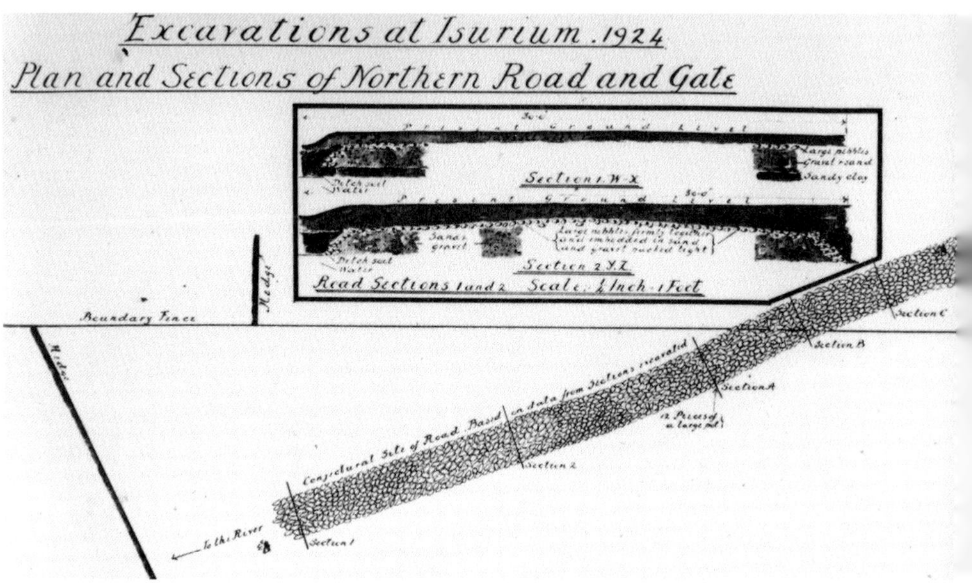

Fig A9 Plan showing the location of the trenches excavated by S C Barber, C A Ridley and G F Dimmock at Aldborough in 1924 (Barber *et al* 1925). *Drawing:* C A Ridley. Reproduced by courtesy of Sir Andrew Lawson-Tancred

Fig A10 Plan showing the trenches excavated by Barber *et al* across the Roman road outside the North Gate (**G33**) in 1924. *Drawing:* C A Ridley. Reproduced by courtesy of Sir Andrew Lawson-Tancred

G34 North Gate of the town and area just within
1924: Trench 1: SE 4071 6670, Trench 2: SE 4069 6670,
Trench 3: SE 4068 6666
1938: Site G: SE 4070 6670, Site E: SE 4072 6670,
Site F: SE 4071 6670

1924 and 1938

The most southerly of the sections cut in 1924 by Barber *et al* (**G33**), section K (fig A11), was complemented by a wider area of excavation (fig A12). Here, numbers 1–3 have been assigned to these trenches as they were not labelled on original plans. Trench 1 revealed elements of the North Gate, including part of the foundation of the western gate pier and an apparent blocking of the eastern portal, although the report is brief and confused (fig A12). A further drawing (plan E) provides evidence for the wall immediately to the west of the gate (Trench 2), including a possible guard chamber or internal tower (fig A13). Soundings within the town *c* 40m to the south revealed foundations that must lie just west of the road leading to the gate. Their plan of this (fig A14) (Trench 3) seems to show a wall flanking the western side of the street, with column bases, conceivably forming a colonnade (fig 2.14). These form part of Building 1.10 in the authors' survey. An inscribed milestone (*RIB* 2277) and architectural fragments were recovered from this excavation (fig A15); one of the plans shows their findspots (fig A14). Architectural stonework – Appendix 4, nos 13, 14 and 37.

Myres *et al* re-examined the gate itself in 1938 (their sites E, F and G), exposing a larger area, including the base of a stone water storage tank just inside the line of the town wall (fig A16). They did not uncover the whole of the plan of the gate. They did, however, cut a section through the road, revealing nine surfaces, and providing some dating evidence. This included material contemporary with the gate construction, which suggested a mid-second century *terminus post quem*. Fragments of stone water tank – Appendix 4, nos 47–48.

Primary references: Barber *et al* 1925; Myres *et al* 1959, 55–8, fig 21, pl IVB.
Other key references: Milestone from Trench 3, *RIB* 2277.
Location: Barber *et al* 1925, plans A and E provide information but are difficult to assess; Myres *et al* 1959, fig 21 gives sound locational information. Accurately mapped in project archive.

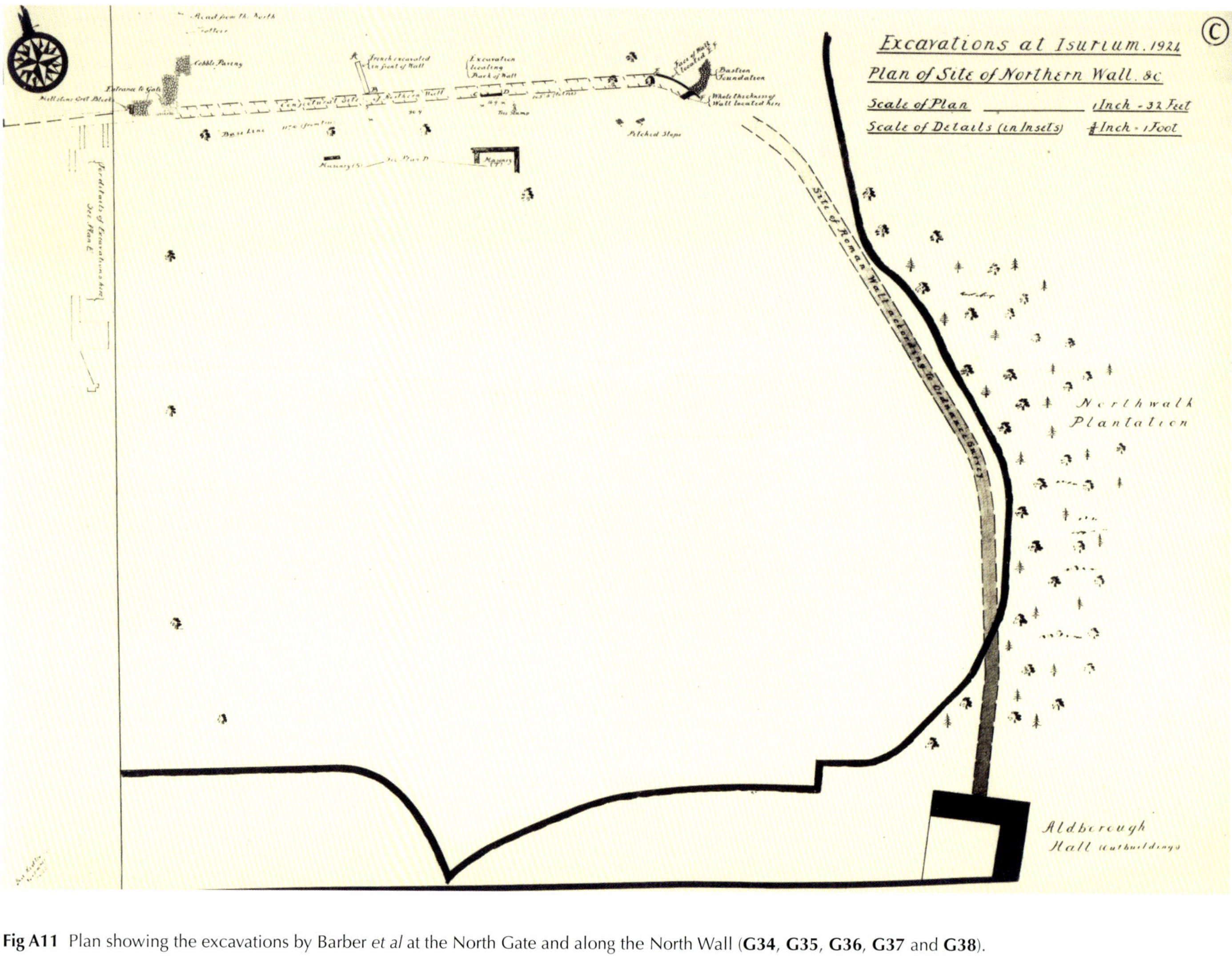

Fig A11 Plan showing the excavations by Barber *et al* at the North Gate and along the North Wall (**G34**, **G35**, **G36**, **G37** and **G38**).
Drawing: C A Ridley. Reproduced by courtesy of Sir Andrew Lawson-Tancred

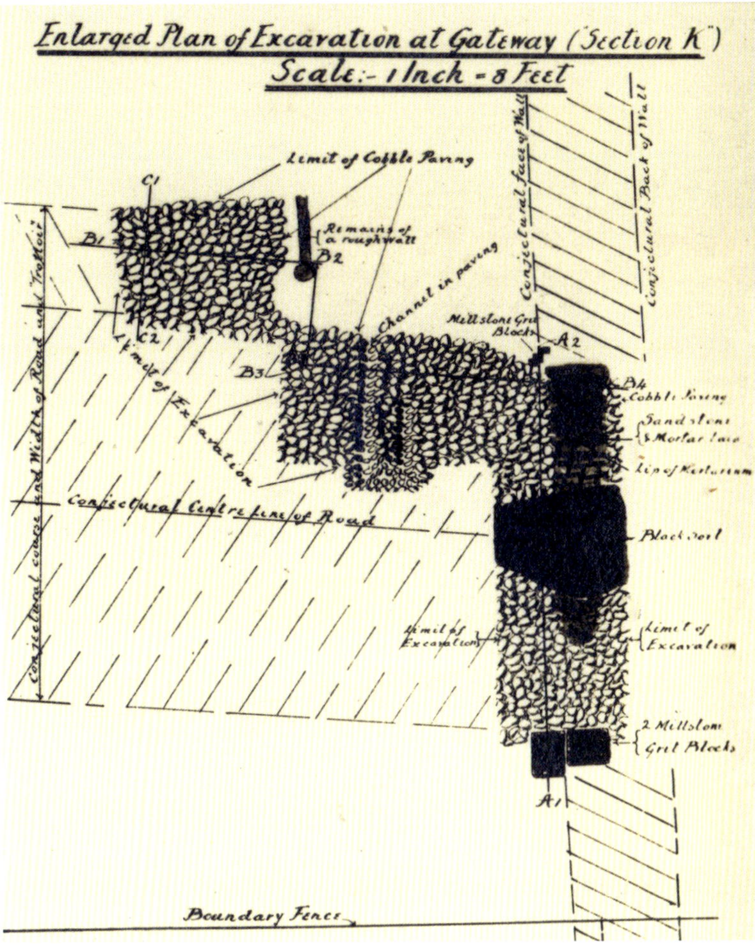

Fig A12 Plan of the excavations (**G34/1**) by Barber *et al* at the North Gate in 1924. Note: north is to the left. *Drawing:* C A Ridley. Reproduced by courtesy of Sir Andrew Lawson-Tancred

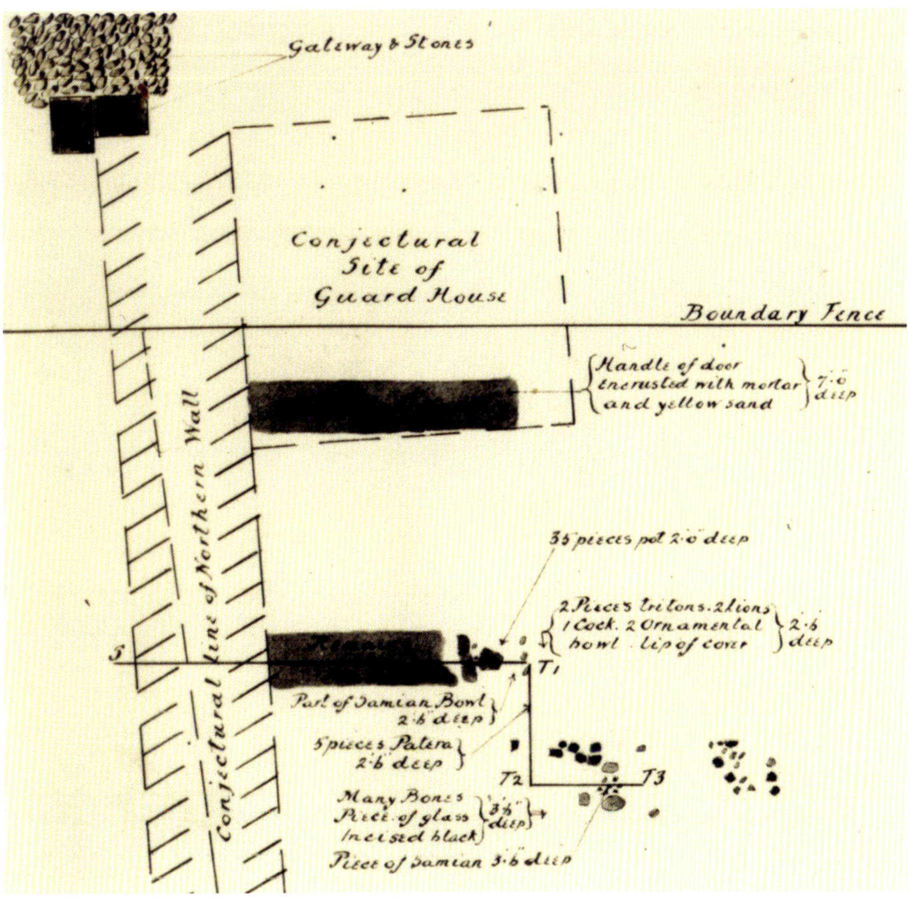

Fig A13 Plan of the excavations (**G34/2**) by Barber *et al* just to the west of the North Gate in 1924. Note: north is to the left. *Drawing:* C A Ridley. Reproduced by courtesy of Sir Andrew Lawson-Tancred

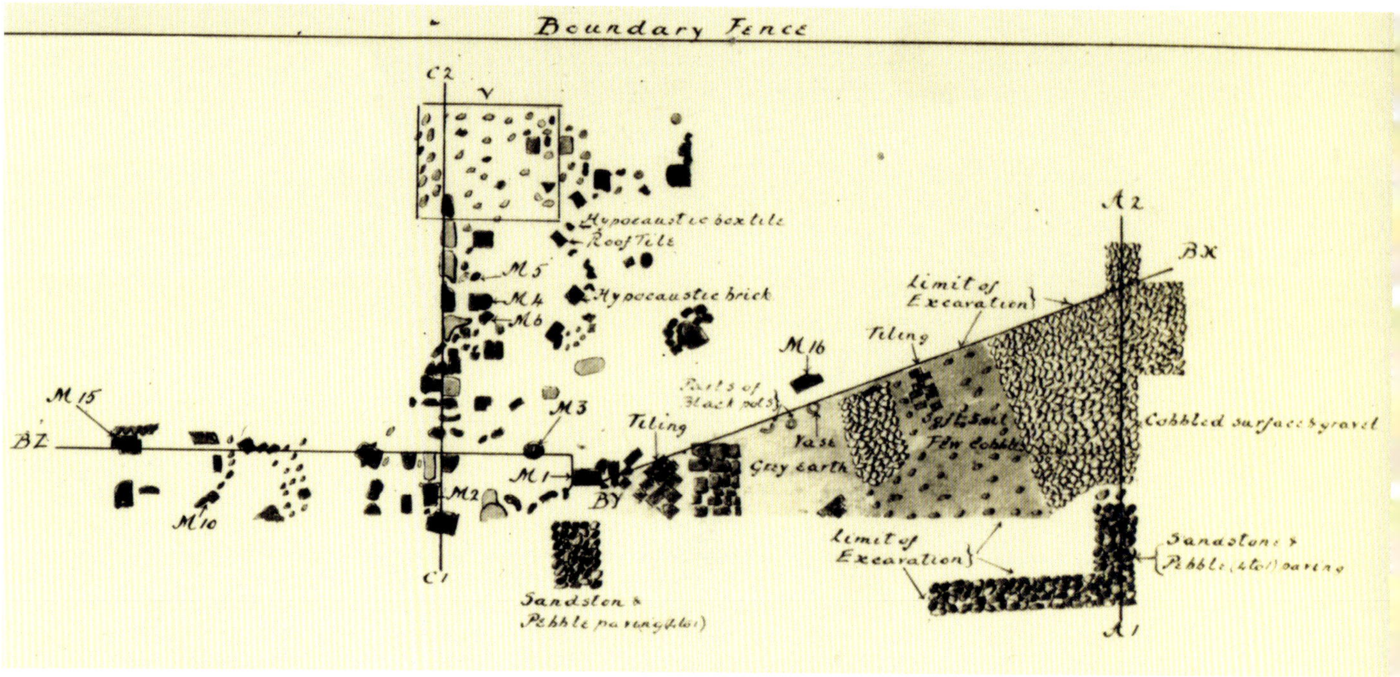

Fig A14 Plan of the excavations (**G34/3**) by Barber *et al* inside the North Gate in 1924. Note: north is to the left. *Drawing:* C A Ridley. (Reproduced by courtesy of Sir Andrew Lawson-Tancred)

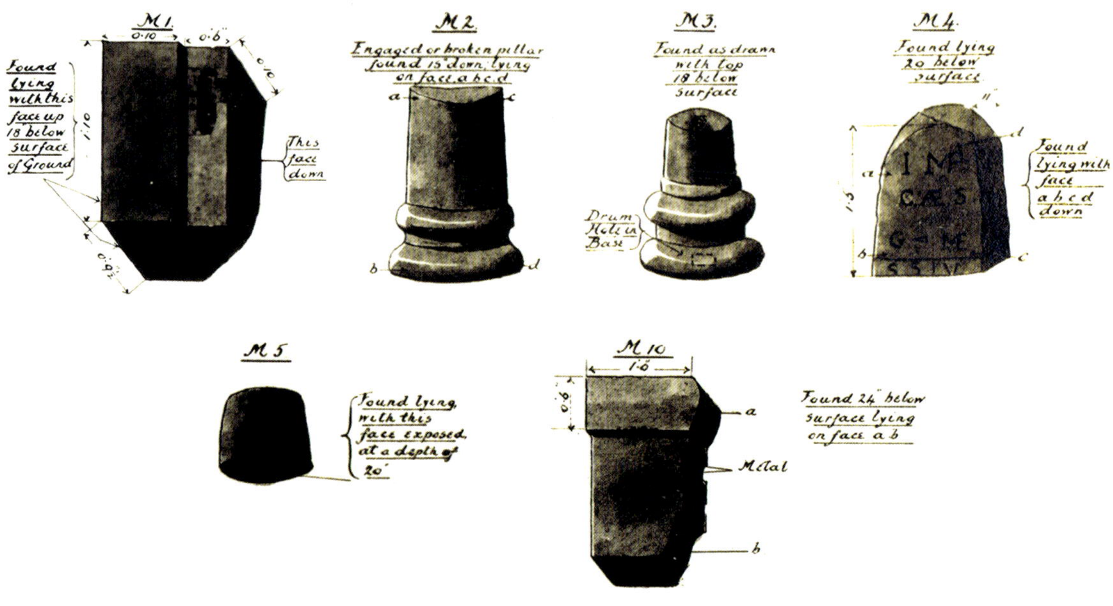

Fig A15 Drawing of the sculpted stone from the excavations by Barber *et al* inside the North Gate (**G34/3**). *Drawing:* C A Ridley. Reproduced by courtesy of Sir Andrew Lawson-Tancred

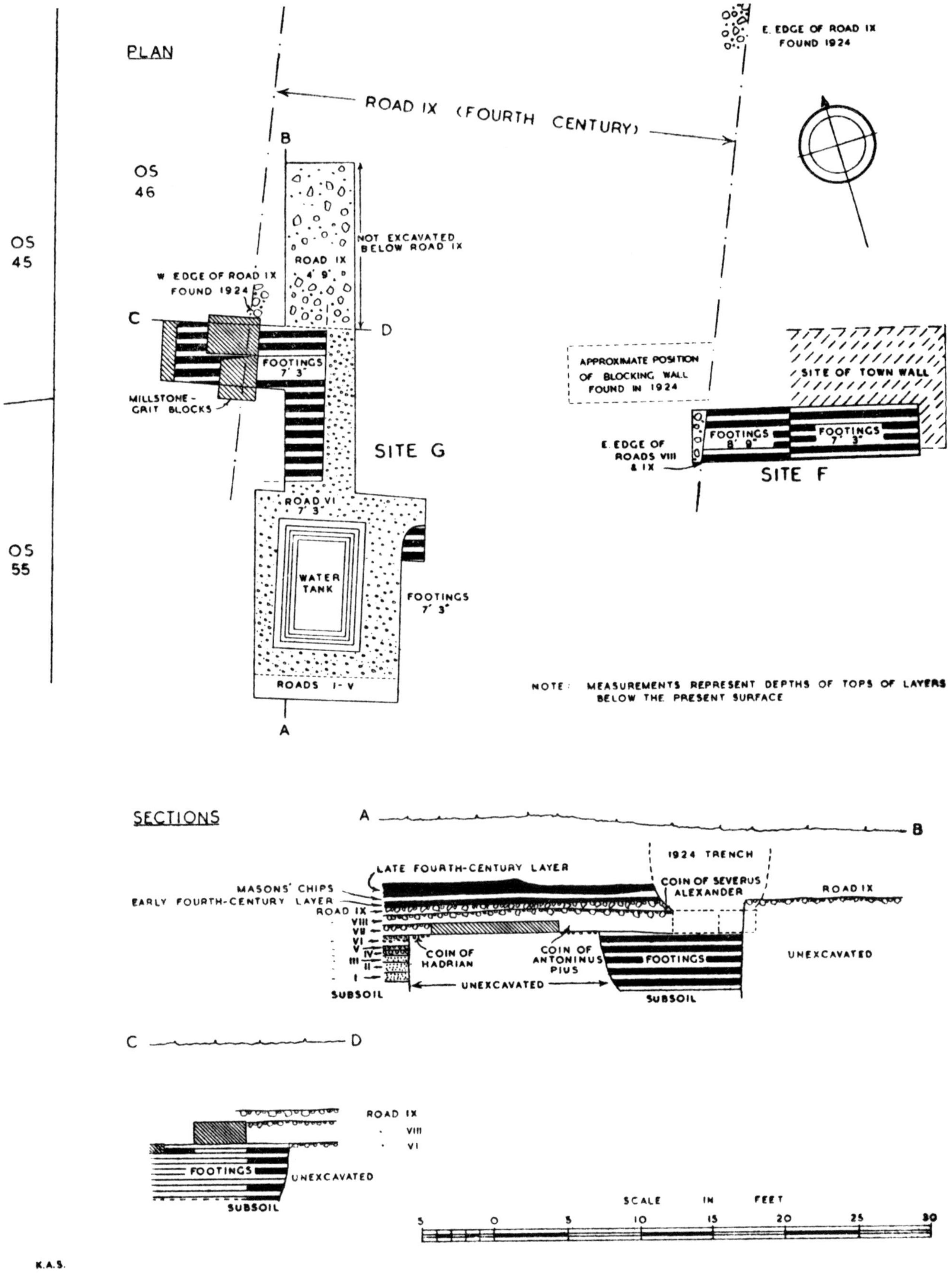

Fig A16 Plan and sections showing the North Gate (**G34/1**) as excavated by Barber *et al* in 1924 and Myres *et al* in 1938. *Drawing:* Myres et *al* 1959, fig 21. Reproduced by courtesy of the Yorkshire Archaeological and Historical Society

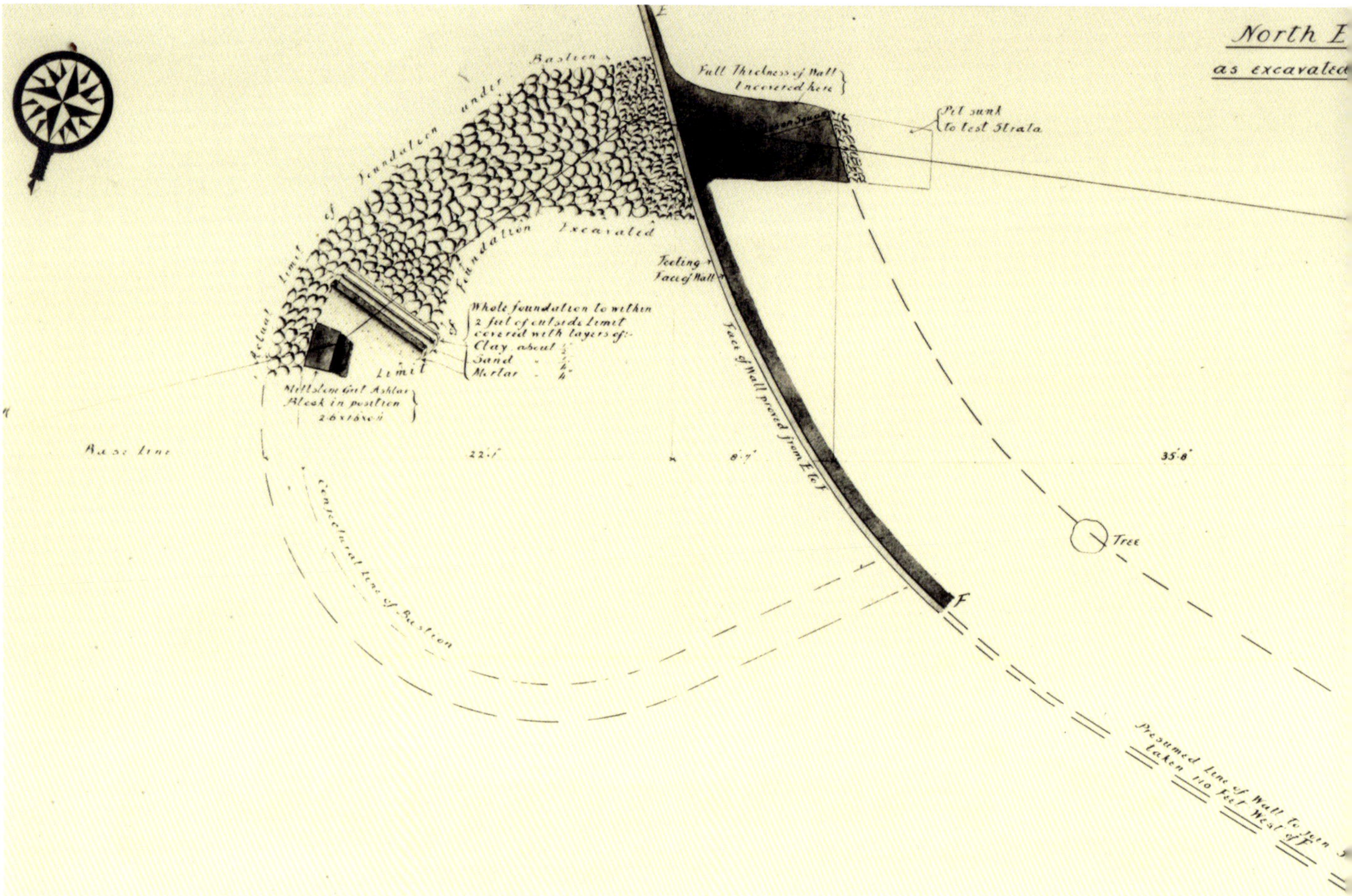

Fig A17 Plan of the excavations by Barber *et al* in 1924 at the external tower on the north-eastern corner of the Town Wall (**G36**). *Drawing:* C A Ridley. Reproduced by courtesy of Sir Andrew Lawson-Tancred

G35 North Wall excavations
Section A–B: SE 4075 6669, Section C–D: SE 4078 6668
1924
The Barber *et al* excavations included the cutting of two sections, one to the north of the Town Wall (A–B), the other to the south, to the east of the North Gate (C–D). The former examined the ditch, and the latter revealed the inner face of the wall (fig A11).
Primary references: Barber et al 1925.
Location: Barber et al 1925, plans A and C. Accurately mapped in project archive.

G36 External tower on north-east corner of Town Wall
SE 4082 6668
1924
The excavations of Barber *et al* revealed part of a semi-circular external tower on the exterior of the Town Wall (figs A11 and A17). Pitched stone foundations were also recorded in an adjacent area within the walls, interpreted as the foot of the internal bank. This was re-mapped by Myres *et al* (fig A18).
Primary references: Barber et al 1925; Myres et al 1959, Site A, 6–7, 50, fig 19.
Location: Barber et al 1925, plans B, C and F; Myres et al 1959, fig 19. Accurately mapped in project archive.

G37 Building within the North Wall
SE 4074 6668
1924
Excavations by Barber *et al* recorded the stone wall of a building as 'Masonry S' (figs A11 and A19). This is perhaps part of Building 2.18 in the authors' survey. This ran east–west and stood eight courses high on river pebble footings.
Primary references: Barber et al 1925.
Location: Barber et al 1925, plan D; Myres et al 1959, Site D, 7, fig 19. Accurately mapped in project archive.

G38 Building within the North Wall
SE 4078 6667
1924
The Barber *et al* excavations also uncovered stone walls of a building recorded as 'Masonry T' (figs A11 and A20). Several walls, standing up to twelve courses high formed the sides of a substantial building with an internal room division. This forms the northern end of Building 2.17 in the authors' survey. This area was re-examined in 2018 (**G106**).
Primary references: Barber et al 1925;
Location: Barber et al 1925, plan D; Myres et al 1959, Site C, 7, fig 19. Accurately mapped in project archive.

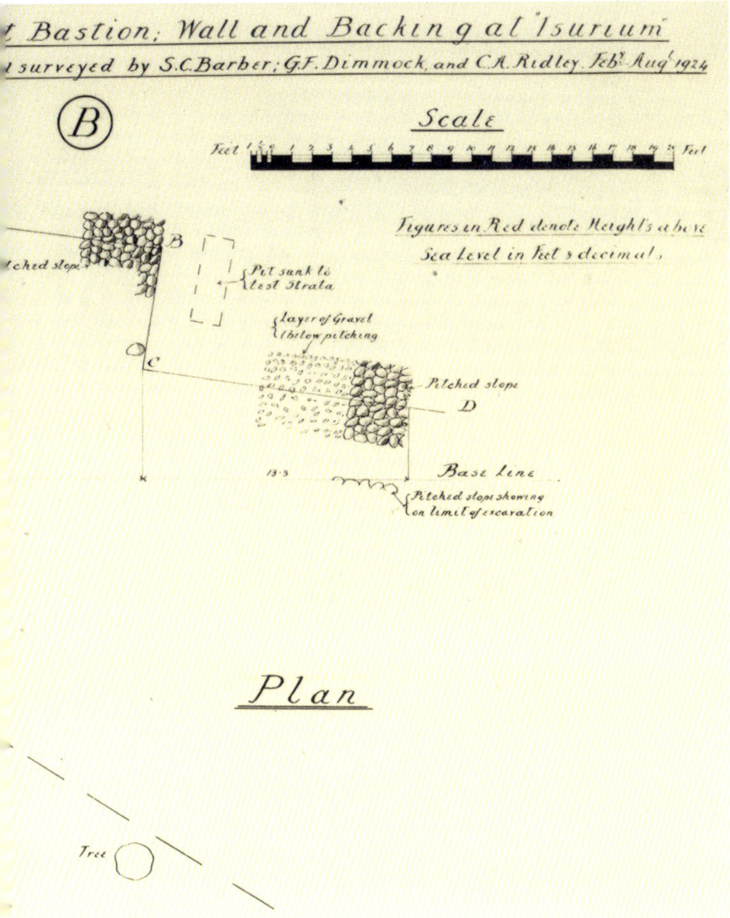

G39 Town Wall to the south of the north-western corner of town
Section I: SE 4052 6670, Section II: SE 4054 6669, Section III: SE 4051 6670

1934–5

The excavations by Myres *et al* involved the cutting of two sections (1934 I, and 1935 III) across the Town Wall about 40m to the south of the north-western corner, and one adjacent trench in the interior (1934 Section II) (fig A21). These located the robbed Town Wall and an external tower. Section III also revealed part of a backfilled first-century AD quarry pit. The Town Wall is given a *terminus post quem* in the middle of the second century, whilst the external tower is dated to the second quarter of the fourth century. A note on a plan showing the excavations by Barber *et al* (fig A9) notes an excavation here in 1923, about which the authors have no further information.

Primary references: Myres *et al* 1959, 12–34, plan figs 3 and 6.

Location: Myres *et al* 1959, fig 3 provides an accurate plan. Accurately mapped in project archive.

G40 Pipeline trench in north-western corner of town
SE 4058 6675

1934–5

A sewerage pipe trench was cut during the winter of 1934–5, and observed by Miss Kitson-Clark, Mr F Kirk Horsell and Mr Kent (fig A21). They identified a robber trench over the line of the Town Wall east of the north-west corner tower, marking its course towards the North Gate. They also noted a great quantity of sand in the northern area of the town, suggestive of levelling and found a dump of samian ware. They recorded that first-century pottery was mostly found close to Manor Farm.

Primary reference: Myres *et al* 1959, 17–18, plan fig 3.

Location: Myres *et al* 1959, fig 3 provides a plan. Accurately mapped in project archive.

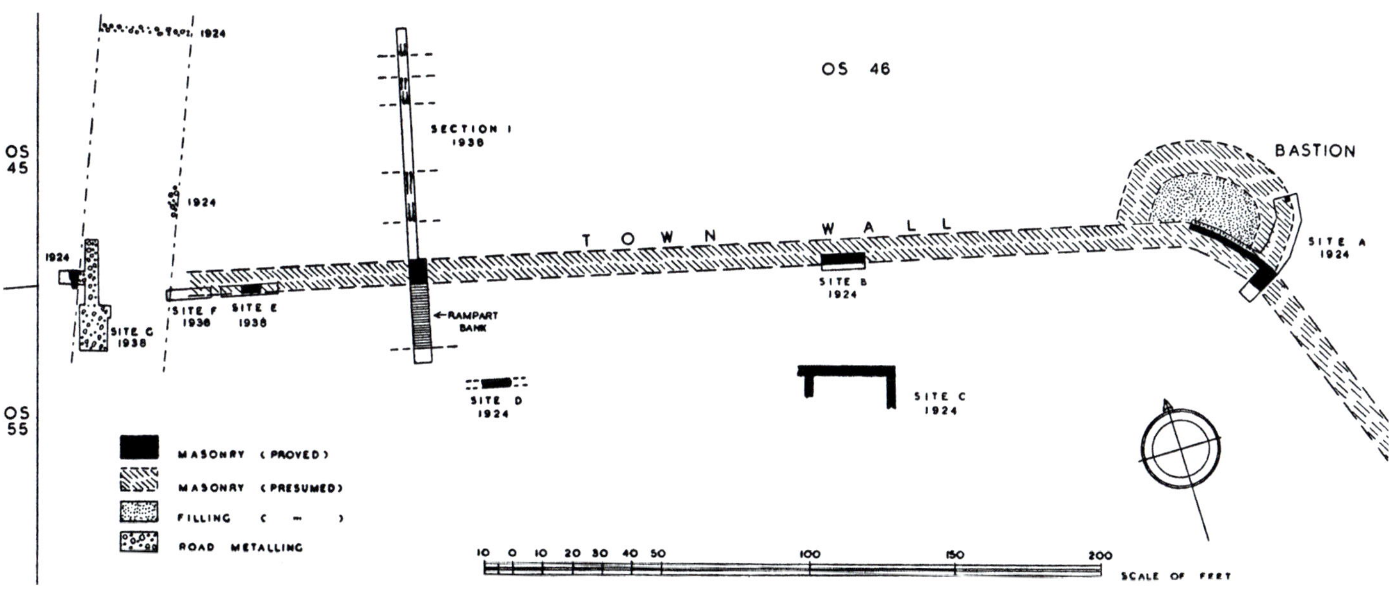

Fig A18 Plan showing the excavations on the north-eastern sector of the Town Wall (**G34/1**, **G35**, **G36**, **G37**, **G38** and **G43**) as excavated by Barber *et al* in 1924 and Myres *et al* in 1938. *Drawing:* Myres *et al* 1959, fig 19. Reproduced by courtesy of the Yorkshire Archaeological and Historical Society

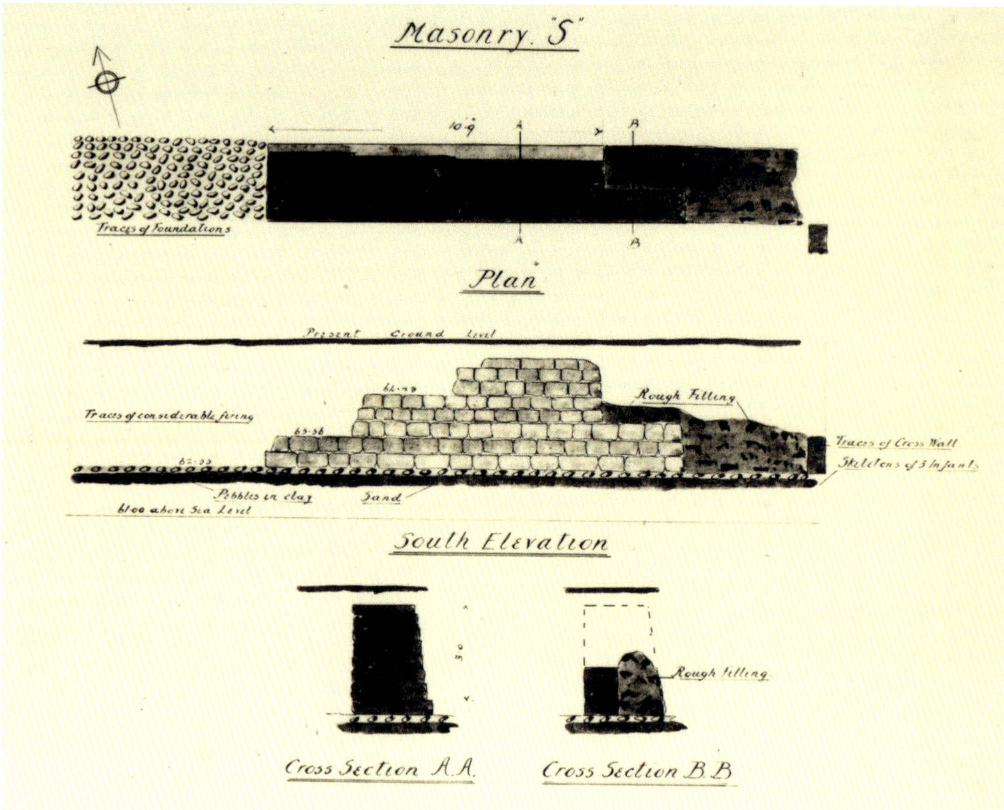

Fig A19 Plan and elevations of the structure excavated by Barber *et al* in 1924 at 'Masonry S' (**G37**). *Drawing:* C A Ridley. Reproduced by courtesy of Sir Andrew Lawson-Tancred

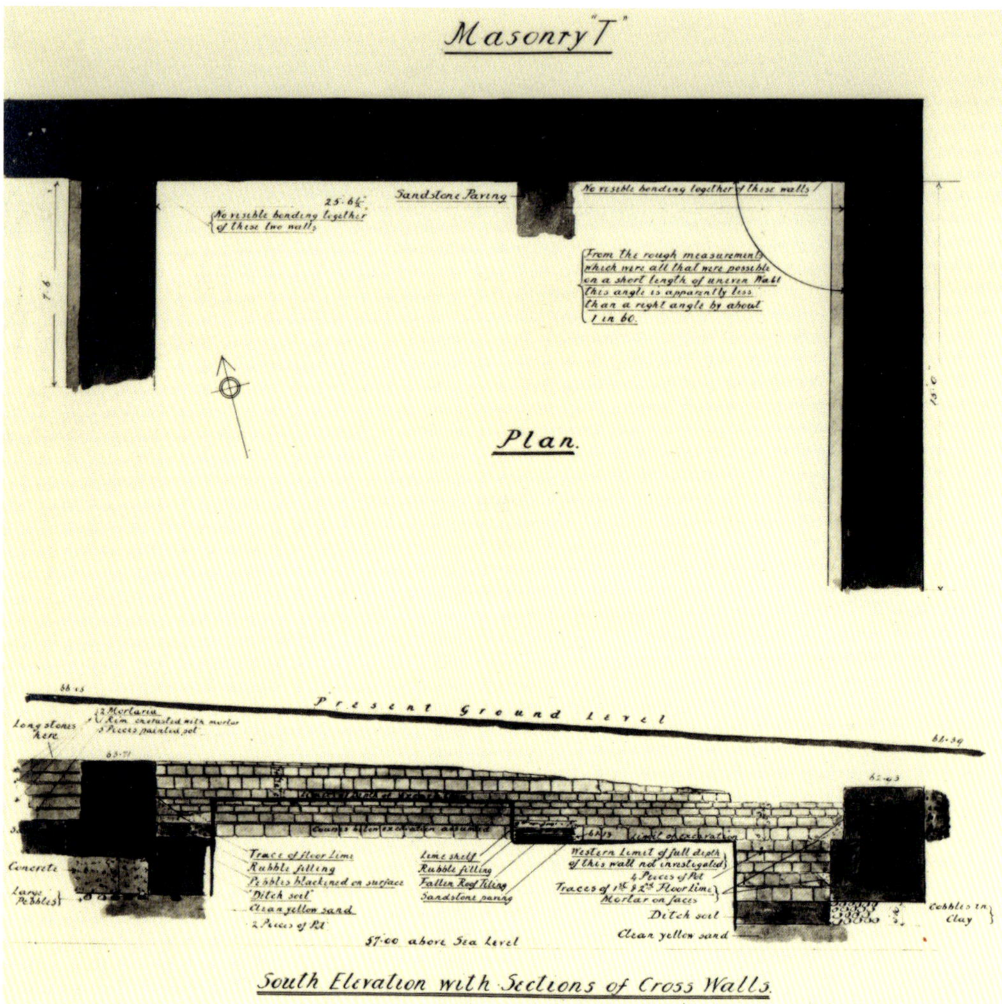

Fig A20 Plan and elevation of the structure excavated by Barber *et al* in 1924 as 'Masonry T' (**G38**). *Drawing:* C A Ridley. Reproduced by courtesy of Sir Andrew Lawson-Tancred

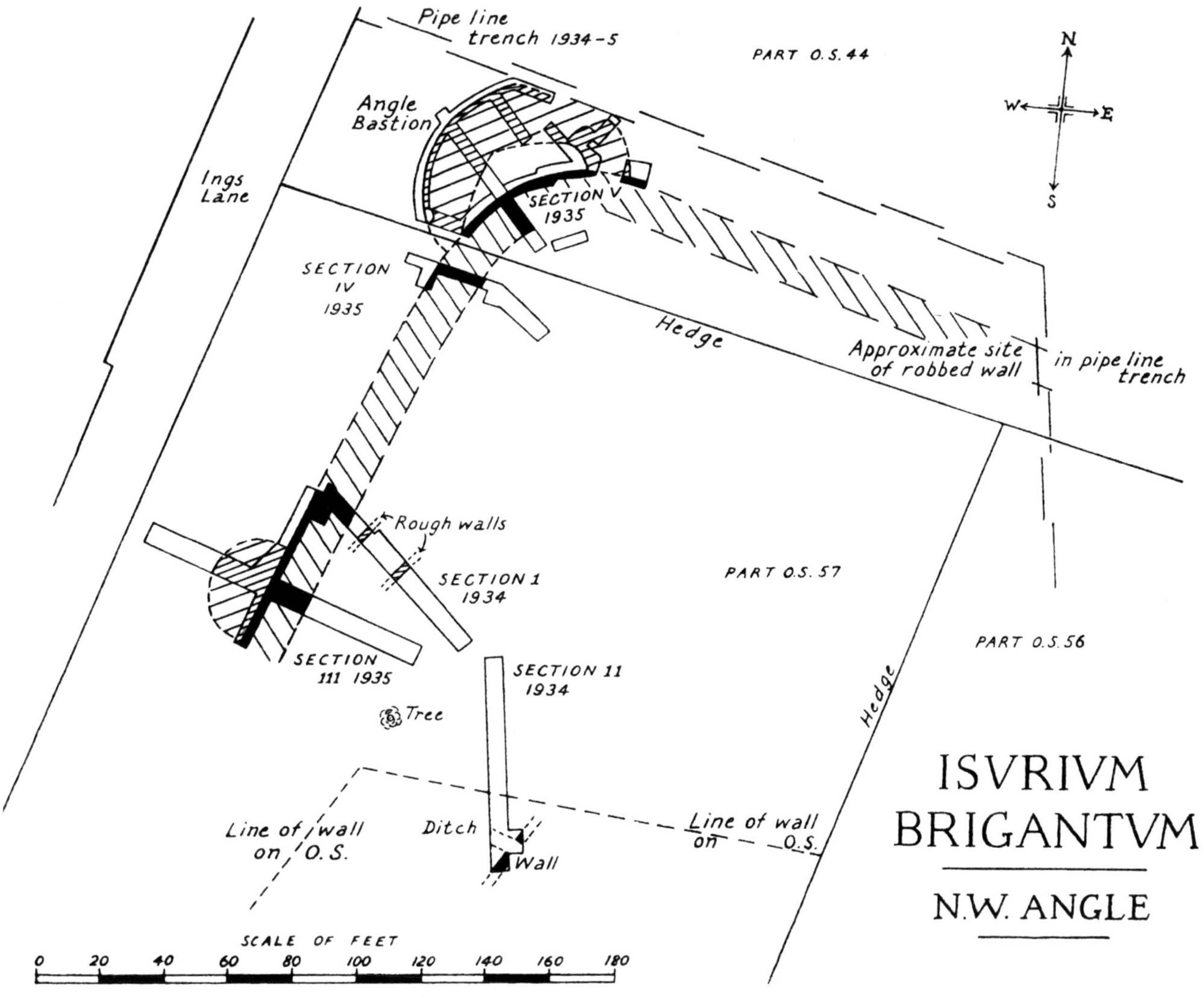

Fig A21 Plan showing the excavations on the north-western corner of the Town Wall (**G39**, **G40** and **G41**) as excavated by Myres *et al* in 1934–5. *Drawing:* Myres *et al* 1959, fig 3. Reproduced by courtesy of the Yorkshire Archaeological and Historical Society

G41 External tower on north-western corner of Town Wall
Section IV: SE 4053 6673, Section V: SE 4053 6674

1935

The Roman Antiquities Section excavations directed by J N L Myres, K A Steer and Mrs A M H Chitty revealed a semi-circular external tower at the north-western corner of the Town Wall (sections 1935 IV and V) (fig A21). The excavators concluded that this was built in the second quarter of the fourth century. First-century deposits, including a beam slot for a timber building, were also recorded in section V).

Primary references: Myres *et al* 1959, 30–34, plan figs 3 and 13.

Location: Myres *et al* 1959, fig 3 gives an accurate plan. Accurately mapped in project archive.

G42 South-eastern corner of Town Wall
Section 1: SE 4068 6609, Section 2: SE 4069 6610, Section 3: SE 4064 6610

1937

Myres *et al* examined the south-eastern corner of the Town Wall (1937 Section 1) (figs 2.15 and A22). They also cut sections close by on the east side (1937 section 2) and a little further west on the south side (1937 section 3). Their work revealed both a rectangular internal angle tower and a semi-circular external tower. The filling of the internal tower to create a platform is dated to the late second century, whilst the external tower has an early fourth century *terminus post quem*. The section across the east wall suggested that its facing had been demolished and rebuilt at some stage, although this was undated.

Primary references: Myres *et al* 1959, 41–9, figs 15–18, pls II and IIIA.

Location: Myres *et al* 1959, fig 15 provides an accurate plan. Accurately mapped in project archive.

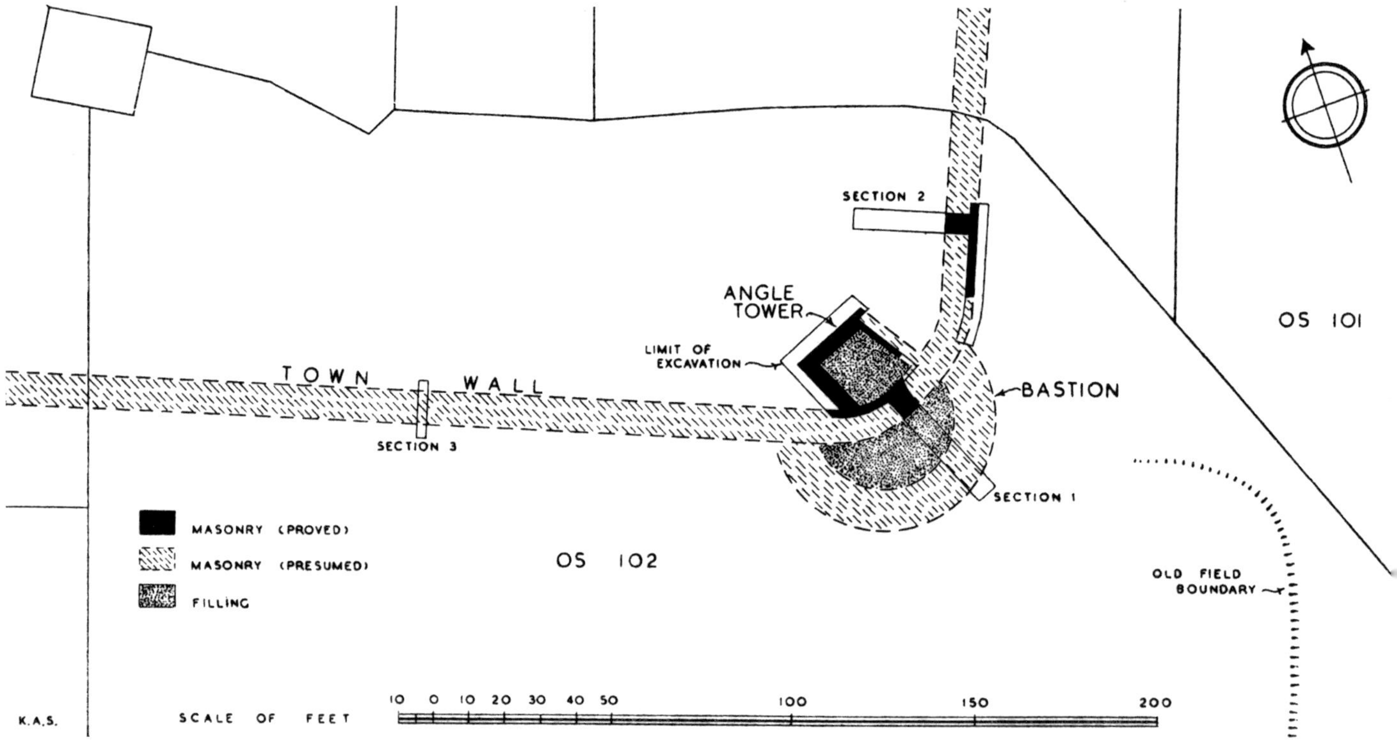

Fig A22 Plan showing the excavations on the south-eastern corner of the Town Wall (**G42**) as excavated by Myres *et al* in 1937. *Drawing*: Myres *et al* 1959, fig 15. Reproduced by courtesy of the Yorkshire Archaeological and Historical Society

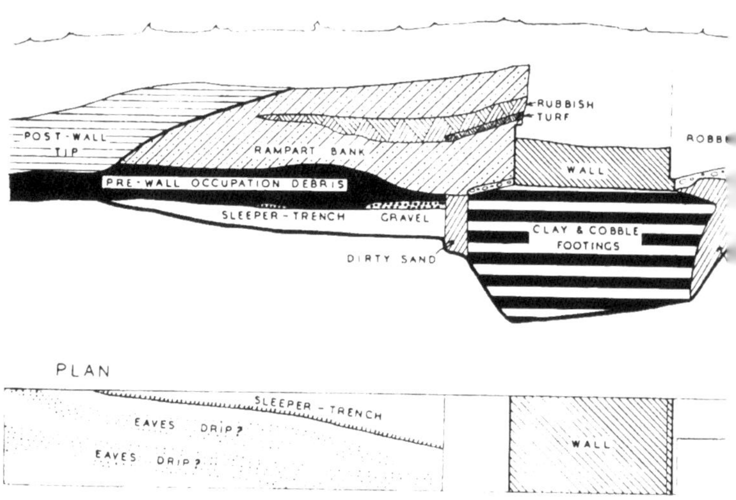

G43 Town Wall to east of North Gate
Section 1: SE 4074 6670
1938
The campaign of excavations by Myres *at al* included the cutting of a long section (1938 section I) across the Town Wall and the ditches to the north (figs A18 and A23). At the base of the sequence the trench revealed beam slots from Flavian timber buildings beneath the bank and to the north of the Town Wall. To the north of the Wall three ditches were located, the inner one contemporaneous with it. The second ditch, which was comparatively small (*c* 2m wide by 1m deep), pre-dated the Wall, and was infilled in the second century. It is not clear whether this formed part of the defences. The third, outermost, ditch, was the latest, but was not fully excavated and could not be dated.
Primary references: Myres et al 1959, 50–5, figs 19–20, pl IIIB.
Location: Myres et al 1959, fig 19 provides an accurate plan. Accurately mapped in project archive.

G44 Trenches south of the former Aldburgh Arms public house, Front Street
SE 4055 6629
1959
A small excavation was undertaken by the Royal Commission on Historical Monuments for England in advance of the construction of a building extension. This revealed walls apparently from a domestic building of Roman date. These may relate to Buildings 4.8 and 4.9 in the authors' survey. No dating evidence was found. The excavations were published by Snape *et al* on the basis of the surviving archive.
Primary references: Snape et al 2002, 33–4, plan fig 3.
Location: Snape *et al* 2002 only provide a small-scale plan. A copy of a survey showing the location of the trenches is held in the Historic England archive at Swindon (CHA01:11), and has been used to locate the excavations precisely. Accurately mapped in project archive.

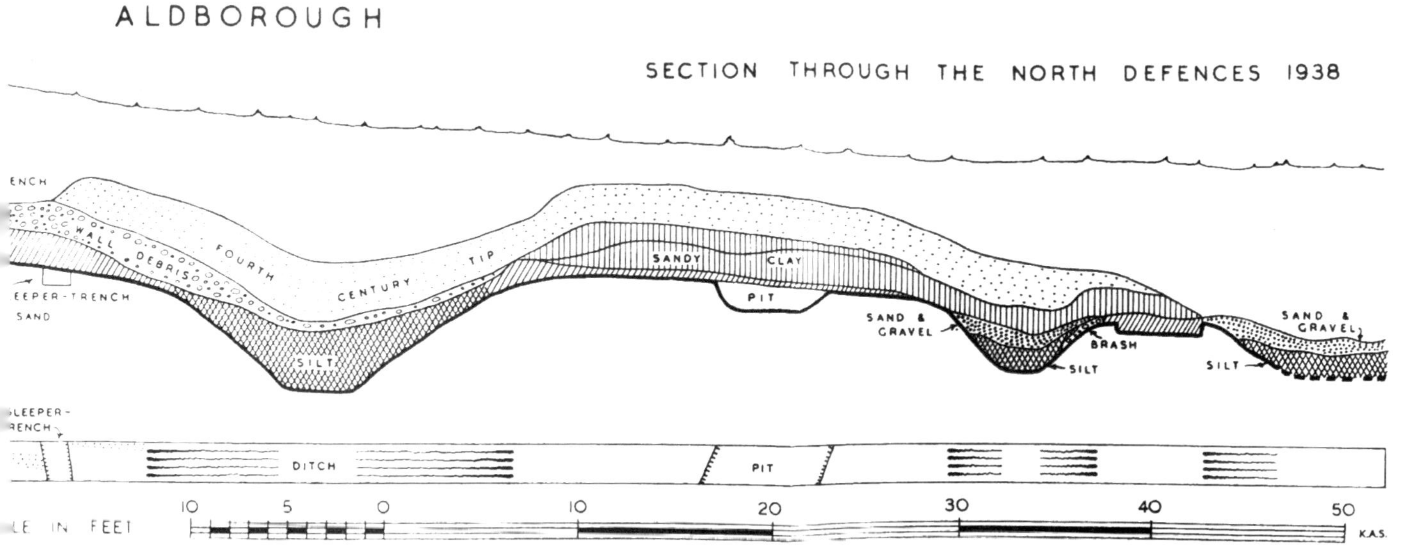

Fig A23 Plan and section of the trench through the North Wall as excavated by Myres *et al* in 1938 (**G43**). *Drawing:* Myres *et al* 1959, fig 20. Reproduced by courtesy of the Yorkshire Archaeological and Historical Society

G45 English Heritage Museum site
SE 4049 6616
1959
A typescript in the Historic England archive in Swindon (CHA/01) records excavations prior to the construction of the museum. These revealed 'traces' of Roman buildings in the north-western corner of the site, although the 'remains were unintelligible and also undateable'.
Primary reference: Historic England archive (CHA/01) in Swindon.
Location: description but no plan in Historic England archive in Swindon.

G46 Town Wall on the western side, in Manor Garden
SE 4042 6646
1960
A brief entry in *Roman Britain in 1960* records the excavation of 'a mound on the line of the W town-wall'. The excavation was undertaken by David Dymond for the Royal Commission on Historical Monuments for England, and a section drawing by him was published by Dorothy Charlesworth. Manuscript notes describe the excavated remains, which included fragments of a building set behind the earth bank at the back of the Town Wall. The structure must form part of Building 4.1 in the authors' survey. It seems likely that the mound represented landscaping of the spoil from the adjacent excavation in the 1840s (**G10**).
Primary references: 'Roman Britain in 1960', 169, in *Journal of Roman Studies* **61** (1961); Charlesworth 1971, 156 and n 9, fig 22.
North Yorks HER references: ENY2329; SNY8739
Location: The location of the excavation is not recorded in the published sources, but notes and a plan in the Historic England archive in Swindon (CHA/01 show that it was located immediately to the south of Aldborough Manor, close to the excavated buildings (**G10**). This is where it is shown on the authors' plan.

G47 'Dominies Lodge', Low Road
SE 4055 6647
1960
A further excavation by David Dymond for the RCHME examined an area that was being developed for the construction of a bungalow to the north of Low Road. A series of trenches revealed a pair of parallel walls and *opus signinum* flooring in a corridor to the north and a room continuing to the south. There are no records to relate the pottery to the excavated stratigraphy. The excavations were published by Snape *et al* on the basis of the surviving archive. This location suggests that the corridor flanked the south side of the Principal East–West street.
Primary references: Snape *et al* 2002, 36–40, fig 6.
Location: the trenches are shown on Snape *et al* 2002, fig 6: a survey plan relating the trenches to the site boundaries is held in the Historic England archive at Swindon (CHA/01 GA 156/6) and has been used to locate the excavations.

G48 'Holmdale', Front Street
SE 4056 6634
1960
A third excavation in 1960 directed by David Dymond for the RCHME examined the plot where cottages had been demolished to build a bungalow. The publication of this work by Snape *et al* on the basis of the surviving archive provides details of a substantial east–west sewer, but also mentions the discovery of other structural remains. The sewer is of great significance as it is likely to have run beneath Street EW8 (above, pp. 44–5). There are no records of the finds from this excavation.
Primary references: Snape *et al* 2002, 34–6, figs 4 and 5.
Location: the general position of the excavations is certain, but Snape *et al* were unable to map the trenches. A reappraisal of the various site plans and surveying records in the Historic England archive at Swindon (CHA01/02/01/001) provides a better understanding of the layout of the trenches, but their precise locations cannot be established.

G49 'Stonehaven', Low Road
SE 4070 6632
1961
Excavations by Dorothy Charlesworth revealed a sequence of timber and stone buildings of domestic character. There were two timber phases: the first with beam slots, the second with post-holes. These are dated to the Flavian to Trajanic/Hadrianic period. The stone structure revealed three phases, with the development of a north–south range of rooms with a corridor to the east. The first stone building is probably later second century.
Primary references: Snape *et al* 2002, 40–7, figs 9–12. This building was erroneously described as a first-century AD bath-house, possibly military (Wacher 1974, 339).
Location: Snape *et al* 2002, fig 9 provides a general location. Accurately mapped in project archive.

G50 'The Castle', Low Road
SE 4070 6645
1962
An excavation led by an amateur archaeologist by the name of J A Dale cut a trench (*c* 30ft long, *c* 3ft deep) in the garden of a house called 'The Castle'. There are no records of this, but Herkes' (1997) discussion and oral accounts (in 2017) from the householder's family and those who visited the dig are consistent with it having cut down into early Roman deposits. Finds included sandstone blocks, tile, wall plaster and coins as well as a quantity of samian ware, including a South Gaulish Dr 15/17 stamped by L Cosius Virilis and dated to AD 75–110 – *NTS* vol 3, die 6d, and a flagon of comparable date.
Primary references: McCann family pers comm; Herkes 1997.
Location: Sir Andrew Lawson-Tancred visited the site as a child and provided an approximate location.

G51 South Gate Lodge, South Gate and defences to the east
Trench A: SE 4055 6611, Trench B: SE 4057 6612, Trench C: SE 4051 6614, Trench D: SE 4057 6612, Trench E: SE 4051 6614, Trench F: SE 4051 6614
1964
Excavations by Margaret Jones in advance of the construction of a bungalow examined the ditches outside the Town Wall in two places. To the west, her trenches C, E and F, examined the primary ditch in front of the Wall and a foundation overlapping this, which is plausibly for an external tower associated with the east portal of the gate. The pottery from the filling of the ditch includes early–mid fourth century material.

To the east, in trenches A, B and D, there were two primary ditches associated with Wall, the inner ditch of which was overlain by the foundations of an external tower. Two later outer ditches were also examined, the outer one only partially. The dating of these features is not certain. The general absence of pottery earlier than the second century is notable.
Primary references: Full excavation report Jones 1971, 40–51, figs 1–8, pls I–IV.
Location: Jones 1971, fig 1 provides an accurate plan. Accurately mapped in project archive.

G52 Sewerage pipe trench to north east of Town Wall
A: SE 4099,6631, B: SE 4075 6681, C: SE 4077 6680, D: SE 4075 6693, E: SE 4100 6635
1964
During the period that she was excavating at the South Gate (**G51**), Margaret Jones also kept a watching brief on a sewerage pipe trench that was cut from the Dunsforth Road across the fields to the north east of the town up to the sewerage works. The Roman road to York was recorded (A). In the northern section, near the sewerage works, two stretches of road metalling were noted, (B) and (C). The authors' magnetometer now shows that the area of C is actually part of a building within the annexe outside the North Gate (above, p. 75). Another section of road was recorded by the new percolators (D). Also significant was a dump of pottery kiln wasters including *mortaria* and coarse pottery dated to *c* 100–40 (E), located *c* 25m north west of Hall Arm Lane. The *mortaria* include vessels with maker's stamps for NATOR.
Primary references: Summary report Jones 1971, 51–4, 59–60, 66–7, figs 2 and 8.
Location: Jones 1971, fig 2 provides an accurate plan. Accurately mapped in project archive.

G53 'Briarwood' and 'Lyndene', Town Wall and defences south of East Gate
Trench 1: SE 4078 6629, Trench 2: SE 4077 6633, Trench 3: SE 4078 6633, Trench 4: SE 4075 6634, Trench 5: SE 4073 6632
1965
Excavations by Dorothy Charlesworth in advance of the construction of two houses just inside the Town Wall to the south of the East Gate focused primarily on the defences. Earlier than the Town Wall was a north–south road (NS5), with evidence of adjacent timber buildings to the west. Other early timber features were found a little to the south east. These features are not well dated, but appear to be largely second century.

The excavation cut the Town Wall and two ditches. The inner ditch was overlain by the foundations for an external tower. These can be equated with Ditches 7.1 and 7.2 in the authors' survey. The pottery from the excavation suggests that the Wall and ditch date to sometime after c AD 170. That associated with the external tower and outer ditch provides a *terminus post quem* of the third quarter of the third century AD.
Primary references: Preliminary results in Charlesworth 1971; full report in Snape *et al* 2002, 48–59, figs 14–19.
North Yorks HER references: ENY5443.
Location: Snape *et al* 2002, fig 14 provides a plan sufficient to locate the trenches reasonably well. Accurately mapped in project archive.

G54 Swimming pool in the grounds of Aldborough Manor
SE 4044 6642
1965
A note in the Historic England archive records that David Dymond of the RCHME observed the trench for the construction of a swimming pool. Deposits to a depth of 5ft were recorded, but no structures were noted.
Primary references: Historic England archive in Swindon (CHA/01).
North Yorks HER references: ENY2329; ENY7398; SNY20806; SNY8739.
Location: Historic England archive in Swindon provides no plan, but its location on the authors' map is based on its existence until recently.

G55 North of the Ship Inn
SE 406 664
1966
An excavation was carried out by Reverend G E Stephens, exposing what was then thought to be a butcher's shop along the road to the North Gate. This identification is highly improbable. It was reported in the *Pateley Bridge Herald*, 20 August 1966. No accurate location or detailed records available.
Primary references: 'Roman Britain in 1966', *Journal of Roman Studies*, **57** (1967), 179.

G56 South of Borough Hill
SE 4058 6627
1977
A manuscript note records a watching brief when houses were built to the south of Borough Hill in 1977. This records 'a section of metalled road with ditches on either side. From its width it was a minor street possibly running along one side the forum'. A single wall foundation was recorded parallel with the street to the west, and a pair of similar walls parallel to it to the east. This perhaps relates to Building 5.2 in the authors' survey.
Primary references: Tyler undated, 14.
Location: Tyler undated does not provide a plan; the general location can be inferred from her description.

G57 North of Sutton Farm
SE 4065 6658
1977(?)
Two unofficial excavations, thought to have been conducted in the field just north of Sutton Farm by two school teachers from Harrogate (assisted by local volunteers). Two trenches were apparently dug, revealing a hypocaust in one and silver coins in the other. No report is known and the whereabouts of the finds is uncertain.
Primary reference: Herkes 1997: A/23.
Location: There is no known plan.

G58 The 'Old Court House', Back Lane
SE 4063 6627
1980
The HER notes a watching brief here with no structures recorded.
North Yorks HER references: ENY1248; SYN6991; SNY7214.

G59 'Penrose House', Front Street
SE 4055 6629
1984
A watching brief was carried out by Colin Dobinson on a foundation trench for a store building to the rear of Penrose House. A feature was noted in the north corner of the foundation trench, though its function or date is unclear.
Primary reference: Dobinson *pers comm.*
Location: Sketch map provided by Dobinson gives accurate location and is mapped in the project archive

G60 Field to north east of East Gate
Trench 1: SE 4095 6638, Trench 2: SE 4096 6639, Trench 3: SE 4094 6639; Trench 4: SE 4089 6641, Trench 5: SE 4089 6643, Trench 6: SE 4089 6640, Trench 7: SE 4090 6642, Trench 8: SE 4090 6645, Trench 9: SE 4094 6644, Trench 10: SE 4091 6639.
1987
A series of small trial trenches was excavated by Colin Dobinson down to the top of the Roman deposits in the field outside the East Gate.
Primary references: Dobinson 1987 provides a summary.
Location: Dobinson 1987, figs 1 and 2 shows the trench locations and are accurately mapped in the project archive.

G61 'The Firs', Low Road
Trench A: SE 4041 6655, Trench B: SE 4042 6654
1987–8
A watching brief and two evaluation trenches overseen by R P Cross on a site to the east of 'The Firs' outside the West Gate in advance of building (now the site of 'Little Ings House'). Roman material was encountered over 1.2m down, interpreted possibly as a demolition or re-deposited context. This lies over the line of the defensive ditches, suggesting that these deposits were ditch infill.
Primary references: Cross 1987a and 1987b.
North Yorks HER references: ENY1670; SNY8096; ENY1671; SNY8097.
Location: Cross 1987a, fig 1 shows trench locations. Accurately mapped in the project archive.

G62 'The Cottage', Back Street
SE 4063 6617
1989
Three trenches hand dug to the north of the house by Kevin Cale. These revealed decaying red sandstone wall courses and Roman roof tiles in the northern part, approximately 0.40m below ground level.
Primary references: Cale 1989.
North Yorks HER references: ENY2179; SYN8575; SYN6978.
Location: The trenches were not mapped in the original report so there is only an approximate location.

G63 'Rosedale', Back Street
SE 4061 6625
1988–9
Watching brief by York Archaeological Trust (YAT) on the excavation into the slope for a garage extension to the north west of the house. Sandstone fragments were found at a depth of 1–1.2m, but no datable material was discovered in this context.
Primary references: Stockwell 1989.
North Yorks HER references: ENY1672; SNY8098; SNY19366.
Location: Stockwell 1989, 2. Accurately mapped in the project archive.

G64 'Sutton Farm', Low Road
A: SE 4064 6656, B: SE 4062, 6656, C: SE 4060 6656, D: SE 4060 6656
1990
Watching brief by York Archaeological Trust (YAT) during the construction of a perimeter drain (A), effluent delivery drain (B), interceptor pit (C) and slurry lagoon (D). A cobbled surface was recorded mid-way down the cut for an effluent drain and painted wall plaster, recovered elsewhere. Across all four trenches red sandstone was noted at a depth of *c* 0.6m.
Primary references: YAT 1990.
North Yorks HER references: ENY2327; SNY8724; SYN6925.
Location: YAT 1990. Accurately mapped in project archive.

G65 'Museum House', Front Street
Trench 1: SE 4048 6614, Trench 2: SE 4049 6614, Trench 3: SE 4049 6614, Trench 4: SE 4050 6614, Trench 5: SE 4049 6613
1991
Archaeological recording in March/April 1991 of five trial trenches for the same investigation as **G66**. Sandstone blocks and cobbles observed.
Primary references: Cale 1991a.
North Yorks HER references: ENY474; SYN770; SNY8573
Location: Cale 1991a. Accurately mapped in project archive.

G66 'Museum House', Front Street
Trench A: SE 4049 6613, Trench B: SE 4049 6613, Trench C: SE 4049 6613, Trench D: SE 4049 6614
1991
Watching brief and trial trenching carried out by Kevin Cale in August 1991 during the demolition and rebuilding of a garage and associated landscaping. Red sandstone and cobbled surfaces were discovered in various locations. The report includes detailed plans and sections and site photos.
Primary references: Cale 1991b.
North Yorks HER references: ENY474; SYN770.
Location: Cale 1991b. Accurately mapped in project archive.

G67 'Well Cottage', Back Street
SE 4061 6618
1992
Planning Officer observed a well during the construction of a conservatory, but no Roman remains.
North Yorks HER references: ENY1921; SNY8397.

G68 Estate Yard, Low Road
SE 4053 6648
1993
A trial trench was excavated by Northern Archaeological Associates in the Estate Yard on Low Lane. Stratified Roman deposits were found at 0.5m, including a metalled surface interpreted as an east–west street. This must be the Principal East–West street.
Primary references: Bishop and Young 1993; 'Roman Britain in 1993', *Britannia,* **25**, 265.
North Yorks HER references: ENY 2332; ENY2334; SYN 8740; SYN8741.
Location: Bishop and Young 1993. Accurately mapped in project archive.

G69 Studforth Farm, Back Street
Trench 2: SE 4061 6614, Trench 3: SE 4062 6614
1993
Trial trenches (2 and 3) were excavated by Northern Archaeological Associates at Studforth House on Back Street. An apsidal wall of mortared sandstone 0.4m thick was discovered cut into the slope, but elsewhere the archaeology was deeper than the trench depth as a result of terracing.
Primary references: Bishop and Young 1993; 'Roman Britain in 1993', *Britannia,* **25**, 265.
North Yorks HER references: ENY 2333; ENY2334; SYN 8740; SYN8741.
Location: Bishop and Young 1993. Accurately mapped in project archive.

G70 Hill View, Chapel Hill
SE 4046 6604
1994
Watching brief for a new porch and bay window. No artefacts of features were observed.
North Yorks HER references: ENY1527; SYN8059.

G71 The Ship Inn, Low Road
TH1: SE 4063 6652, TH2: SE 4064 6651, TT1: SE 4063 6650, TT2: SE 4064 6649, TT3: SE 4063 6648, TT4: SE 4063 6646
1996
An archaeological evaluation was carried out by Kevin Cale at the rear of the Ship Inn in advance of construction of a house ('Severus House'). It consisted of two trial holes (TH1 and TH2) and four trial trenches (TT 1–4) under the foundations and along the access/utilities route. Natural was not reached at 1.04m. A Roman road and kerb were discovered running north–south, with pottery dating to the fourth century AD. This represents the Principal North–South Street.
Primary references: Cale 1996a.
North Yorks HER references: ENY2321; SYN8719; SYN8723; SYN8720.
Location: Cale 1996a. Accurately mapped in project archive.

G72 Sewer on Back Street
A: SE 4070 6639, B: SE 4069 6638, C: SE 4067 6637, D: SE 4066 6636, E: SE 4068 6638, F: SE 4065 6636, G: SE 4066 6635, TT1: SE 4069 6639, TT2: SE 4067 6636, TT3: SE 4066 6635, TT4: SE 4064 6630, TT5: SE 4064 6627
1996
An evaluation and watching brief was carried out by Kevin Cale on behalf of Yorkshire Water when a sewer collapsed. It consisted of: five hand-dug trial trenches (TT1–5); a watching brief on sections of trench (A–G) between manhole covers and seven box type excavations on the line of a stone culvert; and observation of a CCTV scan of the sewer. No road surfaces were found, but a concentration of tesserae indicated a possible disturbed mosaic (in trench E).
Primary references: Cale 1996b.
North Yorks HER references: ENY2325; SYN8727; SYN8728.
Location: Cale 1996b. Accurately mapped in project archive.

G73 'Castle House', Back Street
SE 4065 6629
1996
Excavations for an extension were observed by NYCC, revealing a post-medieval well and north–south sandstone drain, probably associated with the well.
North Yorks HER references: ENY1454; SNY8006.

G74 The Ship Inn, Low Road
SE 4061 6648
1997
A rapid archaeological inspection by Kevin Cale following the commencement of ground disturbance associated with the construction of a kitchen extension to the rear of the pub. Eighteenth- and nineteenth-century landscaping seemed to have disturbed earlier deposits from late Roman to medieval.
Primary reference: Cale 1997a.
North Yorks HER references: ENY2322; SNY8724; SYN8721.
Location: Cale 1997a. Area mapped in project archive.

G75 'Aldene', Back Street
SE 4055 6617
1997
An archaeological watching brief by Kevin Cale during construction of a conservatory and kitchen extension to the south of the main house, close to the southern stretch of the Roman Town Wall. The area had been heavily landscaped in the nineteenth century, removing earlier deposits.
Primary references: Cale 1997b.
North Yorks HER references: ENY927; SYN6978.
Location: Cale 1997b. Approximate location in project archive.

G76 'Rose Cottage', Back Street
SE 4066 6633
1997
Watching brief carried out by Kevin Cale during construction of an extension between the house and garage. This seemed to catch part of a terrace dropping to the north, and an area of cobbling that the excavator concluded was a road surface in the north west of the trench. The ground level had been made up in the twentieth century.
Primary references: Cale 1997c.
North Yorks HER references: ENY567; SNY840.
Location: Cale 1997c. Mapped in project archive.

G77 'Briarwood', Low Road
SE 4077 6632
1998
An archaeological investigation by Kevin Cale during the construction of a garage to the west of the original property. Intact Roman remains were discovered: red sandstone slab and water-worn cobble surface along with fired clay roof tiles and late Roman pottery were preserved under a late Roman deposit. Cale concluded these were the remains of a demolished timber and stone building. The foundation trench was cut into a Late Roman buried soil.
Primary reference: Cale 1998.
North Yorks HER references: ENY48; SNY493.
Location: Cale 1998. Accurately mapped in project archive.

G78 'Aldborough Gate', Chapel Hill
SE 400 658 (centre)
1998
A desk-based assessment was undertaken of a large area between Chapel Hill and Stump Cross, to the south west of Aldborough.
Primary reference: Macnab 1998.
North Yorks HER: SNY9819.
Location: Macnab 1998.

G79 'The Firs', Low Road
SE 4040 6656
1999
Watching brief carried out by Kevin Cale during the demolition of an outbuilding and construction of an extension to the north of the main property. The ground had been made up in the nineteenth century when the original outbuildings were constructed, perhaps due to subsidence over the area of Roman ditches.
Primary reference: Cale 1999a.
North Yorks HER references: ENY2173; SNY8570.
Location: Cale 1999a. Mapped in project archive.

G80 'Hambleton View', Back Street
SE 4062 6625
1999
A watching brief carried out by Kevin Cale during the construction of an extension on the north side of the main house. There was a 1m deep loam deposit containing nineteenth-century finds as well as residual Roman material, suggesting that nineteenth-century landscaping has occurred. Some red sandstone at the deepest part of the trench, suggestive of Roman construction debris.
Primary reference: Cale 1999b.
North Yorks HER references: ENY556; SNY831.
Location: Cale 1999b. Mapped in project archive.

G81 'Pear Tree Cottage', Low Road
SE 4056 6648
2000
A watching brief carried out by Kevin Cale to the north of the property for an extension. In the southern area of the development an east-south-east road surface was discovered with a well-defined camber and robbed kerb on the north side. Cale suggests that this is the same as the road he excavated in the Ship Inn car park (**G71**). This represents the Principal East–West Street. In the northern part of the site, red sandstone fragments suggested constructed/demolished buildings – these seem to be contemporaneous with road and possibly early medieval. There was a deep sandy loam deposit over this, which matches nineteenth-century landscaping in a number of other areas of the town.
Primary reference: Cale 2000.
North Yorks HER references: ENY86; SYN516; SYN232.
Location: Cale 2000. Approximate area of watching brief mapped in project archive.

G82 The Aldborough Institute (Village Hall), Low Road
SE 4053 6645
2001
An exhumation in Aldborough churchyard carried out by Kevin Cale during the construction of an extension to the Aldborough Institute. One grave was disturbed and reburied in a different part of the churchyard.
Primary reference: Cale 2001.
North Yorks HER references: ENY35; SNY8732.
Location: No plan of the works.

G83 Aldborough Manor walled garden
Trench 1: SE 4043 6643, Trench 2: SE 4045 6641
2001
Trial trenches by Field Archaeology Specialists, York University, examined the area for proposed redevelopment at the derelict swimming pool. Two trenches revealed Roman features, no structures, beneath 0.8m of garden soil.
Primary reference: Garner-Lahire 2001.
North Yorks HER references: ENY705; SYN20437.
Location: taken from Garner-Lahire 2001 plan.

G84 Chapel Hill, York Road
SE 4042 6604
2001
Excavation by Northern Archaeological Associates (NAA) of a 2m by 2m wash-out trench on the north side of York Road at Chapel Hill. No archaeological features or finds. Depths and nature of deposits were recorded and are held by NAA.
Primary reference: NAA 2001.
North Yorks HER references: ENY366; SNY8718.
Location: NAA 2001. Point mapped in project archive, but no plan of trench.

G85 'Laurel House', Low Road
SE 4039 6657
2002
A watching by Kevin Cale for the foundations to an extension to the house did not reveal any Roman material.
Primary reference: Cale 2002.
North Yorks HER references: ENY873; SYN8574; SYN6932.
Location: Cale 2002.

G86 Boroughbridge Water treatment works
SE 4070 6686
2002
Watching brief by Tees Valley Archaeology demonstrated that deposits had been destroyed by earlier construction of the sewage works.
North Yorks HER references: ENY1258; SNY7695.
Location: from HER. Approximate location in project archive from aerial photographs showing construction.

G87 Chapel Hill, York Road
SE 4042 6604
2003
Watching brief by Northern Archaeological Associates (NAA) during the excavation of a small trench to locate the water main. The trench was on the north corner of the crossroads on Chapel Hill, north of the York Road. The water main was cut 0.55m into a sandy deposit, and no archaeological features or finds were noted.
Primary reference: NAA 2003.
North Yorks HER references: ENY366; SNY8718 .
Location: NAA 2003. Point mapped in project archive, but no plan of trench.

G88 'Dormer Lodge', Dunsforth Road
1: SE 4084 6651, 2: SE 4077 6651
2004
An archaeological evaluation was carried out by West Yorkshire Archaeological Services during the construction of a garage and extension. The extension (1) was to the north of the property, and a Roman, red sandstone wall was discovered under later contexts. No features were identified in the trench for the garage (2), but Roman pottery was found towards the bottom of a thick, silty sand deposit.
Primary reference: Rose 2004; 'Roman Britain in 2003', *Britannia,* **35**, 275.
North Yorks HER references: ENY2107; SNY8752.
Location: Rose 2004. Mapped in project archive.

G89 'Studforth House', Back Street
Trench 1: SE 4064 6615, Trench 2: SE 4065 6615, Trench 3: SE 4064 6614, Trench 4: SE 4064 6614, Trench 5: SE 4062 6615
2005
Five evaluation trenches were dug by MAP Archaeological Consultancy for a proposed extension and drainage to the south of the property. A series of pits, a linear feature and cobbled surfaces were dated as post-medieval.
Primary reference: Hunter 2005.
North Yorks HER references: ENY2957; SNY10024.
Location: Hunter 2005. Accurately mapped in project archive.

G90 No 1 High Street
SE 4052 6623
2005
Watching brief carried out by Archaeological Services, University of Durham, on an extension to the north of the property. During the excavation of the foundation trenches, Roman finds were identified but no archaeological features were noted.
Primary reference: ASUD 2005.
North Yorks HER references: ENY1591; SNY9423.
Location: ASUD 2005. Accurately mapped in project archive.

G91 Studforth Farm House
Trench 4: 4061 6615, Trench 5: 4061 6615
2006
Two trial trenches (Trench 4 and 5) were dug during the conversion of outbuildings (see also watching brief **G96**). A Roman ditch was identified in Trench 4 under the barn floor, containing pottery from the first–third centuries. Much of the area was thought to have been truncated by post-Roman activity, leaving only discrete Roman features.
Primary reference: Speed 2006.
North Yorks HER references: ENY3215.
Location: Speed 2006. Accurately mapped in project archive.

G92 'Aldene', Back Lane
SE 4056 6617
2007
Watching brief carried out by JB Archaeology during the ground work for an extension and reduced ground levels. The ground level seems to have been raised in the nineteenth century, and the finds were mainly post-medieval.
Primary reference: Buglass 2007.
North Yorks HER references: ENY3952; SYN11698.
Location: Buglass 2007. Point mapped in project archive but no georeferenced trenches.

G93 'Hazeldene', (Coach House), Front Street
SE 4061 6636
2009
Watching brief by MAP Archaeological Consultancy of groundworks associated with the reduction of a floor surface in the coach house, and excavation of a service trench. No archaeological features or deposits were recorded.
Primary reference: Morris 2009.
North Yorks HER references: ENY5514; SYN16319.
Location: Morris 2009. Mapped in project archive.

G94 Electricity sub-station, Front Street
SE 4054 6626
2009
Watching brief by York Archaeological Trust (YAT) during excavation for foundations of a new electricity sub-station. A series of metalled surfaces were found in the driveway cable trench, with finds suggesting a seventeenth–nineteenth century date.
Primary reference: Milsted and Johnson 2009.
North Yorks HER references: ENY5510; SYN16313.
Location: Milsted and Johnson 2009. Mapped in project archive.

G95 'Studforth House', Back Street
SE 4065 6615
2010
A watching brief by MAP Archaeological Consultancy for an extension and associated drainage at the rear of the property. Re-deposited material as a result of levelling in the nineteenth century was noted; otherwise no archaeological features were observed.
Primary reference: Morris 2010.
North Yorks HER references: ENY5513; SNY16318.
Location: Morris 2010 contains no plans. Point mapped in project archive but no georeferenced trenches.

G96 Studforth Farm, Back Street
Test pit 1: SE 4060 6616, Test pit 2: SE 4061 6616, Test pit 3: SE 4061 6615, Test pit 4: SE 4061 6615, Test pit 5: SE 4061 6614, Test pit 6: SE 4061 6615
2010
A watching brief was carried out by JB Archaeology during a barn conversion, consisting of five test pits (1–5) and monitoring ground reduction in a barn (6). Deposits appeared to be re-deposited, but did include some residual Roman material.
Primary reference: Buglass 2010.
North Yorks HER references: ENY5376; SNY15925.
Location: Buglass 2010. Point mapped in project archive but no georeferenced trenches.

G97 Studforth Farmhouse Garage, Back Lane
SE 4066 6614
2010
Watching brief report for monitoring undertaken by Northern Archaeological Associates (NAA) during groundworks associated with the conversion of a derelict cattle shed to a garage. The work included lowering the ground level, and though the foundation trench cut 2.4m down, it is noted as only encountering natural sand throughout.
Primary reference: NAA 2010
North Yorks HER references: ENY5555; SYN16372.
Location: NAA 2010. Area mapped in project archive.

G98 'Hilltop Bungalow', Front Street
SE 4054 6607
2010
A watching brief was carried out by Tees Valley Archaeology during an extension to the front of the property. No archaeological features were discovered, though some re-deposited Roman pottery was found.
Primary reference: Sherlock 2010.
North Yorks HER references: ENY5482; SYN16374.
Location: Sherlock 2010. Point mapped in project archive but no accurate trench locations or plans.

G99 'Olive House', Front Street
SE 4052 6640
2011
Watching brief by Northern Archaeological Associates (NAA) during construction of an extension and manhole. No archaeological features were noted, but descriptions of deposits match those noted in other interventions as Roman. Since the report contained no plans, these deposits cannot be mapped. A significant amount of Roman material was found, as well as post-Roman finds.
Primary reference: Wood 2011.
North Yorks HER references: ENY5819; SNY18781.
Location: Wood 2011. Point mapped in project archive but no accurate trench locations or plans.

G100 Gas mains replacement, various locations
1: SE 4063 6621, 2: SE 4061 6617, 3: SE 4056 6618, 4: SE 4057 6618, 5: SE 4059 6617, 6: SE 4060 6617, 7: SE 4062 6618, 8: SE 4063 6621, 9: SE 4062 6618, 10: SE 4062 6619, 11: SE 4061 6617, 12: SE 4054 6618, 13: SE 4054 6619, 14: SE 4053 6619, 15: SE 4052 6619, 16: SE 4058 6618, 17: SE 4049 6612, 18: SE 4062 6619, 19: SE 4050 6615, 20: SE 4050 6613, 21: SE 4063 6623, 22: SE 4063 6622, 23: SE 4063 6624, 24: SE 4063 6624, 25: SE 4063 6627, 26: SE 4063 6627, 27: SE 4065 6634, 28: SE 4063 6629, 29: SE 4064 6634, 30: SE 4063 6627, 31: SE 4070 6642, 32: SE 4075 6636, 33: SE 4077 6635, 34: SE 4078 6635, 35: SE 4072 6638, 36: SE 4070 6640, 37: SE 4066 6636, 38: SE 4070 6640, 39: SE 4065 6635, 40: SE 4071 6638, 41: SE 4071 6642, 42: SE 4067 6637, 43: SE 4065 6635, 44: SE 4082 6648, 45: SE 4083 6650, 46: SE 4080 6647, 47: SE 4082 6649, 48: SE 4061 6645, 49: SE 4062 6645, 50: SE 4062 6645, 51: SE 4063 6645, 52: SE 4070 6643, 53: SE 4067 6644, 54: SE 4059 6645, 55: SE 4057 6646, 56: SE 4052 6647, 57: SE 4053 6647, 58: SE 4056 6646, 59: SE 4055 6627, 60: SE 4055 6626, 61: SE 4054 6625, 62: SE 4054 6624, 63: SE 4054 6624, 64: SE 4054 6623, 65: SE 4052 6620, 66: SE 4056 6628, 67: SE 4056 6629, 68: SE 4057 6632, 69: SE 4058 6633, 70: SE 4058 6636, 71: SE 4060 6633, 72: SE 4056 6638, 73: SE 4056 6637 74: SE 4053 6641, 75: SE 4055 6638, 76: SE 4051 6644, 77: SE 4051 6644, 78: SE 4051 6645, 79: SE 4049 6648, 80: SE 4048 6649, 81: SE 4048 6649, 82: SE 4048 6649, 83: SE 4047 6650, 84: SE 4048 6649, 85: SE 4051 6647, 86: SE 4050 6648, 87: SE 4044 6652, 88: SE 4041 6653, 89: SE 4035 6656, 90: SE 4028 6659, 91: SE 4039 6654, 92: SE 4034 6656, 93: SE 4049 6648, 94: SE 4050 6648, 95: SE 4049 6648
2013
Watching brief by York Archaeological Trust during gas pipeline replacements around Aldborough in November and December 2012. Trenches 34 (close to the line of the East Wall), 55–8 (to the east of the *forum* just south of the Principal East–West street), 78–86, 93 and 95 (between the Village Hall and West Gate to the south of the Principal East–West street) revealed Roman walls deposits. On the authors' maps trenches have been labelled according to the trench numbers used in their report (for example, **G97**/1, etc).
Primary reference: Johnson 2013.
North Yorks HER references: ENY6757; SNY19691.
Location: Johnson 2013. Accurately mapped in project archive.

G101 'Village Farm', Back Street
SE 4065 6619
2013
An archaeological strip and record was carried out by MAP Archaeological Consultancy during the demolition of an outbuilding, and construction of another building. No archaeological remains were noted.
Primary reference: MAP 2013.
North Yorks HER references: ENY6873; SNY19934.
Location: MAP 2013. Point mapped in project archive but no accurate trench locations or plans.

G102 'Studforth Grange', Back Street
SE 4061 6613
2013
A watching brief carried out by JB Archaeology during works to convert agricultural buildings, including reducing ground levels within the buildings. No archaeological features were found, and there seemed to be re-deposited natural. An old pond appeared to have been filled in in the nineteenth century.
Primary reference: Buglass 2013.
North Yorks HER references: ENY7035; SYN20283.
Location: Buglass 2013. Point mapped in project archive but no accurate trench locations.

G103 'Museum House', Front Street
SE 4048 6616
2016
An archaeological watching brief was carried out by JB Archaeology during construction of an extension to the south of the property. Stone pads were discovered, possibly post pads for a building, but given the location (which must lie over the defensive ditches outside the Town Wall) this conclusion is questionable. Roman pottery was also found.
Primary reference: Buglass 2016; 'Roman Britain in 2016', *Britannia*, 48 (2017), 345–6.
North Yorks HER references: ENY7873; SNY 21883; SNY21884.
Location: Buglass 2016. Accurately mapped in project archive.

Fig A24 Rectified photographic plan of the 2016 excavation (**G104**) showing the walls in relation to those planned in the nineteenth-century plan (**G22**). *Photograph:* Dominic Powlesland; Drawing: Rose Ferraby

G104 English Heritage Mosaic Site
SE 4049 6613
2016
The Aldborough Roman Town Project excavated a small trench to re-investigate the building within which the mosaics on display sit (**G22**) and test the accuracy of the original nineteenth-century plans (figs 3.19 and A24). The work confirmed that the plans were highly accurate, and uncovered part of the hypocaust in one of the rooms. No undisturbed Roman deposits were excavated.
Primary reference: Ferraby and Millett 2016.
North Yorks HER references: SNY22125, ENY8070.
Location: Ferraby and Millett 2016. Accurately mapped in project archive.

G105 Verge north of St Andrew's Church
SE 4062 6644
2017
A trench was dug by the Aldborough Roman Town Project on the verge opposite the Ship Inn in order to investigate the presence, orientation and dating of the north range of the *forum*, as first recorded in 1770 (**G6**) (figs 3.14 and A25). Two interior walls were discovered, confirming the evidence of the eighteenth-century plans (fig 2.5). The walls cut through Flavian deposits with structural features that had been cut into the natural sub-soil. Pottery provides a *terminus post quem* of c AD 120 for the construction of the *forum*. The floor appears to have been robbed-out, probably in the fourth century, with a metal-working hearth cut into the make-up (above, Chapter 4, n 232).
Primary reference: Ferraby and Millett 2017.
North Yorks HER references: SNY22400, ENY7804.
Location: Ferraby and Millett 2017. Accurately mapped in project archive.

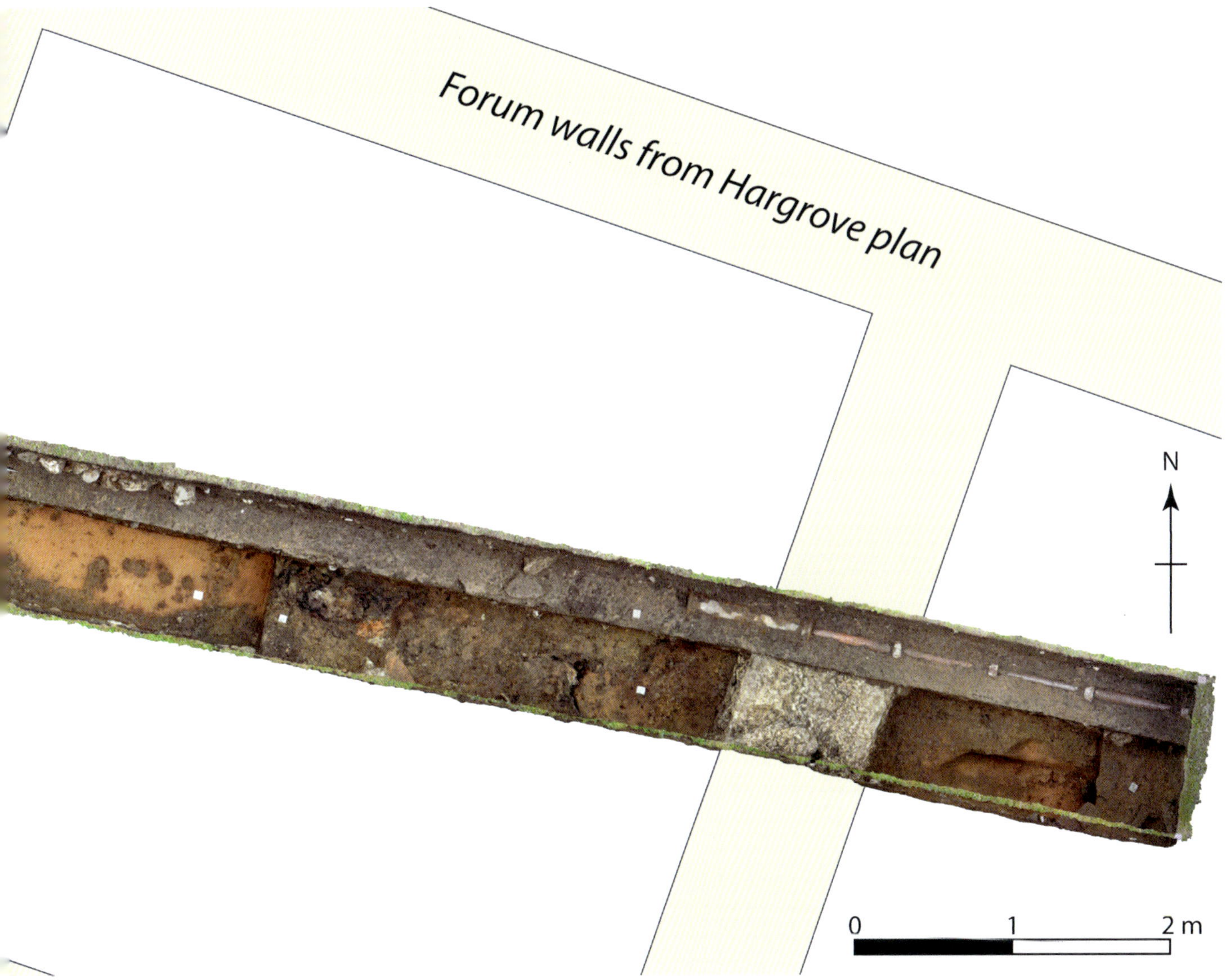

Fig A25 Rectified photographic plan of the 2017 excavation (**G105**) showing the walls in relation to those planned 1770 (**G6**, see fig 2.5). *Photograph:* Dominic Powlesland. *Drawing:* Rose Ferraby

G106 Building in north-eastern corner of the town, just south of the Town Wall
SE 4078 6667
2018
The Aldborough Roman Town Project re-excavated part of the 1924 trench and a new area over 'Masonry T' (**G38**) (figs A26 and A27). The building is known from the fluxgate gradiometry survey to be *c* 60m long (Building 2.17; above, pp. 41–2). The aim was to establish the date and function of the structure. Flavian deposits were located at the bottom of the sequence, and the building was constructed *c* 250–300. After its demolition, there was evidence for late fourth century dumping, which strengthened the bank behind the Town Wall. The trench also confirmed the identification of a street running between the building and the Town Wall.
Primary reference: Ferraby and Millett 2018.
North Yorks HER references: ENY8411.
Location: Ferraby and Millett 2018. Accurately mapped in project archive.

Fig A26 Rectified photographic plan of the 2018 excavation (**G106**), re-excavating 'Masonry T' (**G38**). *Photograph:* Dominic Powlesland. *Drawing:* Rose Ferraby

Fig A27 The 2018 excavation (**G106**) viewed from the south. *Photograph:* Rose Ferraby

Appendix 2
Concordance with *RIB*

***RIB* number and description**	**Gazetteer no./ findspot**	**Comments**
RIB 708 (altar)	Unknown	Ecroyd Smith 1852, pl XXI, no 3. (Appendix 5, no 1) English Heritage Helmsley Store (Accession no 78108257 with unpublished base Accession no 81418111)
RIB 709 (funerary inscription)	Built into a wall in Boroughbridge	Ecroyd Smith 1852, 46, pl XXI, no 8
RIB 710 (funerary inscription)	Perhaps **G7**	English Heritage Helmsley Store (Accession no 78108260)
RIB 2347* (altar with forged text)	**G29**	Found with two uninscribed altars. (Appendix 5, no 3).
RIB 2277 (milestone – Trajan Decius)	**G34/3**	Findspot shown on fig A14 English Heritage Helmsley Store (Accession no 78108261)
RIB 2278 (milestone – Trajan Decius)	Unknown	Ecroyd Smith 1852, 47, pl XXI, no 10
RIB 2411.247 (lead sealing – 'Beneficiarius V…')	Field outside North Gate	Discussed in Chapter 4, above, p. 113
RIB 2429.7 (openwork baldrick pendant)	Unknown	Bishop 1996, no 424
RIB 2429.8 (openwork baldrick pendant)	Unknown	Bishop 1996, no 426
RIB 2448.5 (mosaic label)	**G23**	See also Ling 2007
RIB 2460.52 (LEG VI tile stamp)	Unknown	–

RIB number and description	Gazetteer no./ findspot	Comments
RIB 2460.84 (LEG VI tile stamp)	Unknown	–
RIB 2460.94 (LEG VI tile stamp)	Unknown	–
RIB 2462.7(i) (LEG IX tile stamp)	Unknown	–
RIB 2462.9(xxix) (LEG IX tile stamp)	Unknown	–
RIB 2462.12(i) (LEG IX tile stamp)	Unknown	Ecroyd Smith 1852, 51, Pl XXVIII, 10
RIB 2462.12(ii) (LEG IX tile stamp)	Unknown	–
RIB 2470.2 (COH IIII Breucorum tile stamp)	Unknown	–
RIB 2489.29 (tile stamp M.M)	Unknown	Ecroyd Smith 1852, 51
RIB 3208 (statue base)	Built into Kirby Hill Church	
Roman Britain in 1987, no 97 (lead sealing – 'Provinciae Britanniae Inferioris'	Field outside North Gate	Discussed in Chapter 4, above, p. 112
Roman Britain in 1989, no 68 (lead sealing – 'Dominus Noster')	Field outside North Gate	Discussed in Chapter 4, above, p. 113

Appendix 3
Concordance with *CSIR*

***CSIR* no.** (Vol 1, Fasc 3)	**Description**	**Gazetteer no./ findspot**	**Comments**
CSIR 15	Marble head	Unknown	In Pump Room, Harrogate
CSIR 16	Mercury relief	**G17**	On display in English Heritage site museum (Accession no. 78108258)
CSIR 17	Mercury relief	Unknown	Now in Aldborough church
Not in *CSIR*	Altar with figures in relief	**G15**	Ecroyd Smith 1852, Pl XXI, 7 & pp 23–4, 45 (fig 3.26) = Appendix 5, no 4
Not in *CSIR*	Eroded relief, draped standing figure?	Unknown	Unpublished (project archive no. St 51)
Not in *CSIR*	Fragment of small relief with left side of frame. Head and upper body of figure with hooded cloak. Probably one of three *Genii Cuculati*	Unknown	Unpublished. English Heritage Helmsley store (Accession no. 88106912)

Appendix 4
Architectural stonework

The following list includes pieces that the authors of this volume have identified on site at Aldborough and in the English Heritage stores at Helmsley together with key items that have been published but which can no longer be traced. Included here are only pieces that can be fairly certainly identified as Roman. These have been compared with the manuscript drawings prepared by Tom Blagg in the 1970s–80s during the preparation of his PhD thesis (posthumously published as Blagg 2002). These drawing were kindly made available by Professor A C King. The order of listing here is based on the architectural form.

No.	Brief description	Dimensions (m)	Stone	Ecroyd Smith 1852 ref	Archive ref	Notes
1	Foliate column capital with square top.	Drum dia 0.38; top 0.45 × 0.45; Ht 0.36	Medium grit stone	Pl XIV	St 12	Blagg drawing no 6 = Blagg 2002, 40, 252, Pl CXVII. His Group B capital, with a northern distribution including military sites.
2	Battered and eroded column capital of Provincial Tuscan type. Simple cyma recta above a broad collar, with necking beneath defined at the bottom by a plain astragalus. Slight evidence for clamp hole at bottom. [Pair with no 3.]	Dia at top 0.34; at base 0.40; Ht 0.46	Coarse grit stone	Pl XXII, no 3	St 27	Blagg 2002,142, Type VII, although there is no exact parallel for the collar.
3	Provincial Tuscan capital simple cyma recta above a broad collar, with necking beneath defined at the bottom by a plain astragalus. [Pair with no 2.]	Drum dia 0.32; top 0.37; Ht 0.5	Coarse grit stone		St 59	Blagg 2002,142, Type VII. EH Store at Helmsley (Acc no. 81418139).
4	Eroded Provincial Tuscan capital with large clamp holes in top and bottom. Square top, with cyma reversa moulding. Perhaps similar type to nos 3 & 4 with broad collar beneath, but damage makes this uncertain.	Drum dia 0.3; ht 0.25	Medium–coarse grit stone		St 37	Blagg 2002, 142, Type VII.
5	Section of plain column capital (?).	Dia at top 0.53, dia at base 0.48, Ht 0.34	Coarse grit stone		St 56	

No.	Brief description	Dimensions (m)	Stone	Ecroyd Smith 1852 ref	Archive ref	Notes
6	Eroded column capital and upper part of unfluted shaft with slot cut down one side of drum. Capital of Provincial Tuscan type. Square top above two tall cyma recta mouldings and an eroded astragalus.	Drum dia 0.27; Ht 0.76; slot depth 0.05; Base 0.36 × 0.32	Medium grit stone	Pl XXII, no 6	St 18	Blagg 2002, 132, Type Va.
7	Unworn column capital of Provincial Tuscan type, with square top above a scotia, then two cavetto mouldings with broad fillet above. These each sit above a torus defined by beaded fillets.	Drum dia 0.2; Top 0.36; Ht 0.4	Medium/ coarse grit stone		St 61	Blagg 2002, 136, Type Vc, but no exact parallel illustrated. EH Store at Helmsley (Acc no. 81418138).
8	Column base with torus moulding but with recut hollow in drum.	Base 0.35 × 0.35 Base Ht 0.18; moulding 0.03. Dia of hole in drum 0.18	Sandstone	Pl XXII, no 5	St 14	Blagg drawing no. 7. The recutting is probably 19th century.[2]
9	Column base, double torus moulding separated by scotia, without fillets, below a very eroded cavetto moulding. Square clamp hole. [Pair with no 10.]	Drum dia 0.37; max dia at torus moulding 0.54; Ht 0.33+	Coarse grit stone	Pl XIV beside corridor mosaic	St 16	Blagg 2002, 117, Type IIb. Site **G20** (although note that Ecroyd Smith's drawing shows square bases).
10	Column base, double torus moulding separated by scotia, without fillets, below an eroded cavetto moulding. [Pair with no 9.]	Drum dia 0.39; max dia at torus moulding 0.56; Base 0.56×0.60; Max Ht 0.70	Coarse grit stone	Pl XIV beside corridor mosaic	St 17	Blagg 2002, 117, Type IIb. Site **G20** (but note that Ecroyd Smith's drawing shows square bases).
11	Plain square column base with quarter round moulding defining the base of the unfluted drum.	Drum dia 0.28; Top 0.3; Ht 0.24	Medium fine sandstone		St 57	EH Store at Helmsley (Acc no. 78108384).
12	Column base; assymetrically placed on square base. Crudely carved.	Base 0.50 × 0.50; drum dia 0.34; Ht 0.32+; Offset 0.08 on 2; 0.12 on other 2 sides	Coarse orangey coloured grit stone		St 28	
13	Very eroded column base; double torus moulding. Split so that only ¾ of the diameter survives.	Drum dia 0.3, Ht 0.4	Coarse grit stone		St 50	Too eroded to identify Blagg 2002 type. Barber *et al* 1925, Plan D block M3? **G34/3** see figs A14 and A15
14	Eroded column base with unfluted column above double torus moulding separated by scotia. No evidence for fillets.	–	–	Pl XX, no 4	Not located	Blagg 2002, 125, type VIII. Barber *et al* 1925, Plan D block M2. **G34/3**, see figs A14 and A15

No.	Brief description	Dimensions (m)	Stone	Ecroyd Smith 1852 ref	Archive ref	Notes
15	Square column base with two torus mouldings separated by a narrow scotia. Lower torus has a greater diameter than the upper. [Pair with no. 16.]			Pl XX, no 4	Not located	From site **G3**, illustrated by Drake 1736, vol 2, Pl p xiii. Probably Blagg 2002, 125 Type VIII.
16	Square column base with two torus mouldings separated by a narrow scotia. Lower torus has a greater diameter than the upper. [Pair with no 16.]			Pl XX, no 5	Not located	From site **G3,** illustrated by Drake 1736, vol 2, Pl p xiii. Probably Blagg 2002, 125, Type VIII.
17	Unfluted column drum.	Drum dia 0.24; Ht 0.35	Coarse grit stone		St 58	EH Store at Helmsley (Acc no. 78108383).
18	Unfluted column drum with two grooves at top. Probably semi-engaged column.	Dia 0.27, Ht 0.22	Fine grit stone		St 7	(On English Heritage site, Acc no. 88406419).
19	Unfluted column drum with clamp hole (circular) at visible end.	Dia 0.26, Ht 0.29+ (hole dia 0.08; 0.07 deep)	Fine/medium grit stone		St 9	(On English Heritage site, Acc no. 88406420).
20	Unfluted column drum; with one slightly flattened side.	Max Dia 0.32; 0.28 front to back, Ht 0.31	Medium grit stone		St 22	
21	Unfluted column drum; partially engaged.	Max Dia 0.36; 0.26 front to back, Ht 0.33	Coarse grit stone		St 23	
22	Unfluted column drum, irregular with flat back – secondary erosion?	Max Dia 0.28; max ht 0.34	Medium grit stone		St 24	
23	Unfluted column drum.	Dia 0.35; Ht 0.40	Coarse grit stone		St 25	
24	Unfluted column drum with base buried? Slight evidence for clamp hole.	Dia 0.36; Ht 0.24+	Coarse grit stone		St 26	
25	Unfluted column drum with lower part of column capital? Single line 0.04 from top.	Drum dia 0.48; Ht 0.33+	Medium grit stone		St 32	
26	Unfluted column drum.	Dia 0.30; Ht 0.35+	Medium gritstone		St 34	
27	Battered Unfluted column drum, with clamp hole in end.	Drum dia 0.55, Ht 0.42	Coarse grit stone		St 52	
28	Unfluted column drum.	Drum dia 0.35, Ht 0.35+	Medium–coarse grit stone	–	St 55	

No.	Brief description	Dimensions (m)	Stone	Ecroyd Smith 1852 ref	Archive ref	Notes
29	Cornice, with cyma recta moulding with groove below. (Non-conjoining piece with no. 30.)	L 0.70 x Depth 0.62 × Th 0.23	Medium grit stone		St 3	Blagg drawing no. 1 Thickness suggests a column height of *c* 2.76m. (On English Heritage site, Acc no. 88406415.)
30	Cornice, with cyma recta moulding with groove below. (Non-conjoining piece with no. 29.)	L 0.52 × Depth 0.66 × Th 0.20	Medium grit stone		St 4	Thickness suggests a column height of *c* 2.40m. (On English Heritage site, Acc no. 88406416.)
31	Fine quality but eroded cornice. Plain cyma recta below a fillet and above a quarter round astragal. Below these are plain modillions with a cyma reverse profile. Coffering on the soffits is defined by a groove.	L 0.40 W 0.30, thickness 0.20	Medium grit stone		St 48	See Blagg 2002, 64–8, 92–6. He illustrates a similar cornice from Chester (Pl LXXXI). Thickness suggests a column height of *c* 2.40m.
32	Eroded cornice moulding with a pair of cyma recta mouldings separated by a bead.	Thickness 0.19; Width 0.32; Length 0.31	Medium grit stone		St 60	EH Store at Helmsley (Acc no 88284767)
33	Stylobate with scotia moulding and bead beneath.	W 0.36, depth 0.25, Ht 0.18	Coarse grit stone		St 54	
34	Perhaps a door jamb with recess and plain moulding.	L 0.65 × Depth 0.45×Th 0.23	Coarse grit stone		St 5	Blagg drawing no. 3. (On English Heritage site, Acc no. 88406417.)
35	Threshold (*soglia*) block, in three fragments with hinge and central bolt sockets. Distance from hinge to bolt socket on B–C = 0.52m.	A) L 0.41 × Depth 0.41 × Th 0.18	Very coarse gritstone		St 6A	Width suggests an overall door height of *c* 2.6m. (On English Heritage site, Acc no. 88406418.)
		B) L 0.48 × Depth 0.48 × Th 0.20			St 6B	
		C) L 0.42 × Depth 0.48 × Th 0.20			St 6C	
36	L-shaped corner block. Door rebate?	0.32 by 0.30 Ht 0.20+	Medium gritstone		St 11	(On English Heritage site, Acc no. 88406421.)
37	Block with groove at front and rectangular socket cut into it.	L 0.57, W 0.43, thickness 0.17+	Coarse–very coarse grit stone		St 38	Barber *et al* 1925, Plan D block M1. **G34/3** see figs A14 and A15.
38	Block with hinge pivot hole and two other cut sockets.	'6 ft long' according to Ecroyd Smith's caption	–	Pl XXII, 1	Not located	Ecroyd Smith's caption gives findspot as 'near the presumed site of Western Gate'. **G8**. Location shown on unpublished plan (fig 2.10).

No.	Brief description	Dimensions (m)	Stone	Ecroyd Smith 1852 ref	Archive ref	Notes
39	Block with socket hole.	Drawing says '10 in × 24 in'	–	Pl XXII, 7	Not located	Ecroyd Smith's caption gives findspot as 'near Eastern Gate'. **G16**.
40	Block with hinge pivot hole.	–	–	Pl XXII, 8	Not located	Ecroyd Smith's caption gives findspot as 'near Eastern Gate'. **G16**.
41	Gutter block.	L 1.30 W 0.45, thickness 0.25+	Medium grit stone	Pl p 44(a)?	St 44	Perhaps from **G25**, fig A7.
42	Gutter block.	L 0.47 W 0.42, thickness 0.3+	Coarse grit stone	Pl p 44(a)?	St 45	Perhaps from **G25**, fig A7.
43	Gutter block.	L 0.70 W 0.52, thickness 0.24+	Coarse grit stone	Pl p 44(a)?	St 46	Perhaps from **G25**, fig A7.
44	Gutter block.	L 0.68 W 0.23, thickness 0.15+	Fine grit stone		St 47	Perhaps from **G25**, fig A7.
45	Block, with recesses on 4 short faces; Side of a water tank (cf nos 47 & 48 below).	L 0.58 × Depth 0.73 × Ht 0.23	Heavy grit stone		St 1	Blagg drawing no 4. (On English Heritage site, Acc no 88406413.)
46	Block with axial slot and central groove. Base for a water tank (cf nos 47 & 48 below).	L 0.53 × Depth 0.83 × Th 0.20	Medium grit stone		St 2	Blagg drawing no 2. (On English Heritage site, Acc no 88406414.).
47	Rectangular block with L-shaped groove from the base of a water tank. Pair with no 48 below.	L 0.9 × W 0.54, thickness 0.23+	Coarse grit stone		St 39	From water tank base found inside North Gate (Myres *et al* 1959, Pl IVb). **G34/G**, see fig A16.
48	Block with groove from the base of a water tank (cf no. 46). Pair with no 47 above.	L 0.79, W 0.54, thickness 0.22	Coarse grit stone		St 41	From water tank base found inside North Gate (Myres *et al* 1959, Pl IVb). **G34/G**, see fig A16.

Appendix 5
Stone altars

The following list includes altars that have been recorded on site or previously published.

No.	Description	Gazetteer no./findspot	Comments
1	Inscribed altar dedicated to Jupiter Optimus Maximus and the Matres	Unknown	*RIB* 708; Ecroyd Smith 1852, pl XXI, no 3. Kewley 1970, cat no. 48. English Heritage Helmsley Store (Accession No. 78108257 with unpublished base Accession no. 81418111)
2	Altar with 19th century forged text	**G29**	*RIB* 2347*; Ecroyd Smith 1852, pl XXI, no 6. Kewley 1970, cat no. 618
3	Uninscribed altar	**G29**	Ecroyd Smith 1852, pl XXI, nos 1–2. Kewley 1970, cat no. 619
4	Uninscribed altar with figures in relief on front and right hand side	**G15**	Ecroyd Smith 1852, Pl XXI, 7 & pp 23–4, 45 fig 3.26)
5	Uninscribed altar with mirror? on right side, and patera? on left; focus partly damaged	Unknown	Unpublished (project archive no. St 51)
6	Small altar base?	Unknown	Unpublished (project archive no. St 20)
7	Uninscribed altar top	Unknown	Unpublished (project archive no. St 33)

Notes

Chapter 1

1 Frere 1987, 162ff; Birley 2005, 181; Ottaway 2013, 160.
2 Frere 1987, 110–19; Hodgson 2017, 31–41.
3 Mattingly 2006, 157–8.
4 Dobinson *et al* 2018.
5 Ottaway 2013, 60–5; Smith *et al* 2016, 245–7, figs 7.3–7.4.
6 Champion 2016.
7 Millett 1990, 9–39; Creighton 2006, 14–31.
8 Tacitus *Annals* 12.36. See Haselgrove 2016, 466–97 for the most recent discussion of Cartimandua and Stanwick.
9 Tacitus *Annals* 12.36.
10 Tacitus *Histories* 3.45.
11 Hanson and Campbell 1986, 77–8.
12 Haselgrove 2016.
13 Ibid, 387–8.
14 Ibid, 392–3.
15 Tacitus *Histories* 3.45.
16 Haselgrove 2016, 472–6.
17 Tacitus *Agricola* 17.
18 Ottaway 2013, 93–106.
19 Bishop 2005.
20 Frere 1987, 105–25; Mattingly 2006, 128–60.
21 Margary route 8b – Margary 1973, 428–9.
22 Margary route 82 – Margary 1973, 433–6.
23 Millett 1990, 65–85.
24 Mattingly 2006, 272–3.
25 Ecroyd Smith 1852.
26 Lawson-Tancred 1948, 12.
27 Collingwood 1927, 2–3.
28 Myres *et al* 1959, 9.
29 *RIB* nos 2462.7(i); 2462.9(xxix); 2462.12(i) and 2462.12(ii). Only 2462.12(i) is certainly from Aldborough (Ecroyd Smith 1852, 51, pl. XXVIII, 10).
30 Myres *et al* 1959, 8–9.
31 Published as Wacher 1965, see especially 56.
32 Hartley and Fitts 1988, 40–1.
33 Wacher 1974, 399, n 73 citing *J Roman Stud*, **52** (1962), 166, which reports on excavations on the site of a house called Stonehaven (**G49**). This excavation, by Dorothy Charlesworth, was published by Snape *et al* 2002, 40–7, showing that the building is neither of the first-century AD nor a bathhouse.
34 Dobinson 1988, 10; ibid, 1988–9, 5; see also Dobinson 1995.
35 Bishop 2005.
36 Bishop 1996, 1; 2005, 218–19. *RIB* nos 2460.52; 2460.84 and 2460.94 (*Legio* VI); *RIB* no 2470.2 (*Coh.* IIII *Breucorum*). The attribution of these to Aldborough is not absolutely certain: antiquarian sources mention only one stamp of *Legio* IX.
37 Rivet and Smith 1979, 379–80.
38 Ptolemy *Geography* II, 3, 10.
39 Rivet and Smith 1979, 114–16.
40 Ibid 1979, 311, 379–80. The source for this part of the Ravenna Cosmography is probably fourth century; ibid, 190–200.
41 Wacher 1995, 378–407.
42 Margary route 280 – Margary 1973, 417.
43 Margary route 8a – Margary 1973, 427–8.
44 See Stowe MS, folios 3–5 (quoted below, Chapter 2, p. 12); Turner 1853, 53–4, 134.
45 Margary route 720b – Margary 1973, 406–7.
46 Ottaway 2013, 257–8.
47 PCA 2015.
48 'Roman Britain in 2008', 236 (*Britannia*, **40**, 219–363); Antoni 2008.
49 p. 17, Chapter 2.
50 p. 88, Chapter 4.
51 Wade 1953; Brickstock 2019, 64.
52 Lawson-Tancred 1937, 6–7.
53 Drake 1736; Stukeley 1776; Gough 1789.
54 Turner 1853, 135.
55 Turner 1853, 98–9, 103.
56 Ecroyd Smith 1852.
57 Mark Nicholson Hessey (1828–1909). See Knowles (No Date). The authors are grateful to Mike Turpin for this reference.
58 Lawson 1864, 45.
59 See Myres *et al* 1959, 3 for a note on these excavations, the results of which are integrated into their account of the 1930s work. An unpublished manuscript report on the excavations of 1924 (Barber *et al* 1925) is held in the archive of Sir Andrew Lawson-Tancred.
60 Myres *et al* 1959. See also Chitty 1986–7.
61 Myres *et al* 1959, 7–8 on three sets of structures in the northern part of the town, whilst p. 5, n 4 mentions a cutting through the bank of the supposed amphitheatre that convinced the authors of this volume that the bank was natural (**G15**).
62 Jones 1971.
63 Snape *et al* 2002.
64 Charlesworth 1970.
65 Charlesworth 1971.
66 Johnson and Neal 2002.
67 Bishop 1996, 1–2.
68 Dobinson *et al* 2018; see also fig 4.6 below.

Chapter 2

1 Smith 1907, 85–6.
2 Drake 1736, I, 24.
3 Gibson 1722, 875–6 = *RIB* 709.
4 Gough 1789, 59.
5 Gibson 1722, 875.
6 Drake 1736, 24.
7 Gibson 1695, 716–17.
8 Stowe MS, folios 3–5.
9 Ibid.
10 The identity of WD remains unknown. No candidates can be identified from the contemporary papers published in Lawson-Tancred 1937.
11 Stowe MS, folio 26.
12 Ibid, folio 16.
13 Stowe MS, folio 5. Now identified as Mercury; *CSIR* vol 1, fasc 3, no. 17 (see this volume, Appendix 3).
14 Lukis 1887.
15 Ibid, 281–2.
16 Ibid, 284–5.
17 Ibid, 288–90.
18 Ibid, 292–3.
19 Drake 1736, 24–5.
20 Ibid, figs 1 and 2, opposite p 24.
21 Ibid, 25–6, figs 3 and 4.
22 Ibid, vol II, xiii–xiv.
23 Horsley 1732, 402–3.
24 Stukeley 1776, 73–4.
25 Ibid, 73.
26 York Record Office MS, GB 192 HAR (henceforth referred to as Hargrove MS).
27 Hargrove 1769, 37–40.
28 Gough 1789, 59.
29 Ibid, 59.
30 Ibid, 59, Pl III, figs 7–8 = *RIB* 2347*.
31 Ibid, 59 = *RIB* 2276.
32 Ibid, 59; the coin can be identified as *RIC*, vol 2, 263, cat nos 275, 277 or 278 dated to AD 112–14.
33 Myres *et al* 1959, 5.
34 Hargrove 1818.
35 Ibid, vol II, 359.
36 Hargrove MS.
37 Hargrove 1769.
38 Hargrove MS, vol III, 47.
39 *RIB* 2276. Note that the findspot given in *RIB* vol 1 (first edition) is incorrect. It states that it was found north of Aldborough, on the road to Catterick. It was actually found to the south, on the road to York (SE 42696325).
40 Hargrove MS, vol III, 89.
41 *Gentleman's Magazine* 1787, Part II, 564–5.
42 AAGM database.
43 *Gentleman's Magazine* 1787, Part II, 659–60. Gales' authorship is identified in the AAGM database.
44 *DNB sv.* Hargrove, Ely [*pseud* E H Knaresborough] 1741–1818.
45 Hargrove MS, vol III, 90.
46 *RIB* 710.
47 *Gentleman's Magazine* 1811, Part II, 312.
48 Hargrove 1818, vol II, 359.
49 Moore-Jessop 1849, 75.
50 Turner 1853, 98.
51 Lawson-Tancred 1937, 13, 125–6.
52 Ibid, 198.
53 Ibid, 125.
54 Leach and Pevsner 2009, 97.
55 It may be noted that various features shown on early editions of the Ordnance Survey relate to the layout of the garden. These include 'altars' in the area to the west of the present garden (SE 40314 66422). The Saxon cross also displayed in the garden (SE 40386 66379) was brought from Cundall (Lang 2001, 93–7).
56 Ecroyd Smith 1852.
57 Ibid, Pl III.
58 Ibid, 5.
59 It was visited here by a group from the Archaeological Institute during their annual meeting held in York in 1846, when excavations on the site were also opened especially for them (*Archaeological Institute* 1848, xi).
60 Lawson-Tancred 1948, 13.
61 Ecroyd Smith 1852, 36; Turner 1853, 107. The mosaic is Neal and Cosh 2002, no. 123.17, which was excavated before 1846.
62 Lawson 1864, 45.
63 Ecroyd Smith 1852.
64 Ibid, Pl III, opposite p 13.
65 *CSIR* vol 1, fasc 3, no. 16 (Appendix 3).
66 Fieldwork on the quarry by Rose Ferraby will be published in a forthcoming paper
67 Ecroyd Smith 1859–68.
68 Lawson-Tancred 1948, 13.
69 Letters and Notes of Francis Haverfield, Aldborough, North Yorkshire: Sackler Library Archive, University of Oxford.
70 Moore-Jessop 1849.
71 Turner 1853.
72 Lawson 1864.
73 Leadman 1893.
74 Collingwood 1927.
75 Lawson-Tancred 1948.
76 Myres *et al* 1959.
77 Barber *et al* 1925.
78 *RIB* 2277.
79 Collingwood 1927.
80 Myres *et al* 1959.
81 Chitty 1986–7, 10–11, partly re-published in Millett and Ferraby 2016, 39.
82 Jones 1971.
83 Johnson and Neal 2002; Snape *et al* 2002.
84 Bishop 1996.
85 Brickstock 2019.
86 Wacher 1974, 398–404; revised Wacher 1995, 401–7.

87 Ibid 1995, 402 (first-century baths), 403 (*forum*), 403 (defensive sequence), 406 (by-pass road) and 407 (reduction in defensive circuit).
88 Dobinson 1988.
89 Dobinson 1988–9.
90 Wacher 1995, 401–7.
91 Cambridge University Committee for Aerial Photography image BZG-00062 taken in 1976. This shows part of our streets EW1, EW4 and NS3 (below fig 4.8).
92 Dobinson *et al* 2018 ; below fig 4.6.
93 Herkes 1997.

Chapter 3

1 Verdonck *et al* 2013; 2015.
2 Ecroyd Smith 1852, 13.
3 Stowe MSS.
4 Cf Perring 2002, 65, fig 19.
5 Cf Marsden 1987, 32, figs 17 and 18.
6 Cf Perring 2002, 55ff, figs 15–16.
7 Cf ibid, 66ff, fig 23.
8 Cf Smith 1997, 36–7.
9 Cambridge University Committee for Aerial Photography image BZG-00062.
10 Myres *et al* 1959, 14–16, fig 5.
11 Wacher 1995, 406–7, erroneously placing it in the north-eastern corner of the town rather than the north-western corner.
12 Charlesworth 1971, 155; it is shown in its original course on the first edition Ordnance Survey Map (1852), but had been moved by the time of the second edition (1892).
13 Cf Berry 1951, fig 6.
14 There is possible doubt about the identification of street EW5 since a 1976 aerial photo (Cambridge University Committee for Aerial Photography image BZG-00062) shows a post-medieval farm wall in this area.
15 Cf Rickman 1971, 247–8.
16 Cf Nielsen 1993, fig 1, types I and II.
17 Dobinson *et al* 2018, 55–6.
18 Cf Creighton with Fry 2016, Insula I.1 (fig 5.15) and Insula XXVII.1 & XXVII.2 (fig 5.19)
19 Cf Smith 1997, 117ff.
20 Cf Rickman 1971, 264–70.
21 Cf, for example, Silchester Insula XIV.1 – Creighton with Fry 2016, fig 5.25.
22 In some earlier discussion of the *forum* (Millett and Ferraby 2016, 18–19; Ferraby and Millett 2017), it was suggested that this lay at an angle to the later street grid. Careful analysis of the results of the GPR survey and 2017 excavation (**G105**) has proved this suggestion to be wrong, and confirms that it was aligned with the rest of the street grid.
23 Ecroyd Smith 1852, 17, Pl V.
24 Cf Perring 2002, fig 16.
25 Ferraby and Millett 2017.
26 Cf Perring 2002, 66ff, figs 22–3.
27 Ellis 1995, 169–71.
28 Dobinson *et al* 2018, fig 2.
29 Ecroyd Smith 1852, 23–4.
30 Ibid, Pl XXI, no. 7, but not listed in *CSIR* vol 1, fasc 3 (Yorks); see Appendix 3.
31 Snape *et al* 2002, 62.
32 Ecroyd Smith 1852, Pl IX.
33 *Gentleman's Magazine,* 1811 Part II, 312.
34 Collingwood 1927, 10; Collingwood 1930, 106; Wilmott 2008, 158–9.
35 Myres *et al* 1959, 5, n 4.
36 Jones 1971, 40, n 2.
37 Brown 1959, 261.
38 Wilmott 2008, 50–5.
39 *Gentleman's Magazine* 1811, 312.
40 Ecroyd Smith 1852, 25–6, Pl X.
41 Creighton with Fry 2016, 375–87.
42 The authors could see no evidence for a temple in this area hypothesised by Herkes (1997, 58).
43 Dobinson *et al* 2018, fig 2.
44 Evans and Mills 2018, fig 8.
45 Dobinson *et al* 2018, figs 2–5.
46 Snape *et al* 2002, 52ff, figs 14 and 16.
47 Ibid, 61ff, figs 14 and 16.
48 Ibid, 50, figs 14 and 19.
49 Pearce 2013, 117.
50 Cf Pearce 2013, 35–9.
51 Dobinson *et al* 2018, figs 2 and 8.
52 Evans and Mills 2018, figs 9–10.
53 Jones 1971, 53; cf Dobinson *et al* 2018, 32–3.
54 Dobinson *et al* 2018, fig 2.
55 Fitzpatrick and Scott 1999.
56 This being Margary's route 8b, although he does not note any deviation from a straight course (Margary 1973, 428–9).
57 Margary 1973, 424, route 815.
58 Dobinson *et al* 2018, fig 2.
59 Bishop 2005, fig 39.
60 The authors cannot find any evidence from this area to support the suggestion that there was an amphitheatre hereabouts: Herkes 1997, 59, 63.
61 Margary 1973, 406–7, route 720b.
62 Dobinson *et al* 2018, fig 2.
63 Evans and Mills 2018, fig 11.
64 Ferraby forthcoming.
65 Margary 1973, 406–7.

Chapter 4

1 Ross 2011, 99 Map 2; Bridgland *et al* 2011, 223–4, fig 4.11; this low density of recorded rural sites continues into the Roman period; Horne 2003, fig 4.4; Smith *et al* 2016, 242–5.
2 Roberts *et al* 2010, 55–78.

3 Haselgrove 2016, 415–23.
4 Bridgland *et al* 2011, 221–6; 264–8.
5 Heslop 2008, figs 56–8; Vyner 2018, 22–5.
6 Horne 2003, 59, fig 4.5.
7 Ottaway 2013, 53–70.
8 Another crop mark of an Iron Age enclosure complex was identified in 2018 a little further south at Aldborough Moor Farm (fig 4.1). Tony Hunt's suggestion (in his lecture at the York Archaeology Conference on 17 Nov 2018) that this represents a Roman fort is speculative and looks highly improbable.
9 Manby *et al* 2003, 55, 92–3.
10 Brown *et al* 2007, 149–50; Orton 2007.
11 Brown *et al* 2007, 1–11.
12 Waterman *et al* 1954.
13 Manby *et al* 2003, 68, 96.
14 Nick Wilson, pers comm.
15 For Duel Cross, see below and chapter 2, p. 17; Antoni 2008.
16 Cf Collingwood 1927, 4, proposing an Agricolan date for the deliberate foundation of the town.
17 Breeze 2005, 350; cf Rivet and Smith 1979, 380.
18 Ibid, 350.
19 Haselgrove 2016, 472–6.
20 Ibid, 474–6.
21 Cf Ross 2011.
22 Bishop 2005, 218–19.
23 Wilson 2009, 10; Brickstock 2019, 56.
24 Bishop 2005, 219.
25 Walker 1988; Hobley 1998.
26 SE 336 629, visible on the Google Earth images taken in July 2018. This was previously recorded as an enclosure (NMR Pastscape no. 141172; North Yorks HER no. MNY39135).
27 Wilson 2009, 11, illus 2.
28 Millett 1990, 42–57.
29 Haselgrove 2016, 433–7.
30 Fell 2017.
31 Haselgrove 2016, 466–72.
32 Hodgson 2009, 141–4.
33 Tacitus *Agricola,* xx–xxi.
34 Birley 2005, 67.
35 Wilson 2009, 9–10 critically reviews the evidence.
36 Ambrey *et al* 2017, vol 1, 28, 95–8.
37 Wilson 2002, vol 2 446–51.
38 Ottaway 2013, 104 lists Catterick racecourse, two forts at Bainesse, and another at Scorton.
39 Catterick – St Joseph 1955, 82 – undated; Bainesse – dating to before AD 80 is only speculative (Brickstock *et al* 2007, 113–14); Scorton 'Marching Camp' is later first–second century (Speed 2002).
40 Welfare and Swan 1995, 136.
41 Founded in the early to mid 70s; Abramson *et al* 1999, 290–1.
42 Ottaway 2013, 101.
43 Cf the 'Glen-blocking' forts in Flavian Scotland; Breeze 1996, 56.
44 At SE 472 773, visible on Google Earth images taken in July 2018, and dated by metal-detector finds. Millett and Brickstock 2020.
45 See above, n 26.
46 Poulter 2009, 21–2.
47 Ibid, 28.
48 But cf Collingwood 1927 suggesting an Agricolan foundation for the town.
49 Bishop 1996.
50 Brickstock 2019 (whose conclusions differ).
51 Walker 1988, 281–2.
52 Snape *et al* 2002.
53 S H Willis 2002, in Snape *at al* 2002, 69–79.
54 K F Hartley 2002, in Snape *at al* 2002, 81–91.
55 Snape *at al* 2002, 103–4.
56 Myres *et al* 1959.
57 Bishop 2005, 218.
58 Myres *et al* 1959, 18.
59 Dobinson *et al* 2018, 35, 39–41, 46–7, 50-1.
60 Dobinson *et al* 2018, 35–6.
61 Bishop 1996, 2–3.
62 Four examples: *RIB* 2462.7i; 2462.9xxix; 2462.12i and ii.
63 Three examples: *RIB* 2460.52, 2460.84 and 2460.94.
64 *RIB* 2470.2.
65 Birley 2005, 227–30.
66 Wright 1976.
67 Jarrett 1994, 57.
68 McWhirr 1979, 182–3; Ottaway 2013, 141.
69 *Tab Vind* II, 185 and III, 595.
70 *Vinovia*: *Tab Vind* II, 185 and III, 631; *Cataractonium*: *Tab Vind* II, 185, II, 343, III, 670; *Bremesio*: *Tab Vind* III, 670.
71 Cool and Mason 2008, 297–302.
72 Snape *et al* 2002, 50, figs 18 and19.
73 Myres *et al* 1959, 18–19.
74 Ibid, 33.
75 Ibid, 52, fig 20, Pl IIB.
76 Ibid, 52.
77 Ibid, 53, fig 20.
78 Johnson 1983, 45–8.
79 Ibid, 53.
80 Rickman 1971, 215–21; Johnson 1983, 145, fig 105.
81 Cf Millett 1990, 74.
82 As noted above (Chapter 1, n 33) the suggestion that there was a military bath-house here (**G49**) is unfounded.
83 For example, Gorhambury, building 10 (Neal *et al* 1990, 29).
84 Bishop 2005, 214.
85 Halkon *et al* 2015, 34.
86 Hanson 2007, 48.
87 Ottaway 2013, 96.
88 Ibid, 96.
89 Johnson 1983, 244.
90 Both were small by comparison with Aldborough – each *c* 1ha. Cunliffe 1968, fig 27; 1971, fig 11.
91 Wallace 2014, 154–5; Millett 2016.

92 P Wilson (in Brickstock *et al* 2007, 113) makes a similar point regarding the location of the Bainesse site at Catterick on the River Swale.

93 Wallace 2014, 101, table 23.

94 *RIB* 2404.61 & 2404.62 from Heyshaw Moor, Nidderdale dated to Domitian COS VII = AD 81; *RIB* 2404.63 from Pateley Bridge (S of Greenhow Hill), dated to the reign of Trajan, AD 98.

95 Hirt 2010, 100–6. The published analyses of the Heyshaw Moor lead pigs might suggest that they may have been de-silvered; Gowland 1901.

96 Stowe MS, p 26 quoted above Chapter 2, p. 12.

97 Hanson 1986, 50–1.

98 Ottaway 1993, 69–72.

99 Dobinson 1988; 1988–9, fig 2; Dobinson 2012, plan p 18 (see fig 2.17). The streets he identified largely match the evidence from the geophysics.

100 Throughout this text, the authors take the Roman foot to be 296mm (the so-called *Pes Monetalis*). There has been no attempt to distinguish the *Pes Drusianus* (*c* 332mm), noting the issues in doing this were discussed in Millett 1982.

101 Bowden 2013, 162–7. Recent re-evaluations of Silchester (Creighton with Fry 2016, 436–8, fig 17.1) and Verulamium (Niblett and Thompson 2005, 150–2, fig 4.70) show that *fora* lay at one side of the initial street grid. This pattern is also seen in the earliest stage of London's development (Wallace 2014, fig 37).

102 Millett 1990, 144, fig 62.

103 Wallace 2014, fig 33.

104 Wacher 1995, 378–91, fig 170.

105 Jones *et al* 2003, 82–6.

106 Boethius and Ward-Perkins 1970, 142–8; Millett 2007, 79–80.

107 There is possible evidence for such areas beneath *fora* at London (Wallace 2014, 59–62) and Leicester (Hebditch and Mellor 1973, 7–8, 36–7).

108 The strip between the roadside ditches defining this branch is *c* 22m wide, significantly broader than other major roads (Margary 1973, 20–1).

109 The axis of the bridge lies *c* 89m (about 300 Roman ft) west of street NS1. This distance does not seem to correlate with the measurements used in the layout of the street grid.

110 Dymond 1961; Holbrook 1996.

111 Holbrook 1996, 125.

112 Fitzpatrick and Scott 1999, 125–6.

113 Myres *et al* 1959, 55–6, fig 21. The lowest (levels I–III) are noted as perhaps the foundations for IV, VII–IX are shown as overlying the gate foundation. An unworn *dupondius* of Hadrian, dated to AD 134–8, came from the surface of VI.

114 Welch 2007.

115 Wilmott 2008, 44–61.

116 Myres 1959, 11, 17–18, citing **G40**; Dobinson 1988, 18–20, citing **G39**, **G40** and **G41**; Herkes 1997, 42–3 .

117 **G39**, section III, infilling a quarry.

118 **G34**, **G38**, **G39**, **G40** and **G41**.

119 Millett 1990, 102–3, table 4.4. The date of the timber *forum* at Silchester has subsequently been modified; Fulford and Timby 2000.

120 Myres *et al* 1959, 5.

121 Wacher 1995, figs 6–9.

122 Millett 1990, 72; Gros 1996, 220–9.

123 Breeze 2006, 422.

124 Wacher 1995, figs 6–9.

125 Ibid, figs 6–9.

126 Frere 1987, 193; Wacher 1995, 23.

127 Collingwood 1927, 4; Tacitus, *Agricola* 21.

128 *RIB* 3123; Niblett and Thompson 2005, 150–5.

129 Niblett and Thompson 2005, 150–5; Creighton with Fry 2016, 434–7.

130 Gascoyne and Radford 2013, 77–8; Hurst 1999; Jones *et al* 2003, 56–8.

131 Wallace 2014.

132 Holbrook 2015, 96–100; White *et al* 2013, 171–3.

133 Moore 2011.

134 Creighton 2006, 148.

135 Bowden 2013, 162–7.

136 The possible Augustan parallel at Waldgirmes (von Schnurbein 2003) is much earlier and in a different context.

137 Mattingly 2006, 291.

138 Wacher 1995, 17–32.

139 Wilkes 1996; Millett 1996, 34–5 (but the status of *conventus civium Romanorum* is probably anachronistic by this date).

140 Sommer 1984, 13–26, who, however, concludes that *vici* came under the authority of the *civitas*.

141 *RIB* 2022; Fulford 2006, 68–70. These inscriptions are generally dated to the fourth century (Tomlin 2018, 432).

142 Frere 1987, 110–24.

143 Birley 2005, 121–2.

144 Boatwright 2000, 172 ff.

145 Dobinson *et al* 2018, figs 2 and 3.

146 Wacher 1995, fig 28, nos 2 and 3.

147 Snape *et al* 2002, 58–60.

148 Although Jones' excavations by the South Gate (**G51**) found two primary ditches, this is not seen elsewhere.

149 Charlesworth 1971, 160.

150 Myres *et al* 1959, fig 20; Charlesworth 1971, fig 22.

151 Jones 1971, 76, cf pp 49–50, fig 7 for the stratigraphy and p 58 for the pottery.

152 Myres *et al* 1959, 10–11.

153 Snape *et al* 2002, 58–60.

154 Myres *et al* 1959, 50. The coin was discussed by Charlesworth, who included a re-identification by Dr John Kent (Charlesworth 1971, n 20).

155 Boon 1988, 125–6 suggests that such counterfeits were largely produced under Gordian III and Phillip the Arab.

156 The authors are grateful to Richard Brickstock for his comments on this. He notes that 'the obverse is (or rather was) a female head facing right. The reverse type, Aequitas

(or similar) standing left holding scales and *cornucopiae*, occurs frequently for emperors from Trajan onwards, but not for females. Mattingly recognised the coin as a plated counterfeit; and thought the only female for whom such a coin had been listed (as a hybrid; and therefore counterfeit) was Domna (see *RIC* Septimius Severus 588). He appears to have missed the similar issue for Mamaea (*RIC* Severus Alexander 369A), also listed as hybrid. Despite this, the *terminus post quem* provided by the coin remains AD 193–211: it may well be somewhat later (and was recorded as 'very worn') but not earlier (so Kent had it right).'

157 Myres *et al* 1959, 50.

158 J Evans 2018, in Dobinson *et al* 2018, 55.

159 Myres *et al* 1959, 55–6, fig 21. See above, n 113.

160 Golvin 1988, 284–5. The average arena size is *c* 52m × 37m. For individual comparison Aldborough's arena size (*c* 60m × 40m) is larger than Cirencester (*c* 49m × 41m) and Silchester (*c* 49m × 40m).

161 Mills 2018, in Dobinson *et al* 2018, 55–6; flue tiles of similar date also came from **G106**.

162 Drake 1736, 24.

163 Millett 1990, table 5.1; Mattingly 2006, 268, table 9.

164 For a group of later milestones, see below.

165 *CSIR* vol 1, fasc 3, nos 16 and 17; see Appendix 3.

166 *CSIR* vol 1, fasc 3, no. 15; see Appendix 3.

167 For the Genii Cuculatti, see Toynbee 1964, 105. The Aldborough example is similar to *CSIR* vol 1, fasc 6, no. 485 from Carlisle.

168 Exceptions being Blagg 2002, a foliate capital p 40, type VIII base p 125.

169 Blagg 2002, 105–46.

170 Rowland and Noble Howe 1999, 4.4.2–3, 4.7.1–5, figs 68 and 73.

171 Blagg 2002, 108–12.

172 Rickman 1971, 264–70; Rizos 2013. For a possible comparable example from Housesteads, see Rushworth 2009, 307–11.

173 Still 1995, vol 1, 86–7.

174 Hassall and Tomlin 1988, 504, no. 97 (also mentioned in a note to *RIB* 2411.36).

175 *RIB* 2411.34–36.

176 Birley 2005, 333–6, 397–8.

177 Combe Down *RIB* 2411.37, editorial comment *RIB* vol 2, fasc 1, 88.

178 *RIB* 2411.247 (= Hassall and Tomlin 1987, 373, no. 30, noting that the abbreviation is 'not explicable as the initial letters of *tria nomina*.')

179 Comparable sealings (*RIB* 2411.246 and 2411.267) from Brough under-Stainmore both read BFC, which may suggest that the final letter is from a series.

180 Frere 1987, 185, 202 n 4, with postings along Dere Street including Catterick and Binchester.

181 Jones 1973, 563, 587.

182 Hassall and Tomlin 1990, 376, no. 68.

183 Exact parallels are Tomlin and Hassall 1999, 383, no. 20; Tomlin and Hassall 2002, 369, no. 27; Tomlin 2015, 412, nos 57 and 58; cf also *RIB* 2411.24.

184 Bishop 1996, 3.

185 The suggestion may be supported by a minor peak in coin deposition at this period; Brickstock 2019, 60.

186 Neal and Cosh 2002, 311–14, mosaics 123.13 and 123.14.

187 *RIB* 2022; Tomlin 2018, 432. Cf above, p. 107.

188 Mattingly 2006, 255–91.

189 Millett 1990, 65–9.

190 Mattingly 2006, 262, fig 10.

191 Ottaway 2013, 256–71.

192 Cf Halkon *et al* 2015, chapter 22; Ferraby *et al* 2017 chapter 10.

193 Birley 1986, 66: *RIB* nos 627 (Greetland), 628 (Castleford), 630 (Adel), 1053 (South Shields), 1131 (Corbridge), 2066 (Brampton), 2091 (Birrens).

194 *CSIR* vol I, fasc 4, no. 12. Also illustrated in Tomlin 2018, 322.

195 *Contra* Tomlin 2018, 189.

196 *RIB* 2142 – serving in the Second Cohort of Thracians at Mumrills on the Antonine Wall.

197 *RIB* 2276 (from Duel Cross on the Roman road south of Aldborough); *RIB* 2277 from **G34**; *RIB* 2278 from an unknown location within the town (Ecroyd Smith 1852, pl XXI, 10).

198 *RIB* 2263 (near Segontium), 2268 (Ribchester), 2271 (Lancaster), 2273 (Castleford) and 3517 (Rockbourne).

199 Sauer 2014.

200 Hadrian's imperial titles being IMP CAESAR TRAIANUS HADRIANUS AUGUSTUS, and Trajan Decius's being IMP CAES C MESSIUS QUINTUS TRAIANUS DECIUS AUGUSTUS.

201 Dobinson *et al* 2018; Millett *et al* 2018.

202 Evans and Mills 2018, figs 8–11.

203 Pearce 2013, 117.

204 Jones 1971, 59–60, 66–7.

205 Millett 2006.

206 Halkon *et al* 2015.

207 Halkon 2013, 142–4

208 Rogers 2013, especially Chapter 4.

209 Margary 1973, 406–7, route 720b.

210 Lukis 1875.

211 Branigan 1980, 23, fig 3.3 (wrongly located on his fig 3.1); Scott 1993, 153.

212 Gilyard-Beer 1951. The authors here have taken the view (as Hartley and Fitts 1988, 124 n 15) that this is a villa, not (exclusively) a religious site.

213 PCA 2015.

214 Scott 1993, 152 gives the location as the Deanery; Neal and Cosh 2002, 350, question the veracity of the evidence.

215 Above, pp. 17 and 90.

216 Cf Hayton (Halkon *et al* 2015, 562); note also the discussion by Martins 2005, 111–15.

217 Snape *et al* 2002, 61–2; as noted above (Area 1), there is no evidence to support the identification of a later Roman defensive ditch inside the north-western corner of the

town; Wacher 1995, 406–7.

218 As noted above (pp. 105–6) within the context of the discussion of levelling associated with town planning.

219 Dobinson *et al* 2018, 38.

220 **G106**.

221 Snape *et al* 2002, 62–3.

222 The exception is Silchester where an annexe similar to that at Aldborough lies to the north west of the town straddling the road to Cirencester (Creighton with Fry 2016, 315–16). Its date is uncertain.

223 Millett 1990, 142.

224 Evans and Mills 2018, fig 9.

225 Neal and Cosh 2002, 305.

226 Ibid, 304, 368–78.

227 RCHM 1962, xxxv–xxxix.

228 Millett 1990, 182–3, using 137–216 people per ha based on cross-cultural evidence.

229 Millett 2013, 36–9, using 120–50 people per ha.

230 Dobinson *et al* 2018, 38.

231 Johnson and Neal 2002, 129–30. Radiocarbon samples OxA-9981 (1666±37 BP) and OxA-9983 (1734±34 BP). The calibrated date quoted is the weighted mean of the two samples.

232 Radiocarbon samples SUERC 84781 (1666±26 BP) and SUERC 84782 (1649±26 BP) give a combined date of 343–421 cal AD at 95% confidence. Cf Rogers 2011, 130–4.

233 Loveluck 2003, 152.

234 Dobinson *et al* 2018, fig 7, 41.

235 Brickstock 2019, 64.

236 See Roberts 2014 for the archaeology of Elmet.

237 Faull 1974, 7, 24, fig 1; Loveluck 2003, 155–8, figs 39–40.

238 Bede *Ecclesiastical History*, III, 1; Jones 1971; 1976, 38, n 3.

239 Breeze 2005, 351; Woolf 2004, 7, n 20.

240 Coatsworth 2008, 13–14.

241 'New 7th century remains found at Ripon', *British Archaeology* 24, 1997, 5.

242 Lawson-Tancred 1937, 5; https://opendomesday.org/place/SE4066/aldborough/ (accessed 11 July 2019).

243 Ecroyd Smith 1852, 5 (giving the date as 766); Lawson-Tancred 1937, 5; Lawson-Tancred 1948, 24.

244 Gibson 1722, 876.

245 Gough 1789, 60.

246 Hall 2015, 22–3.

247 The place destroyed by the Danes was Alcluid, on the Clyde, which gets conflated with Aldburgh. The authors are grateful to Professor Lesley Abrahms for discussion of this. See *Polychronicon Ranulphi Higden Monachi Cestrensis; together with the English Translations of John Trevisa and of an Unknown Writer of the Fifteenth Century*, vol 2 (2011), p 66.

248 Charlesworth 1971, 163.

249 Dobinson 2012, 17, illustrates a Viking-age bracelet, and he also mentions two carved bone objects (Dobinson 1988, 36). A strap end dated to 750–100 was found in field-walking just south of the amphitheatre (Millett *et al* 2018: Aldborough SFs.xlsx).

250 Levison 1946, 33–6, 259–65.

251 The late eighth–early ninth century cross in the garden of Aldborough Manor is reliably thought to have been brought from Cundall in the nineteenth century, although one source claims that it was found in Aldborough. It thus provides no evidence to support the idea that there was an early church here. It is carved from two different gritstones that may be re-used from the Roman town; Lang 2001, 93–7.

252 However, the authors' excavation (**G105**) shows that the predominant re-used stone in the church – a coarse gritstone – was not that used in the *forum* walls (which were of Cadeby Limestone, formerly known as Lower Magnesian Limestone). Gritstone was widely used elsewhere in the Roman town.

253 Cf Rippon *et al* 2015.

254 Jones 1971, 40, n 2.

255 *DNB* sv William de Stuteville, d 1203.

256 Brown 1959, 261; Renn 1973, 88.

257 Lawson-Tancred 1937, 7.

258 Lawson-Tancred 1948, 28–31.

259 Chitty 1986–87, 9.

260 Lawson-Tancred 1948.

Appendices

1 The authors are grateful to Colin Dobinson for this reference.

2 The authors are very grateful to Dr David Taylor for his comments on this piece.

Abbreviations and bibliography

Abbreviations

AAGM	Emily Lorraine de Montluzin *Attributions of Authorship in the Gentleman's Magazine, 1731–1868: An Electronic Union List* http://bsuva.org/bsuva/gm2/index.html
CSIR	*Corpus Signorum Imperii Romani*, British Academy, Oxford University Press. vol 1, fasc 3 (*Yorkshire*, 1983); vol 1, fasc 4 (Scotland, 1984); vol 1, fasc 6 (*Hadrian's Wall West of the North Tyne and Carlisle*, 1988)
DNB	*Oxford Dictionary of National Biography* (online edition), https://www.oxforddnb.com/
Hargrove MS	*Manuscripts of William Hargrove* 1777–1825. (Eight Vols). York Record Office manuscript no. GB 192 HAR
NTS	Hartley, B R and Dickinson B 2008. *Names on Terra Sigillata. An Index of Makers' stamps and signatures on Gallo-Roman Terra Sigillata (Samian Ware)*. Bulletin of the Institute of Classical Studies Supplement 102, London (eight vols, 2008–11)
NYCC	North Yorkshire County Council
RIB	*Roman Inscriptions of Britain*, Oxford. Vol 1 (1965), Vol 2 (1990–95), Vol 3 (2009)
RIC	*Roman Imperial Coinage*
Stowe MS	*Survey of the manor of Aldborough, W. Riding, co York, by W.D. a° Doni. 1714. Preceded by an Explanation, describing some of the antiquities of the place; and followed by two plans in pen-and-ink, one of the borough, the other of the manor, of Aldborough*. British Library Stowe MSS 883
Tab Vind II	Bowman and Thomas 1994
Tab Vind III	Bowman and Thomas 2003

Bibliography

Ancient textual sources

Antonine Itinerary
Text and commentary – Rivet and Smith 1979, 150–82

Bede *Ecclesiastical History*
Text and commentary edited by B Colgrave and R A B Mynors, Oxford, 1991 edition)

Ptolemy *Geography*
Text and commentary – Rivet and Smith 1979, 103–47

Ravenna Cosmography
Text and commentary – Rivet and Smith 1979, 185–215

Tacitus *Agricola*
Text and translation – *Tacitus. Agricola with an English translation* by M Hutton (revised by R M Ogilvie), Cambridge Mass, 1970

Tacitus *Annals*
Text and translation – Tacitus. *The Annals Books IV–VI, XI–XII with an English translation* by J Jackson, Cambridge Mass, 1937

Tacitus *Histories*
Text and translation – *Tacitus. Histories Books 1–3 with an English translation* by C H Moore, Cambridge Mass 1925

Vitruvius *Ten Books on Architecture*
Text and commentary – Rowland and Noble Howe 1999

Secondary sources

Abramson, P, Berg, D S and Fossick, M R 1999. *Roman Castleford: Excavations 1974–85. Vol 2 The Structural and Environmental Evidence*, Wakefield West Yorkshire Archaeology Service, Wakefield

Ambrey, C, Fell, D, Fraser, R, Ross, S, Speed, G and Wood, P N 2017. *A Roman Roadside settlement at Healam Bridge: the Iron Age to early Medieval evidence*, (2 Vols), Northern Archaeological Associates, Barnard Castle

Antoni, B 2008. *Hunday Field Farm, Marton cum Grafton, North Yorkshire. Assessment Report*, York Archaeological Trust report no 2008/9, York

Archaeological Institute 1848. *Memoirs illustrative of the history and antiquities of the County and City of York*, Archaeological Institute, London

ASUD 2005. *1 High Street, Aldborough, Boroughbridge, North Yorkshire: archaeological watching brief.* Archaeological Services University of Durham Report No 1226. North Yorks HER: SNY9423

Barber, S C, Ridley, C A and Dimmock, G F 1925 *Excavations at 'Isurium', Aldborough, Yorkshire,* Unpublished Manuscript dated 10 January 1925 in the archive of Sir Andrew Lawson Tancred. A transcription of this manuscript by Mike Turpin is available online: http://www.turpsoft.co.uk/aldborough/1924report.pdf

Berry, C A F 1951. 'The dating of Romano-British houses', *J Roman Studies,* 41, 25–31 (accessed 15 December 2019)

Birley, A R 2005. *The Roman Government of Britain,* Oxford

Birley, E 1986. 'The Deities of Roman Britain', in H. Temporini and W Hasse (eds) *Aufstieg und Niedergang der Römischen Welt II, 18.1,* 3–112, Berlin

Bishop, M C 1996. *Finds from Roman Aldborough: a catalogue of the small finds from the Romano-British town of Isurium Brigantum,* Oxford

Bishop, M C 2005. 'A new Flavian military site at Roecliffe, North Yorkshire', *Britannia,* 36, 135–223

Bishop, M C and Young, G 1993. *Estate Yard and Studforth Farm, Aldborough: Trial Trenches Report.* Northern Archaeological Associates 93/11

Blagg, T F C 2002. *Roman architectural ornament in Britain,* Oxford

Boatwright, M T 2000. *Hadrian and the cities of the Roman Empire,* Princeton

Boethius, A and Ward-Perkins, J B 1970. *Etruscan and Roman Architecture,* Harmondsworth

Boon, G C 1988. 'Counterfeit coins in Roman Britain', in P J Casey and R Reece (eds) *Coins and the Archaeologist* (2nd edition), 102–88, London

Bowden, W 2013. 'The urban plan of *Venta Icenorum* and its relationship with the Boudicaan revolt', *Britannia,* 44, 145–69

Bowman, A K, and Thomas, J D 1994. *The Vindolanda writing-tablets (Tabulae Vindolandenses II),* London

Bowman, A K, and Thomas, J D 2003. *The Vindolanda writing-tablets (Tabulae Vindolandenses III),* London

Branigan, K 1980. 'Villas in the North: change in the rural landscape', in K Branigan (ed) *Rome and the Brigantes: the impact of Rome on northern England,* 18–27, Sheffield

Breeze, A 2005. 'Celtic boundaries and *Isurium Brigantum*', *Northern History,* 42, 349–51

Breeze, D J 1996. *Roman Scotland: frontier country,* London

Breeze, D J 2006. *Handbook to the Roman Wall* (14th edition), Newcastle upon Tyne

Brickstock, R J, Cardwell, P A, Busby, PA, Cool, H E M, Huntley, J P, Evans, J, Makey, P, Ronan, D, and Wilson, P R 2007. 'Catterick metal detecting project 1997-99', *Yorks Archaeol J* 79, 65–153

Brickstock, R 2019. 'Roman Coins from Aldborough: a re-assessment and overview', *Yorks Archaeol J,* 91, 49–70.

Bridgland, D, Innes, J, Long, A and Mitchell, W 2011. *Late Quaternary landscape evolution of the Swale–Ure washlands, North Yorkshire,* Oxford

Brown, R A 1959. 'A list of castles, 1154–1216', *English Historical Review,* 74, 249–80.

Brown, F, Howard-Davies, C, Brennand, M, Boyle, A, Evans T, O'Connor, S, Spence, A, Heawood, R and Lupton A 2007. *The archaeology of the A1(M) Darrington to Dishforth DBFO road scheme,* Lancaster

Buglass, J 2007. *Aldene, Back Lane, Aldborough, Boroughbridge, North Yorkshire: Archaeological Watching Brief.* JB Archaeology Reports. North Yorks HER: SNY11698

Buglass, J 2010. *Studforth Farm, Aldborough, Boroughbridge, North Yorkshire: Archaeological Watching Brief.* JB Archaeology Reports. North Yorks HER: SNY15925

Buglass, J 2013. *Studforth Grange, Back Lane, Aldborough: Archaeological Watching Brief.* JB Archaeology Report. North Yorks HER: SNY20283

Buglass, J 2016. *Museum House, Front Street, Aldborough: Archaeological Watching Brief.* JB Archaeology Report. North Yorks HER: SNY21884

Cale, K J 1989. *Report on a Watching Brief at 'The Cottage' – Back Street, Aldborough (Isurium Brigantum), 5 June 1989.* North Yorks HER: SNY8575

Cale, K J 1991a. *Museum House, Aldborough, North Yorkshire.Archaeological Recording.* North Yorks HER: SNY8573

Cale, K J 1991b. *Museum House, Aldborough, North Yorkshire. Watching Brief and trial trenches.* North Yorks HER: SNY770

Cale, K J 1996a. *Archaeological Evaluation: The Ship Inn, Low Lane, Aldborough.* North Yorks HER: SNY8720

Cale, K J 1996b. *Archaeological Investigation: Back Lane, Aldborough.* North Yorks HER: SNY8728

Cale, K J 1997a. *Archaeological Inspection: The Ship Inn, Low Lane, Aldborough.* North Yorks HER: SNY8721

Cale, K J 1997b. *Archaeological Investigation: Aldene, Back Lane, Aldborough.* North Yorks HER: SNY6978

Cale, K J 1997c. *Archaeological Investigation: Rose Cottage, Back Lane, Aldborough.* North Yorks HER: SNY840

Cale, K J 1998. *Archaeological Investigation: Briarwood, Low Lane, Aldborough.* North Yorks HER: SNY493

Cale, K J 1999a. *Archaeological Investigation: The Firs,*

Low Lane, Aldborough. North Yorks HER: SNY8570

Cale, K J 1999b. *Archaeological Investigation: Hambleton View, Back Lane, Aldborough*. North Yorks HER: SNY831

Cale, K J 2000. *Archaeological Investigation: Pear Tree Cottage, Low Lane, Aldborough*. North Yorks HER: SNY516

Cale, K J 2001. *Archaeological Exhumation in Connection with the groundworks at the Village Institute, Aldborough, North Yorkshire*. North Yorks HER: SNY8732

Cale, K J 2002. *Archaeological Investigation: Laurel House, Low Lane, Aldborough*. North Yorks HER: SNY6932

Champion, T 2016. 'Britain before Rome', in M Millett, L Revell and A Moore (eds) *The Oxford Handbook of Roman Britain*, 150–78, Oxford

Charlesworth, D 1970. *Aldborough Roman town and museum; Dept of the Environment official handbook*, London

Charlesworth, D 1971. 'The defences of *Isurium Brigantum*', in R M Butler (ed) *Soldier and civilian in Roman Yorkshire*, 155–64, Leicester

Chitty, M D 1986–7. 'A personal record of Roman Yorkshire, 1906–43'. *Yorks Archaeol Soc, Roman Antiquities Section Bulletin*, 4, 3–13

Coatsworth, E 2008. *Corpus of Anglo-Saxon Stone sculpture, Vol VIII: Western Yorkshire*, Oxford

Collingwood, R G 1927. 'Aldborough and the Devil's Arrows: handbook for members taking part in excursion no 18', in H E Wroot (ed) *Handbook for Excursions - British Association Meeting Leeds Meeting 1927*, Leeds

Collingwood, R G 1930. *The archaeology of Roman Britain*, London.

Cool, H E M and Mason, D J P 2008. *Roman Piercebridge: excavations by D W Harding and Peter Scott 1969–81*, Durham

Creighton, J 2006. *Britannia: the creation of a Roman province*, London

Creighton, J with Fry, R 2016. *Silchester: changing visions of a Roman town*, London: Britannia Monograph 28

Cross, RP 1987a. *Aldborough (Isurium Brigantum), The Firs: Watching Brief, 18 November 1987*. North Yorks HER: SNY8096

Cross, R P 1987b. *The Firs. Second Report, Watching Brief*. North Yorks HER: SNY8047

Cunliffe, B W, 1968. *Fifth report on the excavations of the Roman fort at Richborough, Kent*, London

Cunliffe, B W 1971. *Excavations at Fishbourne, Vol 1*, Leeds

Dobinson, C 1987. 'Excavations at Aldborough, 1987: interim report', *Yorks Archaeol Soc, Roman Antiquities Section Bulletin*, 5, 3–6

Dobinson, C 1988. *The development of Roman Aldborough: a short survey compiled on behalf of the Roman Antiquities Section, Yorkshire Archaeological Society*. Unpublished manuscript

Dobinson, C 1988–9. 'Roman Aldborough', *Yorks Archaeol Soc, Roman Antiquities Section Bulletin*, 6, 3–9

Dobinson, C 1995. *Aldborough Roman town, North Yorkshire*, London

Dobinson, C 2012. *Aldborough Roman town, North Yorkshire*, (revised edition) London

Dobinson, C, Ferraby, R, Lucas, J, Millett, M and Wallace, L 2018. 'Archaeological field-survey in the environs of Aldborough (*Isurium Brigantum*)', *Yorks Archaeol J*, 90, 29–58

Drake, F 1736. *Eboracum or the history and antiquities of the City of York from its origins to the present time*, London

Dymond, D P 1961. 'Roman bridges on Dere Street, Co Durham', *Archaeol J*, 118, 136–64.

Ecroyd Smith, H 1852. *Reliquiae Isurianae: the remains of Roman Isurium, now Aldborough, near Boroughbridge, Yorkshire*, London

Ecroyd Smith, H 1859–68. 'On a Romano-British Pavement, representing Romulus and Remus, discovered at Aldborough (*Isurium* of the Romans)', *Proc Yorks Geol Polytechinc Society*, 4, 593–604

Ellis, S P 1995. 'Classical reception rooms in Romano-British houses', *Britannia*, 26, 163–78

Evans, J and Mills P 2018. 'The Roman pottery and ceramic building material from field survey in the environs of Aldborough (*Isurium Brigantum*) during the 1980s and 1990s', in Millett, M J, Dobinson, C, Ferraby, R, Wallace, L, and Lucas, J *Research data supporting the publication of "Archaeological field-survey in the environs of Aldborough (Isurium Brigantum)"* [Dataset]. https://doi.org/10.17863/CAM.21743 (accessed 10 Oct 2019)

Faull, M 1974. 'Roman and Anglian settlement patterns in Yorkshire', *Northern History*, 9, 1–25

Fell, D 2017. 'Scotch Corner: a crossroads on the Roman frontier', *British Archaeol*, 154 (May–June 2017), 14–21

Ferraby, R, Johnson, P, Millett, M and Wallace, L 2017. *Thwing, Rudston and the Roman-period exploitation of the Yorkshire Wolds*, Yorkshire Archaeological Report 8, Leeds

Ferraby, R and Millett, M. 2016. *Aldborough Roman Town Project 2016 Excavation Interim Report*, Cambridge https://doi.org/10.17863/CAM.39571 (accessed 1 Nov 2019)

Ferraby, R and Millett, M. 2017. *Excavations at*

Aldborough (Isurium Brigantum) 2017: interim report, Cambridge https://doi.org/10.17863/CAM.39572 (accessed 18 January 2020)

Ferraby, R. and Millett, M. 2018. *Excavations at Aldborough (Isurium Brigantum) 2018: interim report,* Cambridge https://doi.org/10.17863/CAM.39573 (accessed 18 January 2020)

Fitzpatrick, A P and Scott, P R 1999. 'The Roman bridge at Piercebridge, North Yorkshire–County Durham', *Britannia,* 30, 111–32

Frere, S S 1987. *Britannia: a history of Roman Britain,* (3rd edition) London

Fulford, M G 2006. 'Corvées and *civitates*', in R J A Wilson (ed) *Romanitas: essays on Roman archaeology in honour of Sheppard Frere on the occasion of his ninetieth birthday,* 65–71, Oxford

Fulford, M G and Timby, J 2000. *Late Iron Age and Roman Silchester: excavations on the site of the forum-basilica 1977, 1980–86,* London

Garner-Lahire, J 2001. *Evaluation Aldborough Manor North Yorkshire*, Field Archaeology Specialists, University of York, York

Gascoyne, A and Radford, D 2013. *Colchester fortress of the war god: an archaeological assessment,* Oxford

Gibson, E 1695. *Camden's* Britannia *newly translated into English with large additions and improvements,* London

Gibson, E 1722. *Britannia or a chorographical description of Great Britain and Ireland together with adjacent lands,* Vol II, London

Gilyard-Beer, R 1951. *The Romano-British Baths at Well,* Leeds

Golvin, J-C 1988. *L'amphithéâtre romain: essai sur la théorisation de sa forme et de ses fonctions,* Paris

Gough, R 1789. *Britannia: or, a chorographical description of the flourishing kingdoms of England, Scotland, and Ireland, and the islands adjacent; from the earliest antiquity. By William Camden. Translated from the edition published by the author in MDCVII. Enlarged by the latest discoveries,* London

Gowland, W 1901. 'The early metallurgy of silver and lead: part 1, Lead', *Archaeologia,* 57, 359–422

Gros, P 1996. *L'architecture romaine. 1: Les monuments publics,* Paris

Halkon, P 2013. *The Parisi: Britons and Romans in eastern Yorkshire,* Stroud

Halkon, P, Millett, M and Woodhouse, H 2015. *Hayton, East Yorkshire: archaeological studies of the Iron Age and Roman landscapes,* Yorkshire Archaeological Report 7, Leeds

Hall, R 2015. 'Jorvik: York in the Anglo-Scandinavian period, 866–1066', in P V Addyman (ed) *British Historic Towns Atlas Vol 5: York,* Oxford

Hanson, W S 1986. 'Rome, the Cornovii and the Ordovices', in *Studien zu den Militärgrenzen Roms III: 13 Internationaler Limeskongrss, Aalen 1983,* 47-52, Stuttgart

Hanson, W S and Campbell, D B 1986. 'The Brigantes from clientage to conquest', *Britannia,* 17, 73–89

Hanson, W S 2007. *A Roman frontier fort in Scotland: Elginhaugh,* Stroud

Hargrove, E 1769. *The history of the castle and town of Knaresbrough*, Knaresborough

Hargrove, W 1818. *History and description of the ancient City of York; comprising all the most interesting information already published in Drake's* Eboracum *enriched with much entirely new matter,* York

Hartley, B and Fitts, L 1988. *The Brigantes,* Gloucester

Hartley, K P 2002, in Snape *et al* 2002.

Haselgrove, C C 2016. *Cartimandua's capital: the Late Iron Age royal site at Stanwick, North Yorkshire, fieldwork and analysis 1981–2011,* Council for British Archaeology Research Report 175, York

Hassall, M W C and Tomlin, R S O 1987. 'Roman Britain in 1986: II Inscriptions', *Britannia,* 18, 360–77

Hassall, M W C and Tomlin, R S O 1988. 'Roman Britain in 1987: II Inscriptions', *Britannia,* 19, 485–508

Hassall, M W C and Tomlin, R S O 1990. 'Roman Britain in 1989: II Inscriptions', *Britannia,* 21, 365–78

Hebditch, M and Mellor, J 1973. 'The forum and basilica of Roman Leicester', *Britannia*, 4, 1–83

Herkes, S 1997. *Reconstructing the landscapes of Roman Aldborough: the 'anatomy' of a Civitas Capital*, MA dissertation, University of York

Heslop, D H 2008. *Patterns of quern production, acquisition and deposition: a corpus of beehive querns from northern Yorkshire and southern Durham,* Leeds

Hirt, A M 2010. *Imperial mines and quarries in the Roman World,* Oxford

Hobley, A. 1998. *An examination of Roman bronze coin distribution in the western Empire A.D. 81–192,* Oxford

Hodgson, N 2009. *Hadrian's Wall 1999-2009,* Kendal

Hodgson, N 2017. *Hadrian's Wall: archaeology and history at the limit of Rome's Empire*, Marlborough

Holbrook, N 1996. 'Roman bridges in Britain', in P Johnson and I Haynes (eds) *Architecture in Roman Britain,* 120–32, York

Holbrook, N 2015. 'The towns of south-west England', in M Fulford and N Holbrook (eds) *The towns of Roman Britain: the contribution of commercial archaeology since 1990,* 90–116, London

Horne, P D 2003. 'Case study 2: Rural settlements in Roman North Yorkshire, an aerial view', in R A Butlin (ed) *Historical Atlas of North Yorkshire,* 58–61, Otley

Horsley, J 1732. *Britannia Romana: or the Roman*

antiquities of Britain in three books, London

Hunter, K 2005. *Studforth House, Back Street, Aldborough, North Yorkshire: Archaeological Evaluation.* MAP Archaeological Reports. North Yorks HER: SNY10024

Hurst, H R 1999. 'Topography and identity in *Glevum colonia*', in H R Hurst (eds) *The Coloniae of Roman Britain: new studies and a review,* 113–36, Portsmouth RI

Jarrett, M G 1994. 'Non-legionary troops in Roman Britain. Part 1', *Britannia,* 25, 35–77

Johnson, A 1983. *Roman forts of the 1st and 2nd centuries AD in Britain and the German provinces,* London

Johnson, M 2013. *Gas Mains Replacement, Aldborough, North Yorkshire: Watching Brief Report.* York Archaeological Trust, Report Number 2013/08. North Yorks HER: SNY19691

Johnson, S and Neal, D S 2002. 'The re-excavation and study of the Helicon mosaic at Aldborough Roman town', *Yorks Archaeol J,* 74, 113–34

Jones, A H M 1973. *The Later Roman Empire,* Oxford

Jones, G 1971. 'The multiple estate as a model framework for tracing early stages in the evolution of rural settlement', in F Dussart (ed) *L'Habitat et les paysages ruraux d'Europe*, 251-67, Liege. [Republished in *Britons, Saxons, and Scandinavians: the Historical Geography of Glanville R J Jones*, edited by P S Barnwell and B K Roberts, Turnhout 2012, 143–54]

Jones, G 1976. 'Multiple estates and early settlement', in P H Sawyer (ed) *Medieval settlement: continuity and change,* 15–40, London

Jones, M J, Stocker, D and Vince, A 2003. *The City by the Pool: assessing the archaeology of the city of Lincoln,* Oxford

Jones, M U 1971. 'Aldborough, West Riding, 1964: excavations at the south gate and bastion and at extra-mural sites', *Yorks Archaeol J,* 43, 39–78

Kewley, J 1970. *The sculptured decoration on Roman votive altars and pedestals from northern Britain*, Durham University PhD thesis. Available at Durham E-Theses Online: http://etheses.dur.ac.uk/9280/ (accessed 20 Oct 2019)

Knowles, J W No Date. 'York Artists' Online', https://cyc.sdp.sirsidynix.net.uk/client/es_ES/search/asset/1018047

Lang, J 2001. *Corpus of Anglo–Saxon Stone Sculpture Vol. VI: Northern Yorkshire,* Oxford

Larionov, A I 2015. 'Mosaic from Aldborough, Boroughbridge, North Yorkshire: the problem of its authenticity', in S V Maltseva, E Y Stanyukovich-Denisova and A V Zakharova (eds) *Actual Problems of Theory and History of Art: Collection of articles.* Vol 5, 127–136, St Petersburg

Lawson, A S 1864. '*Isurium*', *J British Archaeol Assoc*, 20, 39–51

Lawson-Tancred, Lady Margery 1948. *A guide book to the antiquities of Aldborough and Boroughbridge and a short account of their history,* Boroughbridge

Lawson-Tancred, T 1937. *Records of a Yorkshire Manor,* London

Leach, P and Pevsner, N 2009. *The Buildings of England: Yorkshire West Riding: Leeds, Bradford and the North,* London and New Haven

Leadman, A D H 1893. 'A survey of *Isurium*', *Yorks Archaeol J*, 12, 413–28

Levison, W 1946. *England and the continent in the eighth century,* Oxford

Ling, R 2007. 'Inscriptions on Romano-British mosaics and wall-paintings', *Britannia*, 38, 63–91.

Loveluck, C 2003. 'The archaeology of post-Roman Yorkshire, AD 400–700', in T Manby, S Moorhouse and P Ottaway (eds) *The archaeology of Yorkshire: an assessment at the beginning of the 21st century,* 152–80, Leeds

Lukis, W C 1875. 'Castle-Dykes', *Archaeol J*, 32, 135–54

Lukis, W C (ed) 1887. *The family memoirs of the Rev William Stukeley and the antiquarian and other correspondence of William Stukeley, Roger and Samual Gale etc Vol III,* Publications of the Surtees Society, 80, Durham

Macnab, N 1998. *Aldborough Gate, Boroughbridge, North Yorkshire. Archaeological Desktop Study*. York Archaeological Trust 1998 Field Report Number 2. North Yorks HER: SNY9819

Manby, T, Moorhouse, S and Ottaway, P (eds) 2003. *The archaeology of Yorkshire: an assessment at the beginning of the 21st century,* Leeds

Margary, I D 1973. *Roman roads in Britain,* 3rd edition London

Marsden, P 1987. *The Roman Forum site in London: discoveries before 1985,* London

Martins, C B 2005. *Becoming consumers: looking beyond wealth as an explanation for villa variability,* Oxford: British Archaeological Reports British Series 403

Mattingly, D 2006. *An Imperial Possession: Britain in the Roman Empire,* London

MAP 2013. *Village Farm, Back Lane, Aldborough, North Yorkshire: Archaeological Strip and Record.* MAP Archaeological Practice Ltd Report no 10.110.2012. North Yorks HER: SNY19934

McWhirr, A 1979. 'Roman tile kilns in Britain', in A D McWhirr (ed) *Roman brick and tile,* 97–189. Oxford: British Archaeological Reports International Series 68

Millett, M 1982. 'Distinguishing between the *Pes*

Monetalis and the *Pes Drusianus*: some problems', *Britannia*, 13, 315–20.
Millett, M 1990. *The Romanization of Britain: an essay in archaeological interpretation*, Cambridge
Millett, M 1996. 'Characterizing Roman London', in J Bird, M Hassall and H Sheldon (eds) *Interpreting Roman London: papers in memory of Hugh Chapman*, 33–7, Oxford.
Millett, M 2006. *Shiptonthorpe, East Yorkshire: archaeological studies of a Romano-British roadside settlement*, Yorkshire Archaeological Society Roman Antiquities Section monograph 5, Leeds
Millett, M 2007. 'Urban topography and social identity in the Tiber Valley', in R Roth and J Keller (eds) *Roman by integration: dimensions of group identity in material culture and text*, 71–82. Portsmouth RI
Millett, M 2013. 'Understanding Roman towns in Italy: reflections on the role of geophysical survey', in P Johnson and M Millett (eds) *Archaeological Survey and the City*, 24–44, Oxford
Millett, M 2016. 'Improving our understanding of *Londinium*', *Antiquity*, 90, 1692–99
Millett M and Brickstock, R 2020. 'An early Roman fort at Thirkleby, North Yorkshire', *Britannia*, 51.
Millett, M J, Dobinson, C, Ferraby, R, Wallace, L, and Lucas, J 2018. *Research data supporting the publication of "Archaeological field-survey in the environs of Aldborough (Isurium Brigantum)"* [Dataset]. https://doi.org/10.17863/CAM.21743
Millett, M and Ferraby, R 2016. *Aldborough Roman Town*, English Heritage Guidebooks. London
Milsted, I and Johnson, M 2009. *Electric Substation, Front Street, Aldborough, North Yorkshire*. York Archaeological Trust Report No 2009/87. North Yorks HER: SNY16313
Moore, T (2011). 'Detribalizing the later prehistoric past: concepts of tribes in Iron Age and Roman studies', *Journal of Social Archaeology*, 11(3), 334–60.
Moore-Jessop, C 1849. 'Some observations respecting Aldborough, the *Isurium Brigantum* of the Romans', *J British Archaeol Assoc*, 5, 73–78
Moore-Jessop, C 1862. 'Tessellated pavement', *Gentleman's Magazine*, 213, 614
Morris, C 2009. *Coach House, Aldborough Roman Town, Boroughbridge, North Yorkshire: Archaeological Watching Brief*. MAP Archaeological Consultancy Ltd Report. North Yorks HER: SNY16319
Morris, C 2010. *Studforth House, Back Lane, Aldborough, North Yorkshire*. MAP Archaeological Consultancy Report. North Yorks HER: SNY16318
Myres, J N L, Steer, K A, and Chitty, A M H 1959. 'The defences of *Isurium Brigantum* (Aldborough)', *Yorks Archaeol J*, 40, 1–77
NAA 2001. *Chapel Hill, Aldborough, North Yorkshire: Negative Watching Brief Report*. NAA Reports
NAA 2003. *York Road, Aldborough, North Yorkshire: Negative Watching Brief Report*. NAA Reports
NAA 2010. *Studforth Farmhouse garage building, Aldborough, North Yorkshire: Negative Watching Brief Report*. NAA Reports
Neal, D S, Wardle, A, and Hunn, J 1990. *Excavation of the Iron Age, Roman and medieval settlement at Gorhambury, St Albans*, London
Neal, D S and Cosh, S R 2002. *Roman mosaics in Britain: Vol 1 Northern Britain*, London
Niblett, R and Thompson, I 2005. *Alban's buried towns: an assessment of St Albans' archaeology up to AD 1600*, Oxford
Nielsen, I 1993. *Thermae et balnea*, Aarhus
Orton, D 2007. 'A local barrow for local people? The Ferry Fryston cattle in context', in B Croxford, N Ray, R Roth and N White (eds) *TRAAC 2006: proceeding of the sixteenth annual Theoretical Roman Archaeology Conference, Cambridge 2006*, 77–91, Oxford
Ottaway, P 1993. *Roman York*, London
Ottaway, P 2013. *Roman Yorkshire: people, culture and landscape*, Pickering
PCA 2015. *Bedale, Aiskew and Leeming Bar Bypass*. http://bedale.org/wp-content/uploads/2015/03/BALB-Archaeological-Posters-version-2.pdf
Pearce, J 2013. *Contextual Archaeology of Burial Practice: case studies of Roman Britain*, Oxford: BAR British Series 588
Perring, D 2002. *The Roman house in Britain*, London
Poulter, J 2009. *Surveying Roman military landscapes across northern Britain*, Oxford: British Archaeological Reports British Series 492
RCHM 1962. *An inventory of the Historical Monuments in the City of York: Vol 1 Eburacum. Roman York*, London
Renn, D F 1973. *Norman castles in Britain*, London
Rickman, G E 1971. *Roman granaries and store buildings*, Cambridge
Rippon, S, Smart, C and Pears, B 2015. *The fields of Britannia*, Oxford
Rivet, A L F, and Smith, C 1979. *The place-names of Roman Britain*, London
Rizos, E 2013. 'Centres of the late Roman military supply network in the Balkans: a survey of *horrea*', *Jahrbuch des Römisch-Germanischen Zentralmuseums Mainz*, 60, 659–96
Roberts, I 2014. 'Rethinking the archaeology of Elmet', in F K Haarar (ed) *AD 410: the history and archaeology of Late and Post-Roman Britain*, 182–94, London
Roberts, I, Deegan, A and Berg, D 2010. *Understanding*

the Cropmark Landscapes of the Magnesian Limestone. The archaeology of the Magnesian Limestone and its margins in South and West Yorkshire and parts of North Yorkshire and north Nottinghamshire, Leeds

Rogers, A 2011. *Late Roman towns in Britain: rethinking change and decline,* Cambridge

Rogers, A 2013. *Water and Roman urbanism: towns, waterscapes, land transformation and experience in Roman Britain,* Leiden

Rose, M 2004. *Dormer Lodge, Aldborough, North Yorkshire.* West Yorkshire Archaeological Services Report No 1243. North Yorks HER: SNY8752

Ross, C R 2011. *Tribal territories' from the Humber to the Tyne. An analysis of artefactual and settlement patterning in the Late Iron Age and Early Roman periods,* Oxford: BAR British Series 540

Rowland, I D and Noble Howe, R (eds) 1999. *Vitruvius: Ten Books on Architecture,* Cambridge

Rushworth, A 2009. *Housesteads Roman fort: the grandest station. Vol 1 structural report and discussion,* London

St Joseph, J K 1955. 'Air reconnaissance in Britain, 1951–55', *J Roman Stud,* 45, 82–91

Sauer, E W 2014. 'Milestones and instability (mid 3rd to mid 4th century AD)', *Ancient Society,* 44, 257–305

Scott, E 1993. *A gazetteer of Roman villas in Britain,* Leicester

Sherlock, S 2010. *An Archaeological Watching Brief at Hill Top, Aldborough, North Yorkshire.* Tees Valley Archaeology Report. North Yorks HER: SNY16374

Smith, A, Allen, M, Brindle, T and Fulford M 2016. *The Rural Settlement of Roman Britain,* London

Smith, J T 1997. *Roman villas: a study in social structure,* London

Smith, L T (ed) 1907. *The itinerary of John Leland in or about the years 1535–1543, Parts I to III,* London

Snape, M, Bidwell, P, and Croom, A 2002. 'Aldborough Roman town: excavations by Miss D. Charlesworth, 1961–73, and by RCHME, 1959–60', *Yorks Archaeol J,* 74, 29–111

Sommer, C S 1984. *The military* vici *of Roman Britain,* Oxford

Speed, G 2002. *Hollow Banks quarry, Scorton, North Yorkshire. Archaeological Post-Excavation Assessment.* Northern Archaeological Associates report NAA 02/121

Speed, G 2006. *Land at Studforth Farm House, Top Street, Aldborough, North Yorkshire: Archaeological Evaluation Report* NAA 06/100. HER: ENY3215

Still, M C W 1995. *Roman Lead Sealings.* PhD thesis, Institute of Archaeology, UCL

Stockwell, M 1989. *Rosedale, Back Street, Aldborough, North Yorkshire.* York Archaeological Trust Report. North Yorks HER: SNY8098 & 493

Stukeley, W 1776. *Itinerarium Curiosum; or an account of the antiquities and remarkable curiosities in nature or art observed in travel through Great Britain,* (2nd edition) London

Tomlin, R S O and Hassall, M W C 1999. 'Roman Britain in 1998: II Inscriptions', *Britannia,* 30, 375–86

Tomlin, R S O and Hassall, M W C 2002. 'Roman Britain in 2001: II Inscriptions', *Britannia,* 33, 355–71

Tomlin, R S O 2015. 'Roman Britain in 2014: II Inscriptions', *Britannia,* 46, 383–420

Tomlin, R S O 2018. *Britannia Romana: Roman inscriptions and Roman Britain,* Oxford

Toynbee, J M C 1964. *Art in Britain under the Romans,* Oxford

Turner, T S 1853. *History of Aldborough and Boroughbridge containing an account of the Roman antiquities, Devils Arrows, churches, halls and other curiosities,* London

Tyler, A undated. *North Yorkshire Historic Town Studies – Archaeological Priorities and Needs: Aldborough,* unpublished manuscript

Verdonck, L, Vermeulen, F, Docter, R, Meyer, C and Kniess, R 2013. '2D and 3D ground-penetrating radar surveys with a modular system: data processing strategies and results from archaeological field tests', *Near Surface Geophysics* 11(2), 239–52

Verdonck, L, Taelman, D, Vermeulen, F and Docter, R 2015. 'The impact of spatial sampling and migration on the interpretation of complex archaeological ground-penetrating radar data', *Archaeological Prospection* 22(2), 91–103

von Schnurbein, S 2003. 'Augustus in Germania and his new town at Waldgirmes east of the Rhine', *J Roman Archaeol,* 16, 93–107

Vyner, B 2018. 'The prehistory of York', *Yorks Archaeol J,* 90, 13–28

Wacher, J S (ed) 1965. *The civitas capitals of Roman Britain,* Leicester

Wacher, J S 1974. *The towns of Roman Britain,* London

Wacher, J S 1995. *The towns of Roman Britain,* (2nd edition) London

Wade, W V 1953. 'Coins from Aldborough, Boroughbridge, Yorkshire – *Isurium Brigantum*', *Numismatic Chron* 1953, 132–4

Wallace, L, 2014. *The origin of Roman London.* Cambridge

Walker, D R 1988. 'The Roman coins', in B Cunliffe (ed) *The Temple of Sulis Minerva at Bath. Vol 2 The Finds from the sacred Spring,* 281–358, Oxford.

Waterman, D M, Kent, B W J and Stickland, H J 1954. 'Two inland sites with "Iron Age A" pottery in the West

Riding or Yorkshire', *Yorks Archaeol J*, 38, 383–97

Welch, K E 2007. *The Roman amphitheatre from its origins to the Colosseum,* Cambridge

Welfare, H and Swan, V G 1995. *Roman camps in England: the field archaeology*, London

White, R H, Gaffney, C and Gaffney, V L 2013. *Wroxeter, the Cornovii and the urban process,* Oxford

Wilkes, J J 1986. 'The status of *Londinium*', in J Bird, M Hassall and H Sheldon (eds) *Interpreting Roman London: papers in memory of Hugh Chapman*, 27–31, Oxford.

Willis, S H 2002, in Snape *et al* 2002

Wilmott, T 2008. *The Roman amphitheatre in Britain,* Stroud

Wilson, P 2002. *Cattaractonium: Roman Catterick and its hinterland. Excavations and research, 1958–1997*, York

Wilson, P 2009. 'Holding the line? The Humber frontier and the Roman expansion into Yorkshire reconsidered', in D J Breeze, L M Thoms and D W Hall (eds) *First contact: Rome and northern Britain,* 9–14, Perth

Wood, P 2011. *Olive House, Aldborough, North Yorkshire: Archaeological Watching Brief Report.* Northern Archaeological Associates. North Yorks HER: SNY18781

Woolf, A 2004. Caedualla Rex Brettonum and the passing of the Old North, *Northern History*, 41, 5–24

Wright, R P 1976. 'Tile-stamps of the Sixth Legion found in Britain', *Britannia,* 7, 224–35

YAT 1990. *Sutton Farm, Aldborough. Watching Brief.* York Archaeological Trust Reports

Index

Illustrations are indicated by page numbers in *italics*. The letter 'n' following a page number denotes that the reference will be found within a note. Individual locations and properties within Aldborough are listed under their street name. All places are located in North Yorkshire unless indicated otherwise.